This book analyses the lifelong impact of Beethoven's music on Wagner and its importance for his conception of music drama. Kropfinger charts Wagner's early responses to the composer and considers his experience as a conductor of Beethoven's music. In addition the book addresses Wagner's theory and practice of music drama, which he came to regard as the pre-ordained successor to the Beethovenian symphony. The author discusses this view in the context of the *Ring* cycle, as well as indicating in detail the ways in which Beethoven influenced Wagner both directly and indirectly.

WAGNER AND BEETHOVEN

WAGNER AND BEETHOVEN

Richard Wagner's reception of Beethoven

KLAUS KROPFINGER

Translated by Peter Palmer

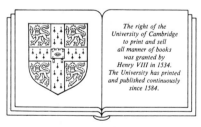

The right of the
University of Cambridge
to print and sell
all manner of books
was granted by
Henry VIII in 1534.
The University has printed
and published continuously
since 1584.

CAMBRIDGE UNIVERSITY PRESS

Cambridge
New York Port Chester
Melbourne Sydney

Published by the Press Syndicate of the University of Cambridge
The Pitt Building, Trumpington Street, Cambridge CB2 1RP
40 West 20th Street, New York, NY 10011, USA
10 Stamford Road, Oakleigh, Melbourne 3166, Australia

Originally published in German as *Wagner und Beethoven*
by Gustav Bosse Verlag Regensburg 1974
and © Gustav Bosse Verlag Regensburg
First published in English by Cambridge University Press 1991 as
Wagner and Beethoven: Richard Wagner's reception of Beethoven
English translation © Cambridge University Press 1991

Printed in Great Britain at the University Press, Cambridge

British Library cataloguing in publication data
Kropfinger, Klaus
Wagner and Beethoven: Richard Wagner's reception of Beethoven.
1. Opera in German. Wagner, Richard, 1813–83
I. Title   II. Wagner und Beethoven. *English*
782.1092

Library of Congress cataloguing in publication data
Kropfinger, Klaus.
[Wagner und Beethoven.   English]
Wagner and Beethoven: Richard Wagner's reception of Beethoven/
Klaus Kropfinger: translated by Peter Palmer.
p.   cm.
Translation of: Wagner und Beethoven.
Includes bibliographical references (p.).
ISBN 0 521 34201 5
1. Wagner, Richard, 1813–1883.   2. Beethoven, Ludwig van,
1770–1829.   I. Title.
ML410.W19K9313   1991
782.1'092 — dc20   90-1505   CIP

ISBN 0 521 34201 5

CE

CONTENTS

PREFACE

This is a revised version of a book first published in German in 1974. More than ever, I have tried to present Wagner's relationship to Beethoven with as little prejudice as possible. It is only away from the beaten track, removed from the aura of the Wagner myth, but also beyond scepticism cultivated for its own sake, that the labyrinthine structure of the *œuvre* becomes evident. Wagner's reception of Beethoven is part of that structure. It therefore needs examining in greater depth and breadth – but even so, this study can only be a partial one: 'drops from the Wagnerian ocean' (*The Times Literary Supplement*, 18 June 1970).

I would like to thank all those who have encouraged and supported this undertaking for their advice and suggestions, as well as their kindness: Reinhold Brinkmann, Harvard; Carl Dahlhaus, Berlin; John Deathridge, Cambridge (UK); Werner Fröhlich, Mainz; Martin Geck, Munich; Günther Massenkeil, Bonn; Wilhelm Perpeet, Bonn; Emil Platen, Bonn; Joseph Schmidt-Görg and Rudolf Stephan, Berlin.

For kindly providing working material and various references I thank Frau Gertrud Strobel, late of the Richard Wagner Archive, Bayreuth, and Dr Joachim Bergfeld of the Richard Wagner Memorial House in Bayreuth. I have also to thank the present director of the Richard Wagner Memorial House, Dr Franz Eger.

I am particularly indebted to the Thyssen Foundation of Cologne for its support, without which neither the work nor the first publication would have been possible. In this connection I am also grateful to Dr Franz A. Stein of the Gustav Bosse Verlag, Regensburg.

I owe the present English edition to the generous co-operation of the Cambridge University Press; the help and sympathy of its music books editor, Penny Souster; the friendly mediation of John Deathridge; and the perceptive translation by Peter Palmer.

I cordially thank Helga von Kügelgen and Volker Schierk, who have always been vigilant critics.

ADDITIONAL ACKNOWLEDGEMENTS

The following English translations are quoted in this text, or have been consulted in its preparation:

Adorno, Theodor, 1981. *In Search of Wagner*, transl. by Rodney Livingstone, London (New Left Books)

Berlioz, H., 1969. *Memoirs*, transl. by David Cairns, London (Gollancz)

Bujić, B. (ed.), 1988. *Music in European Thought 1851–1912* (includes extracts from Hanslick's *The Beautiful in Music* and Wagner's *Opera and Drama* and *Beethoven*, transl. by Martin Cooper), Cambridge (Cambridge University Press)

Dahlhaus, Carl, 1982. *Esthetics of Music*, transl. by William Austin, Cambridge (Cambridge University Press)

Kolodin, I. (ed.), 1962. *The Composer as Listener* (includes extract from Wagner's *A Pilgrimage to Beethoven*), New York (Horizon Press/Collier Books)

Mann, Thomas, 1985. *Pro and Contra Wagner*, transl. by Allan Blunden, London (Faber & Faber)

Schopenhauer, A., 1974. *Parerga and Paralipomena II*, transl. by E. F. J. Payne, Oxford (Oxford University Press)

Wagner, Cosima, 1978/80. *Diaries I and II*, edited by M. Gregor-Dellin and D. Mack, transl. by Geoffrey Skelton, London (Collins)

Wagner, Richard, 1983. *My Life*, ed. by M. Whittall, transl. by Andrew Gray, Cambridge (Cambridge University Press)

1987. *Selected Letters of RW*, ed. by B. Millington, transl. by Stewart Spencer, London (Dent)

1980. *The Diary of RW 1865–1882: The Brown Book*, transl. by George Bird, London (Gollancz)

1979. *Three Wagner Essays*, transl. by Robert L. Jacobs, London (Eulenburg Books)

1973. *Wagner Writes from Paris . . . Stories, Essays and Articles by the Young Composer*, ed. and transl. by R. L. Jacobs and G. Skelton, London (George Allen & Unwin)

GERMAN AND ENGLISH ABBREVIATIONS

BAMZ *Berliner Allgemeine Musikalische Zeitung*
BLW *König Ludwig II. und Richard Wagner. Briefwechsel*, in 5 vols. ed. by
Otto Strobel (Karlsruhe, 1936–9)
GS R. Wagner, *Gesammelte Schriften und Dichtungen*, 12 vols. (Leipzig,
1907)
MGG *Die Musik in Geschichte und Gegenwart*, 14 (+2) vols., ed. by
Friedrich Blume (Kassel, 1949–68, 1973–9)
NZfM *Neue Zeitschrift für Musik*
SB R. Wagner, *Sämtliche Briefe*, ed. by Gertrud Strobel and Werner
Wolf, Vol. I: 1830–42 (Leipzig, 1967); Vol. II: 1842–9 (Leipzig,
1970)
WWV *Wagner-Werkverzeichnis*

CW C. Wagner, *Diaries I and II* (London, 1978–80)
MET *Music in European Thought 1851–1912*, ed. by B. Bujić (Cambridge,
1988)
ML R. Wagner, *My Life* (Cambridge, 1983)
NGW John Deathridge and Carl Dahlhaus, *The New Grove Wagner*
(London, 1984)
SL *Selected Letters of Richard Wagner* (London, 1987)
TWE *Three Wagner Essays* (London, 1979)
WP *Wagner Writes from Paris ... Stories, Essays and Articles by the Young
Composer* (London, 1973)

I

INTRODUCTION

In 1869 Wagner successfully requested a copy of Waldmüller's portrait of Beethoven, which was owned by the publishers Breitkopf & Härtel. This was not the only Beethoven portrait that Wagner possessed. For in December 1851, when he wanted a portrait of Liszt, he said that 'so far I have only Beethoven on my wall, apart from the Nibelung sheet by Cornelius' (*SB*, IV, p. 221). Since his teens, in fact, Wagner had been familiar with Beethoven's outward appearance: in *My Life* (p. 30) he mentions the impression which 'Beethoven's physiognomy, as shown by lithographs of the time' had made on him in 1827. The composer's image accompanied Wagner throughout his life, symbolizing his persistent attempts to comprehend the spiritual phenomenon that was Beethoven, to capture his likeness as both man and artist. What, then, did Beethoven look like to Wagner?

Wagner's mental image of Beethoven is an integral part of that myth of himself, or persona, at which he worked all his life and which he handed on to posterity as something binding and sacrosanct. Both during his lifetime and later on, Wagner's staunch admirers took pains to conserve this 'self-portrait', including those Beethovenian features to which it owes a great deal. The dyed-in-the-wool Wagnerite has always tended to accept statements by Wagner without stopping to consider the background, the context in which they were made. One illustration of this is the way Curt von Westernhagen interprets Wagner's request for a true and not an ideal picture of Beethoven. As Wagner's correspondence with Breitkopf & Härtel and with Robert Krausse, the copyist, shows, it was what made him choose Waldmüller's portrait. Beethoven was to be depicted 'free from any affectation'. But did Wagner actually see in the desired portrait simply the 'real man', i.e. his immediate outward appearance?

Among the portraits painted of Beethoven, Waldmüller's was one of the most suspect and heavily criticized. Wagner knew that, because Breitkopf & Härtel pointed it out to him. No doubt he also knew Schindler's account of the circumstances in which the portrait was produced, and knew how harshly he had judged Waldmüller's labours. Interestingly enough, Wagner rejected this opinion in favour of one which would gain currency at a later period. Unlike Schindler, Theodor Frimmel thought that Waldmüller's Beethoven portrait managed to reawaken a mental image of the Beethoven of the twenties. And Bruno Grimschitz remarks in his study of the painter (1957) that he was capable of memorizing individual characteristics exceptionally quickly. Waldmüller's portrait with the 'hearing eyes' is, he believes, 'one of the best portraits of the great tone-poet'.

Wagner evidently saw in this picture of the 'real man' some quite specific features which he found important. They belong, says Joseph Schmidt-Görg in *MGG*, to a composer already scarred by worry and illness, and above all one who was hard of hearing. The 'hearing eyes' are a sign that his ears were attuned to the sounds within him. Thus in the 'true picture' he wanted, Wagner could see once again the features of the Beethoven he had described in his *Beethoven* essay. This was the composer with 'the vision of an innermost musical world to proclaim' (*GS*, IX, p. 83); the musician who, 'being afflicted by deafness, is now undisturbed by life's noises and listens solely to the harmonies within him' (*GS*, IX, p. 92). The composer as a saint and a redeemer – that was Wagner's contribution to the Romantic image of Beethoven. So behind his apparently straightforward request there lies a specific perception of Beethoven. And it affects Wagner's own myth, too, because his image of 'Beethoven the redeemer is simply an allegory of Wagner the redeemer' (A. Schmitz 1926, p. 183).

Previous research

Although the literature on Wagner has swollen to vast proportions, it does not include many studies that deal in a critical way with the Wagner myth as it relates to the myth of Beethoven. Moreover, the majority of such studies are concerned with individual topics. Only Karl Ipser's *Beethoven – Wagner – Bayreuth* (1953) examines Wagner's reception of Beethoven comprehensively, and as a self-contained subject. (Wyzewa's *Beethoven et Wagner*, first published in 1898, deals with other matters.)

It was Ipser's aim to present Wagner's life as 'a life with Beethoven' not just with the aid of facts and figures, but by postulating the existence of an 'innermost active force'. But his book falls short in this respect: there are long passages comprising merely a stream of facts and quotations. Like the uncritical Wagnerite, Ipser treats his data as symbols with an obvious meaning and function that stand in no need of analysis or criticism. What point is there in his saying, for instance, that Beethoven was born in the same year as Wagner's father? This, to Ipser, is a 'significant conjunction' and no coincidence. As to Wagner's *Faust* Overture, he finds it significant that Beethoven too had planned to set 'Faust' to music. A little farther on he quotes the enthusiastic conclusion to an essay about Wagner's overture, which hailed him as one of 'the few legitimate heirs and successors to Beethoven, the son of the god of music incarnate'. But Ipser never acknowledges Hans von Bülow as the author, and this typifies his liberal and nonchalant use of other writers' ideas and work on the subject of Wagner and Beethoven. In addition to acknowledged quotations, the book includes whole chunks of unidentified 'literary extracts'. (The late Gertrud Strobel has kindly identified Lorenz's *Das Geheimnis der Form bei Richard Wagner* and Engelsmann's *Wagners klingendes Universum* as two of the sources.) Ipser also uses his sources uncritically in various respects. In the first, 1907 volume of his Beethoven biography, Max Koch wrote that Wagner 'was able to hear' Beethoven's Ninth Symphony on three occasions; Ipser presents this as an established fact. And Koch wrongly stated that Wagner had copied out the score of Beethoven's Ninth in Paris. This leads Ipser into claiming that Wagner made 'a fresh copy of the score', which has since been lost. There are many more such errors to illustrate the superficiality of Ipser's approach. The motto of the 'Wesendonck' Sonata, 'Wisst ihr wie das wird', is described as the Norns' question in *Walküre*. Lehrs, instead of Anders, is named as the person to whom Schindler – after an exchange in which Wagner took part – guaranteed to make amends for having criticized him. The significance of this episode is not explained, although a little earlier, Ipser mentions the Beethoven biography on which Wagner and Anders planned to collaborate.

Jean Boyer gives considerable space to Wagner's reception of Beethoven in his book *Le 'Romantisme' de Beethoven* (1938). He outlines the formation and development of the 'Romantic' Beethoven legend and looks at Wagner so thoroughly that this section of his book could be described as an internal monograph. Drawing on Wagner's performance of the Ninth Symphony as well as his writings, Boyer examines Wagner's view of Beethoven chronologically. He particularly stresses the fact that Wagner saw in Beethoven a forerunner of music drama. This idea, he says, was derived from E. T. A. Hoffmann, whose interpretation of Beethoven influenced Wagner's for a long time, until eventually Schopenhauer's influence made itself felt in the *Beethoven* essay. But Boyer also discerns Romantic precursors, especially Novalis and Wackenroder, in major aspects of Schopenhauer's thought. Boyer's survey is broad and richly faceted, while at the same time containing points that call for criticism and debate. What is most open to question is the way he deals with Wagner's concept of music. It is a moot point whether, in *A Happy Evening*, Wagner already takes the view that Beethoven's conception of certain works began with a poetic idea, and that this determined his musical themes. Equally debatable is the claim that in *Beethoven*, Wagner is conforming to Schopenhauer in representing the 'absolute' musician's standpoint. Besides examining what Wagner meant by 'absolute music', we need to explain how he visualized Beethoven's 'idea', and what actively inspired it. Boyer also makes us examine Wagner's interpretation of the Ninth Symphony in greater detail, since this is so closely bound up with the way he experienced Beethoven.

Another major contributor to the subject of Wagner's Beethoven reception is Herbert Birtner with his treatise *Zur Deutschen Beethoven-Auffassung seit Richard Wagner* (1937). Birtner uses the Ninth Symphony to trace the evolution of Wagner's interpretation of Beethoven. He makes the important point that Wagner's experience of Weber's music prepared him for his responses to Beethoven, although it is debatable whether Beethoven was then just 'another object of "enthusiastic veneration" besides Weber and Mozart'. Another valuable comment he makes is that it was only slowly and gradually that Wagner put his personal image of Beethoven to creative, practical use. Here we have some further starting-points for a more intensive study of Wagner's Beethoven experience and its function in his output.

Arnold Schmitz has written a number of works that deal with Beethoven and Wagner. Each is an attempt to explore the interplay between the myths of Wagner and Beethoven respectively. The first, basic work is *Die Beethoven-Apotheose als Beispiel eines Säkularisierungsvorganges* (1926). Schmitz renewed his efforts in *Das Romantische Beethovenbild* (1927), which probably blazed a trail for Boyer's study. His essay *Der Mythos der Kunst in den Schriften Richard Wagners* (1947–50) concentrates on specific features of a development that is linked to the history of ideas. Schmitz offers some illuminating remarks on the 'myth-making technique'. He traces Wagner's 'myth of art' through the composer's writings from the Zurich period to the last years. Schmitz shows how the Beethoven myth – the idea of a 'saint' who embodies man's natural goodness – comes into Wagner's 'art myth', by virtue of the claim that he was going to redeem religion with art's assistance. This amounts to a fusion, within Wagner's own myth of art, of the Wagner myth and the Beethoven myth. Schmitz's studies are an inducement to examine other myths and legends accruing from Wagner's reception of Beethoven, and to observe how they fit in with Wagner's self-portrait. This we shall do in our next two chapters.

Of the objective, critical studies that exist of Wagner and his relationship to Beethoven, Guido Adler's Wagner lectures from the start of the century are the earliest. What is the significance of these lectures? The answer is that they probably represent the first major attempt to grasp Wagner as one phenomenon among others – all of which have equal claims on our attention in an historical context. They challenged the thesis that Wagner's music drama formed the climax to an inevitable development, Beethoven's works constituting a preliminary step. It was also Adler who noted the crucial difference between the invention and treatment of music drama's vocal motifs on the one hand, and purely instrumental motifs on the other. In so doing, Adler provided the basic tools for later research.

Ernest Newman's writings are equally enlightening, especially *Wagner as Man and Artist*, although from the critical viewpoint there is less emphasis on Wagner's relationship to Beethoven. Newman points out some major discrepancies between Wagner's theories and his practice. This is the basic

4

reason why opinions differ so strongly on Wagner's compositional debt to Beethoven, and on the extent to which their techniques can be related and compared, if at all. Such commentators as Walter Engelsmann and Theodor W. Adorno are diametrically opposed in their views on this subject, just as myth and anti-myth are poles apart.

Like Engelsmann, Alfred Lorenz represents the orthodox school of Wagner commentators, except that he tries to demonstrate the music drama's absorption of the Beethovenian symphony by means of a special analytical device: the *Bar* form. At the end of his treatise *Worauf beruht die bekannte Wirkung der Durchführung im I. Eroicasatz* (1924), Lorenz writes as follows:

> The forms piled one upon the other which I have found in Wagner's music drama are rooted not in the type of opera that went before it but in the *Beethoven symphony*, thus confirming the truth of Wagner's claim that the symphony had poured into his drama. (p. 183)

Two objections can be raised to this statement. First, studies by Carl Dahlhaus and Rudolf Stephan have since undermined it by illustrating the inadequacy of the formal patterns Lorenz applied to Wagner's music drama: the *Bar* ('strophe'), the *Bogen* ('arch') and so on. Secondly, even if we apply it to the development section of Beethoven's 'Eroica', the *Bar* form (or rather the scheme of the *Reprisenbar*) does not make sense. In fact it contradicts something that Lorenz himself said. Unlike others, he regarded the close of the development not as 'signalling a victory' but as a 'period of exhaustion' which, he maintained, pointed beyond the development's confines. We may question the correctness of referring to a victory or defeat of the principal theme, but that is not now the point. What is evident is that, having perceived the development's forward impetus, Lorenz subsequently loses sight of it by imposing the *Reprisenbar* on the procedure. For the concept of the *Reprisenbar* implies a 'return of the same thing' [*Wiederkehr des Gleichen*], which is precisely what Beethoven avoids in his developments. To adapt Rudolf Stephan's remark on the schematic character of Lorenz's Wagner analyses, Lorenz does away with all that is best about Beethoven's music, 'its dynamic force, its ceaseless animation'. Lorenz's Beethoven analysis poses two inescapable questions. One is the question of Wagner's own attitude to the dynamic element in Beethoven's music; and, closely connected with this, there is the question of how Wagner viewed the 'reprise'. What is the relationship between Wagner's music drama and the compositions of Beethoven? What sources can we consult on this subject? We shall return to these issues in Chapters 4 and 5.

Otto Daube has tried to give some constructive answers to the above questions in *Richard Wagner. 'Ich schreibe keine Symphonien mehr'* (1960). Daube's main aim was to set forth the sources for Wagner's period of study with Weinlig, but also for the 'actual studies', covering not just Wagner's 'brief half-year' with Weinlig but the whole period from 1828 to the end of 1832. In the *NGW*, however, John Deathridge points out not only that Weinlig evidently taught Wagner over a longer period of time, but also that these lessons may have included classical sonata form as well as studies in counterpoint. Otto Daube's book may be said to hinge on the publication of Wagner's counterpoint studies under Weinlig, together with the previously unpublished Piano Sonata in A major. But on closer scrutiny it is difficult to grant Daube's work as a whole the status of a source-book, because large parts of it are littered with extremely subjective interpretations. Daube avowedly intended them as starting-points for a new and thorough account for the Wagnerian work of art's 'musical anatomy', but they should not go unchallenged. Thus he cites Nietzsche when discussing 'formal parallels' between the symphony and drama, although in the end he rejects Nietzsche – and Thomas Mann and Adorno as well – as an interpretative point of departure. The parallel drawn between cyclical form in the symphony and the *Ring* cycle is arbitrary and totally unfounded: Daube never provides any 'sources'. The same goes for his demonstration of a formal correspondence between the Ninth Symphony and the 'formal miracle of *Meistersinger* and *Parsifal*', where he invokes Alfred Lorenz. A question-mark even hangs over Daube's source-material with regard to the Sonata in A major. Wagner cut the fugato section that originally formed part of the finale, as can be seen from Carl Dahlhaus's edition of the piano music. Daube's edition reproduces the section in full, without comment. His thoughts on this interesting matter are limited to a footnote which dismisses vital details of the sources as negligible. It is up to us to ask if speculation about the reasons for such cuts would truly lead nowhere.

Max Fehr published the two volumes of his *Richard Wagners Schweizer Zeit* in 1934 and 1954 respectively. They have always been essential reading for students of Wagner's reception of Beethoven. The years Wagner spent as an exile in Zurich and Tribschen had an important bearing on his development and on the exact nature of his relationship to Beethoven. Fehr records them from the viewpoint of his activities as a conductor of Beethoven's orchestral music, and as a 'coach' at rehearsals of his string quartets.

Probably the most ambitious recent Wagner book with a close bearing on the present study was published by Egon Voss in 1977, two years after the first (German) edition of *Wagner and Beethoven*. Voss's book is titled *Richard Wagner und die Instrumentalmusik. Wagners symphonischer Ehrgeiz*. Voss has worked as an editor on the Wagner *Gesamtausgabe*, and his book draws extensively on that experience. That fact in itself would suffice to make it interesting. The book's special immediacy is however derived from its central critical point of departure, namely a revaluation and reinterpretation of Wagner as a composer, particularly of instrumental works. Voss has carried a stage further the process of demythologization to which the

6

present study was and still is devoted. He attempts to show how Wagner directed his creative efforts – more or less covertly or knowingly – towards instrumental, i.e. symphonic, music, but also towards symphonic drama, a drama seen as being primarily musical in orientation. Thus Wagner's 'symphonic ambition' [*Ehrgeiz*] serves as a vantage-point from which to look down on a bare stage. The actors have all removed their masks, and the scenery swings to one side or becomes transparent, affording a glimpse of what lies behind it.

This idea has a certain attractiveness, and it seems quite feasible for Wagner's few instrumental compositions to fit in with it. But when we examine this idea more closely, it proves to be fraught with problems. The very phrase 'symphonic ambition' invites contradiction, and here we can quote Thomas Mann:

> But in any case the insinuation of ambition in any normal worldly sense can be dismissed for the simple reason that Wagner was working initially without any hope or prospect of making an immediate impact, which actual circumstances and conditions would not allow – working in a vacuum of his own invention, towards an imaginary, ideal theatre that could not possibly be realized for the present. There is certainly no hint of cool calculation or the ambitious exploitation of existing opportunities in words such as these, addressed to Otto Wesendonck: 'For I see clearly that I am fully myself only when I create . . .'
>
> (*Pro and Contra Wagner*, p. 139)

'Ambition' suggests something external; Thomas Mann's critique delves to the heart of the matter. But if it is still insisted that Wagner had this ambition, then was it not from a false, improper motive that he turned to writing instrumental works from time to time?

By a kind of 'double strategy', it might be argued, Wagner – because he was very aware of his limitations as a purely instrumental composer – ultimately 'slaked' his symphonic ambitions in his music dramas, the latter being 'symphonic dramas'. But this is not the case. Either Wagner was an instrumental fanatic with some kind of secret compulsion to identify himself with the symphony, and was not at all averse to writing any more symphonies, or else his music dramas were the result of a genuine artistic decision, a logical departure as a composer from the instrumental medium of the symphony and from any ambition to write in a genuinely 'symphonic' manner, albeit in the form of 'music dramas'. These propositions cannot both be true. And it is possible to show that Wagner's instrumental works are glosses, experiments and leftovers, and that it is the music dramas which represent his real creative output. It was a musico-dramatic output, not a primarily instrumental one, not one that was the result of 'symphonic ambition'. Dahlhaus describes the instrumental works as mere *parerga* in *The New Grove Wagner*.

If we want to characterize Wagner at all accurately, the only concept which seems to fit is 'intention'. By this we mean first and foremost the unflagging concentration of all one's intellectual and imaginative powers on a single *artistic* goal. But there is also an 'intention' in respect of the artistic objects. In both structure and 'content', or mythical subject-matter, these supremely imaginative products have that 'intentional objectivity' which clearly distinguishes them from any of the products of 'ambition'. Ingarden, in his *Der Streit um die Existenz der Welt* (1965), writes that the 'activity of creating an *intentional object*' consists of actions 'which tend to make permanent, to "fix" in some way the purely intentional objects created therein, and this is achieved by giving these objects some existentially stronger ontological basis that will enable them to outlast the actions which produced them. They will thus become detached from the purely subjective foundation in which they originated and acquire an intersubjective objectivity' (II/I, pp. 204–5).

Such 'permanence' necessarily entails a complete design for the 'intended work'. But the majority of Wagner's symphonic or purely instrumental works – including his late 'symphonic sketches' – lack this for the simple reason that he never completed them. We find a major discrepancy between Wagner's avowed (but temporary!) aims as a composer and his non-realization of symphonic pieces as 'intentional objects'.

There are, however, distinctions to be made here. It would surely be wrong to regard the purely instrumental side of Wagner's creative output as a single entity. Rather it reflects creative impulses arising from a given situation as man and artist: impulses which take various forms because there were different motives behind them. It seems fair to assume that at the start of Wagner's artistic development, the early instrumental works left him the option of being a purely instrumental composer, but that he very soon chose a different path. And via opera, this eventually led him to music drama. Thus viewed, Wagner's symphonic forays and excursions will come to represent transitory impulses arising out of the particular circumstances of his life and artistic career.

Pierre Boulez has summed up the composer's relationship to tradition in the words: 'It can thus be said that a composer does not have a hard-and-fast attitude to tradition; rather his responses are conditioned by his evolution and depend on the current state of his creative development' (*Melos* 27 [1960], p. 294). This holds good for Wagner's relationship to purely instrumental music, and especially the symphony, as a traditional genre.

According to Voss, Wagner's claim that the symphony had evolved into drama was not a true reflection of his views. Instead it reflected his desire to present music drama as a legitimate genre and for it to be acknowledged as such – which would eventually evoke one element in the notorious 'Bayreuth ideology'. This judgment is far too sweeping. Granted, Wagner himself pointed to a whole series of differences (central ones at that) between the symphony and music drama. They include the elimination –

or the redesigning or redeployment – of the reprise; the different design, configurations and development of themes; the harmonic progressions; and the individual structure and form. But looking at it through Wagner's eyes, there are certainly elements in the way he developed his motifs and melodies, for example, that indicate a connection between the symphony and drama. At bottom, however, it was Wagner's broad artistic intention which engendered music drama instead of instrumental works, even though it had had its beginnings in instrumental and operatic pieces, and had passed through several stages of opera composing.

Voss maintains that almost throughout his life, it was Wagner's ambition to become a great and significant symphonist, or at least to compose significant and universally recognized symphonic music. This now seems an exaggeration. Wagner's subsequent efforts in the symphonic realm were more extensive but did not last; after that, there were only sporadic excursions. He cherished no secret yet central, lifelong desire in that respect. Whatever the content and objective by which it is defined, his so-called symphonic ambition was altogether a by-product of his artistic development. If Wagner had really nurtured far-reaching symphonic aims, he would not have cast aside the *Faust* Overture, which he originally conceived as a symphony in Paris in 1839. The thematic sketches and compositional fragments that Voss goes out of his way to enumerate would not have remained mere statements of intent. And towards the end of his life, Wagner would have done more than just talk about future symphonies. He would have actually realized one or other of his initial themes rather than carry on with and complete his final stage-work, *Parsifal*.

After arriving at music drama, Wagner was still driven to the brink of instrumental music time and again. This was for reasons which affected him deeply and were also a provocation. These causes were, however, 'adjusted' very quickly within the music drama's ambit. They included Berlioz (and Beethoven!) in Paris, the symphonic poems of Liszt, those two dogged symphonists Mendelssohn and Schumann, but above all Brahms and – Bruckner. Instrumental music not only survived in the shadow of music drama but even acquired a fresh impetus. This impressed Wagner considerably, and he felt it as a challenge; again and again, however, it was also of instant fascination, for all his woolly anti-Semitism and his fixed art-ideology. The fact is graphically illustrated by Cosima Wagner's diaries, which mention Mendelssohn as an orchestral composer surprisingly often, and not always negatively. In the light of Mendelssohn's unerring skill as a purely instrumental composer, Wagner said such things as 'Mendelssohn would raise his hands in horror if he ever saw me composing' (23 June 1871). Statements like this may be tinged with irony, but the real feelings behind them are complex. They explain why Wagner thought it so important to have at least one entire symphony to his credit in later life, even if it was only the early one in C major. He had once entrusted

9

the score of that very work to Mendelssohn, and he never forgave him for its disappearance!

We can now also understand why, in the end, Wagner wanted to have nothing more to do with the 'Wesendonck' Sonata. Contemporaries of his were casting their 'infinite symphonic shadow'. Do we really wish to embarrass Wagner by puffing up this sketch as a kind of magnum opus of his 'symphonic ambition'? The piece is marginal to a very different order of music that was going through the forward-looking composer's mind. Gutman quite rightly calls it shallow. The 'Wesendonck' Sonata was produced in a specific set of circumstances relating to Wagner's life and career. It stands on the threshold of the composition of the *Ring*. But this is no pointer to music drama as the consummation of the symphony. After all, it was Wagner's aim as a musical dramatist to transpose purely instrumental music into a new – and 'essential' [*eigentlich*] – musical dimension once and for all by giving it dramatic significance. Cosima records Wagner as saying (16 August 1869) that in him, the accent lay on the conjunction of the dramatic poet with the musician; he would not amount to much purely as a musician. Is the idea to unmask this too as a piece of self-ideologizing?

The thesis of Wagner's 'symphonic ambition' appears to be a fresh attempt to solve the problem of how his creative work should really be understood and classified. And it corresponds to the attempt to subsume Wagner's output under the 'idea of absolute music' (Carl Dahlhaus). The notion of assigning Wagner to the realm of absolute music is crucial to numerous studies published by Dahlhaus. It also appears in his extensive contribution to *The New Grove Wagner*, and it undoubtedly has its attractions. There may have indeed been an idea of absolute music lasting from early Romanticism to Wagner and beyond. But if so, we need to ask if, as the result of a change in the musical material, in formal, structural and expressive qualities during the nineteenth century, the content and concept of this idea did not undergo some changes as well. The problem clearly emerges where analysis, by using purely musical categories of form, only partially succeeds in grasping the structure of music drama. This leads on to the question of Wagner's concept of music. Was it really that of an instrumental music which fitted into a purely musical structural and expressive framework, and with which the symphonic drama also fell into line?

Wagner's view of Beethoven can help to enlighten us on this very point. For his reception of the Beethoven symphonies, and also of the other instrumental works, represents a crossroads. Not only does it give a fair picture of the way he summed up Beethoven's instrumental music; it also serves to bring out more clearly the structure of his own range as a composer of music dramas. The one left its mark on the other.

We now come to a matter which looms large both in Voss's book and in the biographical section of *The New Grove Wagner*, which was written by John Deathridge. Establishing the biographical truth is beset with problems. There can be no doubt that Wagner's autobiographical details contain inaccuracies ranging from the inadvertent error to deliberate fabrication. A number of Wagner scholars involved with the *Gesamtausgabe* have pursued this matter further. Their joint findings appear in the *Wagner Werk-Verzeichnis* published in 1986.

For such a strategy, a flair for detective work is constantly needed. There are times, however, when it also resorts to an overdose of scepticism and to distortions that are based on mere hypotheses. Important though this work is, we should always remember that with Wagner we are dealing *de facto* with two levels of biographical truth. Time and again, as an interpreter, Wagner reshaped his life and artistic development. This fact, and the appropriate response to it, surely carries as much weight as the revelation of things 'as they really were' (or could have been). One point is particularly significant. Wagner began to interpret events not after they were over, and from an autobiographical perspective, but so soon as to determine the biographical facts themselves, i.e. that which constitutes the 'actual truth'. This lends weight to what Dahlhaus writes at the end of the chapter in *The New Grove Wagner* headed 'Letters, diaries, autobiography':

Understanding the paths along which Wagner's imagination set off is more important than correcting conscious or unconscious inaccuracies. Yet editorial meticulousness is not to be despised: it is only against the background of empirical truth that the 'poetic truth' can be recognized for what it is – another truth and not a distortion that the exegete is at liberty to dismiss.

It will be essential to take this attitude when it comes to Wagner's autobiographical account of his experience of Beethoven. And in reflecting on the lifelong spell which Beethoven's music exerted on him, and his reactions to it, Wagner was confirming and interpreting his own personality.

Objectives

Any study of Wagner's reception of Beethoven must begin with the source-material. It follows from what has been stated above, however, that the sources should be seen in a wider context. Obviously what rates as a source is chiefly anything that Wagner wrote or said which is directly or indirectly connected with his view of Beethoven. But these statements need to be examined critically, as do the supporting documents that occasionally have to be consulted – press reports and the statements of friends and contemporaries. The use made so far of what Wagner said about his earliest encounter with Beethoven has been wholly uncritical; at best it includes a note on 'poetic licence'. Yet if Wagner's various autobiographical statements are compared, it is impossible to ignore the discrepancies between them. Autobiography, for Wagner, was a means of self-examination throughout his life. Thus the question of his 'Beethoven experience' is bound up with the question of his autobiographical method.

As a follow-up to Wagner's earliest experience of Beethoven, we must look into the profound later impressions that Beethoven's music made on him. This has been considered by a number of previous writers. But have they covered every level and aspect of the experience, and have they comprehended its function? Here again the number of sources is appreciable, but we must also consider the particular situation in which Wagner received his impression and reacted to it. The same goes for his writings on artistic topics. Whom was he addressing, and what private and public circles did he have in mind at the time? Certainly any assessment of all Wagner's remarks on Beethoven must rest on a study of the material ranging from internal textual criticism to a careful exploration of possible 'influences'. Attention must also be paid to Wagner's language. The meaning of individual words aside, insights can be gleaned from Wagner's habit of using a fixed terminology for some very specific musical matters, but not for others.

Any study of extracts from Wagner's writings will confirm that Wagner poses problems as an author. From the viewpoint of his reception of Beethoven, however, it will especially point up the ticklish relationship between his theory and his poetic-dramatic compositions. Up to now Theodor Uhlig's writings have been completely overlooked in this context. Although it was thought that they merely echoed Wagner's, they do in fact add significantly to what he said.

There can be no doubt that Wagner's achievements as a composer far exceed what he achieved as an author. But in assessing the relationship between the two, there is a need to distinguish between the intrinsic merit of Wagner's writings and their interpretative role. Dahlhaus states that the works are the key to the writings, not vice versa. Were this always the case, however, Wolzogen's leitmotif catalogue would still have the importance it used to, and Wolzogen completely fails to do justice to the structural function – i.e. the connective dimension – of Wagner's leitmotifs. Part III of Wagner's *Opera and Drama* is essential reading if we are not to misconstrue his leitmotif as being simply a motif of reminiscence (and there are people who still do this). *Opera and Drama* helps us grasp the point that the leitmotif actualizes a reminiscence and a presentiment at one and the same time.

Wagner's writings are in need of interpretation themselves, but they also assist interpretation, despite all the difficulties. They are not wildly at odds with the compositions of Wagner. Rather they mediate between works and artistic domains, as *Opera and Drama* does.

Originally it was the present writer's aim to examine the overall subject of Wagner's reception of Beethoven. In the course of our researches, however, certain focal points emerged and began to form a whole in themselves. Starting with the autobiographical sources, it then became our objective to observe and describe the core of Wagner's Beethoven experience – its structure and interweaving with the biography – as much as its scope, its roots from the standpoint of reception history and grounding in the 'Romantic image of Beethoven'. The obvious next step was to investigate Beethoven and his works as factors in Wagner's writings on art and in his dramas. Bearing in mind the awkward relationship between Wagner's theory and practice as a composer of music dramas, we made it our aim to explore and sift (at any rate partially) those traces of his understanding of Beethoven that were preserved in his musico-dramatic output. His activities as a conductor and 'arranger' of Beethoven's music were considered only inasmuch as they form an intrinsic part of this cluster of focal points.

Although this study deals with Wagner's reception of Beethoven, his diverse relations to other composers should not be dismissed as insignificant. After all, he himself often spoke of his links with others. Especially in his youth, he said, he owed much to Mozart but above all Weber and, later on, Marschner and Spontini, not to mention Liszt. And even the acquaintance with Meyerbeer's grand opera and the example of Mendelssohn had some effect on him. The reasons for our particular choice of subject are, however, the experience of Beethoven that permeates Wagner's whole life, his almost constant thinking about Beethoven and, not least, his veneration of the composer as evidenced by his works.

WAGNER'S EXPERIENCE OF BEETHOVEN

The initial experience

Autobiographical sources

It is one of the truisms of Wagner research that particular caution is advisable with regard to the autobiographical writings and jottings. That goes not least for *My Life*. Nobody would disagree with Otto Strobel that the composer of the *Ring*, *Tristan* and *Parsifal* chose to view certain experiences in a different light from when they were recent and fresh in his mind. Wagner's letters contradict or amend many details in *My Life* (and as far as facts are concerned, the letters tend to be more reliable than Wagner's other writings).[1]

A full-scale critical study of the way Wagner depicted himself has yet to be written. But research undertaken in connection with the Complete Edition has yielded some important new findings – although some of these, in their turn, have given rise to fresh problems. Recently a start was made on a new edition of Wagner's letters, containing all the available texts.

Cosima's diaries, beginning in January 1869 and ending in January 1883, are an important source which Wagner visualized as a sequel to *My Life*. (The latter is directly followed by his *Annals*: brief, lapidary jottings which go up to the end of 1868.) Cosima's diaries were inaccessible to the public until 1972 under the terms of a will; since their publication they have proved to be very helpful to researchers. Almost inevitably some things are repeated, and there are major difficulties in connection with a textual critique of the originals. But the significance of the diaries is immense. This applies to every aspect of Wagner's reception of Beethoven, including his earliest encounter with the composer. We shall now examine this experience, drawing on a number of statements by Wagner which do not always tally with each other. At the same time we shall endeavour to throw more light on the function of the autobiographical writings and their value as sources, but also on the problems of interpreting them.

Wagner recorded his earliest experience of Beethoven seven times in all. It appears in the following writings, listed in chronological order:

Red Pocket-Book (begun around mid-August 1835)

A Pilgrimage to Beethoven (novella, Paris 1840)
Autobiographical Sketch (1842–3)
A Communication to My Friends (written in Zurich, 1851)
'Music of the Future' (written in Paris, 1860)
My Life (autobiography, begun 17 July 1865, finished May 1880)
The Work and Mission of my Life (original title; 1879)[2]

The above texts differ on the following points:

(i)   the number and the description of works by Beethoven that were crucial to the experience;
(ii)   the time, or commencement, of the experience, and, closely connected with this,
(iii)   the starting-point or cause of the actual experience or its development;
(iv)   the descriptive mode: some accounts present a composite experience, combining a number of elements and describing an intrinsically graduated, lengthier process.

In the earliest source, the *Red Pocket-Book*, Wagner was still particularly close in time and content to the events under review. Significantly, he speaks of just 'Beethoven's symphonies' in general as inspiring a new passion for music in him. Apparently it was not one particular concert but several experiences, several visits to concerts, that fired the youngster's enthusiasm. We are pointing this out because in two more sources (*A Communication* and *The Work and Mission*) Wagner recalls the impression made by 'Beethoven's symphonies'. And where he refers, even less specifically, to Beethoven's 'music' (in the *Sketch* and *'Music of the Future'*), we will at once think of several experiences. This raises the question of whether Wagner's references to just one symphony (*A Pilgrimage, My Life*) represent a stylization of the original experience, undertaken for a definite purpose, under the influence of certain surrounding factors or a fresh experience of Beethoven.

How does the above affect an assessment of *A Pilgrimage*? The most obvious answer would be that Wagner was offering a poetically motivated stylization of the truth, one closely linked to his fictional treatment of his material. But there is more to it than that. It is no accident that the element of stylization appears in that novella, which can be seen as the first expression of Wagner's Beethoven worship. The story tells of a pilgrimage to music's holy of holies, and at its climax the master initiates his disciple into the secrets of his art. Arnold Schmitz sees in this a prefiguration of Wagner's later image of Beethoven, where the latter resembles a saint. Indeed with his Beethoven novella, Wagner took the first step towards consciously fashioning his own myth, his self-image. The artistic enthusiasm attached to the experience was thereby elevated to the status of something unique. Only now did Wagner's first experience of Beethoven achieve that moment of illumination which has always been a talking-point in discussions of Wagner.

It was the rehearsals and/or the performance of the Ninth Symphony under Habeneck which led Wagner back to Beethoven. (Thus *A Pilgrimage* does not just reflect Wagner's Gewandhaus experience, as Guido Adler assumed.) In all likelihood this was the immediate cause of the modifications he made to his own initial source. The original impression, now long past and already growing hazy, became transposed with the immediate experience provided by Beethoven's Ninth, which was *the* symphony. The old experience was returning on a new qualitative plane, so to speak: it marks a rediscovery of Beethoven. It already suggests something of that quest for the past which increasingly drove Wagner to look back on his life, explaining and revising it. Out of this came new 'editions' of his life and experiences.

In *My Life* Wagner is more specific as regards what he wrote in the *Pocket-Book* and names the work that made such an indelible impression on him. Ernest Newman has augmented Wagner's statement by saying that it was on 17 January 1828 that he must have heard Beethoven's Symphony in A major. What prompted Wagner to underline this biographical detail, the fact that he had heard the Seventh Symphony? No doubt his first concern was to make the biographical facts in *My Life* as complete as he could – fuller than in anything previously published. But there was also an inner reason. The Seventh Symphony forms part of a progressive experience. *My Life* sets out Wagner's experience of Beethoven in terms of an ascent: his reaction to Beethoven's death follows on from an acquaintance with the E major overture to *Fidelio*, and the symphony, the crowning experience, comes afterwards. This work's ecstatic rhythmic progressions fascinated Wagner all his life; he had already called it the apotheosis of the dance (*Art-Work of the Future*). In *My Life* he highlights it for the sake of a narrative that is not only detailed but above all vivid and striking. The autobiography projects a new 'truth'. The early experience, which was based on Wagner's hearing of several symphonies, is modified to fit in with a particular pattern of responses.

It is interesting to find that Berlioz wrote with similar emotion of his own Beethoven experience, and that the Seventh Symphony had been the cause of it. In a letter of 1829 he was already writing as follows:

Yesterday I went to the Conservatoire concert, where Beethoven's Symphony in A exploded over us. I was very apprehensive about the superb meditation. The listeners who had never heard it before called for a repeat. What agony! ... Oh, it would have driven me crazy the second time if I hadn't wept tears.

Produced by the most sombre and musing of geniuses, this astonishing work is poised between all the rapture, simplicity and tenderness that joy can offer. There are just two ideas, one being 'I think, therefore I suffer', the other 'I remember, and

16

suffer the more'. Oh, unhappy Beethoven – he too cherished in his heart an ideal world of happiness which he was not allowed to enter.

(Grempler [1950], pp. 193, 281 n. 43)

The parallel with Berlioz goes even farther. In Wagner's account, Beethoven's image 'melded with that of Shakespeare'. Berlioz writes in his memoirs:

In an artist's life one thunderclap sometimes follows swiftly on another, as in those outsize storms in which the clouds, charged to bursting with electric energy, seem to be hurling the lightning back and forth and blowing the whirlwind.

I had just had the successive revelations of Shakespeare and Weber. Now at another point on the horizon I saw the giant form of Beethoven rear up. The shock was almost as great as that of Shakespeare had been. Beethoven opened before me a new world of music, as Shakespeare had revealed a new universe of poetry.

(Berlioz [1969], p. 105)

Their reactions to the composer's death apart, then, important elements in Wagner's and Berlioz's Beethoven experience are the same. Of course they form different patterns, the main difference being that Wagner experiences all at once what Berlioz expresses on two separate occasions. We may wonder if Wagner was aware of Berlioz's descriptions when he dictated the relevant passages in *My Life*. Had Berlioz prompted him to portray his own experience on similar lines, starting out with the auto-biographical data but amplifying, arranging and colouring them in a particular way (Seventh Symphony, Beethoven/Shakespeare)? Wagner might have learnt of Berlioz's memoirs through Richard Pohl. On the other hand Beethoven and Shakespeare had been linked by writers since E. T. A. Hoffmann and Amadeus Wendt.

Different stages in Wagner's Beethoven experience are more or less evident in the *Autobiographical Sketch* and *'Music of the Future'* as well as *My Life*. Admittedly the *Sketch* is the only other account to show it as an escalation, stressing elements that came after the initial cause of it. After mentioning the 'all-powerful impression' which Beethoven's music made at the Gewandhaus concerts, Wagner refers to the music for *Egmont*. It was this which made him want to 'provide a similar music' (*SB* I, p. 97) for the tragedy he had finished (*Leubald und Adelaide*). Thus we find a strong emphasis on the *Egmont* music, at the expense of the initial Gewandhaus experience. All the same the two impressions are seen as forming one complex. In *My Life* (p. 31), Wagner again states that 'I now wanted to write incidental music for *Leubald und Adelaide*, like Beethoven's for *Egmont*.' But here the matter seems peripheral by comparison with the portrayal of the symphonic experience. The reason why he emphasizes it in the *Sketch* is probably that upon his return to Germany, Wagner wanted to present himself as a composer who had been already significantly influenced in his youth by Beethoven, not least in his opera composing. As a note to *SB* I,

17

				Gradations in the experience				
	No. of works involved in 1st experience	Description in source	Date	Starting-point (basic experience)	Development	Climax	Other works in same context	Effect and results of experience
Red Pocket-Book 1835	indefinite (several works)	'Beethoven's symphonies'	1828	—	—	—	—	'Newly fired passion for music' (Logier: *Thoroughbass*)
A Pilgrimage to Beethoven 1840	one work	'a Beethoven symphony'	1828	—	—	—	—	illness and recovery as musician
Autobiographical Sketch 1842–3	indefinite (several works)	'Beethoven's music'	1828	'Beethoven's music'	'B's music for *Egmont* inspired me so much…'	—	—	writes music for tragedy *Leubald und Adelaide*
Communication to My Friends 1851	indefinite (several works)	'acquaintance with B.'s symphonies'	1828	—	—	—	—	passionate allegiance to music
'Music of the Future' 1860	indefinite (several works)	'… I now got to know his [B.'s] music'	1827 1828	Beethoven's death	'I got to know his music…'	—	—	increasingly strong 'bent for music'
My Life 1865–80	one work named	'finally I heard a symph of the master … the A maj Symphony'	1827 1828	Beethoven's death	'I now wanted to learn more about B.': finds *Egmont* music on sister's piano; tries to get sonatas	A maj Symphony	E major overture to *Fidelio*	merging of Beethoven's image and his music, along with image of Shakespeare
The Work and Mission of my Life 1879	indefinite (several works)	'Beethoven's symphonies'	1828	—	—	—	—	impassioned conscious devotion to music

p. 112 confirms, the basic purpose of the *Autobiographical Sketch* was to make Wagner's name known in Germany following his return from Paris. The repercussions of his new Beethoven experience (Habeneck) were, of course, closely connected with the aim of self-promotion: Beethoven's Ninth had inspired Wagner as a composer. It had an appreciable effect on both the *Faust* Overture and *Der Fliegende Holländer*. So in the *Sketch*, Wagner's temporary situation again helped to modify the terms in which he described his original experience of Beethoven.

The context of the experience

We must remember that it was not one particular concert performance but several such experiences which made Wagner resolve to be a musician. At the same time we should bear in mind that his recurring experience of Beethoven often happened within the context of the impression which other composers' music was making on him. As late as 1873, Wagner refers to this *combination of experiences*. For on 9 March Cosima quotes him as saying, 'if I had not received my impressions from Weber and the symphonies of Beethoven, God knows what would have become of me'.

Those statements we have already quoted were nearer in time to the event concerned. But they patently match this brief reminiscence when seen in context. Wagner's earliest statement, the one about a 'newly fired passion for music', reflects a new fit of enthusiasm that was caused by Beethoven. It is, however, unthinkable without a remark which relates to the year of 1826 and similarly occurs in the *Red Pocket-Book*: 'love of music. Passion for Weber . . .' Here Weber triggers off the initial response to music, in advance of Wagner's enthusiasm for Beethoven. And in 1828, Beethoven's music evidently aroused Wagner's passion directly in conjunction with the music of another composer. The full entry in the *Pocket-Book* reads: 'Neglect lessons. Get to know Mozart; Beethoven's symphonies. Newly fired passion for music.' A year later, in 1829, what triggered off a fresh bout of enthusiasm was apparently an enthusiasm for Mozart communicated to Wagner by Kienlen, the Magdeburg conductor. 'To Magdeburg. Discovery of my passion for music Kühnlein [sic].'

Was it entirely instrumental music that always sparked off Wagner's successive bouts of musical enthusiasm? In this respect Beethoven's music was undoubtedly of great importance, especially certain of the symphonies. But there were other contributory factors deriving from the theatre, and hence from opera as well. According to Deathridge, Wagner's claim to have heard Wilhelmine Schröder-Devrient as Fidelio must be untrue, because there is no record of a Leipzig performance of Beethoven's opera in 1829. Be that as it may, Auber's *La Muette de Portici* made such an impact on Wagner that it can still be felt in the *Recollections of Auber* he wrote in 1871. It

19

is hardly conceivable that he missed the performance on 28 September 1829 in which his sister Rosalie played the title role.

The long-term effect of Auber also finds expression in Cosima's diaries. An entry for 9 December 1880 contains some reflections on Wagner's relationship to Beethoven and Auber.

Recently, too, when it was suggested that R. had carried on the Beethoven type of melody, he denied it emphatically, saying that had been something complete in itself: 'I could not have composed in the way I have done if Beethoven had never existed, but what I have used and developed are isolated strokes of genius in my dramatic predecessors, including even Auber, allowing myself to be led by something other than opera.'

This shows that Wagner's long-expressed criticisms of opera actually determined (rather than excluded) the lasting impact of certain features, features which pointed beyond the conventional banalities of 'opera' as such. The point is a crucial one. It leads on to the perception that even in connection with Wagner's earliest musical impressions, Beethoven's symphonic writing left its mark precisely in the context of Wagner's impressions of operatic limits transcended. This is also what makes a performance by Schröder-Devrient important: it went significantly beyond operatic routine. At first, of course, Wagner would hardly have been fully aware of the basic significance of these earliest impressions. But his mind had registered them, and as he developed as an artist, they took on a clear form and thus significance with regard to his own artistic objectives.

So was instrumental music really the sole cause of Wagner's enthusiasm for music? What about those impressions of the musical stage he gained through his family and sisters, not least Rosalie? Did they not also play an extremely important role from very early on? Was it that Wagner began – and (secretly) continued – to write music as an instrumental composer, altogether in line with his enthusiasm for Beethoven, or was it not rather the case that his early musical enthusiasm was already combined with a lively theatrical imagination, and that with the further stimuli of the classical world and literature, this first encouraged him to write for the stage? Did the various criticisms of opera that Wagner voiced as a novice conductor amount to a 'basic critique'? Initially, was it not that he was criticizing the opera of his time and the institutional failings which were bound up with it? And is it legitimate to read Wagner's early work-list selectively, passing over anything, such as the *Leubald* draft, that does not appear to be related to or validated by a genuinely musical ambition?

Let us take as our starting-point Wagner's earliest experience of music as it relates to his other activities. Let us also begin with the premise that very often an artist's early attempts conceal or obscure gifts he will develop and display with panache, once he has realized his potential. Then we shall have to take seriously Wagner's artistic and critical statements in respect of opera and the theatre, hazy and amateurish though they were at the outset, for they point forward to things to come. If we grant equal validity to all the early drafts and trial runs, and extend the young Wagner's work-list beyond 1832, the list will look different to Voss's. Voss leaves out those titles up to the end of 1832 which are marked below with an asterisk, and he does not give the works written up to 1836 in this context.

1826–8, Dresden/Leipzig:
Leubald, tragedy in 5 acts (*WWV* I, pp. 63f.)
Summer 1829, Leipzig:
Sonata in D minor (*WWV* II, p. 64)
1829, Leipzig:
*Aria (*WWV* III, pp. 64f.)
Autumn 1829, Leipzig:
String Quartet in D major (*WWV* IV, p. 65)
Autumn 1829, Leipzig:
Sonata in F minor for piano (*WWV* V, p. 65)
Spring 1830, Leipzig:
*Pastoral opera (*WWV* VI, p. 65)
1828–30, Leipzig:
*Lieder (*WWV* VII, p. 66)
Spring 1830, Leipzig:
*Aria for soprano (*WWV* VIII, p. 67)
Summer 1830–Easter 1831, Leipzig:
*Piano reduction, 2 hands, of Beethoven Symphony No. 9 (*WWV* IX, pp. 67f.)
Summer 1830, Leipzig:
Overture in B flat major, nicknamed 'Drum Tap' (*WWV* X, p. 69)
?September 1830, Leipzig:
'Political' Overture (*WWV* XI, p. 70)
Summer or Autumn 1830, Leipzig:
Overture to Schiller's tragedy with choruses *Die Braut von Messina* (*WWV* XII, pp. 70f.)
?1830, Leipzig:
Orchestral work in E minor (*WWV* XIII, pp. 71f.)
Towards end 1830, Leipzig:
Overture in C major (*WWV* XIV, p. 72)
Beginning of 1831, Leipzig:
*Seven compositions for Goethe's *Faust* I (*WWV* XV, pp. 72ff.)
Beginning of 1831, Leipzig:
Sonata in B flat major, 4 hands (*WWV* XVI, pp. 75f.)
Spring 1831, Leipzig:
Overture in E flat major (*WWV* XVII, p. 76)

Summer 1831, Leipzig:
Piano reduction of J. Haydn, Symphony in E flat major, No. 103 (*WWV* xviii, pp. 76f.)
Autumn 1831–Winter 1831/2, Leipzig:
*Fugues, incl. 4-part vocal fugue 'Dein ist das Reich' (*WWV* xix, pp. 77f.)
Midsummer–Autumn 1831, Leipzig:
Overture in D minor (Concert Ov. No. 1) (*WWV* xx, p. 79)
Autumn 1831, Leipzig:
Sonata in B flat major for piano, op. 1 (*WWV* xxi, pp. 82ff.)
Autumn 1831, Leipzig:
Fantasy in F sharp minor for piano (*WWV* xxii, pp. 84ff.)
End 1831–Beginning 1832, Leipzig:
Polonaises for piano (*WWV* xxiii, pp. 86ff.)
Winter 1831/2, Leipzig:
Overture in E minor and incidental music for Raupach's *König Enzio* (*WWV* xxiv, pp. 88ff.)
?Spring 1832, Leipzig:
Entr'actes tragiques (*WWV* xxv, pp. 91ff.)
Beginning of 1832, Leipzig:
Grand Sonata in A major for piano, op. 4 (*WWV* xxvi, pp. 93ff.)
March 1832, Leipzig:
Concert Overture No. 2 in C major (*WWV* xxvii, pp. 95ff.)
Spring 1832, Leipzig:
*Scena and aria for soprano and orchestra (*WWV* xxviii, pp. 97f.)
?April–June 1832, Leipzig:
Symphony in C major (*WWV* xxix, pp. 98ff.)
12 October 1832, Pravonin nr. Prague:
*'Glockentöne', song for voice and piano (*WWV* xxx, pp. 101f.)
Autumn 1832–February 1833, Pravonin/Prague/Leipzig/Würzburg:
*Die Hochzeit, opera (unfinished) (*WWV* xxxi, pp. 102ff.)
Beginning of 1833–Spring 1834, Leipzig:
*Die Feen, grand romantic opera in three acts (*WWV* xxxii, pp. 32ff.)
September 1833, Würzburg:
*New final allegro for Aria No. 15 from Marschner's opera *Der Vampyr* (*WWV* xxxiii, pp. 120ff.)
August–September 1834, Lauchstädt/Rudolstadt:
*Symphony in E major (fragment) (*WWV* xxxv, pp. 122ff.)
December 1834–January 1835, Magdeburg:
*Overture in E flat major and incidental music for Apel's *Columbus* (*WWV* xxxvii, pp. 127ff.)
Summer 1834–Spring 1836/(1840), Rudolstadt/Magdeburg:
*Das Liebesverbot oder Die Novize von Palermo (*WWV* xxxviii, pp. 131ff.)

'Beethoven and instrumental music' – we can be sure that they made a crucial impact on Wagner. But right from the start, Wagner absorbed these impressions within the context of the theatre, dramatic literature and musically heightened scene-painting and stage effects. This is borne out by Cosima's late diary entry about Wagner's partial orientation to Auber; Wagner's remark was certainly not made for publicity purposes.

It would be flying in the face of all the evidence to confine Wagner entirely to instrumental music and purely symphonic ambitions as far as his real intentions are concerned.

Beethoven's death

Probably the most difficult aspect of Wagner's accounts of his responses to Beethoven is his reaction to the composer's death. *'Music of the Future'* and *My Life* single this out as the starting-point, the event which triggered off all Wagner's successive responses. And bound up with it is the question of when the reaction occurred. According to the other sources it must have been in 1828, because of Wagner's visits to the Gewandhaus concerts after his return to Leipzig. In the two aforementioned accounts, however, Wagner locates his first enduring impression in the year 1827. He tells us in *My Life* (p. 30) that he learnt of Beethoven's death from his sisters: the news 'had just been received'. During 1826–7 he was living apart from his family, who had moved to Prague. But it is still possible that his relatives told him the news, for Beethoven died on 26 March 1827, and Newman records Wagner as paying a second visit to Prague in the spring of that year. Hence the special importance of the sentence 'I asked my sisters about Beethoven and learned that news of his death had just been received.'

Why is it that such a vital part of Wagner's responses to Beethoven emerges so belatedly, and in only two autobiographical documents? Did this reaction really take place at all? Even in the *Red Pocket-Book*, Wagner does not make the least mention of it. Certainly it is a striking fact that his two references to Beethoven's death appear in accounts which are relatively close together in time but were written for different purposes. Beethoven's stated aim in *'Music of the Future'* was to 'give my friends here some information, especially about the formal aspect of my artistic intentions'. All it would supply were some personal details that were of particular relevance in this connection. *My Life*, on the other hand, implied an autobiography which was to be as complete and thorough as possible. So we cannot just say that Wagner mentioned Beethoven's death in *'Music of the Future'* for the sake of completeness. He must have had a stronger reason.

It is worth asking whether the reference was not one more product of Schopenhauer's influence, which could have given Wagner's Beethoven experience a new dimension. The fascination for Wagner of the idea of death as Schopenhauer presented it is well known. The ideas which Schopenhauer imparted to him admit of the following conjecture. Although Wagner never referred to this, it is likely that the idea of metempsychosis, the transmigration of souls, crucially affected the way he wrote about Beethoven's death. Such an explanation gains in cogency when we consider how familiar he was with this idea; it often figures in his writings. (Feuerbach had already broached it in 1834, in his aphorisms *Der Schriftsteller und der Mensch*.)

In *German Art and German Politics* (*GS* VIII, p. 64), Wagner applies the idea of 'reincarnation' to an art fulfilling the classical Greek ideal but designed afresh – and thus in a palpably different sense from the idea of metempsychosis. *On the Destiny of Opera* illustrates another use of the idea. Here a transmigration forms the starting-point, but Wagner is using the term metaphorically.

In practice it was impossible for Shakespeare to act out every one of his roles. The composer, however, achieves this extremely firmly by speaking to us through each of his performers. The soundest technique has infallible laws that govern a transmigration of the soul of the [musical] dramatist into the actor's own body. By giving the beat for a technically accurate performance of his work, the composer becomes totally at one with the musician performing it. If the same could be said of anyone else's work, it could only be that of a visual artist working with colours or with stone, where one might speak of his soul's transmigration into his inanimate material. (*GS* IX, pp. 150f.; see also X, p. 120)

Wagner was, however, already close to the idea of metempsychosis before he encountered Schopenhauer's philosophy. And significantly, it is adumbrated within the context of his responses to Beethoven. The author (who is identical with the narrator) of the story *A Pilgrimage to Beethoven* states:

I no longer partook of any pleasure other than that of immersing myself so deeply in this genius that I finally imagined I had become a part of him; and as this minute particle I began to esteem myself, to hold loftier ideas and views – in short, to become what sensible people are apt to call a fool.

Wagner was aware that one of the religious sources of metempsychosis was Brahmanism, as is evident from *My Life* (p. 530). Here he tells how he assisted Georg Herwegh in finding a suitable framework for 'a vast epic poem':

He had once alluded to Dante's good fortune in finding such an apt subject as the path through hell and purgatory to paradise. This gave me the idea to suggest for the framework of his poem the myth of metempsychosis, which, from its source in the Brahmin religion, through Plato impinged even upon our classical culture. He found this idea not bad at all, so I went even further and sketched the form such a poem should take; he should divide it in three main acts, each in three cantos ...

24

The first part would show the principal figure in his Asiatic homeland, the second in the Hellenistic–Roman world, and the third in his rebirth in the medieval and modern world.

Wagner also applied the idea of reincarnation to family relationships. On 28 May 1879 he wrote a revealing letter to Ludwig II of Bavaria. It describes the theatricality of his birthday celebration a few days earlier and includes the following lines:

> Propped up in the centre of the hall was a new portrait of my wife painted by Lenbach, which was quite incredible in its artistic beauty and perfection. This surprise had been carefully prepared. My son Siegfried was posing in front of the picture, wearing black velvet and with blond tresses (very like the young Van Dyck's portrait). He was meant to be representing – in a symbolical rebirth – my father Ludwig Geyer: he was called 'Ludwig the painter' and was still working on the portrait with a maulstick and brush, as though he were adding the finishing touches... (*BLW* III, p. 153)

But the idea of metempsychosis must have taken a particularly strong hold on Wagner in 1860, when he was planning *'Music of the Future'*. At the beginning of August he wrote to Mathilde Wesendonck:

> Only a profound acceptance of the doctrine of metempsychosis has been able to console me by revealing the point at which all things finally converge at the same level of redemption, after the various individual existences – which run alongside each other in time – have come together in a meaningful way outside time. According to the beautiful Buddhist doctrine, the spotless purity of Lohengrin is easily explicable in terms of his being the continuation of Parzifal – who was the first to strive towards purity. Elsa, similarly, would reach the level of Lohengrin through being reborn. (*SL*, p. 499)

Just as Wagner saw his two opera heroes as being united through a transmigration of souls, so he saw his own creative life as a continuation of Beethoven's on a higher plane, through the same compelling process. The musical dramatist in Wagner was a rebirth, an intensification of the tone-poet in Beethoven. This was symbolized by the fact that the news of Beethoven's death, and the 'strange anguish' Wagner felt at the news, led him to take up the dead master's music. It was the other's death which first really gave life to the musician in Wagner.

This explanation becomes even more obvious when we consider the claim Wagner had already made in Paris in 1840–1 that he alone was qualified to succeed Beethoven, and to round off what Beethoven had struggled to achieve. In that context, the passage we have quoted from the Paris novella takes on a special importance. We might further bear in mind Wagner's view of the redemptive role of art, along with his self-appointed historical task of using art to complete that process of redemption which Beethoven had initiated. And if so, then our explanation shows how an aesthetic precept was simply being extended into the realm of metaphysics.

Response pattern and autobiography[3]

The narrative of *My Life* contains two indications that an extra-musical factor was combined with a musical one in Wagner's response to Beethoven. His 'strange anguish' at the news of Beethoven's death accords with his 'childish dread of the ghostly fifths on the violin'. This emotional state is also part of Wagner's range of responses to the Ninth Symphony, because of the way the Ninth begins. Moreover – and this is our second indication – the musical effect made by the Seventh Symphony combines with the 'impact of Beethoven's physiognomy ... as well as the knowledge of his deafness and his solitary and withdrawn life'. Thus there soon arose in Wagner's mind 'an image of the highest supernal originality'.

Wagner really did experience things on more than one level at once. Let us take the evidence of his oft-quoted letter of 30 January 1844 to Carl Gaillard. This reveals the sharpness of Wagner's perceptions about himself – although, of course, they lack the orderliness of a trained psychologist's. In discussing the creative process, the letter outlines Wagner's artistic make-up:

It is not my practice to choose a subject at random, to versify it & then think of suitable music to write for it; – if I were to proceed in that way I should be exposed to the difficulty of having to work myself up to a pitch of enthusiasm on two separate occasions, something which is impossible. No, my method of production is different from that: – in the first place I am attracted only by those subjects which reveal themselves to me not only as poetically but, at the same time, as musically significant. And so, even before I set about writing a single line of the text or drafting a scene, I am already thoroughly immersed in the musical aura of my new creation, I have the whole sound & all the characteristic motives in my head so that when the poem is finished & the scenes are arranged in their proper order the actual opera is already completed, & its detailed musical treatment is more a question of calm & reflective revision, the moment of actual creativity having already passed. But for this to be so, I must choose only subjects which are capable of an exclusively musical treatment: I would never, for example, choose a subject which a skilled playwright could just as well turn into a spoken drama.[4] (*SL*, p. 118)

The above statement is dealing with the same interaction of musical and extra-musical grades of feeling in Wagner's creative life that occurs in his experience of Beethoven. As a creator of music dramas, Wagner selected only those subjects which presented both dramatic and musical possibilities. This has a parallel in the response mechanism: in the association of a 'strange anguish' at the news of Beethoven's death with the 'dread of the ghostly fifths on the violin', as also in the fusion of the Seventh Symphony's 'indescribable' effect with the impact made by Beethoven's appearance and fate. With both the experiencing process and the creative process, the structure of the underlying artistic make-up is the same.

Wagner's letter to Gaillard is an early (if not the very first) expression of his thoughts about his own creative methods. If we look at his statement in *A Communication to My Friends* (*GS* IV, pp. 267, 316f.), we will be left with the impression that this particular working method crystallized only little by little, from unconscious beginnings. In 1842, two years before the letter to Gaillard, Wagner wrote the essay *Halévy and French Opera*. There he speaks only of the ideal instance of two old friends, a musician and a dramatic poet who are in mutual sympathy, and who arrive jointly at the subject and design of their dramatic creation.

We have found a fundamental agreement between the productive and receptive processes. This suggests that the information about the combined action of the two levels is basically correct. At the age of fourteen or fifteen, of course, Wagner would hardly have perceived any of this. Rather he would achieve an analysis and synopsis only when he had attained to a clear view of himself and, reliving his early impressions and experiences, tried to discern in them the seeds of what came later. It is highly probable that in the course of this self-exegesis, the composer introduced some details which had not been part of the original experience, and modified others which he no longer recalled all that clearly. It will, however, hardly have been mere chance or a whim that led Wagner to use his Beethoven experience to illustrate his own musical awakening and the specific character of his artistic make-up.

Wagner's accounts of his Beethoven experience contain inconsistencies and errors. But to regard them as indicating a general tendency towards untruth and distortion, and to lump them together as failings of which he alone was guilty, would be to misunderstand the task and function of autobiographical writings. The pursuit of autobiography, says Roy Pascal (1960), is a subtle penetration of the past by the present. It is wrong to expect 'to evoke circumstances and experiences as they actually were for the child and young man. We do not need to consult psychologists as to whether this is a feasible task; it is clearly impossible...' (p. 14).

To establish some criteria for an appraisal of Wagner's autobiographical writings, it will be useful to quote Pascal at greater length. Autobiography, he says,

involves the reconstruction of the movement of a life, or part of a life, in the actual circumstances in which it was lived ... But 'reconstruction of a life' is an impossible task. A single day's experience is limitless in its radiation backward and forward. So that we have to hurry to qualify the above assertions by adding that autobiography is a shaping of the past. It imposes a pattern on a life, constructs out of it a coherent story ... This coherence implies that the writer takes a particular standpoint, the standpoint of the moment at which he reviews his life, and interprets his life from it

... Autobiography, as A. M. Clark said, is not the annals of a man's life, but its 'philosophical history'. (Pascal [1960], p. 9)

In the German edition of his study, Pascal goes on to say:

The insight that memory has a shaping function was responsible for the title of Goethe's autobiography. Goethe writes that, modestly enough, he called it *Dichtung und Wahrheit* ['Poetry and Truth'] because of his deep conviction that 'in the present, and indeed even in retrospect, a person builds up a picture of the external world that conforms to the quirks of his own nature'.

So the discrepancies in Wagner's accounts of his Beethoven experience are nothing unusual as autobiographies go. The momentous effect of just one symphony as described in the Paris novella, the emphasis on Beethoven's music for *Egmont* in connection with *Leubald und Adelaide*, the climactic role of the Seventh Symphony in *My Life* – each was prompted by Wagner's particular situation at the time he was writing. The inclusion and highlighting of Beethoven's death in *'Music of the Future'* and *My Life* resulted from a specific philosophical stance, a stance which was influenced by Schopenhauer and the information that he provided on Indian religion. But the development of a response pattern such as is demonstrated by the Beethoven experience in *My Life* was the result of Wagner's perception of his personal creative make-up. He was projecting this back upon the early experience in order to interpret that experience (and also to correct Schopenhauer, as we shall see), no matter how he actually remembered it.

The present study can only give some indication of Wagner's make-up as an autobiographer. If we examined all his writings with this in mind, our findings would probably confirm what is, perhaps, especially pronounced with Wagner: the textural richness of the autobiographical fabric. While our own study may draw certain conclusions from Wagner's accounts of his Beethoven experience, those conclusions ought not to be generalized. All the same, it would hardly be going too far to say that Wagner's Beethoven experience is one of the central strands. According to Roy Pascal (pp. 185–6), the main achievement of the art of autobiography is to give us events that symbolize the essence of the author's personality. It affords an 'intuitive knowledge of some unique experience' (Susanne Langer's phrase) which 'as such is representative of life altogether'. And that can be said of the illumination Wagner received in responding to Beethoven's music.

But Wagner's response to Beethoven is also central in a different sense, in that it gives some indication of his basic approach to autobiography. Doubtless almost every autobiography includes a myth-making element. Looking back, the author interprets the past from a present standpoint, or 'actualizes' [*vergegenwärtigt*] it; he recasts the historical substance as a 'coherent' and 'philosophical' story. With Wagner, however, this myth-making streak is idiosyncratic and especially strongly pronounced. In his autobiographical writings – and not only there – Wagner is constantly addressing the public afresh, and for a purpose. And propaganda is invariably part of the aim. In other words, Wagner was always writing not only for his own times but also for the future, and particularly his own future. Thus his Beethoven experience as stylized in the novella *A Pilgrimage* denotes a meeting that was germane to his future artistic development. Wagner's account in *My Life*, however, is meant to go farther than that and serve the future interests of his own myth or self-image. His autobiographical writing involves not only an 'actualization' [*Vergegenwärtigung*] of past events through 'reminiscence' [*Erinnerung*] but also a 'presentiment' [*Ahnung*]: an inkling of events yet to happen – and of how they would happen. So by studying Wagner's response to Beethoven, we can see his autobiographical writing as being based on the same structure as that used by him as librettist and composer to organize the mythical subjects of his music dramas. Wagner produced quite enough self-explanations to drive home the parallel. As the successive stages of a Wagnerian drama unfold, musical events ('leitmotifs') already familiar to us will be actualized through reminiscence. But thanks to the overall dramatic design, they will at the same time convey a presentiment of future events. (We shall discuss this at greater length on pp. 146–9.) In the same way, Wagner keeps presenting another version of his Beethoven experience, each version being directed towards the future as well as recalling and reviving the past.

Wagner's approach to autobiography corresponds to the construction of myth. This is particularly evident if we remember that the first description of the Beethoven experience in the *Red Pocket-Book* is treated like a 'musical event', a dramatically motivated state of emotion, as it were, like a 'leitmotif'. Wagner has this ability to manipulate his description; besides 'Beethoven's symphonies' he mentions his 'newly fired passion for music'. It was a simple matter to give this emotion fresh nuances, depending on his personal prospects and the consequent purpose of the piece of writing concerned.

This kind of experience made an immediate impact but also had lasting effects. It entitles us to use the term *Erlebnisse* ('experiences', with the nuance of 'lived events') to describe the young Wagner's salient artistic impressions. As a coinage the word at first occurs only sporadically – in the writings of Ludwig Tieck, for instance – in the first half of the nineteenth century. Yet the actual concept was already common in the age of Goethe. And because of the type of experience it represented, and its role in a person's life, the word itself evolved from autobiography. This is illustrated by Wagner's autobiographical writings, including, significantly enough, the entries in his early *Pocket-Book*. Here he expressly records events in his artistic experience that precisely match – and that he uses and reuses in just such a way – the essential meaning of the word *Erlebnis*. As Gadamer defined it, an experience turned into an *Erlebnis* when it was not merely lived through but had a special impact endowing it with lasting significance. The lasting element is what produces the 'material quality' of the *Erlebnis*. It becomes the subject of an autobiographical 'treatment' in which the author surveys and interprets his own life, and endows it with meaning. Cosima's diaries are a good example of this. They contain numerous passages – passages of reminiscence, but particularly reflections on events and landmarks in Wagner's life – which show that it is 'in the very nature of an *Erlebnis* to go on having an effect. As Nietzsche says, all experiences go on for a long time within people of depth' (Gadamer 1972, p. 63). Wagner's earliest experiences stretch right across his life and were the catalysts of its 'poetic truth'. And this confers on the 'poetic truth' of his autobiography a special quality as a statement, one which sets it on a par with the – equally important – 'empirical truth'. Scholars such as Deathridge in *The New Grove Wagner*, Voss and Lichtenhahn have criticized the first in the light of the second. But to do so is at the same time to bring out its own intrinsic character and to confirm its intrinsic value.

Stations and function of the Beethoven experience

Hearing Beethoven the symphonist

Wolzogen tells us that even in old age, Wagner considered it the 'greatest honour to be allowed to listen' to works by Beethoven (Wolzogen [1891], p. 26). Wagner did not say this in connection with a particularly successful performance, a special event. Rather it was said of a Beethoven quartet despite a rough-and-ready rendering of it on the piano, during the customary gatherings at the Haus Wahnfried – a mixture of friendly domestic music-making and absorbed hero-worship.

Beethoven's music constantly inspired Wagner afresh, even prompting him to execute dance steps and gestures. According to Ludwig Schemann, the 'cheerful sections of the String Quartet op. 127' sparked off an uninhibited display of his own cheerful reactions; he danced, leapt about and teased his companions. And according to Cosima's note, not long before his death, on 10 January 1883, he twice came dancing in whilst Liszt was playing the 'Andante of Beethoven's A major Symphony and the Scherzo allegretto of the F major [Symphony]'.

Given the liveliness of Wagner's artistic sensibilities, it is not surprising that he always retained his capacity for fresh experiences. In the latter part of his life, the music of Mozart and especially Bach drew enthusiastic and thoughtful comments from him as well. But the remarkable thing is how far the dynamic responses which Beethoven's art evoked in him are woven into the whole fabric of Wagner's life. And up to now this has never been studied in detail.

Unlike so many youthful artistic impressions, Wagner's earliest Beethoven experience was not overlaid, and eventually ousted, by other happenings. Rather, through the linking together of specific events over a period of years, its structure took on the role of a paradigm. And it was Beethoven's Ninth Symphony that governed the particular pattern of Wagner's successive responses, important stages in his life being associated with it. First there was Paris (1839), then Dresden (1846–9), and later Bayreuth (1872).In all probability Wagner's enthusiasm for the Ninth was kindled soon after the Gewandhaus event in January 1828. In the well-known letter of 6 October 1830 to Schotts, offering them his arrangement of the Ninth for two hands (*WWV* ix), he wrote that he had studied 'Beethoven's splendid last symphony' most intensively for a long time (*SB* I, p. 117). This was no exaggeration. Besides the piano arrangement, he had made a copy of the complete score, a feat which he described in *My Life* (p. 35) as an act of 'arbitrary self-education'. Clearly it was a special type of self-education, for the nocturnal hours he devoted to it were also spent immersed in extravagant imaginings. The open fifths at the start conjured up his very first musical experience, the violins of an orchestra tuning up, and this realm of feeling merged with an existential premonition. As with his earliest experience, a musical feeling of eeriness became entwined with his personal destiny.

On first looking through the score, which I obtained only with great difficulty, I was struck at once, as if by force of destiny, with the long-sustained perfect fifths with which the first movement begins: these sounds, which played such a spectral role in my earliest impressions of music, came to me as the ghostly fundamental of my own life. This symphony surely held the secret to all secrets; and so I got busy over it by painstakingly copying out the score. Once, after having spent a night at this task, I remember being startled by the dawn, which affected me so strongly in my excited condition that I buried myself under the bedclothes with a loud shriek as if terrified by an apparition. (*My Life*, pp. 35–6)

Wagner was surely referring to the same period when he said in *My Life* (p. 429) that he had been driven 'by the mystical influence of Beethoven's Ninth Symphony to plumb the deepest recesses of music'. There is also the passage (p. 175) where he speaks of the 'mystic constellations and soundless magic spirits' he initially associated with the work.

There is good reason to stress the constancy of Wagner's enthusiasm for Beethoven. But to think that there were no crises in this relationship (as Westernhagen does), and that Wagner never had any doubts or criticisms, does not square with the facts. There were times when he wavered over the Ninth Symphony itself. This began with a rehearsal under August Pohlenz in 1830, in the Leipzig Gewandhaus; *My Life* (p. 57) describes Wagner's disappointment and above all his bewilderment. Since he had yet to form a clear idea of the work, he could not maintain all his enthusiasm for it in the face of so negative an impression. The result was that Mozart came more to

31

the forefront. The importance of this episode emerges from *My Life*. Wagner says that with the help of the contrapuntal skills acquired through Weinlig, he had learnt to appreciate and tried to copy the 'light and flowing manner in which Mozart handled the most complex technical problems', especially in the finale of the 'Jupiter' Symphony. In spite of a certain loss of enthusiasm, however, the link with Beethoven was not broken off; rather it became more objective.

For the time being, though, the gap between Wagner and Beethoven was to grow even wider. In a letter of 7 August 1836 to Heinrich Dorn, Wagner described himself as a 'ci-devant Beethovenian'. He thought at the time that he needed to aim for an ideal solution by using some of the components of Italian and French opera. This is quite evident from a letter he wrote to Meyerbeer on 4 March 1837.

Wagner's unsettled attitude to Beethoven during this period becomes plain to behold when we compare his statements in *My Life* about the two earliest operatic events that were associated in his mind with Wilhelmine Schröder-Devrient, the famous singer. He describes his reaction to a *Fidelio* performance as one of helpless enthusiasm:

> I did not know where to turn or even how to begin to produce anything remotely commensurable with the impressions I had received ... I wanted to write a work that would be worthy of Schröder-Devrient: but as that was by no means within my power I abandoned all artistic efforts in headlong despair... (*My Life*, p. 37)

Deathridge assumes that this early *Fidelio* experience is a fiction on Wagner's part, because 'the performance is not mentioned in his diary, the Red Pocket-Book, and there is no trace of it in the theatre records of the period' (*NGW*, p. 7).

The fact that this event does not appear in either source is of course striking. But the omission is surely no positive proof that it never happened. Wagner did not record every major event in his *Red Pocket-Book* by any means. We have also to consider that in *My Life* Wagner says that when he was subsequently Kapellmeister at the Royal Saxon Court, Wilhelmine Schröder-Devrient herself reminded him of his enthusiastic letter to her. As far as the theatre records [*Theaterzettel*] are concerned, there is – according to the City of Leipzig Museum for History – an eleven-day gap for the period in question (April 1829), and it is uncertain whether this gap is because of missing *Zettel* or because there were no performances on those days. Moreover, is it still possible to check *all* the press notices?

It must also be borne in mind that directly before her long Paris engagement (1830), Schröder-Devrient sang in many cities as a guest artist and may have stepped in at short notice on occasion. Thus her omission from the contemporary press organs and *Theaterzettel* does not suffice to show that she did not sing in *Fidelio* at Leipzig in 1829.

And one further consideration is relevant here. In the summer of 1829, Wagner travelled to Magdeburg; can we be entirely sure that he did not go to Dresden as well? There is proof that Beethoven's *Fidelio* was performed in Dresden on 22 and 25 August and again on 11 October, with Schröder-Devrient in the leading role! And even if Wagner did not go to Dresden, would not the reports of her performance that surely reached him have been enough to kindle his imagination? And even if we posit a 'falsification' on Wagner's part, would this not simply be telling us that he was extremely fascinated by Beethoven and wanted to show that Beethoven had legitimatized his own creative work and its intention? But was there, then, ever any need for such a falsification? Does Wagner's extraordinary – and well-documented – early commitment to Beethoven's Ninth not speak for itself?

We can state quite positively that the question-mark behind the documentary evidence regarding the Beethoven experience that Schröder-Devrient sparked off in Wagner only underlines Beethoven's importance to him. It points to a deeper truth.

When Wagner heard Schröder-Devrient in Bellini's opera *I Capuleti ed i Montecchi*, his response was quite different:

The palpable change in my estimate of the German composers I had revered and venerated ... was ... mainly attributable to my impressions of another guest performance in Leipzig by Schröder-Devrient, who carried everyone away with her interpretation of Romeo in Bellini's *Romeo and Juliet*. The effect was unlike anything we had ever experienced. The sight of the boldly romantic figure of the young hero, projected against a background of such obviously shallow and empty music, prompted one at all events to ruminate on the causes of the ineffectuality of most of the solid German music used in drama up to now. Without yet losing myself in these meditations too deeply, I allowed myself to be borne along by the current of my excitable youthful sensibility and was instinctively impelled to cast off that brooding seriousness which in my earlier years had driven me to such dramatic mysticism ... Just as I had sown my wild oats as a student, I now boldly embarked on the same course in the development of my artistic tastes.

(*My Life*, pp. 80–1, slightly amended)

The gulf dividing good from unsuccessful musical interpretations must have made Wagner more discriminating with regard to the qualities of a performance. These experiences formed the background to the lasting effect of later Beethoven performances. Thus a negative experience of the Ninth Symphony paved the way for the especially profound and enduring effect of new and positive impressions. Only now can we fully comprehend the role of the Paris interpretation under Habeneck. On that occasion Wagner first got to know Beethoven's Ninth in a rendering which stood out favourably from other renderings. Later he recalled a rehearsal of the first three movements, 'undertaken by the incomparable orchestra of the Conservatoire'. Suddenly, he wrote, after 'years of bewildering confusion', it put him 'miraculously in touch' with those early youthful days and had 'sown the seeds of an inner change of direction ... as though exerting a magic force'. The memory appears in *My Life* (p. 329).

Wagner refers only to the first three movements of the symphony, and scholars have often followed him in this respect. But it is doubtful whether this account sets out all the facts. Other passages in his writings (such as *GS* xii, p. 82; viii, pp. 166 and 16) admit of the inference that he definitely heard the entire work under Habeneck's direction, including the finale. In some writings he speaks first and foremost of concert performances. It has been established that during his Paris stay – from the autumn of 1839 to the spring of 1842 – Wagner had three opportunities to hear a complete concert performance of the Ninth. It would be unwise to assume that he did not avail himself of them.

We must therefore start out from the premise that Wagner heard Beethoven's Ninth in Paris more than once. But when did he hear Habeneck conduct it; and more particularly, when did Wagner *first* hear him conduct it? Was it, as stated in *My Life*, at a rehearsal of the first three movements near the end of 1839, or was it at a performance of the whole work – very probably the concert of 8 March 1840?

(We have no means of checking the authenticity of the statement on p. 242 of the *Bayreuther Blätter* of 1894 that Wagner first heard the Ninth on 8 March 1840. At all events this statement was not published in his lifetime, i.e. with his knowledge. It does not effectively challenge the hypothesis that *after hearing the rehearsal*, Wagner naturally attended the concert on 8 March 1840 as well, in order to hear the symphony *as a whole for the first time*.)

Because documentary evidence is lacking, we cannot give a definite answer to the above question. But if Wagner heard both Habeneck's concert performance and his rehearsal, why does he make so much of the latter? One suspects that he was particularly impressed by the rehearsal experience. It would have been the first time Wagner had actually heard a Beethoven work in Paris. The impression was wholly fresh and unexpected, and the surprise element associated with this rehearsal made a special impact; the subsequent concert performance would have been tame by comparison. And another factor may have been the evocation, once again, of the original experience of the open fifths at the start. Compared to that, the finale would have come as a let-down, because of the inferiority of Habeneck's rendering of it.

Voss and Deathridge have strongly challenged these propositions. They think it may have been impossible for Wagner to have heard a rehearsal of the first three movements towards the end of 1839. The Conservatoire orchestra played the Ninth Symphony relatively often, and there had already been two performances in 1839, on 10 February and 21 April. For that reason, Voss and Deathridge argue, no rehearsal was scheduled, the next performance not being due until 8 March 1840, which was a relatively

34

long time off. So Voss and Deathridge are very sceptical about Wagner's account in *My Life* – as they are quite entitled to be, in theory. The real purpose of their objection, however, is to show up as a 'mystification' (Voss) the link Wagner declared between the experience of hearing the Ninth rehearsed and his *Faust* Overture. They posit an influence expressly emanating from Berlioz's 'Roméo et Juliette' symphony instead.

Our immediate reaction to this is to say that they are surely right about the influence of Berlioz. But does this necessarily rule out an orientation towards Beethoven at the time in question? One of our reasons for asking this is that there are several possible objections to the theory that Wagner did not hear, and could not have heard, the Ninth in rehearsal.

The basic objection to the standpoint of Voss and Deathridge is that theirs, too, is purely conjectural – starting out from certain pointers. As we have said, we still lack any evidence that would enable us to 'authenticate' the one standpoint or the other. But the anti-rehearsal arguments do clash with counter-arguments that start out from different factors, and that show that Wagner's statement is eminently credible.

Our first counter-argument is based on the fact that Wagner – at two different points in *My Life* (p. 174 and p. 329) – explicitly mentions a *rehearsal*. And why does he speak only of the first three movements? Why mention this point, when the experience would have seemed of much greater significance if Wagner had described it as a concert performance – complete with that choral finale which played such a vital role in his later teleological interpretation? We can hardly suppose that it was a subtle lie designed to provide the counter-argument we have just stated.

The second of our critical factors arises from a closer scrutiny of the rehearsals at which the Conservatoire orchestra played through one or possibly two of Wagner's overtures. Wagner's letters clearly refer to a rehearsal at which quite obviously his *Columbus* overture was played. This was on 4 February 1840 (see *SB* I, p. 379). But on 7 December 1839 Habeneck had already rehearsed a work by Wagner, for Meyerbeer made a note of the rehearsal in his pocket diary. We do not know which work was played on that occasion. Probably it was not the *Columbus* but the *Polonia* overture, or else the Concert Overture in C major. It is altogether possible that Wagner heard the first three movements of Beethoven's Ninth at this rehearsal. As an orchestral trainer Habeneck was keen, persevering and meticulous, and it would not have been odd for him to rehearse a work in between scheduled performances. This thesis is all the more likely because according to Elwart, the last 1839 performance, on 21 April, included only the second and fourth movements. Moreover Habeneck was entirely receptive to special requests, as the rehearsals of Wagner's overture or overtures prove. And the thesis that – with Meyerbeer's help – Wagner persuaded Habeneck to play the Ninth at the rehearsal of 7 December seems an altogether obvious one. For Habeneck's Beethoven performances were already legend when Wagner arrived in Paris, and there can be no doubt that it was Wagner's firm intention to hear them as soon as he could.

Let us now consider the date of the first complete sketch of the *Faust* Overture and the final date of the work. The first is 13 December 1839, the second 12 January 1840. Assuming that Wagner heard the Conservatoire orchestra rehearse the first three movements of the Ninth on 7 December, it is perfectly conceivable that Beethoven's Ninth made some impact on the work he had already started to compose.

All the same, it would be a mistake to view the connection between the *Faust* Overture and the Ninth Symphony as being altogether direct and manifesting itself 'physically' in evidence of Beethoven's fingerprints. Just to leave it at that would be wrong. For in certain areas, Beethoven had left his mark on the atmosphere of Parisian musical life, not just the concert repertoire. There were not only the Conservatoire orchestral concerts but also other Beethoven performances, plus numerous publications, press articles and so forth dealing with Beethoven's personality and his compositions. It was Habeneck's performances that established and increased the general recognition of Beethoven in France. But the critical writings of Castil-Blaze and Berlioz contributed significantly to the spread of Beethoven's fame in that country. Behind the announcement in *Le Siècle* of a quartet 'session' to be held by Pierre Baillot lay the knowledge that this French violinist was an expert in Beethoven's music. And *Le Figaro* helped to popularize Beethoven by publishing extracts from G. E. Anders's translation of the Wegeler-Ries *Biographische Notizen* on 24 February 1839. Despite the hectic time he spent lobbying for work and support, Wagner with his sensitivity to musical atmosphere must have absorbed all this very quickly and developed a new alertness to Beethoven. And even if he did not hear the Ninth before producing his *Faust* Overture, the latter work provided ample scope for mysteriously far-reaching expression. The radiance to be thrown back by Beethoven's last symphony, shortly afterwards, could be combined with thematic material and an instrumentation whose extravagance bears the hallmark of Berlioz.

Voss examines the question of influences in line with traditional research methods. Does the theme in bars 69f. and bars 73–80 of the overture, he asks, correspond more closely to bars 16–22 in the first movement of Beethoven's Ninth or to bars 270f. of the *Coriolan* Overture? But this will not do for various reasons. First of all, when considering the points of similarity and divergence in each case, it is barely possible to make out the decisive factor. Is it the upbeat element and downward-moving curve with its rhythmic readjustment (akin to the Ninth Symphony), or the rhythmic pulse which governs the note-sequence throughout and is notated as a dotted crotchet plus quaver (akin to the *Coriolan* Overture)? And secondly, as evocative devices Beethoven's two themes are similar enough to afford equal access to the associative sphere which Wagner was to delineate as

'Faustian'. From his viewpoint, is it not possible to project Coriolanus's heroic self-assertion at all costs and the Ninth's striving for human brotherhood equally with Faustian ambition upon a common, decidedly far-reaching musical statement?

There is also another obvious counter-argument. Wagner wrote a 'programme' for the Ninth Symphony in 1846. Is it mere chance that this was based on the *Faust* material he used as a programme to boost his Paris overture? Granted, this later association of the Ninth with Goethe's drama could have occurred independently of the *Faust* Overture. But is it not a likelier thesis that Wagner associated all three works with one another within a short space of time? It was, after all, only ten months after finishing the *Faust* Overture, i.e. in November 1840, that he published his novella *A Pilgrimage to Beethoven* in the *Revue et gazette musicale*. This was where he had his first shot at interpreting the finale to the Ninth, which indicates how strongly and quickly the work impressed him all over again in Paris. Surely Wagner was reacting, here, to Habeneck's performance(s)? Moreover the novella depicts Beethoven as a suffering composer, but also as a composer fighting for a revolutionary idea. Here, surely, Wagner is portraying the problems of an artist's livelihood, problems of the kind he was experiencing himself in Paris. And does this not again tie in with both the *Faust* Overture and Wagner's programme for the Ninth? For in the latter, passages from Goethe's drama are used to present the struggle to survive as a precondition of the choral finale, which transcends earthly problems.

So even if Wagner did not immediately associate Goethe's drama with the *Faust* Overture, there was from the outset an internal affinity between them, and it governs the whole character of the overture. This lends a more than passing significance to Cosima's diary entry of 2 August 1879: '*Faust* arrives; he [Wagner] has given me his old copy, which came from Minna and which contains his markings for the *Faust* Overture and the Ninth, and I lay an identical copy at his feet.' We should remember, too, that what Wagner had in mind was not simply an overture. Originally he had intended to compose a four-movement symphony. This in itself brings the projected *Faust* piece closer to Beethoven's Ninth than to the Berlioz composition. And for all the echoes of Berlioz which have rightly been pointed out, we must not overlook another factor. As with the late works of Beethoven, Wagner's slow introduction has the function of an exposition and is already part of the thematic working-out. Hence it is closely related to the Ninth Symphony, where this element determines the opening of the first movement, although in a different way (see Schenker's analysis).

So entirely to reverse the thesis of Beethoven's influence in favour of that of Berlioz is to do Wagner less than justice. Rather, he was combining the two influences – and plainly in a wider sense than merely that of a literal similarity between the notes.

In addition it is by no means the case that in describing his Berlioz experience, Wagner wrote a panegyric that could only be compared to his raptures over Beethoven. Nor can we agree with Voss that Wagner could not have heard a rehearsal of Beethoven's Ninth because there is no mention of it in the early *Autobiographical Sketch* and *A Communication to My Friends*. For the same writings fail to mention the impact of the 'Roméo et Juliette' symphony. It is only in *My Life* that Wagner takes that work as the theme, so to speak, of his Berlioz experience. Exactly the same applies to the rehearsal of the Ninth and his Beethoven experience, and surely this is striking? It should also be noted that even in letters dating from the time of the first performances of 'Roméo et Juliette' (24 November to 15 December 1839), Wagner never mentions the symphony. The first time he refers to it is on 27 March 1841:

permit me on this occasion, therefore, to say only a few things about the personal impression which my acquaintance with Berlioz has left on me. The first piece of his that I heard was his *Romeo & Juliet* symphony, in which the insipidity of the work's outward economy violently repelled me, for all the composer's evident genius.

(*SL*, p. 77)

How do these statements square with what Wagner said some twenty-five years later in *My Life*? Did he not see Berlioz as a thoroughly ambiguous figure, his genius notwithstanding? Surely, despite his criticisms of Beethoven, his statements praising the latter stand out by virtue of their basically positive tone?

Berlioz, then, may have stimulated and guided Wagner's composition of the *Faust* Overture, but his was not the only influence. It was Beethoven who determined the background, the work's essential, interior dimension. At the time Wagner was having a hard struggle to find his artistic bearings (see also Lichtenhahn [1972], pp. 143–60), and trying to reconcile opposing or rival artistic trends. This makes a combination of several influences especially plausible.

What is certain is that in view of his difficult outward position and divided inner state, Wagner very soon came to regard Beethoven as a new guiding light. Berlioz and Beethoven were rival but not mutually exclusive influences. Already in Paris, however, Beethoven very soon overshadowed the figure of Berlioz. The prime example of this is, within the context of Wagner's Beethoven novella, the *Faust* Overture.

No matter which of Habeneck's performances Wagner heard, Habeneck's interpretation of Beethoven is closely connected with the importance the composer assumed for Wagner during his stay in Paris. He was undoubtedly expecting insights from Habeneck that had been hitherto denied him. Surely Habeneck was bound to see those things that had been beyond a conductor like Pohlenz? As his retrospective remarks make clear, Wagner was partly enthusiastic, but partly disappointed. Although

Habeneck had rehearsed the first three movements better than anyone else, the finale to the Ninth evidently suffered by comparison, even when he was conducting. There is a contemporary witness to this. Anton Schindler made two extended visits to Paris in 1841–2 and attended the Conservatoire orchestra's rehearsals and concerts. In both his diary and the pamphlet *Beethoven in Paris* (1842), Schindler is full of praise for Habeneck and his players, but he also makes a number of critical comments. His opinion of the performance of the Ninth Symphony, while generally couched in superlatives, is not so positive with regard to two passages in the finale, the recitative on the double basses and cellos and the melody of 'Freude, schöner Götterfunken'. Schindler thought both were too slow. His comment on the 'Freude' melody is particularly revealing:

Habeneck took the melody of 'Freude schöner Götterfunken' at an extremely slow tempo, so that it sounded as woeful as the preceding recitative on the basses. Here he was being misled by a faulty translation of the words. ([1842], pp. 39f.)

Wagner's own disappointment can still be sensed in what he wrote thirty years later in *On Conducting*. While acknowledging all Habeneck's merits, he denies him any genius, and that remark is bitter indeed. But after his bad rehearsal experience with Pohlenz, Wagner had gone away sorry and confused. This time, on the other hand, he tried to solve the finale riddle, fired by the impression of the first three movements, and driven by a desire to improve on Habeneck's interpretation.

Thus Wagner had his reasons for passing over the problematic finale in his reports from Paris, as also in later references to the impressions of his first stay. But it became the central topic of a work in which he endeavoured to explain the riddle – the 1840 novella *A Pilgrimage to Beethoven*. Its significance in the present context is that it was Wagner's first attempt to elucidate Beethoven's Ninth Symphony, and it established the basic drift of his later interpretations. His explanation begins with the finale. In private conversation Beethoven confides his most intimate artistic plans, and thereby the answer to the finale, to his young visitor, who is Wagner's poeticized self-portrait. Here Wagner arrives at that interpretation which was later to harden into dogma.

Let those wild primal emotions that stretch out into the infinite, that are represented by instruments, be contrasted with the clear, definite emotions of the human heart, represented by the human voice. The addition of the second element will work beneficently and soothingly upon the conflict of the elemental emotions... (Kolodin [1962], p. 33)

What governed Wagner's reading of the Ninth was a process beginning with the sense of expectancy aroused by the first movement, through the open fifths. A programmatically conceived interpretation starting with the finale becomes clear-cut only with the onset of a specific period, which we can identify as the Paris years. This interpretation too underwent a development. Its stages are measured by the extent to which the mainly emotional aspect, based on the first movement, was integrated with the mainly intellectual aspect, which was based on the last movement. What characterizes the Paris stage is this. The difference in quality between Habeneck's performance of the earlier movements and the finale on the one hand, and Wagner's varying responsiveness to the first and last movements on the other, inspired Wagner with a single aim. This was to understand the work from the perspective of the finale (although the interpretation would not yet include every factor). Words, even though Schiller had written them, were directly blocking the 'poetry' that mattered to Beethoven as Wagner saw him.

Wagner had Habeneck to thank for a clearer and firmer definition of his image of Beethoven. Nonetheless, Habeneck was a 'typical' Frenchman. Clarity in the phrasing of a melody, technical perfection, mechanical work-throughs until it was all stupendously polished: these were the attributes that Wagner recognized in him. But only Germans, he thought, were capable of a true understanding of Beethoven.

whether one could say that the French completely *understand* German music is another question, the answer to which must be doubtful. Certainly it would be wrong to maintain that the enthusiasm evoked by the Conservatoire orchestra's masterly performance of a Beethoven symphony is affected. Yet when one listens to this or that enthusiast airing the various opinions, ideas and conceits which such a symphony has suggested to him one realises at once that the German genius is still very far from being completely grasped. (*WP*, pp. 36–7)

The above lines already reveal a chauvinistic attitude. Eventually, thirty years later, this would lead to Wagner's embarrassing association of a pride in military conquests with the 'memory of our great BEETHOVEN' (*GS* IX, p. 125).

One thing is sure. Wagner's Beethoven experience in 1839 compensated him for the personal humiliation of the frustration he felt as an artist in Paris.[5] After his earlier confusion, he now encountered Beethoven's music as a new and astonishing phenomenon. It was also an encouraging one in a situation that was forcing him to scrape a living from musical hackwork. Thus his Paris experience marked the start of a twofold reorientation. He started thinking about Beethoven, and thereupon about German music. Beethoven became the catalyst of his own artistic qualities and aims. This is seen in such compositions as the *Faust* Overture and *Der Fliegende Holländer*, but also in his numerous literary pieces.

Wagner always experienced events in a hyperactive way. At the same time as he sensed and digested their inner meaning, he would be actively carrying on, converting or delineating the experience. This again was determined by the basic pattern of his responses. In *A Communication to My*

Friends, he himself saw a connection between artistic receptiveness and the artistic urge to communicate. He made a distinction between the 'poetic' urge of the artist and the absolute urge to communicate. The one, he said, was 'only determined and shaped by the capacity for receiving vital impressions', whereas the other grew from a receptiveness which kept life's impressions at bay.

This pattern of artistic reactions was developed during the years in Paris. And if Paris signified a complete reorientation for Wagner, this affected not only the composer, critic and writer on music in him, but also the conductor. It was Paris that actually produced this side of Wagner, the conductor who was to perform Beethoven's music and all but overload it with his ideas on interpretation. For the conductor as for the composer, 'poetic receptiveness' turned into the 'strength of the urge to communicate', and thereby became a stimulus to musical performance.

Performing the Beethoven symphonies

Although Wagner conducted a large number of Beethoven's orchestral works, one group stands out from the others. On the whole it is the symphonies that predominate. Wagner never performed the First and Second Symphonies, which he thought were too indebted to Mozart and not independent enough (see Chapter 4). The same applies to the Fourth Symphony, which he very rarely conducted. Besides the Third, the Fifth and the Sixth, the Seventh is particularly important: it inaugurated his conducting career in Zurich. Between 1850 and 1855 he gave five performances of both the Fifth Symphony and the Seventh. The latter's importance is underlined by the influence that Wagner's interpretation had on Nietzsche, who attended the performance he conducted on 20 December 1871 in Mannheim.

The Ninth's significance for Wagner is undisputed, even though he performed it only five times in all. He gave it three times in Dresden (1846, 1847 and 1849), once as part of his London conducting engagements in 1855, and finally on 22 May 1872. These rare performances had a particular emphasis, the London concert apart.[6] At the time of the Dresden concerts, Wagner was just really starting to face the artistic and social problems of his day, which he did more and more purposefully. At the time the foundation stone of the Bayreuth Festspielhaus was laid in 1872, he was at last approaching the summit of his artistic endeavours.

When Wagner arrived in Dresden he had already made greater strides as an artist than was immediately evident. *Rienzi*, the opera with which he made his brilliant debut at the Saxon Hoftheater and which earned him the post of court Kapellmeister, had been already superseded in an artistic sense by *Der Fliegende Holländer*. This was a Paris offshoot, so to speak, of the unfinished 'Faust' symphony. (Wagner's statement in a letter to Uhlig that with this opera he had won through 'from all the mistiness of instrumental music to the resolution of drama' is one we should take seriously.) With his *Holländer* opera, the composer had already distanced himself from an aesthetic outlook with which he was again being confronted in Dresden. Reactions to the first performances were not wholly unfavourable, but they bore no comparison to the earlier enthusiasm for *Rienzi*. This fact, combined with a poor reception for *Tannhäuser* and with the practical and administrative problems Wagner was facing as a conductor, must have brought it home to him that a situation akin to his situation in Paris was only just around the corner. He was feeling much the same despair as when he had composed the *Faust* Overture. Thus it was quite natural for him to be seized, in the end, by 'a great longing for the Ninth Symphony', and also for him to draw on Goethe's *Faust* in the programme he wrote for the performance on Palm Sunday, 1846. *My Life* reflects the strength of his renewed response to the work when he got out the score:

What I did not dare to admit to myself was my knowledge of the utter lack of a solid foundation for my existence as an artist and as a member of society, headed as I was in a direction in which I could not help seeing myself without prospects and a stranger within my profession and in my daily life. My despair over this, which I tried to conceal from my friends, was now transformed by this marvellous Ninth Symphony into brightest exaltation. It is simply not possible that the heart of a pupil has ever been captivated with such rapturous force by the work of a master as mine was by the first movement of this symphony. Anyone who came upon me by surprise with the open score before me, as I went through it thinking how best it could be performed, would have been startled to hear my wild sobs and see my crying, and would no doubt have asked themselves in some amazement whether this was proper behaviour for a Royal Saxon Kapellmeister.[7]   (*ML*, pp. 329–30)

Wagner was particularly struck by the first movement once again. This is also borne out by an entry in the *Brown Book* (p. 93): '[1846] Back in country: (last opera was Tell; lingers disagreeably; dispelled by 1st theme of 9th Symph.).'

The basic mood of Beethoven's first movement, coloured afresh by depressing experiences and forebodings, Wagner now presents, however, as a battling towards 'Freude', towards joy. He describes the gulf to be bridged between the first and last movements at the end of his programmatic exegesis of the first movement:

At the close of the movement this gloomy, joyless mood, swelling up to gigantic proportions, seems to encircle the universe with a view to taking possession in fearfully exalted majesty of this world that God created – for *joy*.   (*GS* II, p. 58)

This joy, according to Wagner, is attained via the spiritual intermediate stages embedded in the inner movements. But here he goes further than the Paris novella and claims that resolution in favour of joy also signifies a resolution in favour of the word. For, to Wagner's mind, only the word is capable of expressing this feeling clearly. Intellectually his elucidation of the whole symphony takes its cue from the finale, but from an emotional angle his starting-point is the first movement. To Wagner, the word 'joy' entitled him to invest the original musical experience with emotional values that were bound up with the wretchedness of his existence. For it was those emotions which made him feel the finale as a spiritual break-through and look upon the word – the word 'joy' – as the only possibility of such a breakthrough, and as its token. (Wagner's friends Uhlig and Ortlepp took a similar view of the symphony as marking a progression from despair to joy.) Wagner now regards personal experience and reflection, musical feeling and the word, the first movement and finale as parts of a whole that are meaningfully inter-related.

In his programme Wagner was not only providing – as he himself said – pointers towards a better understanding of the Ninth in performance. In an artistically heightened form, he was also proclaiming for his own benefit the idea of battling through. But it was vital to him that there should be an intensive communication between an interpreter and his audience. And so he wanted a further purpose of his programme to be the union of all the work's performers and listeners in 'joy', or in other words the brotherhood of men. The events of 1849 subsequently led him to combine this enthusiasm with a revolutionary fervour. The idea of 'joy' merged with the idea of a better, truly honourable existence.

Glasenapp's point ([3/1894–1911], II, pp. 343, 538ff.) that Wagner wrote his article *Revolution* under the impact of the third and last Dresden performance of the Ninth Symphony is supported by the structure of this text, for it resembles the way he constructed his programme for the music. Both texts are based on the idea of a victory over unbearable, tormenting conditions. In both cases the development reaches its climax with a redemptive breakthrough to human happiness. The main difference is that in the later text, the abstract idealism of the programme's pathos has become orientated to the revolutionary ideal and transposed into the revolutionary idiom. In Goethe's *Faust*, problems to do with man's own nature are seen as the cause of his sufferings. But Wagner now defines his wretched state as the result of social and corporate injustice, to be overcome through the revolutionary trinity of 'liberty, equality, fraternity'. Although not stated outright, this solution clearly lies behind the article's construction and choice of words. Schiller's 'Freund' and 'Brüder' are now exemplified by this kind of sentence:

Henceforth let there be not hatred, not envy, not disfavour and enmity amongst you; as *brothers* shall all of you who are now alive recognize yourselves and be free, free in your desiring, free in your actions, free in your enjoying, to recognize the value of life.   (*GS* XII, p. 249)

Wagner also uses the word 'Freude' several times. The abstract 'joy' of the programme becomes a concrete social objective, which is to be grasped as human 'happiness'. The revolutionary article even includes literal echoes of Schiller's text: 'and with the heaven-shaking cry, *"I am a human being!"*, the millions hurtle ... down ...'[8]

There is a variety of evidence that this association of the Ninth Symphony with revolution was in many people's minds in Dresden. Gustav Adolf Kietz wrote of the third performance on 1 April 1849: 'The effect of the marvellous work was positively intoxicating in these turbulent times, it's impossible to describe its impact on the audience, you need to have experienced it!' And Theodor Uhlig makes the point that Beethoven, having now 'attained his professional goal', was revealing 'his socialist awareness'.

It is surely also of relevance that Michael Bakunin – Hans Mayer's 'natural revolutionary' – attended the final rehearsal (Newman says the actual concert). This was at the risk of being arrested by the police, whom he normally took good care to avoid. At the end he shouted his acclaim for the work. His words were: 'Everything, everything will perish and nothing will remain – *one* thing only will not perish but last for ever: the Ninth Symphony.' This could be interpreted as either irony, flattery or genuine admiration for Beethoven's Ninth. But however we may interpret it, everything indicates that it was Wagner who aroused his manifest interest in the symphony. Wagner achieved this by giving his programme for the work a revolutionary immediacy, by linking the work with political events.

This association must have got through to the public, and we may assume that Wagner was known as its originator. It is even probable that such ideas were in public circulation before 1849. There is hardly an alternative explanation for a press notice relating to the first Dresden performance in 1846, quoted by Dinger:

Our authorities are to be envied for the confidence they enjoy on Palm Sunday, when thousands are calmly entrusting their lives to them in order to hear a music whose sounding-board seems to anticipate a fire or débâcle: 'The grey goose will be caught at last.'

(Alfred Meissner records that Wagner was already convinced in the autumn of 1846 of a fundamental political change; he indicated, moreover, that revolution was already complete in many people's minds. See Newman II, n. 3.)

Against the background of the above press comment, an entry in Wagner's *Brown Book* dating from 1849 can be similarly seen as an allusion to his interpretation of the Ninth. He recorded as follows the shout of a guard he encountered during the uprising:

1849 ... 8th May: ... At St Ann Barricade guard shouts 'Well, Mr Conductor, joy's beautiful divine spark's made a blaze.' (3rd perf. 9th Symphony at previous Palm Sunday concert; Opera House now burnt down. Strange feeling of comfort.)

(p. 97)

But did Wagner give his symphonic programme its revolutionary directness under the pressure of his own grinding existence as an artist? Did the breakthrough to 'joy' therefore acquire a new, subjective dimension of experience? This was almost certainly the case. Wagner was identifying himself with revolution, albeit after his own fashion. He was not the kind of anarchist that Bakunin was, but neither was he a 'revolutionary' in any doctrinaire sense. What made him tick as a revolutionary is described by Thomas Mann as follows:

> Thus Wagner became a revolutionary. He did so as an artist, because he hoped and believed a complete transformation would result in more favourable conditions for the arts and his own art – a national drama compounded of myth and music. He constantly denied being a truly political animal and never concealed his distaste for the doings of the various political parties. If he supported and took part in the 1848 revolution, that was because of his general leanings rather than the revolution's concrete targets, which his true dreams and desires far exceeded ...
>
> (*Pro and Contra Wagner*, p. 178, amended)

This view is supported by Eduard Devrient's diaries.

In 1849, then, Wagner responded to the Ninth Symphony in a very particular way. The finale stood for his salvation from an ignominious life as a Kapellmeister; after being rescued, he would begin to create true art. At the beginning of June 1849 he was again in search of a Paris spring. And in the rhythm of the wheels of the carriage taking him there, he thought he could hear the tune of 'Freude, schöner Götterfunken'.

Experienced in this way, the word 'Freude' became a symbol of brotherhood, a symbol of man's redemption in general and of Wagner's release into an artist's unfettered existence. It meant a breakthrough to the word, to a new language, and music's redemption would entail the 'all-embracing' [*allgemeinsam*] art-work uniting all men on Wagner's part. With the word 'Freude', Beethoven's historic deed was made manifest:

> Thus, through the most unheard-of possibilities of absolute music, the Master pressed forward ... until he reached the point where a seafarer will start measuring the ocean's depth with his sounding-lead ... Briskly he cast anchor, and this anchor was the *word*. But this was no arbitrary, insignificant word ... This word was – '*Freude!*' And with this word he cries to mankind: '*Seid umschlungen, Millionen! Diesen Kuss der ganzen Welt!*' – And *this word* will be the language of the *art-work of the future*. –
>
> The *last symphony* of Beethoven is music's redemption from its intrinsic element in the name of an *all-embracing* art. It is the *human* gospel of the art of the future. There cannot be any *progress* beyond it, for it can have an immediate sequel only in the supreme art-work of the future, the *all-embracing drama* [das *allgemeinsame Drama*], the artistic key to which has been forged for us by Beethoven.   (*GS* III, p. 96)

Wagner's response to the Ninth Symphony in a time of revolution led to his conception of the *Art-Work of the Future*. It was a response that constituted a threshold value. Wagner now includes the Ninth in his theoretical writings; he absorbs it aesthetically. Until 1872 it disappears from his concert programmes almost entirely.

After some initial hesitation, however, Wagner did direct concerts of Beethoven's music in Zurich. He began by conducting the Seventh Symphony on 15 January 1850. A total of some thirty further Beethoven performances followed during the concert seasons of 1851–5. Then, in 1856, he suddenly refused to go on conducting. Later on, he explained his decision in *My Life* (see p. 531) by saying that the Zurich Music Society had not allowed him to strengthen and improve the orchestra in the ways he wished. No doubt other factors were the difficulties surrounding his London concerts in 1855 and his projects as a composer. But there was probably a further reason for the decision. On 23 November 1856, independently of his Zurich withdrawal, Wagner took part with Liszt in a concert at St Gall and conducted the 'Eroica' Symphony. A letter he wrote to Otto Wesendonck a week later is a clear indication of his feelings: 'It's no longer a pleasure for me to do Beethoven symphonies at all: I have played them almost to death.'

Such a remark cannot be attributed to exertions of the kind undertaken by performers who were as busy as Hans von Bülow or Anton Rubinstein. What lay behind this temporary flagging of Wagner's interpretative powers was his exaggerated conducting of Beethoven. Wagner's conducting was governed by the belief that as a tone-poet [*Tondichter*], Beethoven wanted to say more than could ever be expressed in 'absolute music'. His technique, so-called, was primarily exegesis, his equipment being the 'programmatic explanation'. The substance of the piece in question would be condensed into this programme, and it was then a matter of constantly reviving it. Furthermore it was a matter of presenting its contents, the 'poetic object', through the medium of music. The extraordinary imagination and expressive intensity that Wagner repeatedly demanded of himself as a conductor[9] was bound to have the result he describes.

It was no accident that he returned to composition at around the time he gave up conducting. As a creator of music dramas, Wagner considered himself to be the successor to Beethoven the tone-poet. (We shall return to this subject in Chapter 4.) As a conductor he had actively approached Beethoven in spirit, but had overtaxed his interpretative powers while trying to emulate him. It was only in music drama that his articulated response could be fully developed. Thus if Wagner is to be regarded as creatively succeeding Beethoven as a tone-poet, we must also regard the symphony as being 'resolved' [*aufgehoben*] in the music drama.

Quartet studies

Wolzogen tells us that in conversation, Wagner himself distinguished between a symphonic style which was addressed to everybody – the *oratio directa* with its 'simple symphonic thematic construction' up to the Ninth Symphony – and the intimate style of Beethoven's quartets. Beethoven's symphonies were speeches to mankind. Both Wagner's own personal experience and the public response to the Ninth had brought that home to him. Having guided the Beethoven symphony into 'the bed of this musical drama' (*GS* VII, p. 97), Wagner saw the symphony's public function as having been transferred to the 'all-embracing drama' [*das allgemeinsame Drama*]. This is also reflected in his later relationship to the Beethoven symphony. For he had not given up performing Beethoven's works for good: from about 1860 he was again conducting the symphonies. But the function of the performance had changed. Whereas earlier, Wagner had presented Beethoven's symphonies as straightforward speeches to the masses, they now served as marginalia, as it were, to the drama. Nothing illustrates this better than his performances of the Ninth. On three occasions he associated it with the common people; but in 1872, when the foundations of the Festspielhaus were laid, the symphony symbolized the foundation stone of music drama. During his Dresden years Wagner had seen the Ninth as embracing all mankind, but now it was Wagner's closed community that the work was celebrating. The increasing predominance of his own music in his concert programmes during the 1860s is another indication of the same process.

Whilst using Beethoven's symphonies as a public commentary on his music drama, Wagner was making an intensive study of the string quartets. Once again it was a concert in Paris which marked the crucial experience. In October 1853 Wagner and Liszt heard a performance of Beethoven's E flat major and C sharp minor quartets (op. 127 and op. 131) by the Maurin-Chevillard Quartet, which was recognized as one of the best in existence. Wagner compared this event with the 1839 orchestral performance under Habeneck (see *ML*, p. 503). The rendering of the C sharp minor quartet was particularly impressive. It probably induced Wagner to concentrate on rehearsing this work with a Zurich ensemble (the Heisterhagen-Schleich Quartet) in 1853–4. He provided a 'programmatic explanation' for the performance on 12 December 1854. Op. 131 was played again in an evening of chamber music in 1855. And when Cosima and Hans von Bülow visited him at his Zurich home in 1857, Wagner laid on some music for string quartet that had been rehearsed under his supervision.

It was not, however, until 1870–1 that Wagner resumed this study of chamber music in a really intensive way, with the Tribschen Quartet. In all there were seven sessions in Tribschen between 30 December 1870 and 26 March 1871, and they were devoted almost exclusively to Beethoven's late quartets. Max Fehr records that the works studied were opp. 127, 132, 130, 131, 133 and 135, as well as the first two 'Rasoumovsky' quartets and opp. 74 and 95. Along with the centenary essay, these sessions formed

Wagner's very personal musical contribution to the Master's hundredth anniversary. It was a celebration among friends:

> For we had retired to the chamber; not, unfortunately, into that cosy parlour where Beethoven imparted to a few breathlessly listening friends all those ineffable things which, he believed, could be understood only here and not in a large hall, where he thought it necessary to speak to the people, the whole of mankind with great, graphic gestures ... *(GS* x, p. 183)

Formulated as a criticism of current instrumental music-making, this passage indicates what Wagner's ambition was. Like Beethoven, he would reveal the secrets of the last quartets in the privacy of the 'cosy parlour'.

Wagner's chamber music sessions show how much the significance and function of his response to Beethoven had altered since the music drama had 'resolved' ['*aufgehoben*'] the Beethoven symphony. The momentous performances of the Ninth in Dresden were peak experiences in the sense that they brought the work and mankind into harmony. They were matched by the Zurich performances of Beethoven, which already represented a fusion of the tone-poet as re-creator with the creative dramatist in Wagner. And from that point onwards, Wagner's inner dialogue with Beethoven shifted more and more into the intimate world of chamber music. The propagandist gesture of later symphony performances had its counterpart in the close-knit circle. The beginning of the nineteenth century had seen what Ludwig Finscher calls the transposition of chamber music into the bourgeois living-room. The same thing was now happening again, although on a different level. For it was precisely Beethoven's late quartets, being part of a reaction against this bourgeois concept of chamber music, which became the works Wagner used for 'practice' and 'amusement'. And even now, the difficulties created by their esoteric character and their technical demands were of some consequence. In exploring the esoteric sphere, the student could skip over matters of execution and indeed compositional technique only too quickly. On the other hand a high-minded show of absorption in the work called for a technically adequate realization of it. Elements of the connoisseur and the dilettante are equally present in Wagner's relationship to Beethoven's chamber music.

We see here an idiosyncratic fluctuation between domestic music-making, with its levelling effect, and real pretensions to chamber music. But the gatherings in Bayreuth were probably the first to show this absolutely clearly. Often Joseph Rubinstein would play the quartets – rather badly – on the piano, with Wagner indicating the tempi. Wagner persisted in having individual passages practised in detail, such as the transition from the first to the second movement of op. 131 (a passage he also points out in the essay *On Conducting*). He even considered passing on his ideas in a teaching capacity. On 5 August 1877 he wrote to August Wilhelmj:

I am contemplating the idea of teaching young people something else before I die –
i.e. interpretation. Could you assure me of your pupils' assistance here in Bayreuth
from 1 January to 30 April, particularly for quartet playing & advanced themati-
cized interpretation in general? (*Bayreuther Blätter* XXVIII [1905], p. 234)

Altogether, Wagner took a more relaxed attitude to Beethoven's quartets during this late period, and did not burden them with so many ideas.
But the associative context still formed a part of his response. Wagner's
'receptive powers' were now finding an outlet through a constant flow of
'communications' issued among a small circle of friends. Such powers
correspond to the creative experience of an inspired musician that we find
in the *Beethoven* essay – an experience where the sound, rhythm and
expressive gesture are inseparably linked.

3

THE ROMANTIC BACKGROUND
AND BEETHOVEN BIOGRAPHY

The 'Romantic image of Beethoven'

As Walter Wiora has shown, music as the 'primal language of the soul' and as the 'geometrical meeting-point' of various 'trans-musical' ideas was a basic fact of the Romantic universe. So was the experience of an intermingling of musical and extra-musical qualities; so too was the intention that the arts should complement one another.

It has been remarked by Wellek, Blume and others that Wagner was much indebted to the categories of Romantic thinking about music as developed in the critical and imaginative writings of E. T. A. Hoffmann, Novalis, Wackenroder, Tieck and Friedrich Schlegel, as well as in Schelling's philosophy. Knopf and Fries have particularly remarked on the links between the Romantic movement and Wagner's *Gesamtkunstwerk*, the 'total work of art'.

In addition the Romantic interpretation of Beethoven's artistic personality and his works was a major stimulus for Wagner. Summing up these exegetical studies as the 'Romantic image of Beethoven', Arnold Schmitz has subjected them to critical analysis and has considered their transmission basically from the viewpoint of the history of ideas. In the process, the Romantic layers of the Beethoven image were stripped away to expose important sections of a portrait which is faithful to history. Beethoven no longer resembled a child of nature and a revolutionary, a magician and a priest – attributes created through an inspired act of forgery. A 'Classical' Beethoven took the place of the specifically Romantic composer.

E. T. A. Hoffmann

In spite of the foregoing comments, the 'Romantic image of Beethoven' should not be consigned wholly to the realms of poetic fantasy and the bizarre. This is especially evident from E. T. A. Hoffmann's picture of Beethoven. Hoffmann's was the first significant attempt at an appraisal of the composer. Too much stress has been laid on his romanticizing tendencies, for Hoffmann's reviews are not just Romantic effusions. His examination of Beethoven's music may be lacking in subtlety by our

50

standards, but he does go in for objective description and incisive analysis. In his reviews of the Fifth Symphony, the *Coriolan* Overture and the two trios of op. 70, both his paeans of praise and his sometimes very acute summaries of the formal construction are confined to the opening and closing paragraphs. Only now and then does he lard the actual analysis with enthusiastic interjections, referring to the effect of individual passages. For the rest, this section traces the sequence of musical events, the motivic and thematic construction, the order of the themes and their inter-relations, contrapuntal and harmonic features, and the instrumentation. Here Hoffmann displays the same *Besonnenheit*, or 'self-possession', that he repeatedly observes in Beethoven.

'Self-possession' is a key idea with regard to Hoffmann's appreciation of Beethoven. By this term he does not mean (to quote Schmitz) 'a magician's irrational self-possession'. Rather he uses it to characterize the carefully controlled formal process:

> Only that artist who controlled the eccentric flight of his genius by means of the most diligent study of art, thereby achieving a supreme self-possession, and is now master of the interior realm of sounds, knows clearly and firmly how he can most effectively apply the most striking artistic resources available...
>
> (Hoffmann [1963], pp. 36f., 137)

This meaning of the word 'self-possession' is underlined by its close connection with 'structure'. Hoffmann uses the latter on many occasions. In his writings on Beethoven, where it occurs specifically as an 'inner structure', it means a musical construction that has been governed by reason, all enthusiasm notwithstanding. And precisely this 'inner structure' – the clearest illustration of Beethoven's constructional method – is based on 'self-possession':

> only an intensive examination of the inner structure of Beethoven's music [will show us] the Master's great self-possession, which is inseparable from true genius and is fostered by the unremitting study of art.   (*Ibid.*, p. 37)

Certainly E. T. A. Hoffmann's consideration of structural relationships ties in with something that is not usually remarked on at all. He made it a point of principle never to discuss a work without having studied the score. He also quoted from the scores in his reviews whenever possible, and he pleaded for the publication of Beethoven's instrumental works in that form, so that people could study them really thoroughly.

> May more auspicious conditions in the arts enable the publishing trade to issue the scores of Beethoven's instrumental compos[itions]: what a more than rich treasure trove it would open up for the artist, the connoisseur!   (*Ibid.*, p. 144)

That 'self-possession' which Hoffmann found in Beethoven – a controlled enthusiasm leading to an organically constructed work of art – was a new feature of the 'Romantic image of Beethoven'. And it shows

Wagner's relationship to Hoffmann in a new and different light. Wagner may have taken Hoffmann's idea as the starting-point for that study of symphonic form in which he tried to do justice to Beethoven's originality. According to Wagner (*GS* I, pp. 144f.), Beethoven 'infinitely extended symphonic form ... so that with daring, yet always self-possessed freedom, he could follow his impetuous genius into regions which only he could attain'. In neither diction nor content is this statement conceivable without Hoffmann's idea of self-possession.

Equally influential, of course, were Hoffmann's spirited comments on the intrinsic nature and special powers of instrumental music. Although so many Romantic writers took up this subject that it hardly seems possible to say where Wagner got it from, Hoffmann was surely a direct model once again. For he had been the first to appraise Beethoven's instrumental music, and Wagner's writings echo this acclamation. Thus *On German Musical Life* contains the line:

While Beethoven's mighty genius was opening up a new world of daring romanticism in his instrumental music, a light from that magic region shed its radiance upon German opera.   (*WP*, pp. 47–8)

In his programme for the Ninth Symphony, to be sure, Wagner was clearly drawing on another Romantic author. There is a passage where he refers to the 'infinite and indefinite expression' of purely instrumental music as being prerequisite to the choral finale (*GS* II, p. 61). Here he quotes Ludwig Tieck's description in *Phantasus* of the 'insatiable yearning that strays from and returns to itself, that ineffable longing which cannot be fulfilled'. Originally, to be sure, this line had a negative slant; Tieck dismissed Beethoven's symphonies as being the music of a madman. And the drift of Tieck's statement determines the function of the quotation in Wagner's programme: it is meant to underline the necessity of Beethoven's recourse to the medium of words. In other respects, however, Wagner's attitude is patently a detached one, since he points out that Tieck was judging from his own particular angle. He concludes by saying: 'It is almost as if Beethoven were impelled by a similar awareness about the essence of instrumental music when he conceived this symphony.'

But when Wagner is talking of the 'ineffable' element [*Unaussprechliche*], the expressive power of instrumental music that Beethoven did so much to heighten, the tone is unmistakably positive – for all Wagner's reservations about absolute music. He does not mention Hoffmann by name, or quote him. Nonetheless his view surely derives from Hoffmann's poetic enthusing over the 'ineffable' power to which Beethoven dedicated himself. This applies not only to Wagner's *Halévy and French Opera* (1842), where he invokes the 'magic of the *ineffable*', but even to *Opera and Drama*, where the 'ineffable' is an important component in Wagner's musico-dramatic conception.

Adolf Bernhard Marx

Wagner's Paris novella *A Happy Evening* (1841) contains references to another author besides E. T. A. Hoffmann. It also pursues a contrasting line of thought, based on whether or not Beethoven's works were derived from certain 'ideas'. This proposition cannot be traced back to the reviews of Hoffmann. True, Hoffmann refers at one point to the possibility of abstracting 'both the idea and the structure' of Beethoven's instrumental works from his music's spirit and character: see Hoffmann [1963], pp. 120f. But despite the 'wondrous images' in which he clothes his feelings, he is still convinced that Beethoven is speaking an 'unknown language', i.e. that of the 'ineffable'. It was, we suspect, A. B. Marx and not Hoffmann who encouraged Wagner to discuss and enlarge upon the subject of Beethoven's 'idea' in his novella, for Marx had already discussed this subject in several essays in the *BAMZ*.

Wagner undoubtedly refers in the novella to Hoffmann's dialogue, *The Poet and the Composer*, and for that reason a possible connection with Marx has never been considered. Yet the focal point of Wagner's discussion, the 'idea', is never mentioned by Hoffmann. Where it does appear is in a review by Marx of Beethoven's op. 111, couched in epistolary form and presenting an argument between three persons.[1] Implicitly, then, Wagner's *A Happy Evening* could also be a discussion of the thoughts Marx had expounded. If so, by ruling out the 'idea' as the determining factor Wagner is refuting Marx, who believed that Beethoven's music reflected his personal tragedy. (We are assuming that Marx identified himself with the young artist in his review, and not with the reviewer.) Marx himself, to be sure, backed down by saying that the 'idea' took shape without any reflection on Beethoven's part.

There is, however, a further connection – a thought which so clearly leads to Wagner as to make his partial dependence on Marx almost certain. Marx is discussing the recipient's personal involvement, which helps to determine the content:

> I conceive the effect of a work of art as being the product of its idea and the character of the recipient, and the fact that art offers every different individual what is suited to him seems to me a proof of its divine nature.

> (*BAMZ* [1824], p. 99)

There is an obvious link between the above and a passage near the end of the novella, stating that everyone ought to enjoy music 'according to his strength, his capacity and his disposition' (*WP*, p. 187).

A Happy Evening, then, includes two strands of the Romantic interpretation of Beethoven, but the author endorses only one of them, the one deriving from Hoffmann. Nonetheless, the concurrence of these trends, and the fact that Marx's 'idea' is discussed at all, establishes the angle from

53

which Wagner would examine the problem of the content of Beethoven's work. It initiated a process whereby he came increasingly close to Marx's outlook, without actually identifying himself with it. (The basic difference – at any rate at the time of *Opera and Drama* – is that Wagner postulates a 'poetic object' in Beethoven's compositions which exceeds the powers of 'absolute music', whereas Marx's 'idea' remains within purely musical limits.)

Like 'self-possession', the concepts of the 'ineffable' and the 'art-work of ideas' [*Ideenkunstwerk*] are important links between Wagner and the Romantic view of Beethoven. But there are also other connections, and they have to do with the interpretation of individual works.

According to Linda Siegel, one aspect of Wagner's debt to Hoffmann is that 'the composer paid particular attention to those compositions of Beethoven that Hoffmann had reviewed'. This needs amending on two counts. Firstly, Wagner did not pay anything like the same attention to all the works reviewed by Hoffmann; examples are the Mass in C and the piano trios op. 70. And secondly, his interpretation of the *Coriolan* Overture is only partly in line with Hoffmann's. Like Hoffmann, Wagner associated the work with Shakespeare's drama instead of the play by Collin for which it was written. But he also drew on Marx for his programmatic explanation. Marx's account of the overture in the *BAMZ* resembles a rough draft for Wagner's text. Marx wrote as follows:

If we imagine the proud, violent, high-minded young man, expelled from the popular party, and deserted by the nobles for whom he went to war against that party – victoriously closing in on Rome at the head of her mortal foes, refusing any compromise, deaf to all entreaties, and then, his bitter hatred and his vengefulness having been conquered by naive love and reverence for his mother, being expelled for the second time and wandering by himself in oblivion and the dark, or (as other historians believe) being executed by his suspicious soldiers because of his compromise – that gives us the gist of the overture. (*BAMZ* [1825], p. 396)

Wagner's explanation begins:

Coriolanus, immensely strong, incapable of feigning humility and expelled from his native city for that reason, and waging all-out war on the city in league with her foes until, moved by his mother, wife and child, he finally abjures revenge, and is punished with death by his associates for having thus betrayed them – this *Coriolanus* I may assume to be familiar to everybody. (*GS* IV, p. 173)

Marx's reviews filled a gap at least partially, and for the time being, because there were a lot of Beethoven works that E. T. A. Hoffmann had not discussed, especially the late compositions. Wagner must have been particularly interested by the detailed review of the Ninth Symphony which the *BAMZ* had published in 1826. If we compare certain passages in it with Beethoven's words of explanation in *A Pilgrimage*, the impression is that here again Wagner was drawing on Marx for inspiration. For both of them draw a contrast not between the word and instrumental music, but between the infinite, restless roving of instrumental language and the pacifying element in human song.

With Marx the relevant passage reads:

As in landscapes and other natural phenomena outside of man, the formations and combinations in the world of instruments are infinite . . . Song is in contrast to this, being forever pure in itself, the special gift of man, who is nature's supreme creation, and with its simplicity conquers the protean world of instruments by its supreme spiritual content.

Beethoven, it seems to us, has expressed this view in the Choral Symphony . . . It was not an incidental final chorus for an instrumental piece (one having no need of a foreign ending) that he was after, not a setting of Schiller's ode, not the musical expression of its content or even its words – but only song, the simplest mode of human musical language, which he wanted to celebrate by its victory over the world of instruments. To him this superiority appeared so certain and inevitable, and *singing* in itself so innate to man and so powerful within him, that he let the voice take command and conquer by virtue of what it is, so to speak . . .

(*BAMZ* [1826], p. 375)

Wagner's Beethoven says:

In instruments, the primal organs of creation and nature find their representation . . . they but repeat primal feelings as they came forth from the chaos of the first creation . . . With the genius of the human voice it is entirely otherwise; this represents the human heart, and its isolated, individual emotion . . . Let these two elements be brought together, then; let them be united! Let those wild primal emotions that stretch out into the infinite, that are represented by instruments, be contrasted with the clear, definite emotions of the human heart, represented by the human voice. The addition of the second element will work beneficently and soothingly upon the conflict of the elemental emotions, and give to their course a well-defined and united channel; and the human heart itself . . . will be immeasurably strengthened . . . and made capable of feeling clearly what was before an uncertain presage of the highest ideal, now changed into a divine knowledge.

(*The Composer as Listener*, ed. I. Kolodin, 2 [1962], p. 33)

As we have seen, the areas in which Wagner agrees with Hoffmann and with Marx partly overlap. It may also be assumed, however, that Marx was reiterating some of Hoffmann's ideas, with modifications. In 1823, the year after Hoffmann's death, Marx wrote an essay titled 'On Assessing Hoffmann as a Musician' for Zacharias Werner's *Aus Hoffmann's Leben und Nachlass*. Significantly, this essay deals with Hoffmann more intensively as a writer on music than as a composer. Although Marx would later specifically acknowledge Hoffmann's particular kind of 'dilettantism', he saw in the author of the 'Fantasy Pieces' somebody who lacked a proper musical training. First and foremost, however, Marx's essay reveals a detailed knowledge of Hoffmann's writings and reviews. Moreover, as he recalled in his memoirs, he had seen the posthumous writings. He praised

Hoffmann's reviews when mentioning them in subsequent essays, and his own Beethoven monograph includes extracts from Hoffmann's review of Beethoven's Piano Trio op. 70(ii).

The close link between Marx and Hoffmann had been already observed by contemporaries. Eduard Krüger remarked in 1847 that Marx's earlier reviews in his own periodical (1830) and the 'excellent little book' on *Painting in Music* resembled Hoffmann in tone and outlook. We can give individual examples to support this. Marx's phrase 'restless driving' [*rastloses Treiben*] corresponds almost exactly to Hoffmann's 'continuous, ever-increasing urging and driving' [*fortdauernden, immer steigenden Drängen und Treiben*] in his review of op. 70(i). And like Hoffmann, Marx thought Beethoven the most important representative of instrumental music, 'sovereign in the magical world of instruments'. Beethoven's genius, he wrote, was bearing him away upon virgin, unexplored paths.

When Marx had founded his musical periodical in 1824, he had declared that a general and complete recognition of Beethoven was one of his chief aims. This too can surely be ascribed to Hoffmann's example. Marx was carrying on his endeavours to fathom the originality of Beethoven's work and to impart it to the public at large. So it may be the case that Marx not only prompted Wagner to discuss Beethoven's 'idea', as a key to the compositions; he also alerted him to the importance of studying the scores – a point that was stressed by both Marx and Hoffmann with particular reference to Beethoven. We have already shown what influence they had on Wagner's 'programmatic explanations'.

In expounding Beethoven's works Wagner referred to their social function. This brought him in line with another aspect of the Romantic interpretation of Beethoven. Its importance will become clear if we remember that the contemporary (and later) response to Beethoven was largely made up of rejection based on prejudice, barely comprehending reserve and, in Adolf Sandberger's words, fairly cheap eulogies. Nowadays the Romantic interpretation of a work's unintelligible and 'bizarre' features as parts meaningfully related to the whole seems exaggerated. So does the projection of the enigmatic into a Romantic infinity. But precisely those elements once helped to make the music concerned more intelligible.

Beethoven's attitude to Romantic critics

Beethoven is known to have taken note of the pioneering Romantic critics, whose writings he appreciated. We cannot say which of Hoffmann's stories or reviews he knew. A letter he wrote to Hoffmann on 23 March 1820 does not enlighten us on this point. (Schmitz assumes that it was Hoffmann the critic he was writing to.) That Beethoven was acquainted with at least one review by Hoffmann can be gathered from Schindler, who observed a swing in critical opinion following the appearance of a review of the Fifth

Symphony and another of the Sixth. Beethoven had then expressly enquired after the reviewer's name. Like Schindler, he thought that the author would be Amadeus Wendt. It has since been established that the review of the Sixth Symphony was by M. G. Fischer, but that E. T. A. Hoffmann wrote the other; the excerpts quoted by Schindler remove the last remaining doubts. In addition it is possible that Beethoven's *Romantische Lebensbeschreibung des Tobias Haslinger allhier in drei Teilen* was inspired by Hoffmann's writings. Hoffmann is frequently mentioned in Beethoven's conversation books. One of the conversations engendered the canon 'Hoffmann, sei ja kein Hofmann', which Beethoven offered to Schott, together with the *Romantische Lebensbeschreibung* and two more canons, on 22 January 1825. (This canon, with its punning title, was not a reference to E. T. A. Hoffmann, but it was surely a discussion of the writer which sparked it off.)

For his part, Amadeus Wendt wrote an essay entitled *Gedanken über die neuere Tonkunst, und van Beethovens Musik, namentlich dessen Fidelio*. It was published in Leipzig in 1815. Beethoven's opinion of it – not an unreservedly positive one – has been recorded.

The composer was unstinting in his praise when it came to what A. B. Marx published in his Berlin periodical. In a letter written to Schlesinger on 19 January 1825, Beethoven states: 'I hope he [Marx] will carry on revealing more and more of what is higher and true in the realm of art; little by little this might achieve a reduction in mere syllable-counting.' As Sandberger has noted, this refers to a passage in Marx's essay *Etwas über die Symphonie und Beethovens Leistungen in diesem Fache*. The phrase 'syllable-counting' may also have been an allusion to the aforementioned review of Beethoven's op. 111. There Edward, one of the partners to the dialogue, objects to the practice of merely 'anatomizing' a sonata instead of comprehending it on the artistic level. Underlying this is an aim which Marx sets forth in detail in the same essay: that of discovering the active central 'idea' in a work, i.e. the 'higher' aspect. This, he maintains, is the only way to understand and judge the work as a whole.

People are always talking about form, by which they appear to mean something which is here for all time, a standard for all works of the mind. But is form something autonomous? Is it anything other than the revelation of the idea, the incarnation of the thought behind the art-work? Every mature, sound idea must reveal itself as such in the art-work ... every idea has created a form for itself.

(*BAMZ* [1824], pp. 97f.)

Beethoven was apparently impressed by the notion of the 'idea' as Marx expounded it. This 'idea', this governing artistic aim, could be used to justify any deviations from the established mould and ingrained criteria. Beethoven rejected the fanciful interpretations of someone like Dr Iken, but in spite of the odd reservation, he endorsed in principle the discovery of 'what is higher and true', i.e. the 'idea' as Marx defined it. This has undoubtedly influenced the exegetical history of his compositions. Schindler contributed to it, because although he referred chiefly to Wendt, he mentioned Marx time and again as a model. Schindler distinguished between interpreting [*Deutung*], in the sense of intimating [*Andeutung*], and 'analysing in the manner of the modern Beethoven interpreters': the one was acceptable but the other was not. But to accept Marx's Beethoven interpretation meant sanctioning its 'idea' and, ultimately, was simply a precondition of those interpretations that Schindler later condemned as 'eccentric aberrations in the analysis of Beethoven's music by cheer-leaders for the "music of the future"'. In moving on to the 'art-work of ideas', Marx was pursuing a trail that Hoffmann had blazed for him. At the same time it was a decisive change of course – and one that Wagner too would follow.

Wagner's knowledge of literature on Beethoven

In the preceding section we adumbrated Wagner's links with E. T. A. Hoffmann and A. B. Marx. These links are confirmed by what he himself said about his reading of both authors. Wagner knew Hoffmann's fictional writings very well: from his sixteenth year onwards he read them over and over again. He would also have read Hoffmann's reviews of Beethoven, given his enthusiasm about both the one and the other. Moreover the fantasy piece *Beethoven's Instrumental Music* (the fourth piece in *Kreisleriana*) must have aroused Wagner's interest in similar reflections by Hoffmann.

Statements by Wagner about Marx, on the other hand, are very sparse. There is an important account in *My Life* (p. 349) of his 1847 visit to Marx.[2] He mentions in passing that in his earlier writings and musical criticism, Marx had seemed to him 'replete with fire and energy'. As is apparent from a look at the texts, Wagner was referring to essays and reviews in the *BAMZ* but also more extensive works like *On Painting in Music* (1828), *General Music Theory* (1839) and *The Theory of Musical Composition* (1837–47). Wagner will surely also have been aware of the essay *Organization of Musical Life* [*Organisation des Musikwesens*], which came out a year after his visit. Marx's disagreeable experiences in this field were among the subjects they discussed.

Wagner may have taken note of Amadeus Wendt's and Ernst Ortlepp's interpretations, which romanticized Beethoven. But that was only because Ortlepp was a friend of Wagner's, while his uncle Adolf had married a sister of Wendt. He mentions Wendt in *My Life* (p. 23) as 'the not unfavourably regarded aesthetician'.

Wagner's interest in writings on Beethoven was not, however, confined to those which were mainly concerned with interpretation. He was just as keen to collect historio-biographical data. He had an insatiable thirst for information – and not only information about Beethoven. He never wasted a chance to gather material; and so people with whom he was in touch invariably took on the role of informants. Let us give just two out of many possible examples. In 1832 Wagner used his stay in Prague to collect 'a lot of very authentic information' about Mozart's *Figaro*. The informant in this instance was Dionys Weber, the director of the Prague Conservatoire, who had been an 'eye- and ear-witness' (*GS* XII, p. 210) to Mozart's conducting. And on his trip to Vienna in 1848, Wagner took the opportunity to inspect the then unpublished manuscript copies of Bach church cantatas in the possession of Johann Theodor Mosewius (see *ML*, p. 366).

Glasenapp speculates that during his Prague visit, Wagner not only asked Dionys Weber about Mozart and the performance of his music, but also raised the subject of Beethoven with Tomášek. To this we can add further speculations of the same kind. It is fair to assume that he questioned Rochlitz, who gave his C major Symphony a cordial reception in 1832. At all events he knew Rochlitz's memoirs of Beethoven, which were published that year. As for Wilhelmine Schröder-Devrient, whom Wagner idolized as an artist, she had made her name as Fidelio in 1822, when Beethoven was still alive to see her.[3] Wagner had already made her closer acquaintance in Magdeburg, and he worked with her when he was court Kapellmeister in Dresden (1843–9). His assistant conductor in Dresden was August Röckel. The latter was able to pass on the memories of his father, Joseph, who had experienced Beethoven at rehearsals for the 1806 *Fidelio*, in which he sang Florestan.

Particularly noteworthy is Wagner's acquaintance with Joseph Fisch-hof. This dates from the time of his visit to Vienna in 1848 (see *ML*, p. 367). During his two-week stay, Wagner spent a lot of time with Fischhof. Although his main object was 'to discuss plans for reforming the Viennese theatres' (Strobel), he also wanted to see Fischhof's manuscript collection. Wagner knew that it contained some original Beethoven manuscripts including op. 111, which particularly struck him. He probably also inspected the *Fischhofsche Manuskript*, a collection of letters, documents and jottings by and about Beethoven.

The subject of Beethoven came up again when Wagner called on Rossini in 1860. Although there is no mention of it in *A Recollection of Rossini* (1868), it figures in Edmond Michotte's record of their conversation. Wagner tried stubbornly to stick to the subject of Beethoven and kept returning to Rossini's visit to the composer's lodgings in 1822.

In 1839, Wagner had made friends with the Paris librarian G. E. Anders, who was a native of Bonn. This friendship was of great value to Wagner's knowledge of the literature on Beethoven. He describes Anders as 'a pupil of Forkel's and one of the most painstaking and erudite of music bibliographers' (*GS* XII, p. 85). Anders had already assembled 'a copious amount' of 'very detailed and meticulous information about Beethoven and his works' (*SB* I, p. 453) for a projected biography when Schindler stole a march on him. (So far it has not been possible to inspect Anders's material, which is currently in the possession of the former St Petersburg Conservatoire. In any case he was in the habit of writing all his notes in a private code.) Doubtless Wagner joined Anders in closely examining Schindler's book, for soon afterwards they obviously agreed that Wagner should write the projected biography on the basis of Anders's material, consciously distancing himself from Schindler's approach. In a letter to August Lewald, Wagner describes Schindler's biography as 'to a large extent ... very incomplete, besides being written incoherently, and in a dull and clumsy way' (*SB* I, p. 471). We can be quite certain that the critical scrutiny of Schindler involved a detailed study of the first important source-work on Beethoven, the *Biographische Notizen* (1838) of Wegeler and Ries. This was because Schindler's book contained a polemic against a French translation of these 'Notes' which had been made by Anders. Whilst Schindler was visiting Paris, a meeting was called at the premises of the publisher Maurice Schlesinger. Its purpose was to reject and refute the allegations of the 'Ami de Beethoven' – as Heine ironically called Schindler. Wagner describes the episode as follows:

After Anders had shown him line for line that he had not permitted himself the slightest significant addition to the original Notes, the flashing eyes of Beethoven's liegeman grew moist, and ... he ... assured him ... that he ... solemnly swore to make *handsome amends* in the second edition of his book.   (*GS* XII, pp. 82ff.)

We may assume that this was sufficient incentive for Wagner to read the second edition. Hence he would also have seen Schindler's appendix, 'Beethoven in Paris', where the results of his stay in Paris are viewed from the angle of somebody else.

It was in Paris, if not earlier, that Wagner came across Seyfried's *Ludwig van Beethoven's Studien im, Generalbaß, Contrapuncte und in der Compositions-Lehre*. This had appeared in a French translation by Fétis in 1833, a year after its first publication. There was an appendix with a wealth of biographical data, and the whole work was a talking-point among Habeneck's circle. Wagner had a chance to catch up with Berlioz's review of the French edition in the *Journal des débats*.

Periodicals and journals in general were an important source of information for Wagner, at any rate at times. By his own account he stopped reading magazines in Dresden, but from the time of his Zurich exile onwards, he again read all kinds of journals. Of musical periodicals, he mentions the *Neue Zeitschrift für Musik*, whose chief attraction for him lay in the essays of Uhlig, and the *Signale für die musikalische Welt*. He also mentions the *Rheinische Musik-Zeitung*, of which he had a poor opinion, and the *Gazette musicale*.[4] In addition he read the *Deutsche Monatsschrift für Politik, Wissenschaft, Kunst und Leben*; and he mentions the weekly *Deutsches Museum* in connection with an article by Otto Gumprecht on Beethoven's Seventh

Symphony. Apparently Wagner consulted other periodicals as well, because he speaks to Uhlig of trips 'to the museum to read the newspapers' (*SB* IV, pp. 356, 397). In all probability he knew David Friedrich Strauss's essay on the Ninth Symphony, which appeared in the *Augsburger Allgemeine Zeitung* (1853).

It is fair to assume that Wagner read the essays on Beethoven that were published in the aforesaid journals even if he thought them misguided. This applies in particular to the years of his Zurich exile, for those years are distinguished by the intensity of his involvement with Beethoven, in that Wagner's theoretical studies and conducting activities helped him achieve a new dimension in his conception of music drama.

Naturally the above paragraphs are only a partial indication of Wagner's familiarity with contemporary journals. As a glance at his correspondence and Cosima's diaries will show, he still took note of musical journals later on in his life. Sometimes there were personal motives for this, such as the correction of wrong reports, the printing of letters from himself or from his friends, and the publication of his own articles. If Wagner wanted to influence the public with the press's help, he also needed to pick up the 'signals' it was transmitting from the outside world. And all along, these signals included information and articles about Beethoven.

To judge purely by the contents of Wagner's library at Wahnfried, his later reading-matter about Beethoven was rather one-sided. But Cosima's diaries indicate that he did not limit himself to that branch of Beethoven research whose orientation he himself had significantly influenced. He owned writings by Ludwig Nohl, for whom Beethoven was an obsession; Wagner described him to Ludwig II as a 'researcher into the most minute details of Beethoven's life' (*BLW* II, p. 241). Apparently Wagner set no store by the works of Alexander W. Thayer, although they are still indispensable today. On the other hand he was interested in Gustav Nottebohm's investigations into Beethoven's sketches. He saw in the initial skimpiness of these sketches a similarity with his own first jottings (see Cosima's diary entry for 15 May 1875).

The projected Beethoven biography

The biography of Beethoven that Wagner planned to write in Paris never came to fruition, either then or later. Wagner scholars have always regretted this, and rightly so, although the point has been laboured. All the same, the rudiments of his conception can be inferred from statements in letters, from one of the Paris novellas and from the centenary essay. Furthermore Julius Rühlmann, who was a trombonist with the Dresden court band and a follower of Wagner, suggests that Wagner's 'programmatic explanations' also contained elements of this biography. In 1854

Rühlmann reviewed a pamphlet which followed Wagner in its interpretation of Beethoven's symphonies. After expressing his regret that Wagner did not produce the biography, he went on to say:

But what Wagner intended to produce is shown by his programmes for individual Beethoven works ... which were just fragments of the larger study. Not only would Wagner have thereby achieved another lasting memorial to himself; he would also have spared us the embarrassing fact that we still lack a Beethoven biography in the artistic sense, and that a foreigner might have to beat us Germans to it, as in the case of Mozart. (*NZfM*, 41 [1854], pp. 114 f.)

For his remark about a biography 'in the artistic sense', Rühlmann had the support of Wagner himself. He was probably even familiar with the letter Wagner had written from Paris to Theodor Winkler in Dresden, over ten years earlier:

Our biography of Beethoven will be a book in 2 volumes, each having 30 sheets of medium-sized print, containing an accurate and detailed account of both the great master's artistic and domestic life, written in persuasive and, to match its subject, perhaps imaginative terms. Our book will avoid any pedantic display of scholarship, being more of a great novel about an artist than a sober listing of data and anecdotes arranged in chronological order; but for all that, there will be no statements that cannot stand up to the most thorough and meticulous historical scrutiny. At the same time, however, there will be woven into the historical account a detailed review and description of the great musical epoch which was produced by Beethoven's genius and extended from his works to all the more modern music. Among other things, this biography will include a complete catalogue of Beethoven's works in chronological order – something we have never had up to now – together with facsimiles and the like. At all events it will be the fullest and most detailed work that anyone could publish about Beethoven. (*SB* I, p. 483)

We suspect that both Wagner and Anders had contributed ideas to this extensive and complex project. Anders would have been the one behind the complete work-list, inclusion of facsimiles and extensive account. Wagner, for his part, would have suggested adopting the imaginative style of a novel. As we mentioned on p. 60, they wanted to get right away from Schindler's biography, with its 'sober listing of data and anecdotes'. Anders had introduced his 'Détails biographiques sur Beethoven' with the sentence 'La biographie de Beethoven est encore un ouvrage à faire.' By this he meant 'la vie intime', the inner life of Beethoven, and Schindler's biography had merely served to underline the point.

But what did Wagner mean by an account that would be like a novel, yet stand up to the 'most thorough and meticulous historical scrutiny'? Here the 1840 novella *A Pilgrimage to Beethoven* provides the answer. The framework of Wagner's story is the contrast between two travellers who are both heading for Vienna, and who meet up with each other several times on their journey. Both want to see Beethoven. One of them is a wealthy

Englishman riding in a carriage, and his motives are those of a sensation-hungry tourist. The other, the narrator, is travelling by foot, impelled by his extreme enthusiasm; it is he who is making a pilgrimage. Certain autobiographical elements may have been involved here. Wagner travelled to Prague and Vienna in 1832, and he may well have worked impressions of that journey into his novella.[5]

Arnold Schmitz has rightly seen Goethe's *Von Deutscher Baukunst* (1772) as providing the literary and intellectual model for the pilgrimage. What Goethe called a pilgrimage to the tomb of the 'holy *Erwin*', the architect Erwin von Steinbach, corresponds to the journey to Wagner's 'holy Beethoven'.

One possible literary precedent for Wagner's English traveller has not been hitherto acknowledged. It occurs in the writings of Heine. In the third volume of his *Salon* (1837), under the heading 'Florentine Nights II', Heine writes:

when you meet Englishmen in a foreign country, their weaknesses are all the more glaring because of the contrast. They are the gods of boredom, chasing from one country to another in gleaming carriages, and leaving a grey dust-cloud of sadness in their wake wherever they go. There is also their curiosity without interest, their well-heeled clumsiness, insolent stupidity, four-square egoism and delight in melancholy subjects.   (*Sämtliche Werke* [1912], VI, p. 423)

We recognize Heine's English traveller in the character of Wagner's patiently insistent Englishman. The latter is riding to Vienna in an elegant carriage, and in his failings he is in marked contrast to the 'pilgrim'. In addition to this, however, there is documentary evidence of English visitors to Beethoven.[6] It is even known that the composer reacted negatively to a visit by Alexander Kyd.

In his use of biographical details, Wagner concentrates on Beethoven's physiognomy, his physical movements, clothes and domestic circumstances. He mentions Beethoven's dishevelled, shaggy grey hair. The narrator recognizes the countenance he remembers from 'a good portrait', and refers to his 'gloomy, unfriendly expression'. (Here Wagner's description draws on the portrait which Ferdinand Schimon painted in 1818–19). Beethoven moves with 'short swift steps', and his attire is 'pretty untidy'. It is even likely that some of the circumstances of the pilgrim's visit were taken from a report published in the *Neue Zeitschrift für Musik* in 1838. For this too relates how the visitor, who is a young artist, writes a few lines to Beethoven, is turned away by the housekeeper but is then admitted after all. He mentions Beethoven's firm step, recognizes him from an illustration, notices the tangled white hair, and is shocked by the composer's deafness. Beethoven gives him writing instruments so that they can start a conversation.

Having now indicated some details of Beethoven's gloomy outward appearance, Wagner's narrator proceeds to trace it to its spiritual cause: 'Of course I knew all about Beethoven's deafness and had prepared myself. But it smote my heart to hear that hoarse, broken voice say: "I cannot hear"' (*WP*, p. 78). Only with this elevation of his personality to the tragic level – which is also a heightening of the artistic figure – does Wagner's Beethoven become the worthy goal of the pilgrimage. The visit takes the pilgrim into the 'sanctuary' and culminates in his initiation into the Master's plans.

Wagner's novella illustrates his quest for the living Beethoven and for the true content of his creative output. And his way of imaginatively entering the composer's milieu is an indication of his treatment of biographical facts. Beethoven's opera *Fidelio* had been staged in 1822 with Wilhelmine Schröder as Fidelio. Wagner knew of this event: his pilgrim sees the performance before calling on Beethoven. Following Wegeler, Wagner incorrectly refers to the 'new revised version of the opera which, under the title of *Leonore*, had already been played in Vienna and ... damned' (*WP*, p. 76). But more important is the fact that he telescopes this historical event in Beethoven's career with his own *Fidelio* experience of 1829, which he owed to Schröder-Devrient. Beethoven biography merges with autobiography: by imaginatively fusing together two separate periods, Wagner transforms the historical past into a fictive past in which he has actively shared. This background is, however, crucial to the fact that what his Beethoven says about the Ninth Symphony reflects the composer's artistic position at the time he wrote it. After all, he started on it in 1822, the year in which Wagner sets his Beethoven–Fidelio experience. So what the pilgrim knows after his visit is not an interpretation; he knows what the Master's intentions were. This is a pointer to Wagner's myth-making, his imaginative exegesis of personal experience.

The happiness I felt at receiving out of Beethoven's own mouth these clues to the understanding of his gigantic last symphony, which he had at the most just completed and which nobody knew – this happiness is something which even now I find impossible to picture.   (*WP*, p. 81, rev. Kropfinger)

In point of fact, Beethoven only completed the Ninth in 1824.

Wagner's Beethoven offers his 'clues' against the background of his critical attitude to *Fidelio*, and in conjunction with the remark that it is impossible to write 'a true musical drama'. This is extremely significant. It established the context within which Wagner would classify *Fidelio* and the Ninth from the viewpoint of historical developments, and feel justified in 'resolving' upon 'musical drama'.

A Pilgrimage illustrates one other facet of Wagner's use of the details of Beethoven's life. This is his amalgamation of the life and the music, especially under the impact of Beethoven's deafness. The idea of the composer as 'a poor devil, deaf as a post', who 'might have his own ideas' –

words that Wagner puts into Beethoven's own mouth – assumes a programmatic significance in Wagner's 1846 explanation of the Ninth Symphony. This is reflected in the additional remarks on it which he threw out anonymously in the Dresden press. Wagner had a concrete biographical point of reference. In the following passage he alludes to the thoughts of suicide which Beethoven expressed in the Heiligenstadt Testament, which was then already accessible.

> But now he was to be robbed of his special source of happiness – he became deaf and could no longer hear his own glorious language! Why, he was on the verge of wanting to deprive himself of speech itself as well; but his guardian spirit restrained him; – whatever he must have felt *now*, he continued to speak out in notes; – but his feelings were now to grow rare and wondrous ... he had only his own heart to consult...
>
> (*GS* xii, pp. 204f.)

The deaf Beethoven was living all alone, but his desire was for joy. The unfolding of the Ninth up to the finale is to Wagner's mind the expression of Beethoven's striving for joy.

The biographical aspect of Wagner's interpretations emerges quite clearly from his programme for the C sharp minor quartet, op. 131. Wagner offers a kind of review of 'all the moods' of the composer's 'rich inner life' (*GS* xii, p. 348), viewed as a succession of states of mind. This again is based on the well-worn idea of Beethoven as a suffering human being, consumed by his longing for joy. What finally awaits him, however, is not joy but painful resignation.

After revising the ending, Wagner included the above programme in his centenary essay so as to give a 'picture of a day in the life of our saint' (*GS* ix, pp. 96f.). Here the aim was to build into his interpretation the basic biographical fact of the tension between 'the paradise of his inner harmony' and the 'hell of his dreadfully unharmonious existence'. To be sure, this is now at odds with Wagner's premise that there could never be a direct link between the life and the music. But what he begins by denying, he proceeds to achieve by a subterfuge. Beethoven embodies the essence of music, and Wagner will use the life to illuminate it; this intention is clearly stated. The 'personal' Beethoven is 'the focus of the rays of the wondrous world emanating from him' (*GS* ix, p. 87).

The biographical features with which Wagner begins can be summed up in three characteristics. One is Beethoven's 'emancipating tendency' in his art', i.e. the 'extension of the artistic sphere'. Another is his inward-looking musical mind, and his optimistic religious faith is the third. Symptoms of Beethoven's emancipating urge are the signs of violence, defiance, wilfulness and the independent streak in his character. Wagner exaggerates Beethoven's features considerably in the process. Thus he writes of the composer's 'almost savage independence' and relates this behaviour to the 'prophecy of his innermost musical vision', which make him seem constantly 'like a man truly possessed'. This feature is connected with Beethoven's completely introspective cast of mind, his deafness being its outward sign. This in turn is reflected in his countenance. His forbidding, defiantly intent expression is proof of the inner vision. Particularly indicative of the way Wagner exploited the details of Beethoven's outward appearance, or physical traits, is the interpretation he puts on the measurements of his skull. The skull, he tells us, was 'of quite unusual thickness and solidity', protecting a brain 'of abnormal sensitivity' so that it 'could look purely inwards and pursue a great heart's universal vision in peace and quiet' (*GS* IX, p. 90).

It is, however, this introspective, intuitive vision that produces the 'serene' element in Beethoven's works, the innocence regained. Beethoven's serenity is bound up with his belief in man's original goodness. For Wagner the best confirmation of this idea was Beethoven's study of Bach, and it is linked with the image of Beethoven as a saint. In his painful dealings with the external world, his faith ultimately retains its advantage. In the end, Beethoven harmoniously resolves the hell of a 'dreadfully unharmonious existence, once again purely as an artist' (*GS* IX, p. 96).

Wagner's method was to process biographical data with a view to explaining Beethoven in the context of the drama of the future. Beethoven's attitude to his surroundings is closely linked with his artistic aims, his deafness leading him to focus his gaze inwards. It was his 'period of blissful isolation' (*GS* IX, p. 100) which brought about his religious optimism, but it also went hand in hand with 'an instinctive tendency to extend the scope of his art' (*GS* IX, p. 98) and led to the Ninth Symphony. In both the Paris novella and the centenary essay, Wagner's use of biographical details was governed by the same idea. This was that Beethoven's music was the necessary preliminary to his own composing – and the Ninth Symphony, the bridge to music drama.

Although the Paris biography that Wagner intended to write with Anders was never realized, their plans are not a complete mystery. As Rühlmann thought, the 'programmatic explanations' were spin-offs from that project, and so were *A Pilgrimage* and the Beethoven centenary essay. True, they differ in form and emphasis according to period, purpose and historical context, spiritual and intellectual. But in every case, Wagner visibly processed and worked over biographical material in the same way. In 1840, he would hardly have produced a Beethoven biography where the data and presentation could stand up to 'the most thorough and meticulous historical criticism', and it would certainly not have been that comprehensive and illuminating work which orthodox Wagner devotees are still vaguely hinting at. Rather Wagner would have produced the biography 'in the artistic sense' that he described to Winkler as possessing a deliberately imaginative language and the narrative style of a 'novel about an artist'. These are features which he defined through his actual use of them. The use of the novella form can be termed 'artistic'; so can Wagner's linking of the life with his programmatic explanations and the biography with the *œuvre*, as well as his technique of tracing his own work back to Beethoven's.

4

BEETHOVEN'S ROLE IN
WAGNER'S WRITINGS ON ART

Wagner as a writer

The problematic nature of Wagner's writings

I am not talking about his theory. If it were not something so completely secondary, not so wholly a retrospective and superfluous glorification of his own talent, then his creative work would undoubtedly have become just as untenable as the theory: and nobody would have taken it seriously for a moment without the work, which appears to validate it as long as one is sitting in the theatre, but which in fact validates nothing but itself. Has *anybody* ever seriously believed in this theory, I wonder? ... it is true enough: there is not much to be learned about Wagner from Wagner's critical writings.   (*Pro and Contra Wagner*, p. 47)

Thomas Mann expressed the above views in 1911; later he would qualify them, as in 'The Sorrows and Grandeur of Richard Wagner' (1933), addressed above all to the theory of the *Gesamtkunstwerk*. What fascinated him all his life was the immediate artistic experience of Wagner's compositions, with their significance for his own creative work. The theorist in Wagner was suspect to the author in Mann. While his approach may have been a partial one, Mann still represents the critics of Wagner the theorist, the musical philosopher and aesthetician. Wagner has an undisputed place in a cultural tradition that we acknowledge and reproduce. But even today his theoretical statements are regarded with a certain amount of misgiving and prejudice.

It is inaccurate to say that Wagner's theory was made up of afterthoughts. Rather his writings formed a necessary reflective counterpart to his composing, and they always sprang from an immediate cause and were meant for public consumption. We could describe them as occupying a position between Wagner's own past and his future; while recalling the first, they are anticipating the second. *Opera and Drama* illustrates this particularly clearly. True, it is precisely *Opera and Drama* which has been used indiscriminately in the interpretation of works before the *Ring* cycle, but this should not lead to the overall conclusion that Wagner's writings are invalid as commentaries on his musical works. To categorize his theoretical texts as an irrelevance would be to dismiss all artists' statements about art as immaterial.

68

The argument as to which came first, the art or the theory, is beside the point. And it is just as pointless to play off the music dramas against the theory, although the former are unquestionably the more important and the more consistent. What matters is the inter-relationship of the two, and the tensions which appear when we start examining this are a significant part of the phenomenon. The gaps between the theory and artistic practice, like the discrepancies between them, are aspects of a complex larger relationship which must be identified as a whole.

Wagner was quite aware of the problematic nature of his writings, and a catalogue of his own comments about them would hardly obviate the complexity of the situation, with its inherent contradictions. It would be a mistake, however, to assign more weight to one particular group of statements by him – contradictory as they so often are – than to another. The motives behind Wagner's writings were neither purely financial nor purely emotional. Nor was he prompted solely by artistic considerations or artistic politics. Despite his self-criticism, he did not disown anything that he had written. And although he repeatedly asserted in his letters to Uhlig that he had said all he had to say in terms of theory, this was only a passing phase. His compulsion to express himself constantly, and on every subject, was evinced in a rhetoric which not only dominated his conversations but also materially affected the style and dimensions of his writings. One moment he says that he has had enough of writing once and for all; the next he says that he considers it far less important to write operas than publicly to state his views on prevailing artistic conditions (*SB* iii, pp. 166, 172). Wagner's renunciations of theorizing represented transitions rather than complete breaks. To communicate by theorizing was just as necessary to him as communicating through a work of art. The urge to be writing all the time is perhaps most apparent where Wagner, having reached the peak of his aversion to 'theoretical speculation', dissociates himself from it simply in order to gain a fresh vantage-point. It was a special form of 'the art of transition'. Writing to Frédéric Villot in 1860, Wagner describes the mood he was in when he began '*Music of the Future*':

It would have seemed utterly impossible to immerse myself once more in that labyrinth of abstract speculation; indeed the revulsion I now feel at the thought of re-reading my theoretical works makes me realize what a thoroughly abnormal state of mind I was in when I wrote them, a state of mind which may occur once in the life of an artist but can hardly be repeated.

(*TWE*, p. 13)

In the same preface, Wagner accounts for the weaknesses in his writings as follows:

I called that condition abnormal because I was under a compulsion to treat as a theoretical problem what I had come to feel absolutely certain about in my artistic perceptions and production; I had to make it completely clear to my reflective consciousness and so abstract contemplation was necessary. To an artist nothing is more alien and repugnant than that kind of thinking, so utterly opposed to the usual nature of his own. He cannot bring to it the required calm composure of the professional theoretician; rather, he is impelled by a passionate impatience which prevents him from giving the necessary time and attention to matters of style; he wants to put into every sentence the picture of the whole that is constantly in his mind; he doubts whether he has succeeded and the doubt drives him to make the attempt again, so that eventually he works himself into a state of irritation and excitement completely unknown to the theoretician. Aware of all the error and failure, and upset still further by his awareness of it, he hurriedly finishes off his work, telling himself with a sigh that when all is said and done he can only expect to be understood by one who already shares his artistic standpoint.

(TWE, p. 29, slightly amended)

Seldom are Wagner's comments on his own writing activity as profound and revealing as the above remarks from '*Music of the Future*'. It was in fact the theoretically adequate production of the 'picture of the whole' which left Wagner palpably struggling and always really eluded him, or could only be achieved with the assistance of metaphors. His metaphors are a symptom of his problems with terminology. It seems impossible to analyse them because of their lack of a scientific basis. In point of fact, however, they represent new departures and perspectives in his artistic thinking, which is precisely why they need to be analysed. (See Kropfinger, *Musica* 38 [1984], pp. 422–8.)

Admittedly the disquiet due to inner uncertainty that Wagner mentions had a further cause, and one which he does not examine in this context. It does emerge from a letter he wrote to Uhlig at the time he was writing *The Art-Work of the Future*. This shows he was aware of some quite specific gaps in his account and in the material he was using. And it is significant that he was apparently thinking of quite different gaps to those which strike us today and which, to go by Wagner's letters, were also noted by Uhlig.

Theodor Uhlig's contribution

When Wagner first settled in Dresden, Theodor Uhlig stood in the opposite musical camp. But because of their common admiration for Beethoven, and after the performance of the Ninth Symphony in 1847, Uhlig became a staunch and selfless friend to the composer. During the first years of Wagner's exile, up to his own death on 3 January 1853, he was undoubtedly Wagner's most important associate in Germany apart from Liszt. Wagner encumbered him with a variety of tasks – tasks which may have been beyond his physical capabilities.

Both Uhlig's theoretical writings and Wagner's letters to him tell us a lot about their association (Uhlig's letters to Wagner have not survived). Uhlig's dependence on Wagner is evident from a mere glance at his writings. At times he would go so far as to take over whole paragraphs from a letter by Wagner, as well as faithfully obeying his advice on how to organize his statements. This applies to the essay he wrote on the poetic substance of Beethoven's works [*Über den dichterischen Gehalt Beethovenscher Tonwerke*]. (Ludwig Frankenstein's edition of Uhlig's writings omits part of this essay, which appeared in the *NZfM* 37 [1852], p. 166. See Wagner's letter of 15 February 1852.) What has been virtually ignored up to now, or at any rate has received only the occasional passing mention, is the fact that Uhlig had criticisms to make of Wagner. There are even signs that he provided the author of *The Art-Work of the Future* with a fresh or at least a deeper insight into certain musical aspects of his own compositions and Beethoven's.

When Wagner sent Uhlig the manuscript of the *Art-Work of the Future*, he was conscious of the gaps in his statements. He wrote in his covering letter:

As you see, the piece has become fairly substantial: if I had to expand on individual points, there was also much I had to leave out of consideration altogether – but only, I hope, things of no great importance.

And only two paragraphs further on Wagner writes:

This will be my last literary work: much could be added to it that I have for the most part outlined in only the most general fashion: – but if I needed to do all that myself, it would only go to show that I had missed the target: if so, there is nothing one can do about it; but if I have been understood and have persuaded others, albeit a handful, of my conviction, then others must and shall accomplish everything that is the prerogative of the *many*, and not of *one individual*. I am particularly staking my hopes on you!   (*SB* iii, pp. 166f.)

It is likely that so explicit a challenge was scarcely necessary to secure Uhlig's participation. Wagner's account apparently stung him into action. Judging by Wagner's reply of 27 December 1849, Uhlig's initial response was one of unqualified approval. But as he re-read the essay more carefully, this obviously gave way to a cooler, critically appraising attitude. Wagner promptly reacted to this in his letter of 12 January 1850:

There is so much I would say to you, and so much to write in response to your letter ... Let me just say this: if after reading through my Art-Work of the Future one more time you can't make out my plan clearly, I must have expounded it badly. Our divided modern art's genetic origin in the Greek total work of art could only be shown clearly by bringing out with great precision the crucial point where this art became indirectly and no longer directly representational, passing from tragic drama into so-called plastic art [*bildende Kunst*]. If you read it as my intention simply to discuss and compare the different art-forms one by one, you mistook my meaning, or I expressed myself unclearly: I have grouped all the art-forms according to the nature of each in such a way as to use them to demonstrate the whole evolution of art up to our modern art concepts, in conjunction with the whole evolution of the human personality in general. Here I had to be completely

71

impartial to conform to the outward allocation of space, and that is why I even felt obliged to apologize in a footnote for dwelling on music at such length (relatively speaking). But if I wish to prove that the plastic arts, being artificial forms that have simply been abstracted from real art, must come to a complete stop in the future, and thus reject out of hand the survival of these plastic arts of painting and sculpture, although they profess to be today's principal art-form, you would probably agree with me that the issue could not and should not be settled without further ado. – Well, let me know when you have taken another look at the piece. I quite understand too that in the main, only music interested you: perhaps I shall help to make up for that on another occasion. (*SB* III, p. 209)

The above letter tells us that Uhlig was criticizing two points in particular. These points are features of Wagner's exposition which have been at the centre of Wagner criticism ever since. There is in fact no need to refute his account of the intrinsic differences between the individual arts. With regard to both the decline of ancient Greek drama and his proposed revival of the 'total work of art', Wagner does not really explain the above differences in terms of genetic history. His concept of historical evolution is governed by a rather abstract idea of development. This is related to Wagner's caricature of the individual arts, which becomes downright grotesque in the case of the 'plastic arts'. And it is striking that Uhlig evidently thought Wagner had not given enough attention to music, of all things. This suggests that despite his support for Wagner, his close attachment to 'absolute music' was still colouring his outlook.

The main outlet for Uhlig's criticisms was his essay *Die natürlichen Grundlagen der Instrumentalmusik im Hinblick auf Beethovens Sinfonien*. He did not dwell on those points where he differed from Wagner, because he was adopting the latter's thesis of a development aimed at uniting the arts within drama. But the divergences became clear when we compare the corresponding passages. Furthermore Wagner appears to have taken up Uhlig's account in one respect, although without really revising his views.

There are three main points on which Uhlig differs from Wagner. Firstly, he confines himself to musical matters; there are none of Wagner's elaborate and unrealistically one-sided ideas on classical art and the separation of the arts. Secondly, he takes the trouble to elucidate specific features of the historical development of music, at least sketchily. And in the process, he also endeavours to pin down the way that individual genres and trends in music interact and correspond to one another.

Bypassing Wagner's speculations on the separation of the arts, Uhlig goes back to the real and 'natural' foundations of music by 'looking up historical documents'. This brings him closer to the historical facts. He goes back as far as the union of dance and music in the art of the minnesinger and troubadour, for whom he adduces a shared basic form of two, four and eight bars strung together. In the same way as Wagner, Uhlig polemically exaggerates the contrast between church music, song and dance. But he is at pains to do a certain amount of justice to the intricacy and complexity of musical developments, and to define the relations between the symphony and dance. He suggests that instrumental music did not select the dance as just a foundation for its larger forms. This is in marked contrast to Wagner's wholesale description of harmonized dance as the 'basis of the richest art-work of the modern symphony' (*GS* III, p. 90). For Uhlig, interestingly enough, the connection between dance and the symphony is based entirely on what he calls the main characteristic of dance, namely dance rhythm, the 'regular, frequent return' of a short motif. Wagner may have been influenced by Uhlig when he wrote in *Opera and Drama* that dance melody was originally at one with song melody, thus departing somewhat from his abstract aesthetic dance formula.

There is a possibility of Wagner's having acknowledged corrections by Uhlig's and even of his having adopted them. This is not as unlikely as may seem at first glance, thanks to the influence of those Wagner apologists who still regard all his ideas as the products of his own special genius. Wagner's letters to Uhlig are full of statements in which the theorizing composer proclaims his respect and admiration for Uhlig as a violinist and theorist. This was a remarkable amount of approval and recognition for Wagner to express. It covered writings which ranged from the two essays, *Die natürlichen Grundlagen der Instrumentalmusik* and *Beethovens Sinfonien im Zusammenhange betrachtet*, to Uhlig's later treatise *On the Closing Scene of Tannhäuser*. Wagner's reaction to the Beethoven essays is particularly noteworthy, because he acknowledged Uhlig's painstaking corrections:

> Since returning to Zurich I have procured every issue of the Neue Zeitschrift für Musik for the first half of this year, and have read not only *all your* essays *but* also most of the other contributions. I began by reading only your essays: they have given me enormous pleasure, and what is more, they have often *taught* me as well. Thank you very much. All I can say is that you are a master of your subject. Your thoroughness is devastating, and nobody with an ounce of sense will want to argue with you but only to learn from you. Your two essays on the Beethoven symphonies are of the most vital importance... (*SB* III, pp. 365f.)

This was not the only way in which Wagner showed his approval, for he went so far as to quote Uhlig. In December 1850 he wrote to him:

> I have no idea, by the way, what you've got against your article about Lohengrin in the Zeitschrift für Musik. If I thought there was anything at all you might have misgivings about, it was the pragmatic account of the action; for the rest you have told even me things I didn't know, or at any rate shown me things I already knew in a fresh light deriving from your own perceptions, for which I can only thank you most sincerely. You are probably well aware that I have learnt a good deal from you generally: in my new [literary] work I've actually had to quote you at one point – Be pleased with yourself! (*SB* III, pp. 478f.)

Here Wagner was referring to the essay *Drei Tage in Weimar: Das Herderfest: Richard Wagners Oper 'Lohengrin'*, which Uhlig published in the *Neue Zeitschrift für Musik*. The quotation he mentions must have appeared in

Opera and Drama, because that was what he was working on at the time of his letter. We can also say roughly where the quotation came from: it must have been the musical section of the above Uhlig essay or another essay by him.

Of course Wagner's attitude to quotations was, as we have noted, a lax one. Something in him jibbed at a literal repetition of what had been said already, as is clearly expressed in a letter to Uhlig:

> As a rule I dislike this quoting; there is something pedantic about it: what has once been publicly stated belongs to everybody and is no longer the property of the person who said it. In this sense I would always forgive myself for plagiarism because I would not be able to regard it as such. (*SB* III, p. 504)

Nonetheless Wagner quoted his Dresden friend, just as he said in his letter. There are two references to Uhlig in the manuscript of *Opera and Drama*. (See my 1984 edition, pp. 406 and 421.) Significantly, both are concerned with the limitations of pure music.

In the first passage Wagner criticizes attempts to compose 'dramatic' music, since music is simply 'an art of *expression*' (*GS* III, p. 243, and my 1984 edition of *Oper und Drama*, p. 34). A note in his manuscript states: 'There was a pertinent and exhaustive discussion of this by T[heodor] U[hlig] a while ago in the N.Z.f.M.' The comments to which Wagner refers can be traced to both *Die natürlichen Grundlagen der Instrumentalmusik* and *Beethovens Sinfonien im Zusammenhange betrachtet*. Each includes a section dealing with the relationship between pure instrumental music and programme music (or what Uhlig calls 'representational, descriptive and pictorial music'), and drawing a firm distinction between them. What is particularly important is that Uhlig fully acknowledged 'representational music', which he called a 'transitional genre'. This helps us to locate the second reference to Uhlig in Wagner's manuscript. It occurs precisely where Wagner is describing 'tone-painting' as a necessary evolutionary phase. (See *GS* IV, p. 188, and *Oper und Drama* [1984], p. 346.)

To be sure, there are also similarities between *Opera and Drama* and Uhlig's writings which are not expressly noted in Wagner's manuscript. Moreover we should bear in mind that Wagner was in the habit of reading things into a text. He wrote to the Princess Marie Wittgenstein that whenever he read a book, it was rarely the actual words on the page that he read, but rather what he read into them (*SL*, p. 365).

Taking this attitude into account, we will notice a correspondence between certain passages in Uhlig's *Drei Tage in Weimar* and Wagner's *Opera and Drama*. The passages in question are devoted to a description of the motivic permutations in Wagner's musical works, and the overall unity they achieve. This is how Uhlig puts it:

> Naturally Wagner never renounces ... the primal musical form, the theme ... but he abandons those artificial forms [i.e. the established trappings of operatic form]

74

whenever their deployment would obstruct his drama's quiet but steady progress
... Hence Wagner's operas contain melodies in abundance but few self-contained
musical numbers: the music is closely connected with the poetic text in which the
drama is inexorably developed to begin with. But if there is one art that is capable of
achieving its effect through repetition, and also needs to do so, that art is music ...
Hence he [Wagner] replaces the musical theme, artificially enlarged into an aria or
conventional operatic number, with the principal motif of the essential musical
theme, elevated to a standard characteristic. That is to say, the most significant
musical ideas run through his whole opera like a crimson thread, and the opera
thereby acquires a musical unity in a far higher sense than it would from stringing
together a miscellaneous selection of self-contained numbers.

(Drei Tage in Weimar [1913], pp. 333f.)

Wagner writes as follows:

Previously opera composers had not even attempted to create a unified form for the
whole work of art: each individual vocal piece was formally entire in itself, bearing a
resemblance to the other musical pieces in the opera as regards outward structure,
but never really connected with them in terms of a form-dictating content.
Unconnectedness was the very hallmark of operatic music. Only the individual
musical item had an intrinsically coherent form deriving from the calculations of
absolute music, preserved through custom, and forcibly imposed on the dramatist
... Once they are precisely differentiated melodic elements that completely realize
their content, the dramatic action's principal motifs will, as they suggestively ...
recur, come to constitute a unified artistic form extending not only across shorter
dramatic sections but across the whole drama, binding it together ... This
represents the achievement of a completely unified form... (*GS* iv, pp. 201f.)

There were structural aspects of Beethoven's instrumental music of
which Wagner was aware at that time. He had already recognized their
relevance to his own composing. There were others he first perceived with
the aid of Uhlig's powers of analysis. We cannot tell exactly where the
dividing-line comes. But it should be clear from the foregoing statements
and quotations that Uhlig did not merely confirm Wagner's views and fill
them in. He also supplied Wagner with important insights regarding the
structure of music and its formal design. (Uhlig was conscious of this fact,
as is shown by his reply in the *NZfM* to a critic who accused him of
depending on Wagner's ideas.) And this would tally with artistic experience. At the start of the 1850s, Wagner had a new road ahead of him. The
difference between his subjective intention and the objective state of the
arts was forcing him to give up a 'more or less unconscious artistic
productivity' for a new creative phase that was determined by 'permanent
reflection' (*GS* vii, p. 89). There was an extra motive for the interest
Wagner took in Uhlig's analytical insights into Beethoven's compositions –
as well as into Schumann's, for example. As is proved by Wagner's remarks
on the 'poetic object', the fascination Beethoven held for him was combined with a challenge. He felt that he had not only to explain the

mysteriousness of Beethoven's works from the viewpoint of content, but also to understand them from the compositional angle. Before tackling the *Ring*, he needed to explore artistic resources and extend his musico-dramatic material. This made Uhlig an indispensable 'translator' of the motifs and structure of Beethoven's compositions. And by the same token, Uhlig's writings must be considered by any modern student who seeks to know more about Wagner's change of direction as a composer, and the background to it.

Aspects of the exegesis of Beethoven

The symphony and drama

(a) The symphony and the sonata

Nonetheless the new form of dramatic music must have the unity of a symphonic movement for it to constitute, as music, a work of art, and it will achieve this by being most intimately connected with the whole drama and stretching right across it instead of just covering isolated smaller, arbitrary parts of it. The aforesaid unity will then result from a fabric of basic themes running through the whole work, themes which, as in a symphonic movement, contrast with and complement each other, assume fresh shapes, separate and combine: the only difference is that it is now the dramatic action taking place which governs the separating and combining, whereas in the symphony the rules for this were originally derived from dance motions.
(*GS* x, p. 185)

If we begin with this much quoted passage, an even better title for Wagner's essay *On the Application of Music to Drama* (1879) would be 'On the Application of the Symphony to Drama'. The latter would not only come closer to the heart of the matter; indirectly, it would also immediately point to Beethoven as a major preliminary to the conception of 'music drama'. In the introduction to the fifth and sixth volumes of his collected writings (*GS* v, p. 4), Wagner calls his literary essays 'variations on the great theme'. And the Beethoven symphony is undoubtedly one of the 'leitmotifs'.

What Wagner associates with the word 'symphony' has many different levels of meaning. On this very issue there is a distant as well as an intimate side to his relationship to Beethoven. To be sure, his examination of formal and technical matters is not as comprehensive as it might be; and his writings do not reflect the true systematist's objectivizing tendency. Wagner is selective, making both aesthetic and historical value-judgments. He emphasizes certain aspects of musical composition while excluding others or relegating them to the sidelines. In addition he often dispenses with the specialist terminology that was already current in his day, and when he does use it – as in the cases of 'theme' and 'motif' – he does so in an unorthodox way. (Wagner never cared much for the 'equerries of the

Musical Forms Riding School', as Hans von Bülow called them.) The problem facing Wagner as an author is always evident from the particular case, and it is the findings that determine the method. Our task is to identify the technical and/or formal questions which his aestheticizing language conceals; to do our best to show up any concrete statement behind it.[1]

One method of tackling this is to locate passages of text that correspond to one another, and to treat the context as a potential commentary and key. As we shall see, Uhlig's writings also play an important part in this. The textual correspondences oblige us, however, to focus on the points of contact between drama and Beethoven's compositions, thereby leading to that more far-reaching question which is central to our theme. The question is this: in Wagner's study of Beethoven and music drama, are the word usage and verbal content mutually related? And what are the implications of this for Wagner's reception of Beethoven, for the link with the conception of music drama and ultimately with drama itself?

In many instances Wagner hammered out his interpretation in respect of Beethoven's symphonic works, or used them to develop it. But even where this is not expressly stated, his statements are mostly valid for Beethoven's sonatas as well. Only in one instance, albeit a very important one, is this definitely not the case. It does not apply to those passages that are concerned with the *Sprachvermögen*, the expressive powers of the orchestra, which Beethoven carried a crucial stage further. For by *Sprachvermögen*, Wagner means not only the quite special rhythmic incisiveness of Beethoven's music, but also the individual sound of the various orchestral instruments.

It can be gathered from Wagner's writings that he associated the symphony with the sonata from a formal viewpoint, especially where Beethoven's works were concerned. Thus in 1870 he wrote in his centenary essay:

One may say that Beethoven was and remained a sonata composer, because with the vast majority of his works and the finest of them, the basic form of the sonata was the veil through which he looked into the realm of sounds, or through which, emerging from that realm, he would make himself understood by us ...

(*GS* IX, pp. 81f.)

And a few years earlier, in his *Report on a German School of Music to be Established in Munich* (1865), he had written:

In attempting to define the sum of German music today, we would place the Beethoven sonata directly alongside the Beethoven symphony; and to cultivate the performer's sense of what is right and beautiful, there is from the viewpoint of schooling no happier and more instructive method than to begin with an education in sonata performance, so as to develop the faculty of sound judgment when performing a symphony. (*GS* VIII, p. 150)

Basically Wagner always refers to the sonata pattern, or at any rate certain aspects of sonata form, when examining formal questions to do with the symphony and sonata. In *Opera and Drama*, for example, he writes:

These forms achieved coherence by virtue of the fact that an already finished theme would alternate with a second middle theme, and the decision as to when to repeat it would be musically motivated. The activity of the larger, absolute instrumental piece of music, the symphonic movement, was made up of the alternation, repetition, contraction and expansion of the themes, and they alone determined that activity, while the symphonic movement strove to acquire a unified form from the coherence of the themes and their return, a coherence that could be justified if possible in terms of feeling. (*GS* IV, pp. 201f.)

(b) The sonata as a 'problematic form'

We will search Wagner's writings in vain for a detailed description or even definition of sonata form, as it became crystallized in nineteenth-century theory. Nor can we pin down his concept of the structure of sonata writing with any great accuracy. Clearly he was not interested in formal nomenclature such as the A–B–A scheme that A. B. Marx propounded. Wagner saw this framework, but to try and reduce his idea of sonata form to this formal scheme would not be appropriate. His musical thinking was too subtle for that. It was his very lack of schematicism about the framework for the sonata which enabled him to grasp what was special about Beethoven's construction of motifs and themes, up to the late quartets with their specifically form-creating structures. In his last years Cosima recorded him as saying it might be of some benefit to the symphony 'if one did not feel obliged to compose in four movements, and if one shaped the motives – first, second, return to the first – into movements' (18 October 1878). This shows that his thinking about symphonic form was far from static.

In early instrumental works like the A major and B flat major sonatas, Wagner adhered to sonata form in the construction of the first movement. All the same, his attitude to it was a critical one from an early date. Wagner saw in the sonata anything but a form to be adopted unquestioningly. He came to regard it more and more as a 'problematic' form about which people could disagree (Robert Schumann's view of it was not uncritical either). And Wagner saw it as doubly problematic. Firstly it was no longer an *intrinsically* fixed scheme, because Beethoven had overcome this inner paralysis, so to speak. Secondly, even Beethoven had found himself restricted by the architecture, the outer framework of sonata form. To remove this restriction was an integral aspect of Wagner's dramas with their new, musically dramatic structures.

Wagner noticed early on that Beethoven's personal realization of sonata form differed from that of his predecessors, particularly Mozart. In *German Opera* (1834) he wrote that Beethoven expressed 'mighty events' in the 'freest symphony' (*GS* XII, pp. 2f.). Seven years later, in the novella *A*

Happy Evening, he followed this very sweeping statement with the comment that Beethoven had 'infinitely expanded the form of the symphony'. Beethoven, he went on, had discarded 'the proportions of the traditional periodic structure, wrought to their highest beauty by Mozart', in order for his turbulent genius, 'daring, and yet at the same time reflective', to be 'free to take wing in realms to which it alone could penetrate' (*WP*, p. 184). The perceptions about form that this extravagant Hoffmannesque language undoubtedly clothes are difficult to establish. Apparently Wagner was referring to Beethoven's unschematic musical construction, for which Marx uses the term 'period with open-order after-phrase' [*Periode mit aufgelöstem Nachsatz*] or 'extended period'. It is interesting that at that time, Wagner already saw a greater flexibility of the periodic construction as making for an increase in 'dramatic truth'. In his essay *Halévy and French Opera* (1842), he contrasts Halévy's method of composing with Auber's.

A liking for sealed-off, rhythmical period construction is very noticeable in Auber's music in general. It undeniably bestows on his music a good part of that clarity and intelligibility which make up one of the most important requirements of dramatic music, whose effect should be instantaneous ... But the moment it ceases to chime with the dramatic truth, this pronounced liking for great rhythmic and melodic regularity and neatness becomes tiresome and lacking in impact. Now bearing in mind also that this ... *brilliant* one-sidedness in the design of the actual melody is not commensurate with the universal expression of tragic feeling, a rhythmic–melodic structure of this type will often seem like a resplendent casing set on top of the dramatic situation, as though the latter were being framed and put under glass.

(*GS* xii, p. 136)

It is Halévy's method which Wagner prefers. For he goes on to say that Halévy has 'escaped the spirit of conventional rhythms and melismata' and followed the 'free, unrestricted road of the *creative poet*, where the only condition is truth of expression'. And there is a ready connection between Wagner's positive assessment in the novella of a freer type of periodic construction and his statement in the essay that along with French influences, Halévy revealed 'the clearest and loveliest traces of *Beethoven's* spirit'.

The gap between Wagner's Paris statements and what he wrote in *'Music of the Future'* (1860) is considerable. This applies not only to their respective dates but also to their content. The Paris novella, like the essay on Halévy, was concerned with breaking down a standard periodic structure of melody. In the article he wrote eighteen years later, Wagner wanted to abolish an inwardly ossified sonata scheme and allow the parts to grow together melodically instead. At this stage, then, he was tackling a far more extensive problem:

In Beethoven's predecessors, even in symphonic movements, you still find these perilous blank spaces between principal melodic motives ... Beethoven, supreme genius that he was, so managed matters that these embarrassing intermediate

79

passages completely disappear: his principal melodic motives are linked by music which itself possesses to the full the character of melody.

(*TWE*, pp. 37–8, amended)

Wagner's fundamental new insight is based on a much deeper exploration of Beethoven's thematic–motivic processes and their formal relevance.[2] It brings home to us what Beethoven had achieved by overcoming the inner ossification of the sonata, that 'problematic form'. The same insight underlies a passage in Wagner's Beethoven centenary essay. In connection with Beethoven's repeal of musical formalism he writes:

For the element in Beethoven's musical construction which is so important in the history of art is this: all the technical devices whereby an artist can behave conventionally towards the outside world, in order for him to be understood, themselves attain a supreme importance as a direct outpouring. As I remarked before, there is nothing added, nothing encloses the melody, and everything turns into melody instead, every voice in the accompaniment, every rhythmic note, even the rests... (*GS* IX, p. 87).

It is not only as regards the interaction between form and motif – the inner structure of sonata writing, as it were – that a more precise definition of Wagner's ideas in his writings can be recognized. The same goes for the outer construction, the external scheme of the sonata. In contrast to his standpoint in *Opera and Drama*, Wagner later incorporated the tripartite sonata movement into his thinking (*On Franz Liszt's Symphonic Poems*, *On the Application of Music to Drama*). These reflections suggest something of a text-book schematicism. But Wagner's concept of sonata form transcended it. In this respect, Theodor Uhlig's comparison of the sonata writing of Mozart and Beethoven provided him with crucial insights. We must not let this be obscured by the fact that he did not put them in any strict order from a theoretical viewpoint.

What Wagner established through these reflections, however, was that in spite of his motivic–thematic processes, Beethoven was still tied to the sonata framework or, to be more precise, the reprise. This mattered where dramatic considerations required the music to follow a different course – which was in the overture. It was here that Wagner's criticism of Beethoven began. This, the second aspect of the sonata as a 'problematic form', also marked the start of Wagner's task as a dramatist. Not that Beethoven's thematic–motivic processes became irrelevant in Wagner's eyes as soon as he turned to dramatic composition. On the contrary, Wagner regarded both aspects of the sonata as a 'problematic form' as equally significant, although from different angles. But to prove our point, we now need to take a closer look at Wagner's efforts to develop his conception of music drama, to mark out and formulate his position as a dramatist during his first years in Zurich. For the first time amid the vicissitudes of his relationship to Beethoven and of his dramatic problems, a situation now arose in which those two aspects of the sonata became mutually permeable. This was, of course, over and beyond any surface connections which could be interpreted and summed up as straightforward 'influences'.

(c) Uhlig's essay 'Die Wahl der Motive'

What would the role and function of music be in the 'drama of the future'? Wagner's basic idea was that of the genesis and configuration of musical themes and motifs (he speaks of 'melodic moments') in accordance with a poetic aim. The basic motifs growing out of this poetic aim serve to convey 'plastic elements of feeling'. The composer has to condense such motifs into melodic elements, and 'in complete agreement with the poetic aim' he must by means of their 'well-determined mutual repetition' organize them in such a way that 'even the supreme integrated musical form will come about entirely of its own accord' (*GS* IV, p. 201). This abstract model for a thematic framework is, however, still orientated much more to *Lohengrin* than to Wagner's practice in the *Ring*. In order to translate his theory into a new reality – a reality of which he had only a vague idea at the time of *Opera and Drama* – Wagner needed to evolve a new technique of motivic development and working-up. An indication of the gap between theory and practice is a letter Wagner wrote to August Röckel in 1854, whilst he was working on *Rheingold*. Here he briefly refers to the working-up technique he was now employing:

> In time I believe I shall be able to tell you about its [*Rheingold's*] composition. For now let me add merely that it has become a close-knit unity: there is scarcely a bar in the orchestra which does not develop out of preceding motifs. But these are not things one can communicate. (*SL*, p. 310, amended)

Opera and Drama says nothing about this development of each successive bar from preceding motifs. Wagner's theoretical model lags behind the subtle technique of motivic and thematic working-out that he would later develop in practice. The same thing is reflected in his account of the thematic framework of Beethoven's music. *Opera and Drama* merely refers to the thematic 'alternation, repetition, contraction and expansion' in symphonic writing. This seems just as rudimentary as Wagner's theoretical axioms, compared with the statements we have already cited from his later *'Music of the Future'* and Beethoven centenary essay. And we may take it that Wagner's deeper analytical delvings into the internal melodic structure of Beethoven's symphonic writing were not merely a reflex of the new dimension in his own composition technique. Rather he was carrying on a continuous dialogue with Beethoven's music while developing as a composer.

It is true that Wagner had already considered Beethoven's works from the opera composer's standpoint, picking out specific aspects of their composition. But now it was a matter of realizing a new basic design for musical drama, and of finding out which elements in Beethoven's composition technique would lend themselves to the purpose.

We can perceive that Wagner did in fact ponder these questions from the importance he ascribed to them in his correspondence and conversations with Theodor Uhlig. At all events he saw fit to mention in *My Life* that when Uhlig visited him in the summer of 1851, they discussed 'important aspects of the manner in which Beethoven develops his themes' (*ML*, p. 471). But what particularly interested Wagner in this context were Uhlig's writings, including one with the title *Die Wahl der Motive* – 'The Selection of Motifs'. It looks as though in this particular area he owed more to Uhlig's theories than has been hitherto supposed.

At the beginning of 1851, Wagner sent Uhlig a copy of the second part of *Opera and Drama*. In his covering letter he wrote: 'I liked your "Instrumentalmusik" very much . . . Now I am eager for the second article, which I shall probably need to quote in my third part' (*SB* III, p. 504). It is clear from *My Life* that the 'second article' must be a reference to *Die Wahl der Motive*. Looking back to 1851, Wagner says in his autobiography seventeen years later:

He [Uhlig] had soon acquired the literary skill to give expression to our concord of views [on artistic matters] and gave proof of it in a superb, lengthy essay about instrumental music . . . In addition, he sent me another rigorously theoretical work on the construction of musical themes and movements, which has remained unpublished to this day. This evidenced an original grasp and intensive study of the methods employed by Mozart and Beethoven, and particularly of their highly characteristic differences. In its thorough and exhaustive discussion of the subject, it seemed to me to constitute a suitable basis for a new theory of the more advanced aspects of musical structure, through which the mysterious process employed by Beethoven might be fully elucidated and worked out in greater detail to furnish a practical system for further use. (*ML*, p. 466)

Although Wagner seldom praised anyone else's theoretical work, he had already mentioned Uhlig's essay in similarly appreciative terms on 5 April 1856, in a letter to Breitkopf & Härtel. And it is a noteworthy fact that here, a good twelve years earlier, he lays particular stress on the description of Beethoven's motivic construction, acknowledging Uhlig's 'instructive' importance for his own creative work.

Without being at all aware of exaggerating, I think this essay – a fairly comprehensive and detailed one – must be considered one of the most important of its kind to have appeared so far, perhaps the most important in many ways. Dispensing with all polemics, it ranges over the weighty subject of motivic construction, clearly demonstrating the difference between *Beethoven* and his predecessors in this respect, and with its perfectly lucid analysis of the method concerned, it offers the most practical and successful guidance in one's own motivic construction, so that it is fair to regard it as an extremely helpful instructive work as well.

(Uhlig [1913], pp. 9f.)

There is no further mention of the essay in Wagner's correspondence with Uhlig. Nor did he receive it during the author's lifetime; it was evidently one of the manuscripts he arranged to be sent to him after Uhlig's death in 1853.

The foregoing quotations suggest that in the realization of his own theoretical conception, Wagner was significantly influenced by Uhlig's essay, i.e. its analysis of Beethoven's thematic construction and working-up technique. The essay's date of origin does not contradict this hypothesis. Judging by Wagner's letter to Uhlig and by the excerpt from *My Life*, which plainly refers to the period when the letter was written, namely the beginning of 1851, the essay already existed at that time. Hence it did not arise out of their exchange of views when Uhlig visited Switzerland in the summer of 1851, as Westernhagen repeatedly assumes, but originated some time before then. Accordingly it was the essay that no doubt sparked off the conversation, and not vice versa. Another argument in favour of an earlier date is the title's similarity to that of another – again very extensive – piece by Uhlig. This already came out in 1851 and was called *Die Wahl der Taktarten*. Moreover there is a passage in a letter of Hans von Bülow's which can be readily associated with the unpublished manuscript. On 7 November 1849 Bülow wrote to Uhlig:

> Your letter and enclosure ... were a very pleasant surprise, and I thank you most cordially for the agreeable hours I have spent reading your 'giant manuscript', which is both interesting and informative ... [Your text] has given me a satisfying explanation of so many facets of Beethoven's compositions that were new to me, as well as their organic structure. I hope very much that the work will appear in print sooner or later ...   (H. von Bülow 1 [2/1899], pp. 197f.)

Since Uhlig's *Die Wahl der Motive* has disappeared, it seems impossible to tell exactly what Uhlig's ideas were on Beethoven's method of 'constructing musical themes and movements', ideas that Wagner and Bülow stressed were highly important. We can, however, reconstruct the gist of the essay with the help of Uhlig's other work. His treatise *Sinfonie und Ouvertüre*, which Rühlmann published in the *NZfM* after Uhlig's death, contains paragraphs which are devoted to sonata construction and put a particular emphasis on 'organic unity'.

> This fundamental modification of Mozartian form by Beethoven can be seen at its clearest in nearly all the first movements of his symphonies. The closing section looks newly invented, the development section completely transformed, and the counter-theme, second or subsidiary theme (i.e. the so-called second main idea) is restricted to its appearance in the first main section and a reappearance in the second. Against this, the whole further course of the movement is made to depend on a principal theme which fully takes up the first half of the first main section, along with the whole of the development and equally the whole final section. Accordingly the development and final part now assume the utmost importance and they become sections around which the whole movement revolves, whereas in

the old form, this fulcrum was found in two juxtaposed themes (first and second main idea) which remained juxtaposed until the end of the movement, without letting themselves coalesce in a really organic unity.   (Uhlig [1913], p. 380)

These statements are notable. If we think of the German text-book definition of sonata form, especially as cited in the works of Birnbach and Marx, Uhlig's definition is a compound of progress and stagnation. Uhlig is still honouring a backward viewpoint inasmuch as bipartite sonata form evidently provides his starting-point, going by his reference to a first and a second main section. But there are two further sections he includes in his survey, namely the 'development' and 'final part', which militate against a bipartite scheme. By final part [*Schluss*] Uhlig means the section we generally describe as the coda, and there can be little doubt that what he calls the development is the same as the development section in orthodox sonata form (Marx's 'second part'). Therefore what Uhlig actually has in mind is not a bipartite or even tripartite structure, but a structure with four parts. He places so much emphasis on the Beethovenian coda, along with the development, as to grant this coda the status of a formal section in its own right.

We will find confirmation of this elsewhere. In the *NZfM*, Uhlig commented on Wagner's statements in *Opera and Drama* about the way Beethoven 'gives birth to melody'. Using the first movement of the 'Eroica' Symphony, Uhlig expounds Beethoven's completely new type of thematic genesis as follows:

Strictly speaking (the later) Beethoven takes a route which is quite the opposite of that taken by his predecessors . . . and researches in this area have yielded one of the most remarkable fundamental differences between Beethoven and Mozart – although most composers have still not the slightest inkling of it . . . the main theme of the first movement of Mozart's G minor Symphony is, the way Mozart commences the movement, a perfectly finished melody based upon the primal form of all instrumental music, dance-song or song-dance. Mozart applies traditional contrapuntal procedures to this finished melody's segments (motifs) in the so-called development section of the movement; and this development section is followed by an essentially unaltered repetition of the main theme. In the first movement of Beethoven's Heroic Symphony, on the other hand, the main idea is in itself only a short, four-bar motif, and at the beginning it is only adumbrated three times in a very isolated manner. In the first third of the second part, the motif's individual segments assert themselves quite independently in totally new con-figurations (this replaces the Mozartian development). In the middle third, the whole motif is treated completely afresh without any element of repetition (this replaces the Mozartian recapitulation). But only in the final third of the second part does the new, independent and perfectly finished melody grow from the short principal motif: not until here is the main musical idea of the whole movement achieved – at a point where Mozart generally likes to break off briefly, with a few harmonic–rhythmic phrases that are more or less germane to his main theme.

(*NZfM* 36 [1852], p. 28)

The above text adds significantly to our impression of the contents of Uhlig's essay *Die Wahl der Motive*. For it examines the way Beethoven's thematic construction supports the formal process and spurs it on. Instead of being fully developed from the outset, his themes are potential ones which evolve stage by stage. This is the distinguishing feature of what Beethoven himself called his 'new route'. Uhlig's statements must have provided Wagner with fresh insight, encouragement and support all at the same time. That they continued to influence him is borne out by what he said to Draeseke in 1859 about the 'single, perfectly coherent melody in the first movement of the 'Eroica'. (This was before *'Music of the Future'*, which dates from 1860. Wagner owed his observations basically to Uhlig and not to what he had previously put in writing himself, as Dahlhaus [1988, pp. 225f.] assumes.) And clearly, Wagner must have discovered a sonata framework that transcended the simple A–B–A scheme through Uhlig's exposition, if not sooner. This is another reason for not limiting Wagner's idea of sonata form to the A–B–A type, as Voss does, for example. On the contrary, Wagner's concept of the form went beyond those of Marx and Birnbach.

With his reference to a closing section or coda, Uhlig had set forth a criterion which does in fact characterize Beethoven's symphonic writing and is taken into account by modern analysts. Kurt von Fischer has written: 'The works of Beethoven's middle period, too, often expand the coda into a second development. This means that more thematic working finds its way into the closing section.' Moreover it is evident from Uhlig's remarks on *Opera and Drama* that he considered both development and coda from the viewpoint of Beethoven's development technique. In *Sinfonie und Ouvertüre*, too, the attention he pays to the 'first' main theme uppermost in the 'development and close' hardly lends itself to any other explanation. And indeed Beethoven – unlike Haydn, for instance – always found it a particular problem to build the second subject into the development (see Westphal [1965], p. 75).

On the other hand we cannot generalize as much as Uhlig did; this objection also applies to the coda. Beethoven did not eliminate the second theme entirely. For example, he uses it in the development section of the Piano Sonata op. 14(ii), the Second Symphony and the 'Appassionata' Sonata. In the 'Eroica' Symphony he falls back on the rhythm of the second theme as well as introducing a new theme. The second theme forms part of the coda in the 'Waldstein' and 'Appassionata' Sonatas.

Uhlig's approach as a whole is markedly one-sided, for all his perspicacity about important formal relationships and processes. While he does not overlook the 'counter-theme, second or subsidiary theme' in either the exposition or the reprise, there is an obvious tendency to place undue stress on the predominance of the main theme, in the interests of a thorough unification of the whole movement. This, however, ties in with the idea of the melodic integration of the entire course of a movement. And barely ten years later, in *'Music of the Future'*, Wagner was to identify this as a particular consequence of Beethoven's composition technique. For Wagner, too, the 'growing together' of a movement into a 'really organic unit' instead of a thematic 'juxtaposition' was an important feature of Beethoven's style.

In attempting to reconstruct the contents of the lost manuscript, we have cited some statements by Uhlig that contain crucial perceptions about Beethoven's working-up technique. We can add to those statements in greater detail with the help of Uhlig's other essays. This brings us to a subject involving another set of questions to do with Wagner's attitude to the symphony and sonata, namely his interpretation of the symphony as a 'dance form'.

(d) The symphony as a form of dance

Various objections have rightly been raised to Wagner's derivation of the symphony from the dance. The critics range from Ferdinand Hiller to Adorno, and there is no need to repeat them now. But what is true in general of Wagner's grasp of musical (and other) matters again applies in this particular instance. Historical and aesthetic data were forced into imagined patterns that corresponded to his artistic aims. Such manipulations intensified the critical focus. The interpretation of Beethoven's Seventh Symphony, the 'apotheosis of the dance', as a 'Dionysian revel' may have contributed to this. But it is on this work that people agree most – even Wilhelm Furtwängler, no great admirer of Wagner's 'programmes', is said to have acknowledged the phrase 'apotheosis of the dance'. Certainly the Seventh Symphony could be used to account for Wagner's view of strongly rhythmic musical motions as a development and refinement of what began as an accompaniment to dancing.

In order to assess Wagner's position correctly, we must also remember that there was a tradition behind his association of the symphony with the dance. The close links between music – in its purest, instrumental guise – and dance are an important part of the Romantic view of music. But this body of aesthetic opinion partly obscures some formal and compositional considerations that were at least equally relevant to Wagner's approach to Beethoven. Very probably Uhlig helped to expound and define them. His statements not only shed light on these highly complex connections; they are also a commentary on, and at least a partial key to, Wagner's terminology.

In *The Art-Work of the Future* (1849), Wagner was already deriving Beethoven's construction of melody from 'harmonized dance'. He praises this melodic construction as a 'language' which, 'in long, connected lines and in larger, smaller and indeed the smallest fragments', turned into 'sounds, syllables, words and phrases' at the poetic hands of the Master (*GS* III, p. 92). This already contains a glimmer of the special structure of a Beethoven work. But Wagner's writing is determined far more by his treating music metaphorically as 'language' and by Romantic enthusiasm than by efforts at analysis.

In contrast to Wagner, Uhlig expressly describes melody based on dance as 'motivic melody'. In his essay of 1850, *Beethovens Sinfonien im Zusammenhange betrachtet*, he writes:

> If we consider the individual movements of Beethoven's symphonies from this standpoint, we shall find that they are made up exclusively and in a markedly strict way firstly of dance rhythm and then, with very few exceptions, of dance melody as well; for nearly all the structures of these movements appear to have arisen as rhythms of 2, 4 or 8 beats, and out of short motifs that frequently recur.
>
> (Uhlig [1913], p. 187)

Here Uhlig is examining primarily the small-scale basic motivic structure of melody, and its periodic arrangement. It is only in passing that he refers to 'short motifs that frequently recur' and thus to an element in the working-up technique. He says more about this in his 1851 treatise, *Die Instrumentalmusik*:

> So in an individual Beethoven movement the particular content is developed in an altogether necessary manner, and the listener's guide to this development is the one main musical idea, which usually appears at the start in the form of a short motif.
>
> (Uhlig [1913], p.140)

Thus the course of a movement depending on one main theme, to which Uhlig refers in *Sinfonie und Ouvertüre*, is produced in a special way. The basic requirement is that a central idea, the 'main musical idea', should come at the start of the movement, and that it should be brief, precise and memorable. This is conducive to frequent repetition and 'motivic melody' as well as an organic unity, while also enabling the listener to follow the course of the movement. This coherence, this structural logic, entitles us to assume the presence of an overall 'philosophical plan', whereas Haydn's and Mozart's movements seem to Uhlig to have been constructed bit by bit. Uhlig believes that with Beethoven, the orderly recurrence of the main musical idea is no standard repetition but a modification and variation: it signifies development on the basis of thematic–motivic working. This view crops up in another passage, where Uhlig mentions the 'various ways' in which the main idea is realized ([1913], p. 189).

Despite its brevity, the above attempt to reconstruct Uhlig's treatise will give some idea of the points which particularly interested Wagner. These show that Wagner's study of Beethoven was bound up with his own creative work. Carl Dahlhaus has shown that when Wagner began to compose his *Ring* cycle, he was faced with one particular problem. This was the question of how to reconcile the wealth of motifs needed to spread a coherent motivic network across an entire drama with a restriction on the number of 'melodic moments', for these, according to *Opera and Drama*, had to 'spring only from *the most important motifs* in the drama' (*GS* IV, p. 201). Wagner's solution, says Dahlhaus, was to develop the necessary variety of motifs from a handful of primary motifs. And he was surely assisted in this by one of the fruits of Uhlig's analysis, as exemplified in the 'Eroica' Symphony. We mean a main idea that is set forth as a short motif at the beginning, and that is worked up in various ways on its frequent recurrences, while also acting as a guide for the listener. (Westernhagen is surely wrong in saying that Wagner was the first to perceive the secret which enabled Beethoven to create a completely organic movement from a single starting-point.)

Uhlig's view of sonata form was of course one-sided, as we have said. He overstresses the degree to which the musical development depends on one main idea, and effectively denies any thematic dualism. The aesthetic root of this outlook reaches back into the eighteenth century. It can be observed in Uhlig's essay on *Instrumentalmusik*:

Rich in its capacity for expression though instrumental music may still seem if restricted to the possible characters of the dance, it is in fact restricted from the angle of its own completeness. For if in a short piece of music there is hardly any reason to depart from what must be the one basic mood, the given reason for doing so in a longer movement must be carefully avoided so as not to jeopardize the necessary determination in expressing the one basic mood, so as not to leave the listener asking: 'Sonate, que me veux-tu? ... Sonata, what am I to make of you?'

(Uhlig [1913], pp. 182f.)

Here Uhlig is quoting Fontenelle, and it shows the extent to which his outlook was affected by the old prejudice that music was a language which was less than absolutely intelligible. And like H. C. Koch and others before him, he tried to compensate for this lack by adhering to the 'one basic mood' in a piece of music. Although his consideration of forms was largely adequate, there is a certain amount of distortion. Uhlig's interpretation was constricted by an old prejudice against instrumental music.

As his outlook indicates, Wagner consciously or unconsciously harboured a prejudice which had the same origins. Nevertheless, writing from the dramatist's viewpoint, he throws the position of instrumental music into even sharper relief:

This was very clearly the beginning of the strangely confused ideas about the essence of music that the predicate 'dramatic' engendered. As an art of *expression*, music ... can only be *true*, and herein it has naturally to relate only to what it is meant to express ... But any music that wants to be more and, not content with relating to an object to be expressed, wants to be this object as well is no longer music at bottom, but a fantastic monstrosity abstracted from music and poetry...

(*GS* III, p. 243)

The above observation shows the 'problematic form' of the sonata in a new light. In line with the prejudice we have described, purely instrumental thematic construction and working-up are regarded entirely from the angle of their dramatic power. Beethoven's technical feats as a composer have suddenly become insignificant from an aesthetic standpoint.

> Let us just refer again to the character which the basis we have indicated [i.e. the dance air] has impressed once and for all on both the Haydn and the Beethoven symphony. This character completely excludes dramatic pathos, so that in their most intricate complications the thematic motifs of a symphonic movement could never be explained in terms of a dramatic action, but only from an entwining of ideal dance figures ... Two themes of diametrically opposed character never confront one another within a movement; however much they may seem to differ, they will always simply complement one another, like the masculine and feminine halves of the same basic character.
>
> (GS x, p. 178)

It looks, however, as though from the second half of the 1850s Wagner had definite ideas on the relation between form, thematic material and thematic working-up – ideas that fall into the area of a differentiation according to genres. Given the composer's dramatic aims, these relations were necessarily disorderly in the symphony. But matters changed when the dramatic statement created a form of its own in accordance with the thematic material. That was why, in 1857, the symphonic poem of Liszt met with Wagner's approval. On the other hand Wagner criticized the form from which Liszt's new orchestral form was derived, the overture:

> But not only the overture but also every independent instrumental piece owes its form to the dance or march, and a series of those pieces or a piece combining several dance forms was called a 'symphony'. Even today, the formal nucleus of the symphony lies in its third movement, the minuet or scherzo, where it suddenly emerges in the most naive fashion in order to reveal, as it were, the formal secret of all the movements ... For this rule [of the dance] requires a process of alternation instead of the *development* which dramatic material calls for. And for all forms that are basically derived from the march or dance, this process has established itself as comprising a lively initial period, then a gentler, quieter one and finally the repetition of the livelier period ... Without such an alternation and recurrence, the symphonic movement as we have known it up to now is inconceivable. And what obviously amounts to a minuet with a trio and repeat of the minuet in the third movement of a symphony can be shown to provide the formal nucleus of all the other movements, albeit less obviously (and tending more towards variation form in the second movement particularly). It will now be evident, however, that where a dramatic idea is at odds with this form, the immediate result will be the necessity of sacrificing the development (the idea) to the alternating process (the form), or vice versa.   (GS v, pp. 189f.)

For Wagner the critical nub of the matter is the reprise, whch he calls the *Wiederkehr* or recurrence. If a tripartite structure is rendered formally complete by the 'return of the same thing' [*Wiederkehr des Gleichen*], this becomes a drawback where the nature and treatment of the thematic material are pointing beyond its 'return'. Beethoven's 'Leonore' Overture No. 3 is a particularly clear illustration of this:

But anyone with eyes in his head can see from this particular overture the inevitable disadvantage to the Master of adhering to the traditional form; for who ... will disagree with my saying that the flaw in it is the repeat of the first part after the middle section, which distorts the work's idea to the point where it becomes unintelligible, all the more so because in all the other parts and especially the conclusion, we can see that the Master's one consideration was the dramatic development?

(*GS* v, p. 90)

By criticizing the reprise in an overture, Wagner was also criticizing the form of the sonata movement. As the above quotation confirms, Wagner finds sonata form's second 'problematic' aspect to be relevant precisely where, in his opinion, Beethoven yields to the formal scheme – where there is a need to adopt an even more critical attitude to the sonata than Beethoven's. Granted, the latter's working-up technique over-rides the internal limits of the scheme, but the reprise still stands in the way of a real, i.e. dramatic development. For the reprise commences 'unheedful of the fact that the dramatically stirring course of the middle section, devoted to thematic working-out, has already led us to an expectation of the close' (*GS* x, pp. 180f.).

The foregoing observation makes one other thing clear. Here, at least, Wagner firmly distinguishes between the symphony and the overture. The distinction is that the symphony is not dramatic, whereas the overture is at least potentially dramatic. The Beethoven symphony affords us the most enchanting sight of what could be expressed in symphonic form, and it is 'at its finest and most satisfying where his expression was wholly attuned to that form' (*GS* v, p. 189). The demands Wagner made on the overture, on the other hand, were those of a dramatist. He saw a discrepancy between the dramatic idea, which promotes development and needs to be creatively unfolded, and the return of the same material which the scheme dictated. And inevitably, this exposed the sonata's limitations.

As a critic of the sonata, Wagner rightly starts out from the premise that the sonata movement is – 'in essence', let us note – tripartite. This includes an awareness of structural subdivisions and distinctions within this formal framework as outlined in the aforementioned statements by Uhlig. It is therefore surprising that Wagner sees the 'reprise' in the 'Leonore' Overture No. 3 as being so fixed when it has been substantially altered.

Why did Wagner particularly use the overture to elaborate on the critical element in sonata form, and why did he exaggerate it like this? The reason lay in Liszt's new compositions, which he had taken as his yardstick. He saw Liszt's symphonic poems as overcoming the tension between content (idea) and form (recurrence). If Beethoven's 'Leonore' No. 3 distorted the work's idea to the point where it became unintelligible, the only remedy would have been:

to discard that repetition completely, thus throwing over the form of the overture, i.e. the purely motivated, originally symphonic dance form, and taking this as a starting-point for the construction of a new form. But which would be the new form? – ... 'programme music'. (*GS* v, pp. 190f.)

For Wagner, then, the study of the sonata as a 'problematic form' was founded not only on the ambition and requirements of music drama. Another reason was to defend the symphonic poems of Liszt. This, however, was also one reason why Wagner finally harboured a desire to compose 'symphonies' himself in this or a similar style.

'Theme' and 'motif'

Wagner used the words 'theme' and 'motif' as synonyms. This becomes evident when we compare the passage in *My Life* about Uhlig's essay on the selection of motifs with what Wagner wrote to Breitkopf & Härtel. In the first he writes of Uhlig's work 'on the construction of musical themes and movements', while in his letter he refers to an analysis of the 'motivic construction'. This is not an isolated example as far as Wagner's written statements are concerned. The two terms are again interchangeable in his article *On the Overture* (1841). But this applies not only to his remarks on Beethoven's compositions or on instrumental music in general. We also find it in Wagner's identification of the 'musical moments' in his own music dramas. In *On the Application of Music to Drama* he describes the terse, chordally treated syncopated phrase in the song of the Rhinemaidens ('Rheingold! Rheingold!') as both a theme and a motif (*GS* x, pp. 189, 190). And in *A Communication* he speaks of 'thematic motifs' (*GS* iv, p. 322). Since we could equally well use the reverse of this epithet, 'motivic themes', it proves that the two words mean the same thing.

Wagner's use of words merits special attention inasmuch as A. B. Marx's composition theory had established in a definitive way a precise distinction between a theme and a motif. J. C. Lobe had also helped to clarify the terms in his *Compositions-Lehre* of 1844, where he discusses 'thematic working' in particular detail. Is Wagner's use of the two terms as synonyms just verbal laxity on his part? Or does it mask a particular purpose, either deliberately or unconsciously?

With Marx, 'theme' means the same as a phrase in song-form [*liedför-miger Satz*]. It thus signifies a periodic construction divided into an antecedent and consequent, these in their turn being based on a configuration of motifs. Wagner also describes formations of this kind as themes (*GS* iii, p. 94), as when referring to 'modern composers with their second themes' – which also indicates a subtlety of perception going beyond the A–B–A scheme. Wagner writes of the 'second theme' in the second movement of Beethoven's Seventh Symphony, meaning the melody that joins with the main theme from bar 27, at first in the inner parts. It 'clings', as he puts it, to the main theme that does duty as a continuous rhythmic pattern, and is articulated in accordance with that theme's periodic subdivision.

This, however, is marginal to Wagner's thinking. What he concentrates on is the short, concise motif. Beethoven's innovations, he remarks, are based on the ability to be 'constantly shaping rhythmically plastic motifs anew' (*GS* x, p. 178).

Wolzogen reports that starting with the addition of the words 'Es muss geschehen!' ('It must be done!'), Wagner described the four opening notes of Beethoven's Fifth as the 'world-renowned first main theme of the C minor Symphony'. Wagner takes the same view in his essay *On Conducting* (1869), where he attributes to Beethoven the following direction for performing the opening bars:

And now observe my quite specific thematic intention in placing this sustained E flat after three stormily short notes, and what I wanted to say with all the equally sustained notes which come afterwards . . .   (*GS* viii, p. 283)

Here Wagner interprets a musical motif, namely the first four notes of the movement, as a motto – a kind of leitmotif. But at the same time he speaks of a 'thematic intention'. This is an especially clear sign that for Wagner, 'theme' and 'motif' had the same musical connotations. Statements from his last years confirm this. With regard to the theme of the fugue in Beethoven's C sharp minor quartet, op. 131, he saw everything as depending on the first four notes at the start. Then, Cosima reports him as saying, Beethoven devoted himself to the fugal working-out, which in itself was 'not very interesting' to a musician. (See Cosima's diary entry of 11 December 1880.)

The deeper reason for the above viewpoint is suggested by the word 'intention'. In order to explain it we can, without doing violence to Wagner's ideas, turn to his concept of the 'poetic intention' in *Opera and Drama*. This embraces everything that Wagner saw as the author's function in music drama: the overall poetic conception, and also that disposition which intervenes, so to speak, at certain points, and by which the course of the drama is governed continuously. Hence the phrase 'thematic intention' indicates the following. Behind the musical motif, Wagner perceived it as the intention of Beethoven as tone-poet to express a particular poetic object in notes of music, and to deploy the 'thematic motif' in accordance with this aim. It is precisely when writing about Beethoven that Wagner uses the word 'motif' (or 'theme') not in a purely musical sense but in the poetic sense, as it were. This attitude is unequivocally argued in the language of his Zurich period as follows: 'And what this essence entails is that Beethoven's longer compositions are only secondarily music, but that first and foremost they contain a poetic object' (*SL*, p. 251).

The meaning of 'motif' as used in the exegesis of Beethoven's music corresponds to the double meaning that Wagner assigns to it in the context of his idea of music drama. At the turn of the century, Guido Adler was already remarking on his equivocal use of the word. The 'plastic emotional moments' in which the poetic aim is condensed fall on the ear as musical motifs; the poetic motif as a conditioning factor goes hand in hand with the musical motif as an element conditioned by it. And when Wagner refers to the (musical) theme, he means simply the 'principal motif of the dramatic action, turned into the melodic moment' (*GS* IV, p. 202). 'Theme' and 'motif' are used as synonyms in connection with Wagner's own creative work, as well as in connection with Beethoven's. (This does not, however, exclude the analytical distinction between thematic complexes – structures with a thematic function – and individual motifs or leitmotifs.)

Wagner's use of 'theme' and 'motif' as synonyms is revealing in another respect as well. Neither does he employ the first for thematic structures as Marx defined them, nor does he apply the second to those small and very small musical details for which Marx reserved the word 'motif', meaning the 'nucleus' or 'motive power' of musical events. Wagner never uses the term 'motif' in connection with the segmentation of Beethoven's themes, or with his method of fragmentation [*Absplitterung*]. When describing the structure of a Beethoven first movement in '*Music of the Future*', for instance, he skirts round the subject thus:

What we see is a dance-melody split into its tiniest fragments, each one of which – it may amount to no more than a couple of notes – is made interesting and significant by a pervasive rhythm or significant harmony.   (*TWE*, p. 38)

As Wagner saw it, this method of fragmentation was a major requirement if the whole sonata movement was to be integrated melodically, thus paving the way for 'infinite melody' – *unendliche Melodie*. What must be asked nonetheless is how much importance he really attached to the fragmented Beethoven motif, or what Adorno calls the 'elaborate empty' detail, as a separate unit. And the answer must take into account that Wagner did not select a particular term to describe these particles, although they are very characteristic of Beethoven and of great stylistic significance. Compared with the status which the 'plastic structure' as a shape or *Gestalt* (*GS* x, p. 149) acquires through being called a motif, Beethoven's 'elaborate empty' details remain anonymous in Wagner's vocabulary. They do, however, fall within the scope of a different concept, namely 'melody', but this only serves to underline their anonymity. Wagner explicitly states that melody – 'dance melody' – is split up into its component parts, and not that musical details (i.e. motifs in a different sense) are fitted into a melodic line. Athough he praised the 'one perfectly coherent melody', he does not seem equally appreciative of all the stylistic levels of Beethoven's music. For Wagner there was a limit to thematic–motivic working, despite the prominence he gave to the splitting-up of melody.

93

Wagner evidently regarded the farther limit as coming where the melodic flow was lost in the ramifications of the structure, in Beethoven's *durchbrochene Arbeit*.[3] Here it will be useful to look at Wagner's performance practice. Besides the problems of tempo (agogics) and dynamics, he was mainly concerned with retouchings to the orchestral writing, and to the musical structure as well. The purpose of this was to 'bring out' the melody. Particularly good examples are the changes Wagner made to bars 138–43 and 407–14 in the first movement of the Ninth Symphony. These affect both the flute and the oboe line. In both parts the individual cast of the melody has been ironed out. Wagner accounted for his action by saying that for a number of bars he had always felt there was 'a melodic hiatus', i.e. a 'complete lack of clarity', and had suffered repeatedly as a result (see *TWE*, pp. 112–19). His action shows that he was ignoring the detail, the motif that mattered in Beethoven's melodic design. All that mattered to Wagner was a melody which hung together, which flowed continuously and could be heard to do so.

In Beethoven's late quartets the thematic–motivic ramifications determine the musical structure far more strongly still. How, then, did Wagner hear these quartets? Cosima provides some information in a diary entry for 19 March 1878. Wagner was toying with the idea of scoring

the first movement of Beethoven's E-flat Major Quartet, for instance, for an orchestra more or less the same as that for the [*Siegfried*] *Idyll*. You would see how the themes would stand out, how something played on the horns would become clearer, whereas even in the best performance so much is lost, things are not separated out.

In contrast Wagner is recorded as saying on 30 January 1871 that the 'tremendous concision' of the last quartets made them harder to perform; 'everything in them is solid core and they no longer contain any frills'. That was why they had the reputation of being incomprehensible, although, 'properly played, they are thoroughly melodious and indeed virtually popular.' So Wagner appreciated the delicacy of the musical fabric. He saw the possibilities for a worthy interpretation – but here again, he saw the evocative power of Beethoven's motifs as a challenge. What he wanted was to use the elements of his own musical language to render those evocations graphically explicit.

Variations in the concept of melody

Wagner's opponents persisted in saying that he was lacking in melody. This sounds strange in view of his frequent use of the word 'melody' as a theorist and the various nuances he gave it. It is almost as though he wanted to conjure up in his aesthetics what the critics missed in his music.

There is hardly another word in Wagner's vocabulary that occurs so often and has the same diversity of meanings. This in fact shows how fascinated he was by the phenomenon of melody. 'Primal melody', 'instrumental melody', 'dramatic melody', 'absolute melody', 'patriarchal melody' and 'primal patriarchal melody', 'verse melody', 'orchestral melody' and not least 'infinite melody': these were just some of the phrases he coined. In their variety, they support Wagner's statement that melody is the musical form whose 'special cultivation' determines 'our musical history' (*GS* IX, p. 146). In *'Music of the Future'* he states:

> To say that a piece of music has no melody is in a higher sense tantamount to saying that the composer has failed to create a form that grips and stirs our emotions; and that this is so because his lack of talent and originality has forced him to fall back on hackneyed melodic phrases that make no impact. (*TWE*, p. 37)

To be sure, Wagner's attack on melody constructed from 'hackneyed melodic phrases' was aimed not so much at the untalented composer, but more at the ossified melodic formulae of traditional Italian opera and its German imitators. (Schumann remarked of Italian melody that you could recognize it even before it started.) The key critical concept with regard to this phenomenon is 'absolute melody'. In the following passage Wagner takes Rossini as a polemic example:

> He [Rossini] had realized that the only thing that was alive in opera was absolute melody . . . Instead of studiously mugging up scores he raised his sights and listened to people who sang their music by heart, and what he heard was what amid all the orchestral trappings had lodged in the ear most spontaneously, *naked, ingratiating, absolutely melodic melody*, i.e. melody that was all melody and nothing else, that slips into your ear, although you don't know why, and that you sing to yourself, without knowing why . . . (*GS* III, pp. 251f.)

What Wagner meant by 'absolute melody', however, only becomes really clear in a different context. This is where he talks about the folk song. He perceived in folk song the 'primal maternal melody' (*GS* IV, p. 142), the origin of all melodic development generally. Admittedly, it is a development leading away from that natural oneness of the word and melody that also contains the emotional basis of the 'purely human'. In the end, this progressive alienation culminates in the complete negation of what melody was originally. According to Wagner, opera composers were now using folk tunes solely as ossified melodic formulae. Wrenched away from the original oneness of words and music, melody becomes 'absolute' and is merely stuck on top of the poetry, so to speak, without being organically united with it.

> The folk song was the result of a direct, closely interacting, simultaneous combination of poetry and music – an art which, in contrast to the deliberate techniques of the civilized art which is almost the only kind to be still grasped, we hardly like to call art but could perhaps describe as a spontaneous depiction of the popular spirit

with artistic resources ... The person living in luxury listened to this folk song only from a distance ... only the tune drifted up to his magnificent quarters from the meadow, whereas the lyric was lost on the breeze. Supposing this air to be the flower's enchanting *aroma*, and the lyric to be the *body* of the flower ... then the person living in luxury would extract this aroma ... He would then sprinkle this fragrant extract on his dreary and boring life ... and the artistic offspring of this unnatural fertilization was nothing other than the *operatic aria*.   (*GS* III, pp. 249f.)

In Wagner's view, the same thing has happened with instrumental melody, which can be traced back to the folk dance-air:

If hitherto this [operatic] melody had been artificially inseminated as *song* melody ... its avid listening now finally became focused on that point where the melody, once more removed from the singer's mouth, had acquired an additional lease of life from the instrumental mechanism. Thus *instrumental melody*, translated into the melody of operatic song, became the agent of the proposed *drama*: – indeed the unnatural genre of opera was bound to come to this!   (*GS* III, pp. 276f.)

'Absolute melody' is absolute, says Wagner, because it is unconditional. That is to say, it is not the product 'of a lyric [*Wortvers*] that is obliged to shape itself to the melody' (*GS* IV, p. 168). The hallmark of its genesis is a construction that lacks inner necessity. Its stock in trade are the melodies of the folk song and dance (alienated from their origins), but it is applied by transferring these 'from the instruments to the singer's voice'.

Wagner particularly deplores the fact that the 'rigid formalism' which instrumental music has already overcome is being automatically applied in 'opera'. This stereotyping is in contrast to the powers that instrumental music has achieved. In instrumental music – and here Wagner is referring to Beethoven's works – there is a configuration of fragments from a 'melody which has been cut up, hacked apart and atomized', because the composer is endeavouring to wrest a maximum of clarity, as it were, from the vagueness of music. But when applied to opera, this method would only give rise to 'frivolous, insubstantial melody'. For the languages of words and music would get into a chaotic tangle, and despite a semblance of 'characteristics', it could only result in emptiness (see *GS* III, pp. 286ff.).

Wagner used the concept of 'absolute melody' to condemn the melodic procedures of traditional opera and its negative exponent, Rossini. He saw them as signifying a disregard and misinterpretation of – indeed a disdain for – a step that Beethoven had already taken. With Beethoven's kind of melody, he thought, the die was cast, and it would lead musicians to the one true objective of art. Beethoven had freed melody from the influence of fashion and changing tastes, and raised it to an 'eternally valid, purely human standard' (*GS* IX, p. 102).

To Wagner, Beethoven's melody represented a return to the spontaneity of folk song. This was ideally achieved in the finale of the Ninth Symphony, 'a proof of the most sublime naivety'. (A. B. Marx similarly referred to the 'folk tune' in the finale.) This interpretation is paralleled by two phrases coined at different times. One was 'patriarchal melody', from *Opera and Drama*, and the other was the 'melody of this good man' in the Beethoven centenary essay, where it is synonymous with 'divinely sweet, pure and innocent human melody'. Wagner uses the 'melody of this good man' to cover both the simple modesty of the melodic form and his interpretation of the finale as a breakthrough from darkness to light. What he means by the phrase is that the tune of 'Freude, schöner Götterfunken' is an artistic manifestation of the idea that 'man is good after all!' To be sure, the influence of Schopenhauer's metaphysics of music makes Wagner play down the importance of the verbal side. It is, he says, the intrinsic character of the human voice that basically conveys the meaning (*GS* IX, p. 101). With its aura of religious solemnity, Beethoven's melody performs a function which is akin to

the intimate sound of a chorus with which, we feel, we are being called upon to join in, so that we ourselves can take part as a community in the ideal worship of God, as really happened in the chorales of S. Bach's great Passions.   (*GS* IX, p. 101)

In 1849–50 Wagner had described the finale of the Ninth as affirming a revolutionary pathos, artistically heightened. The contrast between his two interpretations could not be more glaring.

The 'melody of this good man', as Wagner interpreted it, also incorporates a formal element. This is not explicitly stated, but it can be inferred from various hints and is ultimately confirmed by looking at the context. References to formal aspects occur in the following lines:

It is quite apparent that Schiller's words have only been fitted to the actual main melody in a makeshift way, even clumsily; for it is all on its own at first that the melody unfolds before us in its full breadth, performed only on instruments, and fills us with an ineffable sense of joy at having attained to paradise.

Never has the highest art produced anything that was artistically simpler than this air with its child-like innocence, which wafts over us as though with a holy tremulousness when we first perceive the theme, whispered by all the basses of the string section in unison.   (*Ibid.*)

What does the aforesaid artistic simplicity involve? The answer will become clear when we look at Wagner's preceding statements, dealing with Beethoven's artistic route to this final form of melody via his earlier symphonies. It is Wagner's premise that 'the same urge that was behind Beethoven's rational perception in constructing his *good* man' also governed the way he produced 'the *melody* of this good man' (*GS* IX, p. 98). He sees Beethoven's Third Symphony as being a rudimentary version of the 'prime example of innocence':

It is almost feasible to say the Master was already following this course in his

'Eroica' Symphony: its last movement's uncommonly simple theme, which he used again in workings-up elsewhere, seemed to him the right basic framework for this...   (*GS* IX, p. 99)

The formal aspect of this 'prime example of innocence' emerges from Wagner's survey of the finale of Beethoven's Fifth. Wagner comments (and the present author cannot agree with the interpretation put on this passage by Ashton Ellis or by Martin Cooper in *MET*, p. 6):

The course he was following is more apparent in the jubilant closing movement of the C minor symphony, where the simple march tune proceeds almost entirely on the tonic and dominant, in the natural scale of the horns and trumpets, and the great naivety of this is all the more appealing because now the preceding symphony [i.e. the 'Eroica', not the Fourth] seems to be just an exciting anticipation of it...   (*Ibid.*)

Wagner regarded the finale of Beethoven's Ninth as the climax to a development that was going on in the Third and Fifth Symphonies. What he meant by the 'good man's' melody was above all a melody building entirely upon the simplest harmonic relations and unfolding within them. Essentially, therefore, this is a formal conception which starts with the harmonic structure.

The above becomes clearer still when Wagner is speaking of 'patriarchal melody'. For this melodic concept, too, is developed from the finale to the Ninth Symphony – from the melody 'Freude, schöner Götterfunken'. It corresponds to the 'oldest patriarchal national melodies', and Wagner means by it a melody which 'almost never moves out of a particular key' (*GS* IV, p. 148). For Wagner, Beethoven's 'Freude' melody marks a return to 'patriarchal restrictions', the 'Christian development' having previously cultivated the modulation as a 'most enormously versatile power'. A nostalgia for that 'restricted family melody' was inevitably associated, in Beethoven, with a desire for the poet: 'Beethoven, the boldest of swimmers, clearly expressed this nostalgia; but he not only struck up that patriarchal melody once more, he also spoke the verse that went with it' (*GS* IV, p. 149).

What Wagner described as Beethoven's return to patriarchal melody was not, of course, a regression into the past. It was part of the evolutionary spiral, the negation of a negation, and thus an affirmation of artistic progress:

But the evolutionary course of everything human is not a return to the old ways, but progress: everywhere we look, the return is not a natural one but achieved by artifice. Even Beethoven's return to patriarchal melody was, like the melody itself, something achieved by artifice.   (*GS* IV, p. 150)

The aforestated viewpoint is based on Wagner's idea that the original unity of poetry and music came about because in the earliest lyric poetry, 'the words and the line of verse sprang from the note and the melody' (*GS*

IV, p. 143). This route had been blocked when poetry and music were separated. To overcome their separation the process must be reversed, the verbal phrase giving rise to the melody. In the choral finale, however, this connection is achieved not directly but via the intermediate stage of patriarchal melody. Only the latter, as a skilfully contrived analogy to primal melody, allows the poet and composer to reach a rapport and be finally united. 'Freude, schöner Götterfunken' does not effect an immediate union of words and music. This is only produced in the course of the development:

But it was not Beethoven's artistic purpose merely to construct this melody either. Rather we notice how just for a moment he deliberately relaxes his power of melodic invention enough to arrive at music's natural foundation, where he could reach out his hand to the poet but could also seize the poet's hand. When this simple, limited melody makes him feel hand in hand with the poet, he moves on to the poem itself. Creating music out of this poem to match it in spirit and form, he progresses to ever bolder and more varied structural devices until finally, with the resources of a poeticizing musical language, he is producing hitherto unsuspected miracles – miracles like 'Seid umschlungen, Millionen!', 'Ahnest du den Schöpfer, Welt?' and finally the perfectly intelligible blending of 'Seid umschlungen' with 'Freude, schöner Götterfunken!'. Now compare the broad melodic construction displayed in the musical realization of the whole of 'Seid umschlungen...' with the melody which, using the resources of absolute music, the Master simply spread as it were over the line, 'Freude, schöner Götterfunken'. This gives us a precise understanding of the difference between ... patriarchal melody and melody arising out of the poetic intention with regard to the verbal line.   (GS IV, pp. 159f.)

Here Wagner refers to the form of the movement. For he points to the piece's 'ever bolder and more varied structural devices', founded on the spirit and form of the poem. This could hardly relate to anything but the formal development. But exactly which formal aspects did Wagner have in mind? The text following on from the above quotation provides at least a partial answer. It shows that Wagner was thinking of differences in the harmonic design when he contrasted 'patriarchal melody' with melody arising out of 'the poetic aim with regard to the verbal line'. He again explicitly links the former with the 'most restricted key-relationships', whereas the other type of melody, he says, is capable of expanding the narrower key-relationship by linking up with other related keys. And this can be extended until the 'primal relationship between the notes as a whole' is attained.

The musical events in the choral finale to Beethoven's Ninth do in fact support Wagner's distinction. On the one hand the 'Freude' melody sticks to the key of D major – passing through the submediant and the dominant of the dominant. The melody of 'Seid umschlungen', on the other hand, begins in G major and modulates to F major before passing through the dominant of G major (related to C major) to the key of G minor, the key in which 'Ihr stürzt nieder, Millionen' begins. After this, however, the harmony gradually returns to D major, and the themes of 'Freude, schöner Götterfunken' and 'seid umschlungen, Millionen' are combined (double fugue). A harmonic linking of keys that extended as far as the 'original relationship between the notes as a whole' had a considerable formal significance in Wagner's conception of music drama. This can be seen from his description of the 'poetico-musical period' as one of the music drama's basic formal units, for its shape is based on the harmonic development governed by the poetic aim. So the harmonic links extending as far as the 'original relationship between the notes' in the choral finale are both a preliminary to the 'poetico-musical period' and a contrast to the 'Freude' melody with its very restricted key-relations. And this underlines the formal aspect of the epithet 'patriarchal melody'.

This concept enabled Wagner to reconcile the shape of the 'Freude' melody – which he surely recognized as an instrumental one – with his interpretation of the finale as a bridge to the verbal realm. As so often, it was not the true facts of the matter which determined the interpretation. Rather, an idea based on Wagner's philosophy of history outweighed the empirical findings.

'Infinite melody' – a philosophical and compositional concept

Along with 'leitmotif', Wagner's 'infinite melody' [*unendliche Melodie*] is one of those formulations which have long been adopted by other arts besides music. It appears in literary studies and in the history of art. Admittedly there is a negative side to this widespread and varied use of the phrase: the difficulty of finding an exact definition. This goes right back to the phrase's beginnings. Often Wagner's formulations and theoretical statements are inextricably bound up with the question of whether he was propounding a philosophical concept or one that had to do with composing and composition technique – or both of these. This particularly applies to 'infinite melody'.

The above point has been made recently by Fritz Reckow. He objects to the traditional reading of the phrase as a purely technical term. In his opinion there are no concrete reasons whatever for saying that Wagner himself intended the expression to be understood as denoting a compositional 'unendingness'. Reckow's aim is to establish 'what Wagner himself meant when he actually uses the expression *unendliche Melodie*'. The essay culminates in the thesis that Wagner only wanted to say that the melody concerned was timeless, 'eternally valid' and 'intelligible for all time'.

It is crucial to this thesis that Wagner (allegedly) uses the term only once, in *'Music of the Future'*, and 'patently avoids it' before and afterwards, 'both in describing technical processes and in making compositional value judgments'. Further, Reckow argues that the paragraph in which the phrase occurs does not contain a single technical term relating to the process of composition. Since the publication of Cosima Wagner's diaries, however, we can no longer accept the statement that Wagner used the term *unendliche Melodie* only once. On the evidence of the diaries he undoubtedly referred to it again later. But these late documents are only additional sources. Wagner's *'Music of the Future'* will itself suffice to show that conclusions which are quite different from Reckow's can be drawn from the larger context.

Reckow sees the one paragraph as supplying the context, but this must be questioned. It is advisable, when interpreting individual passages in Wagner, to consult other writings of his, and indeed his whole literary output. To begin with, then, we must check whether *'Music of the Future'* itself does not need to be referred to more extensively. The phrase in question appears in a paragraph reading as follows:

> In truth, the measure of a poet's greatness is that which he does not say in order to let what is inexpressible silently speak to us for itself. It is the musician who brings this great Unsaid to sounding life, and the unmistakable form of his resounding silence is *unendliche Melodie*. (*TWE*, p. 40, amended)

Does *unendliche Melodie* appear solely in the context of this paragraph and round it off? Or does the whole paragraph – culminating in the epithet – form the climax to a wider argument, one that has yet to be defined more precisely? Reckow himself describes this paragraph as 'the well-prepared climax to the whole article, in both language and content'. But what are the consequences for an appraisal of the context we want? We seem to have every reason to ask whether and how far we need to widen the context.

On going into the above question, we find straight away that the passages which are germane to *unendliche Melodie* cannot be limited to this one paragraph. Although the latter clearly accentuates it, it will be obvious, too, that a train of thought beginning much earlier has been leading up to it. It represents the culmination of the statements preceding it, and those statements inevitably and crucially affect the content of the phrase. In elucidating Wagner's *unendliche Melodie*, we must bear in mind that it lies at the centre of a thorough examination of 'melody' which is built into the entire essay. The cadences of Wagner's language are another indication of this. What he offers us is not just a string of ideas but the development of these ideas – a verbal compression extending even beyond the paragraph concerned before eventually petering out. Hence the context of the phrase embraces subsequent paragraphs as well, and the connection between what comes before and what comes after it has a decisive bearing on its content.

In particular, the fact that Wagner was developing his arguments as a 'theoretical justification' illustrates the unified thinking behind a much wider context. It is the justification of a claim he has been making for *Tristan*. He has said that by using a web of words and lines of poetry to prefigure 'the whole layout of the melody', the melody and its form are given a wealth 'which would otherwise be utterly impossible'. Wagner then states:

I cannot do better than round off this communication by providing you with a theoretical justification for that answer. I will attempt this by concentrating at last solely upon the musical form, the melody. (*TWE*, p. 36)

Wagner proceeds to say that melody is the only form of music. By this he does not just mean that music and melody are identical. His main wish is to indicate the outward appearance of the melody that will confirm his thesis. But what stands as its ideal and, as it were, 'pre-set' realization (without having a definitive outline or being 'proved' as yet) is the melody of *Tristan*.

Wagner embarks on his 'justification' with the negative example of the kind of music that is notable for 'lovely passages' and also for their opposite, namely a partial absence of melody. Precisely this kind of writing, Wagner complains, is mistakenly praised time and again as the perfect example of melody:

Those shrill cries for 'melody, melody!' so often raised nowadays by the superficial dilettanti in our midst only serve to convince me that their conception of melody is drawn from works where, along with melody, you have a dearth of melody which makes the melody they cry for so very precious. (*TWE*, *ibid.*)

In his reference to partial melody or absence of melody, Wagner is dialectically turning on its head the accusation that his own music lacked melody. It reflects the polemical undertones in the essay as well as telling us something about the way he presents his argument. More important, however, is this early reference to a formal element. We mean melody which is introduced only sporadically, as it were: this doubles the enjoyment of the superficial dilettante because he can divide his time between music and conversation. But Wagner now counters his negative example with a melody which differs from 'actual' melody, although the latter is only implied. He emphasizes its formal element indirectly but from what he regards as a crucial angle, the angle of audience behaviour.

Such music [which is played whilst the audience is chatting] virtually comprises the whole score of an Italian opera: the portion that is actually listened to probably amounts to no more than a twelfth. An Italian opera must contain at least one aria worth attending to ... A composer capable of gaining the attention of the audience as many as a dozen times would be hailed as an inexhaustible melodic genius. Imagine such an audience suddenly confronted with a work every bar of which demanded the same amount of attention throughout its entire length! You couldn't blame it for feeling rudely torn out of its normal listening habits – how could it possibly be expected to recognise its beloved 'melody' in a thing which at its best could hardly be considered more than a refinement of that musical noise which in its simpler form serves the purpose of promoting pleasant conversation? And, what is more, this stuff positively demands to be listened to! The audience would clamour for the restoration of its six to twelve melodies in order to be sure of having time for the conversation which is the evening's chief purpose.

(TWE, pp. 36–7, slightly amended)

In the above passage Wagner is contrasting his own work, as containing a 'positive' form of melody, with the 'negative' background of traditional, hidebound operatic form. If intermittent melody is responsible for the fitful attentiveness of opera audiences, a quite different form of melody is needed to make them pay constant attention from beginning to end. So far, they are not capable of showing such attention, at any rate not easily or properly.

Between the negative and positive poles of his idea of melody, Wagner now interposes the outline of a 'development' which approaches his melodic ideal. The protagonist of this development is Beethoven. Beethoven's pioneering achievement in the melodic field lay, to Wagner's mind, in his handling of a specific, narrow form of melody, namely its dance form. This he developed into a new melodic quality, so to speak.

There are, therefore, three points of support for Wagner's 'justification'. One is the 'negation' of melody (meaning 'partial' melody). Another is the exact opposite, the 'affirmation' of melody, whose actual form has still to be decided. The third is melody in its 'dance form'. And although the last, like 'partial' melody, is a narrow basic form contained within prescribed formal limits, it undergoes a development. At the hands of Beethoven it achieves an entirely new quality representing an important advance towards the ideal melodic form.

Here Wagner's exposition overlaps with the ideas on sonata form discussed earlier in this chapter. The criteria of a true melody cannot be met by the melody of a conventional symphony, which is tailored to the formal confines of regular periodic construction. For here, albeit far more with Mozart than with Haydn, the melody is completely isolated, just as in opera. And the intervening spaces are filled by music 'which we must call unmelodic since it scarcely rises above the level of mere noise' (*TWE*, p. 37). Only Beethoven's method of splitting up the actual dance melody into its tiniest fragments was calculated to eliminate these awkward intermediate spaces altogether:

And the outcome, never before achieved, of this procedure was the expansion of a melody, through the richest development of all the motives it contained, into a continuous large-scale piece, which in itself constituted a single, perfectly coherent melody.
(*TWE*, p. 38, slightly amended)

Up to this point in the exposition, there could still be some doubt as to whether Beethoven's melody is a significant link in Wagner's 'theoretical justification', or integrated into the argument leading up to *unendliche Melodie*. But Wagner now dispels any such doubts. First, there is his comment that the varied, ever-changing articulation of the dance melody, split up into its tiniest fragments, constantly grips the listener 'through a movement so plastic' that he cannot escape its impact for a single moment. Forced to listen so intently, we are obliged to acknowledge melodic significance 'in every harmony, even in every rest'. Clearly this ties up with the constant attention Wagner has previously asked to be paid to his ideal melody. And his reference to fragmented dance melody confirms that the public's constant and undivided attention depends, or ought to depend, on a specific form of melody. At the same time the description, with its emphasis on the fragmented dance melody, suggests that Wagner saw melodic 'form' as a function of a quite specific compositional technique. Secondly, Wagner says at this stage of the argument that his concern is with the application to opera of Beethoven's 'single, perfectly coherent melody'. It is, he observes, striking that 'although German masters have applied this essentially instrumental technique quite closely to music for both choir and orchestra as well, they have never made any real use of it yet in opera'.

He then proceeds to discuss this application of Beethoven's technique to opera. This is a tricky thing to deal with because it is not really a matter of applying the method to the traditional 'operatic' form, and of joining this music up with its 'libretto'. Rather, a dramatic poem itself should provide a poetic counterpart to a symphonic form. Here Wagner is evidently referring back to the poetic text for *Tristan*, where 'the web of words and lines' already prefigures 'the whole layout of the melody'.

The proposed utilization of Beethoven also depends on another requirement, one which is directly connected with his melody. And only this melody makes it possible for the dramatic poem, as the counterpart to a symphonic form, to be 'in perfect conformity with the fundamental principles of drama'. In the minuet or scherzo, a melody by Beethoven still comprises 'a primitive dance music which could easily be danced to'. But in the other movements of a symphony, especially the first movement, this possibility becomes increasingly remote. 'The dance that would exactly fit his music – this idealized form of a dance – is in fact to be found in the *dramatic action*' (*TWE*, p. 39, rev. Kropfinger).

This, to Wagner's mind, is as far as the symphony can be taken. Although Beethoven's melody demands to be complemented by a staging of the dramatic action, the 'note of tragic passion' cannot be sounded too strongly, or else the listener will be compelled to ask about the music's poetic content – 'that unsettling "Why?"'. And only the dramatic poet, being aware of what such a subtly designed melody demands of him, is capable of a solution.

It is interesting to compare the above view of the Beethoven symphony with the view of it that underlies Wagner's conception of drama in *Opera and Drama*. We find that the requirements for 'applying' the symphony to the drama have become more subtle. This is the case precisely because of Wagner's emphasis on matters of form and his way of looking at them. In the earlier essay it was the orchestra's 'powers of speech', the poetically motivated shaping of plastic motifs, that led ineluctably to the new form of the drama – against the background of the Ninth Symphony, representing the bridge to the word. But this is now achieved by the 'single, perfectly coherent melody' characterized by the 'richest development of all the motifs it contains', and by the dramatic action which such melody effectively encloses within itself. In his earlier argument, Wagner stated that the musical developments which Beethoven brought to an historic climax led inexorably to his own conception of the drama. His 'theoretical justification' in *'Music of the Future'* is simply a fresh version of this.

But what is also clear, now if not before, is that Wagner includes in the formulation *unendliche Melodie* ideas which are much broader in scope than indicated by that one paragraph in *'Music of the Future'*: certain formal and technical characteristics of Beethoven's melody are paramount. The three paragraphs that we are now going to quote represent the final approach to the climax of Wagner's text. In them he refers to the poet's task and function in the integration of Beethoven's melody. This is simply the last step in Wagner's 'theoretical justification'. The method whereby the melody in *Tristan* is prefigured in the poetic fabric, according to how it is expanded and differentiated, is justified on material and historical grounds. Since these statements culminate in the phrase *unendliche Melodie*, there can be little doubt that it was coined basically for the 'melody' in *Tristan*. The 'utmost freedom' in the poetic conception to which Wagner refers is simply another way of expressing the procedure in *Tristan* already described. This starts with Beethoven's melody, but surpasses it by resorting to the possibilities contained in the poetic design.

Since I have already set forth my grounds for this assertion, it now only remains to consider the matter from the point of view of melodic form and indicate how a truly complementary dramatic poem can give this form a fresh vitality and breadth. A poet who is fully aware of the inexhaustible expressive possibilities of symphonic melody will feel impelled to match in his own sphere the subtlest, most intimate nuances of that melody, which can stir us to the depths with a single harmonic shift. The narrow confining limits of 'operatic melody' will no longer cow him into providing a dull meaningless canvas. On the contrary, by watching the musician he will discover a secret the musician himself does not know – that melodic form is capable of an infinitely greater development than the symphony has so far made possible. Intuitively divining this development, he will anticipate it by designing his poem with the utmost freedom.

Thus the poet will say to the symphonist, who still clings timidly to the original dance form, not daring to push his mode of expression beyond its narrow limits: 'Plunge boldly into the sea of music; with my hand in yours you can never lose contact with the things that all men understand. For with my help you are in constant touch with the firm ground of a dramatic action, and the scenic represen-tation of such an action is the most immediately understandable poem of all. Frame your melody boldly, so that it pours through the whole work like an uninterrupted stream; in it you will be voicing what I leave unsaid, for only you can say it; while I in my silence will still be saying it all, because it is your hand I am guiding.'

In truth, the measure of a poet's greatness is that which he does not say in order to let what is inexpressible silently speak to us for itself. It is the musician who brings this great Unsaid to sounding life, and the unmistakable form of his resounding silence is *unendliche Melodie*. (*TWE*, pp. 39–40, revised)

In '*Music of the Future*' Wagner reserves the qualifying adjective *unendlich* or 'infinite' for his own melody. Prior to the climactic phrase 'infinite melody' it only appears in his statements on melody within a comparative form, in the phrase 'infinitely richer development'. Subsequently it occurs in connection with the 'forest melody' metaphor: 'the infinitely richly ramified detail', 'the infinite multitude of voices awakening in the forest'. But in other essays Wagner uses the word in comments on Beethoven's melody. In *The Art-Work of the Future*, he states that Beethoven's 'powers of speech' are 'infinite'. Our study of Wagner's relationship to the symphony and sonata has already shown that by 'powers of speech' [*Sprachvermögen*], he means an aspect of composition: the speech of the orchestra and the instruments in musical figures. Even in this essay we cannot ignore the compositional aspect. The comment that Beethoven's powers of speech are infinite is meant as a summing-up. It refers to the instrumental 'speech' discussed previously, whose salient feature Wagner described as a capacity for both 'the most unrestricted expression and most limitless treatment' of melody. 'Every letter of this language', he wrote, 'was an element infinitely full of soul, and the choice was unlimited' when it came to articulating those elements (*GS* III, p. 92). Behind this there lies a statement, albeit a very general one, about the specific technical basis for any development of Beethoven's 'powers of speech' as an 'element infinitely full of soul'. Beethoven, says Wagner, composes both 'in long, coherent lines and in bigger or smaller and indeed the tiniest fragments'.

The essay *On Conducting* also uses the adjective 'infinite' to describe Beethoven's melodic layout. Again, however, the statement is a very general one, and the word 'melody' does not appear. This essay ascribes to the finale of the 'Eroica' the 'character of an infinitely extended variation movement' (*GS* VIII, p. 292).

It has now been established that Wagner includes formal and also technical aspects of Beethoven's melody within his concept of 'infinite melody'. We are therefore justified in drawing on these aspects to elucidate the term, especially as certain features of Beethoven's melodic construction already bore the attribute 'infinite', in a compositional sense, in *The Art-Work of the Future*. Moreover the description of these details closely matches the description Wagner gave ten years later in *'Music of the Future'*. In the earlier essay he mentions 'long, coherent lines' and 'bigger or smaller and indeed tiniest fragments' of which melody is made up. The later essay refers to the splitting up of dance melody 'into its tiniest fragments'. Both of these relate to the thematic–motivic structure of the compositional layout, i.e. its technical features. So Wagner seems to have regarded a diversity of melodic elements and their articulation as one feature of Beethoven's melodic 'infinitude', and the rich spectrum of expressive values that went with it as another. In addition Wagner describes the actual working-up and fragmentation technique in *'Music of the Future'* along with the musical process – although in a very general way, without using specific terms. The chief innovation is that he also points out certin formal consequences of this working-up technique: 'The expansion of a melody, through the richest development of all the motifs it contained, into a continuous large-scale piece...' Here, as we have already noted, Wagner was presenting an important aspect, namely the 'melodic' integration of transitional and intermediate paragraphs by dint of thematic–motivic work. How much bearing did this have on the content of the phrase 'infinite melody'? The answer is that Wagner contrasted Beethoven's melodic form with the 'narrow form of melody', including traditional 'operatic melody' in particular, which was precisely why he took Beethoven as the model for his own melodic construction. As we have seen, what Wagner meant by the 'narrow form of melody' was a stringing together of unconnected, sporadic melodies that were only 'interpolated'. Consequently an essential requirement for 'infinite melody' is the removal of these internal melodic dividing-lines, supported by the scope for variation in continuous thematic–motivic working-up.

But the removal of the internal confines does not automatically entail melodic 'endlessness'. Very probably the phrase does not even cover the idea of *unendliche Melodie* as 'endless melody', in the sense of transcending the external melodic limits. And so the lack of this attribute cannot be used to argue in principle against the technical meaning of the phrase, as Reckow does. On the other hand it would certainly seem to make sense to connect Wagner's term with the melody's uninterrupted and also constantly significant flow. (See Dahlhaus in the *NGW*, pp. 114–15.)

If, however, Wagner's *unendliche Melodie* represents both uninterrupted continuity and melody every moment of which is significant, he must be employing highly sophisticated technical procedures. The question of whether the term is chiefly an aesthetic or a technical one now ceases to seem so important. Wagner was aiming in his music for a melodic continuity that would constantly maintain the same high 'level of meaning'. This called for a method of deriving his melodic motifs and distributing them among the interwoven voices that kept the melodic substance intact. And here Beethoven's thematic–motivic working-out, as practised in the late string quartets in particular, constituted a crucial model and also a preliminary stage.

Wagner said that if melody ceased and was replaced by some kind of working-out, the effect would be lost. According to Egon Voss, this excludes Beethoven's method of thematic–motivic derivation and any such technical meaning from the range of meanings covered by 'infinite melody'. But this claim does not stand up to examination. Voss is quoting only part of what Wagner said, and quoting it out of context. The full statement reads:

'The only time Beethoven was not concise is in the finale of the great B-flat Major Sonata, which your father alone can play, and in which I got more enjoyment out of his virtuosity than out of what was being played. Conciseness seems to be the secret of music; when melody ceases and is replaced by some kind of working out, the effect is lost. Beethoven is the first composer in whom everything is melody; it was he who showed how from one and the same theme a succession of new themes arise which are complete in themselves.'   (CW, 10 June 1870)

What does 'working out' mean in this context? The answer will only become clear if we remember which Beethoven work Wagner is talking about, also bearing in mind the important idea of 'conciseness'. Wagner is passing judgment on the fugal finale of the 'Hammerklavier' Sonata. By 'some kind of working out' he undoubtedly means Beethoven's fugal writing in general, of which he was fundamentally critical. To quote from Cosima's diaries again: 'As far as fugues are concerned, these gentlemen [Beethoven and Mozart] can hide their heads before Bach, they played with the form, wanted to show they could do it, too, but he showed us the soul of the fugue' (15 January 1872).

But this fussing with counterpoint – which Wagner regarded as lacking in significant melody – was diametrically opposed by the melodic compactness of Beethoven's late quartets. Here Wagner's aforementioned reference to the enormous concision of these works assumes a particular importance. For he was referring to the constant significance of the musical fabric, to the fact that everything was of the 'essence' and nothing was 'decoration'. And what could that mean but the particularly concentrated thematic–motivic working-out in the late Beethoven quartets? When, however, motivic and thematic connections are worked as closely as they are in these quartets, they will at the same time develop a musical expressiveness. For that reason it would not be right to regard Wagner's remarks in *'Music of the Future'*, including the remarks on *unendliche Melodie*, simply as statements about Beethoven's 'expressive power' (as suggested by Voss). In dwelling on musical expressiveness, Wagner was surely aware of the musical material this required, and of methods of working it up. Particularly in *'Music of the Future'*, his vocabulary and phraseology are based on the knowledge that technical components are combined with aesthetic ones.

This is supported by Wagner's later remark to Cosima that for the musician, everything was 'tempo, structure' (20 December 1869). On 14 November 1882 he was to say of Beethoven's Sonata in A, op. 101:

The first movement of this A Major Sonata is an excellent example of what I mean by *unendliche Melodie* – what music really is. The change – four bars here, boom-boom, then another four bars – is extremely clumsy. But Beethoven is unique in that respect.

Cosima then mentions Bach as an example of this 'infinitude', and Wagner replies: 'Yes, and what is all the more curious is that it is actually done without melody. Indeed, one can even say that compared with it the square melody is a decline ...'

What does Wagner really mean by this brief comment? One clue is the mention of 'square melody', the kind of melody that both Bach and Beethoven have already surpassed. In addition we need to look at the structure of the first movement of the Sonata in A. Beethoven's sonata does more than just illustrate that, in Schenker's words, 'the second idea in a sonata movement need not produce a new motif at all'. Rather, this first movement's exposition can be used to show that it is not just a modulation already beginning in the consequent phrase of the first idea that overcomes the rigidity of the four-bar unit. What is mainly responsible for this is the fact that 'the modulating consequent phrase at the same time supplies the first part of the second idea, so that this shares its motif with the first idea – and it was the character of the consequent phrase that brought it about' (Schenker). It is a thematic–motivic and formal combination which meets Wagner's definition of conciseness. And it embraces Beethoven's thematic–motivic technique and compactness as a pre-condition that was automatically part of his conception and practice.

Although Wagner was obviously relating to Beethoven in the conception of *unendliche Melodie*, Beethoven's melody is not identical with it. Beethoven's contains some important features of melodic 'infinitude', but 'infinite melody' only arises out of its 'infinitely richer development': the raising to a higher power, as it were, of the individual elements.

But what are the compositional criteria? How far do they tie in with those elements in Beethoven's music which Wagner termed 'infinite', and what constitutes the above heightening? Wagner himself provides an answer, in the very paragraph that introduces the concept of infinite melody. The relevant lines are 'It is the musician who brings this great Unsaid to sounding life', and the immediately following 'unmistakable form of his resounding silence'. There is a particularly close connection between all this and the preceding sentence: 'Frame your melody boldly ... in it you will be voicing what I leave unsaid ... while I in my silence will still be saying it all, because it is your hand I am guiding.'

What does Wagner mean by 'resounding silence'? The following passage from *Opera and Drama* offers an answer:

So if we seek a precise definition of that expression which, since it was a complete one, would also make for a complete content, we would describe it as the one which can best communicate to the feelings a most all-embracing intention of the poetic intelligence. Such an expression is an expression *which encloses the poetic intention within all of its elements, but also conceals it from the feelings within all of them, or in other words – realizes it.* (*GS* IV, p. 199)

Wagner's 'resounding silence' is nothing less than the poetic intention hidden from the rational mind. And this brings us to Wagner's motivic technique. For in his drama the poetic intention unfolds with the help of poetic motifs condensed into emotional values, i.e. 'melodic moments' (motifs), and linked together by virtue of 'presentiment' [*Ahnung*], 'actualization' [*Vergegenwärtigung*] and 'reminiscence' [*Erinnerung*]. This is also related to the interaction between the text ('verbal melody'), the dramatic action and the 'orchestral melody'. For 'resounding silence' succeeds in conveying emotional values which speech conceals – has to conceal.

The compositional features of this procedure correspond to those features of Beethoven's melody that Wagner had already construed as 'infinite'. It is precisely 'this melody's subtlest and innermost nuances' which are to undergo an 'infinitely richer' development through 'infinite melody'. It is, however, the motivic inter-relations which determine the bold extent of the melody. It then 'pours through the whole work' in a continuous stream, overcoming the 'narrow form' of operatic melody once and for all.

To be sure, this represents a special kind of overcoming. It is this particular heightening, compared to Beethoven, that justified coining the term 'infinite melody' at all. For despite all the complexities and nuances, Wagner regarded the emotional distinctions in instrumental music as being constantly subsumed in one basic emotion. (This point has been made in our section on the symphony and drama.) The music in music drama, however, was not bound by this restriction. The 'expressive elements in the orchestra' must never be determined by the musician's choice but only '*by what the poet intends*' (*GS* IV, pp. 199f.). Hence the 'infinite' multiplicity of possible, established emotional values and contrasts replaces the symphonic movement's unified basic emotion. A whole range of independent, quasi-definitive emotional units takes the place of the emotional nuances in the separate movements of an instrumental work: nuances which are always tuned, as it were, to the same wave-band.

Wagner himself indicates the above points following the crucial paragraph of '*Music of the Future*', in passages which must be regarded as forming part of the same context. This would be evident even without his concluding remark, 'You can well imagine what a great number of technical details I have had to pass over in this sketchy . . . account' (*TWE*, p. 41). Wagner refers to the orchestra as the 'instrument' whose assistance in the creation of 'this melody' – quite plainly the aforestated 'infinite melody' – is indispensable. Here he is alluding to the same complex state of motivic relations in the music drama. By becoming so intimately involved in the motives of the action, the orchestra 'will embody the harmony which alone makes possible the melody's specific expression'. It will also 'maintain the melody in a state of uninterrupted flow' (*TWE*, p. 40). In his next paragraph, Wagner expressly introduces the 'single great forest melody' as a metaphor to describe 'this great melody . . . spanning the whole compass of a music drama'. These statements, too, adumbrate elements of composition technique, as does the reference to the melody's infinite wealth of detail.

Without doubt, however, it is also possible to discern a 'philosophical' meaning in the phrase *unendliche Melodie*. Taking up Lotze's ideas, Reckow sees the word 'infinite' as denoting something timeless and eternal, a 'state of elevation above all conditions of origin, preservation and change'. And this is exactly what Wagner was striving for. The intended effect of the drama, he wrote, was an impression that carried such irresistible conviction 'that before it, all deliberate reflection dissolves into pure human feeling'. Because of his involuntary emotional involvement, the listener necessarily helps to create the work of art (see *GS* IV, p. 186). And when his affections are thus tied to the dramatic action, he becomes dramatically integrated, so to speak. He resembles a visitor to a church who is struck by its atmosphere of solemnity; rather than enquiring after the technical data of its construction, the 'ground-plan' or 'building joints', he loses himself in the experience. In the process, all emotional values boil down to Wagner's 'pure human feeling'. The listener experiences the infinite diversity of the different elements as a single, eternal unity. This transition from the infinitely diverse to what is eternal and single combines the compositional and 'philosophical' aspects of the term 'infinite melody'. And to sum it up, Wagner chose the 'metaphor' of the forest melody.

To give you a final idea of this great melody which I visualize spanning the whole compass of a music drama I shall again employ a metaphor. I am concerned here only with the impression this melody must make upon the listener. Its wealth of detail, branching out in infinitely many different directions, should be apparent not only to the expert but also to the naivest layman once he has attuned himself to listen. First of all, therefore, it must convey an impression rather like that which a beautiful forest makes upon the solitary visitor who comes there from the noisy city on a summer evening . . . When under the spell of that impression the listener seats himself and, liberated as he is from the noise of the city, perceives afresh, hears with new ears, listens ever more intently, he becomes increasingly aware of a multitude of voices in the forest – new ones keep on entering, each different and such as he had never heard before; they gather strength as they accumulate; louder and ever louder. And yet, even though the voices are so numerous and the songs so various, the radiant, swelling tones only seem to be that single great forest melody which had first arrested him – just as the sight of the deep-blue night sky arrests him, and then the longer he loses himself in the spectacle the more clearly he perceives the multitude of dazzling stars. Afterwards the melody will be forever resounding in his mind, though he will never be able to hum it – to hear it again he must go back to the forest, and on a summer evening. (*TWE*, pp. 40–1)

For Wagner, this rapture over the vision of the infinite, this eternal echo of the aesthetic experience, was undoubtedly linked with the claim of 'eternal validity'. Beethoven had already redeemed melody from the dictates of fashion and the 'singer of fashion' (*GS* III, p. 96). And Wagner, after all, was raising the melodic elements that Beethoven had prepared to 'infinite melody'. So who could deny that his music was timeless?

Wagner wrote *'Music of the Future'* in Paris during the summer of 1860 as a 'preface' to a French prose translation of his opera texts. This was in the aftermath of three concerts which he had put on as the intended foundation of his further undertakings in Paris. The concerts were given on 25 January, 1 February and 8 February 1860, and the resulting clamour resolved into two clearly opposing viewpoints. One, according to *My Life*, was reflected in the 'fury of our opponents', who vented their spleen in the press; the other in the kind of admiring enthusiasm that had seldom, if ever, come Wagner's way up to then. This was voiced largely by non-musicians. Chief among them were Baudelaire and the novelist Champfleury, who wrote an enthusiastic letter assuring Wagner of his respect and support (see also *ML*, p. 606). But what must have seemed particularly encouraging, irrespective of immediate events, was the sympathy and admiration of Frédéric Villot, who was already a devotee of long standing. Wagner had good cause to recall him in *My Life*:

a most valuable addition to my circle of French acquaintances was made in M. Frédéric Villot. He was curator of paintings at the Louvre, an extremely sensitive and cultured man whom I had met one day at the shop of the music dealer Flaxland ... where he had come to inquire as to the whereabouts of the score of *Tristan* which he had ordered; quite amazed by this, I had asked him, after we were introduced and I had learned that he possessed the scores of my earlier operas as well, how he could derive enjoyment from my dramatic compositions without a command of the German language, as I could not understand how he could otherwise make much sense of music so closely interwoven with the poetry; he responded with the spirited remark that it was precisely my music which served as the best possible guide to a comprehension of the dramatic poetry, whereupon I formed a strong attachment to the man and was very pleased to be able to maintain a stimulating association with him. When I subsequently produced a very comprehensive preface to the translation of my operatic poems, I could think of no one to whom it could more worthily be dedicated. (*ML*, p. 613, rev. Kropfinger)

It is not surprising that Wagner chose to examine the interplay of text and music in this preface addressed to Villot, since Villot had shown an exceptional insight into this question. He had approached it by means of a 'mutual illumination of the arts' [*wechselseitige Erhellung der Künste* – to quote the asthetician Oskar Walzel]. With the help of *Tristan*, Wagner was able to demonstrate particularly well how right Villot had been to apply this method in order to understand the work.

The more personal side of Wagner's 'preface' was accompanied by a polemically worded sally against public opinion. In his account of his melodic procedure, Wagner was replying to those critics for whom the only yardstick was the currently popular accusation of lack of melody. One such critic was Berlioz. On 9 February 1860 Berlioz had published an article headed 'Concerts de M. Richard Wagner. La Musique de l'avenir' in the *Journal des débats*. Wagner addressed his reply to Berlioz personally. Under the heading *A Letter to Hector Berlioz* it appeared in the *Journal des débats* on 22 February and in the *Presse théâtrale* four days later (*GS* VII, pp. 82–6; see also Newman III [1966], p. 19). There is little doubt that Wagner's 'preface' was also conceived as a public commentary on this letter. It was surely Berlioz's critique which prompted him to call his preface '*Music of the Future*' – a term which, he alleged in *A Letter to Hector Berlioz* (*GS* VII, p. 83), Berlioz had got from 'Professor Bischoff in Cologne, a friend of Ferdinand Hiller's'. (Bischoff had not however 'invented' this term – see Riemann, *Lexikon* [1967], 'Sachteil', 1082.) By their nature, Berlioz's imputations and charges inevitably provoked Wagner into once more defending his melody, especially the melody of *Tristan*.

Berlioz had such remarks as this to make on the aims of the 'school of the future':

Supposing it says to us: 'One must do the opposite of what is laid down by the rules. We are tired of melody; we are tired of melodic design; we are tired of arias, duets, trios, of pieces where the theme develops in a regular way; we are fed up with consonant harmonies, with the preparing and resolving of simple dissonances, and with modulations which are natural and realized with skill' ... If that is what this brand-new religion preaches, I am a long way from professing it ... I raise my hand and swear: Non credo.   (*A travers chants*, pp. 314f.)

In the same critique Berlioz wrote of the prelude to *Tristan*:

I have not yet mentioned the instrumental introduction to Wagner's latest opera, Tristan and Isolde. It is strange that the composer had it performed at the same concert as his introduction to Lohengrin, since he has followed the same plan in both. Once again it is a slow piece starting pianissimo, rising gradually to fortissimo and then returning to the initial dynamic, with no theme beyond a kind of chromatic moaning, but full of dissonant chords whose harshness is increased by some long appoggiaturas in place of the real note in the harmony. (*Ibid.*, pp. 310f.)

Incidentally Wagner had dedicated his *Tristan* score to Berlioz as the 'great and dear composer of Roméo et Juliette', but had criticized the latter work in *On Franz Liszt's Symphonic Poems* (1857).

In view of these public criticisms by Berlioz, the implied rebuff in *'Music of the Future'* is again as obvious as it is understandable. But as in the case of Eduard Hanslick – only more so in this instance – Wagner resorted to the indirect answer in order to ward off his critic and to make his position clear and secure.

In his defence Wagner put forward 'infinite melody' as the key idea. Very probably (and this has not been noticed or considered before) it was Champfleury who prompted him to do this. In his short pamphlet *Richard Wagner*, Champfleury had directly challenged those who were accusing Wagner of a lack of melody: 'An absence of melodies, the critics were saying. Each fragment of every one of Wagner's operas is simply one vast melody, akin to the spectacle of the sea.' The phrase 'each fragment' refers to the operatic extracts performed at the concert of 24 January 1860; Champfleury dated his pamphlet '27 January night'.

It is fair to assume that the above quotation particularly appealed to Wagner, bearing in mind his concept of the 'single, perfectly coherent melody'. But starting with those melodic features which he thought were already 'infinite' in Beethoven's music, yet which his own melody surpassed, he substituted another epithet for Champfleury's. Instead of *vaste melodie* he wrote *unendliche Melodie*. Nonetheless he must have been also attracted by Champfleury's sea metaphor, since it suggested the timeless element which he associated with his melody.

In conclusion, everything seems to indicate that 'infinite melody' was a combination of two factors: the connection with a specific work – *Tristan* – and a particular occasion – the pattern of events in Paris. But the phrase also combines a topical element with one that is 'beyond time'. Although related to a particular situation, it ranged far beyond the immediate scene in what it was claiming and implying. And both these aspects of the term seem to have deterred Wagner from re-using or repeating it. The immediate cause disappeared along with the contemporary Parisian scene. As for later on, Wagner may then have flinched from the slogan-like use of a term which, once uttered, promised nothing short of an 'infinite', i.e. timeless, effect.

'Absolute music'; 'programme music'; 'music drama'[4]

(a) Wagner and the term 'absolute music'
The term 'absolute music' is generally associated with the 'autonomy of art' in Hanslick's sense, for it was Hanslick who proclaimed 'form animated by sounds' [*tönend bewegte Form*] to be the essence of music. In fact, however, he wrote only of 'pure, absolute musical art' [*Tonkunst*]; his book on *The Beautiful in Music* never actually uses the phrase 'absolute music'. By contrast, there were times when Wagner was using it quite frequently. Moreover he was responsible for coining the phrase, and it

appeared in his writings some years before Hanslick published his famous polemic. Where and when did Wagner use it, and what are its meaning and function?

Wagner first referred to 'absolute music' when he was living in Dresden. In the 'programme' for Beethoven's Ninth that he wrote in 1846, he remarked of the finale:

> Observe how the Master anticipates the addition of speech and the human voice, as a foreseeable necessity, with the help of this moving recitative for the orchestral basses, which, already on the verge of bursting the bounds of absolute music, seems to meet the other instruments in vigorous, emotional speech, pressing for a resolution... (*GS* II, p. 61)

Three years later, in a letter to Baron von Biedenfeld dated 17 January 1849, Wagner wrote:

> The Greeks, and perhaps even our own medieval dramatists in part, were able to bestow upon the stage play the advantages of musical expression without thereby altering this play in any substantial way: in our own day, by contrast, the heroes of absolute music (i.e. music divorced from the art of poetry), and especially Beethoven, have raised the expressive potential of music, notably through their handling of the orchestra, to the level of a completely new artistic force which had earlier scarcely been dreamt of, even by Gluck himself; yet throughout this development, music was bound to have an important influence on drama... (*SL*, pp. 142–3, slightly amended)

'Absolute music' frequently occurs in two works that Wagner wrote soon after the Biedenfeld letter: *The Art-Work of the Future* (1849) and especially *Opera and Drama* (1850–1). Here, Wagner also resorts occasionally to the synonymous phrase 'absolute instrumental speech' (or 'absolute instrumental music'). In the following passage from *Opera and Drama* he uses it to outline the advantages and drawbacks of 'absolute music':

> In creating such moods [of expectancy] as the poet needs to awaken for us with our own indispensable help, absolute instrumental speech has already proved to be all-influential; for it had the peculiar effect of evoking vague feelings of expectancy, and this was bound to become a drawback whenever it was seeking a clear definition of the feelings evoked. (*GS* IV, p. 187; *Oper und Drama* [1984], p.345)

And finally, the term 'absolute music' appears in *On Franz Liszt's Symphonic Poems* (1857):

> Let me tell you what I believe: *whatever associations it may enter into, music can never cease to be the supreme, the most redemptive art*. It is of music's essence that through and within music, that which all the other arts merely suggest turns into the clearest certainty, the most immediately decisive of truths. Take the clumsiest dance or the feeblest piece of doggerel: the accompanying music will ennoble even these (providing it takes them seriously, rather than deliberately caricaturing them); for, thanks to its peculiar seriousness, it has a character so chaste and wonderful that it transfigures

all it touches. But what is just as clear and sure is that music can only be heard in forms taken from a real-life relation or manifestation which, while originally foreign to music, only receive their deepest significance through it, by virtue of the revelation, as it were, of that music which is latent within them. Nothing is less absolute (as regards its manifestation in life, that is) than music, and the advocates of an absolute music obviously don't know what they are saying. Challenge them to indicate a music outside of a form taken from bodily movement or a line of speech (in accordance with the causal connection), and that would baffle them.

(*GS* v, p. 191)

The variant 'absolute instrumental speech' makes it clear that Wagner's concept of absolute music is identical with his concept of instrumental music. One facet of this idea became more and more significant: the thesis that instrumental music is music which is not linked to poetry. Wagner makes this explicit in the Biedenfeld letter.

Another facet of the same idea can be inferred from the 1841 novella *A Happy Evening*, where the narrator is stating the agreement finally reached about the essence of music. As yet there is no direct mention of 'absolute music'. But it is evident from the context that here Wagner was fore-shadowing an important aspect of it:

What music [instrumental music] expresses is eternal, infinite and ideal. It speaks not of the passion, love and longing of this or that individual in this or that situation, but of passion, love and longing in themselves, and furthermore in all the infinite variety of motivations which arise from the exclusive nature of music and which are strange to, and beyond the expression of, every other form of language.

(*WP*, p. 187)

In *Opera and Drama* Wagner confirmed that 'absolute music' only expressed generalized feelings. This includes a shift in his attitude, a previously positive view of the concept giving way to an ambivalent one. He points out this music's ability to express 'moods' or feelings, but at the same time he regards the communication of merely vague feelings as a shortcoming.

Wagner adopted a particularly critical attitude towards the individual arts during his first years in Zurich. This was when his search for a conception of music drama had entered a crucial phase. He regarded the evolution of instrumental music as something of an ascending line on a graph, a line that had peaked in Beethoven. Now instrumental music was in need of poetry to complement and 'redeem' it:

in short, as soon as *Beethoven* had written his last symphony, – the whole musical fraternity could do any amount of darning and patching in an effort to produce an absolute man of music, but this could only result in a colourfully darned and patched man of fantasy, and not a wiry and sturdy man of nature. Haydn and Mozart could and needs must be succeeded by a Beethoven; the tutelary spirit of music required him urgently, and in a flash he was here; but in the field of absolute music, who can aspire to follow Beethoven in the way that he followed Haydn and Mozart? The greatest genius would not be able to achieve anything further in that area, simply because the spirit of absolute music no longer needs it...

(*GS* III, pp. 100f.)

Wagner never actually said that he was not going to write any more symphonies. But the above statements express his conviction that the possibilities of purely instrumental music including the symphony had been exhausted. It seemed to him a crime against historical developments in music, and against music generally, to go on composing purely for instruments. Music's capabilities and expressive tendencies, he thought, should not be tied any more to the symphony and sonata. And to misuse the resources of instrumental music altogether in opera composing seemed to him equally wrong.

This critical attitude is crystallized in Wagner's term 'absolute music'. His early Zurich writings draw instrumental music as a separate art from poetry into a critical survey of everything which is 'absolute'. By this he means everything seen as being associated with the claim to an unlimited significance and function, self-enclosed and self-justifying.

Wagner writes of 'absolute music', the 'absolute musician', the 'absolute man of music', the 'absolute artist' and the 'absolute opera singer'. He mentions 'the absolutely musical', 'absolute musical speech', the 'absolute art-work', 'absolute recitative', the 'absolute aria', 'absolute melody', 'absolute operatic melody' and the 'absolute art of singing'. He also refers to 'absolute fashion', 'absolute respect' and 'absolute verbal language'. In every case the critical nuance is unmistakable. The copious use of the adjective 'absolute' reflects what Hans Sedlmayr has called an inherent value judgment. It indicates Wagner's rejection of any compartmentalizing, and thus a drive towards integration with the target of the 'Gesamtkunstwerk', the total work of art.

The critical function of the adjective 'absolute' was probably inspired by Ludwig Feuerbach, whose writings Wagner had started reading in 1848–9 if not earlier. The treatise *Zur Kritik der Hegelschen Philosophie* (1839) could have served as a model for Wagner. In it, Feuerbach is fundamentally against vindicating the 'totality, the absoluteness of a particular historical manifestation or existence ... as a predicate' – especially as Hegel propounded it.[5]

(b) Beethoven and 'absolute music'
Although Wagner was critical of 'absolute music', he did not postulate its 'decline', as Dahlhaus maintains (*NGW*, p. 75). His critique makes certain distinctions. He developed his concept of absolute music in relation to instrumental music. The latter's 'power of speech' must be credited to Beethoven, but at the same time Beethoven's intentions go beyond such music's bounds, making it uniquely and unmistakably clear. This point is

especially clear from Wagner's appraisal of the Ninth Symphony. According to his programme, the instrumental recitatives are close to leaving the realm of absolute music, and the frontier is finally crossed with the introduction of words.

Wagner describes Beethoven's exact position in the Zurich writings, particularly *The Art-Work of the Future* and *Opera and Drama*. Beethoven's instrumental music is now involved in the problems attaching to 'absolute music'. The infinitely enlarged 'powers of speech' are all to the good; on the other hand the very richness and density of the musical language are making it unclear, indeed incomprehensible.

Wagner expresses his ambivalent attitude in a metaphor which is not easy to explain. The mysterious side of Beethoven's works induces him to refer to 'sketches'.

In works from the second half of his artistic career, Beethoven is generally incomprehensible – or rather, open to misunderstanding – in the very places where he wants to express a particular individual content in the most comprehensible way. He goes beyond what unthinking convention acknowledges as the intelligibility of absolute music, i.e. that which bears some kind of recognizable resemblance to the dance-air and vocal air, in both its expression and its form. Instead he uses a language which often seems an arbitrary display of temperament and which, not being part of a purely musical context, is only articulated by dint of a poetic intention – the very thing that music could not express with the clarity of poetry. Most of Beethoven's works from that period must be seen as involuntary attempts to construct a language which would meet his desire, so that often they seem like sketches for a painting on whose *object* the artist had decided, without being sure how to organize it in an intelligible way. The actual painting he was unable to execute until he had attuned its object to his powers of expression, i.e. had grasped it in its universal meaning and transposed its individual element back into the characteristic colours of musical composition itself, thereby 'musicalizing' the actual object up to a point. Had the world set eyes on these really finished paintings in which Beethoven expressed himself in a refreshingly clear and intelligible way, the misunderstanding of his works that the Master promoted would certainly have had a less confusing and mesmeric effect.   (*GS* III, pp. 279f.)

This paragraph from *Opera and Drama* has been misinterpreted. Wagner, it was assumed, regarded all Beethoven's works from 'the second half of his artistic career' as sketches. But Wagner was writing of a majority of works; he describes other Beethoven compositions as 'essentially finished paintings'. Which works does he mean, and from which period?

No clear-cut division of Beethoven's output into separate periods is to be found in Wagner's writings. There is no definite indication, even, of whether he preferred to divide it into two periods or into three. The writings tend in the main to favour two periods. (As Kurt von Fischer notes, so did Liszt, but disregarding dates of origin and opus numbers.) This classification is supported by the selection principle Wagner applied as a conductor of Beethoven. The early works, he thought, subsisted on

Mozartian themes and ended with the Second Symphony. He began his programme for the Third Symphony by saying that with this work, Beethoven 'started off in a direction that was quite personal to him' (GS v, p. 169).

The hallmark of this personal direction, in Wagner's view, was Beethoven's 'poetic content', and it first came into play in the 'Eroica' Symphony. The above statement can therefore be related to the extract we have quoted from *Opera and Drama*, which refers to Beethoven's 'poetic intention'. So what Wagner calls the second half of Beethoven's career begins with the 'Eroica'.[6]

But which are the works of his 'second' period where Beethoven went beyond what was conceivable in 'absolute music', i.e. within the bounds of the dance-air? In which of his works did he aspire to a poetic language, although his commitment to music prevented him from achieving it? Which of Beethoven's compositions did Wagner regard as 'sketches'?

On this point, too, Wagner remains vague. But let us assume that the purpose of his Beethoven 'programmes' was to foster at least here and there an understanding of the works that an unintelligible presentation of the 'object' was hindering. Then we can regard as sketches in Wagner's sense of the word all the works for which he wrote a programmatic explanation, apart from the Ninth. So the 'Eroica' Symphony, the *Leonore* Overture No. 3, the *Coriolan* Overture and the String Quartet in C sharp minor must have been 'sketches' of this kind. And judging by what Wagner wrote in *The Art-Work of the Future*, where he retraces Beethoven's route to the Ninth Symphony, he seems to have regarded the Fifth and Sixth Symphonies, at least, as preliminary stages, or further 'sketches'. In his anonymous announcement at the time of the first Dresden performance in 1846, Wagner had already declared that compared with Beethoven's last symphony, all the earlier works were 'like sketches and preliminary studies'. Without them, he wrote, it would have been impossible for Beethoven to brace himself up to conceiving the Ninth (see GS xii, pp. 203f.).

In Wagner's view, the Ninth Symphony meant the 'redemption of music from its intrinsic element for an *all-embracing art* [zur *allgemeinsamen Kunst*]' (GS iii, p. 96). Even though it might need explaining, he calls it Beethoven's most accomplished painting, the work with which Beethoven 'cast out the anchor, this anchor being the *word*'.

Wagner distinguishes between several kinds of 'paintings'. First there are the fictive compositions, as it were; here Beethoven pictured the subject-matter or 'object' without adequately realizing it. Then there is his 'most accomplished painting', the Ninth Symphony. This in turn is in contrast to the 'essentially finished paintings' where the actual object is, in a way, converted into music again. That is to say, the object has been reconciled with the 'absolutely musical' possibilities, within the bounds of the 'dance air and vocal air'.

What Wagner meant by 'essentially finished paintings' emerges from something which Wolzogen quotes him as saying:

It is amazing how firmly Beethoven, after his bold attempts in the Eroica to pass beyond traditional symphonic form, returns later on, and especially in the Seventh and Eighth Symphonies, entirely to the original dance form, which it is always a very serious matter to abandon.

(Erinnerungen, p. 29)

So although forming preliminary stages in relation to the Ninth, Beethoven's Seventh and Eighth Symphonies were not 'sketches' but 'essentially finished paintings'. This was because Wagner evidently saw no discrepancy here between the composer's intention and what a symphony that was a form of dance comprised in terms of content. It is worthy of note that Uhlig described these two symphonies – the Ninth aside – as the focal point of Beethoven's instrumental music. In both, Uhlig claimed, Beethoven provided 'a whole consisting of four movements with the unmistakable character of a dance' (see Uhlig [1913], pp. 190, 201 ff.). And both symphonies contained just one basic mood: serenity [*Heiterkeit*].

Wagner's 'sketch' metaphor is not the only one that reflects his ambivalent attitude to Beethoven's works and especially towards his relationship to 'absolute music'. This attitude finds even clearer expression in the metaphor of Columbus.

Beethoven made the same mistake as Columbus, who was only looking for a new route to the old India that was already known, but actually discovered a new world instead; Columbus too took his mistake to the grave with him: he made his companions swear on oath that they took the new world for the old India. And thus, even though completely beset by error, his deed took away the world's blindfold and taught it in the most conclusive way to recognize the real shape of the Earth and the unsuspected riches it contained. – Now, thanks to Beethoven's mighty mistake, we have discovered music's inexhaustible powers. (*GS* III, p. 278)

Wagner uses the Columbus metaphor to emphasize that for him, the artistic course taken by Beethoven was a 'mistake'. Like Columbus, Beethoven went in the wrong direction, but that was precisely why he stumbled upon some discoveries which – unintended as they were – he failed to recognize. In concrete terms, Beethoven went wrong by trying to represent what was 'artistically necessary' (a specific poetic content) in something 'artistically impossible', i.e. 'absolute music', instrumental music. Even though his attempt to represent the poetic object intelligibly was doomed to failure, he still opened up 'music's inexhaustible powers'. But he made its limitations clear by not only exhausting but also overtaxing its possibilities.

If we look at the historical reality, it will be obvious at once that Wagner's view was very wide of the mark. The picture of Beethoven as vainly seeking to realize his 'poetic intention', while unwittingly perfecting instrumental music – from the evolutionary and aesthetic angle, this is an anticipation of Wagner the dramatist. While proclaiming Beethoven's discoveries to be a binding heritage, the Columbus metaphor was also justifying the drama of the future. Wagner saw his own aims as being vindicated not only by the concluding Ninth Symphony but also by Beethoven's 'sketches', the compositions that revealed his 'mistake'.

(c) Beethoven's 'poetic object'

Wagner sharply contrasted Beethoven's 'particular individual content' with the capacity to make known the ineffable or inexpressible in 'absolute music'. What that 'content' actually amounted to was, to Wagner's mind, a secret as stimulating as it was unyielding. In *Opera and Drama* he describes the 'content' of Beethoven's compositions as being his 'in truth, *unexpressed secret*' (*GS* III, p. 281). This was more than a casual remark: it reflects a fierce and protracted tussle with a problem that has faced exegetes of Beethoven's music up to our own times, namely the problem of Beethoven's 'idea'.

Wagner refers not only to an 'idea' but also to the 'philosophical idea' (*GS* I, p. 145). More often he speaks of the 'content', either 'particular' or 'individual'; first and foremost, however, he speaks of Beethoven's 'poetic object'.

Only little by little did Wagner develop the notion that Beethoven's music represented a 'poetic object'. He still saw this view as being ultimately irrelevant to the origin and musical design of a work in the novella *A Happy Evening*. This emerges from the following comments by 'R':

When a musician is moved to sketch out a composition, no matter how small, he is acting under the influence of a feeling which in the hour of conception dominates his entire being. The feeling may have been occasioned by some external event or it may have sprung from some mysterious inner source . . . in the mind of the musician the feeling always takes a musical form and expresses itself in tones before it has been cast into notes. Profound, passionate feelings which hold sway over our emotions and ideas for months and years are the ones which impel the musician to those broad, all-embracing conceptions to which, among other works, we owe the existence of the 'Eroica'. Profound feelings of suffering or elation may be occasioned by external events since we are human beings whose destinies in the nature of the case are governed by extraneous circumstances; but such feelings, when they impel the musician to create, have already been transmuted into music. Thus in the moment of creative inspiration the determining factor is no longer the external event, but the musical feeling which it engendered . . . (*WP*, p. 186)

Wagner already thought Beethoven's 'idea' was something that was worth considering. But it could not become more than a motivating element; it was no shaping element that established the structure and form of a work. It was not, to quote Carl Dahlhaus, a component of the actual musical work. In Wagner's novella, the narrator states that Beethoven began planning a symphony in accordance with a 'philosophical idea' before inventing the musical themes for it. But 'R' counters this by saying that during the actual creation, the composer is guided solely by musical feelings, and not by an 'external event'.

Compared with this statement, the view which Wagner expressed to Uhlig in his letter of [13] February 1852 signifies a complete *volte-face*:

What is characteristic about Beethoven's great orchestral works is that they are real poems in which an attempt is made to represent a real object ... would the vague and disjointed note-spinning of modern instrumental music be possible if composers had understood the true essence of Beethoven's tone-poems? And what this essence entails is that Beethoven's longer compositions are only secondarily music, but that first and foremost they contain a poetic object. Or might it be argued that this *object* was perhaps taken simply from the music? Would that not be the same as if the poet were to take his theme from language, the painter his from colour? (*SL*, pp. 250–2)

In *A Happy Evening* a work was determined by the musical feeling, and the external occasion was not important to the actual design. But now the musical element is peripheral, whereas the 'poetic object' is of the first importance.

In the meantime Wagner had changed his mind about the respective positions of composer and listener. This crucially affected the change in his interpretation of Beethoven. Although he had denied in *A Happy Evening* that an 'external manifestation' or 'philosophical idea' was important to the creation of music, the same did not apply to musical reception. This point is generally overlooked, but it emerges from the sentence following on from Wagner's statement on the essence of music: 'Let each according to his strength, his capacity and his disposition take from it what he is capable of feeling and enjoying!'

With his programmatic explanations, however, Wagner began to ensure there was ample scope for subjective musical experiences and associations. Above all, his Beethoven programmes were intended to stimulate the individual enjoyment of music and indeed to bring it about in the first place. Their function was to bridge the gap between the work and the listener (and so they were invariably performing a social function as well).

There are two levels to the breadth of tolerance in the subjective experience of music associated with Wagner's 'programmes'. There is the level of the commentator, and there is also that of the listener, who will be more or less adjusting his own musical experience to the programme provided for him. But with regard to their mutual relationship, the view Wagner initially put forward, in his programme for the Ninth, is fundamentally different from the later view he expressed in the letter to Uhlig. At the beginning of the programme he states:

Anyone who was not yet able to achieve a closer, intimate acquaintance with this wonderfully significant composition will have great difficulty in understanding it on a first hearing. This would seem to justify the attempt to assist that probably sizeable audience in the said situation, not to an absolute understanding of Beethoven's masterpiece (for this is only likely to come of personal intuition), but, with the help of some pointers, at any rate to a perception of the artistic organization, which is so idiosyncratic and still so completely new and unparalleled that it could escape the less well-prepared and hence easily confused listener.

(*GS* II, p. 56)

Here Wagner's attitude indicates reservations with regard to both the work and the public. He was undoubtedly setting down his own interpretation of the Ninth. But he did not claim to be providing an authentic reading, any more than he was forcing it upon the listener. The programme does not affect 'absolute understanding' achieved by dint of 'personal intuition'.

By 1852 Wagner had come a long way from such 'pointers'. His effort to help people understand Beethoven was now associated with a desire for his interpretation to be recognized as the only authentic one. The scope afforded to the listener's own experience is reduced, being swallowed up by the interpretative claim, which Wagner now connects with an illumination of the 'poetic object'. He sees himself as 'having exactly the same feelings, the same mental training, indeed almost the same powers' as Beethoven. His interpretation of the composer, he thinks, is almost completely identical with Beethoven's intentions. But his endeavour to give an authentic explanation of the 'ideas' of Beethoven the tone-poet and to formulate them in a programme depended on the recognition of the 'poetic object' (or 'idea') as an integral part of Beethoven's composition.

Wagner does not appear to have become fully aware of the 'poetic object' and all that it implied until the start of his Zurich exile. This was when his conception of the drama was taking shape on the theoretical level. And even within this short space of time – roughly between 1849–50 and 1852 – his outlook varies. In *Opera and Drama* he speaks of Beethoven's 'poetic intention' with complete conviction, but in his letter to Uhlig of 26 February 1852 we read:

I at least cannot view it differently, because I have now become quite clear in my own mind that *I*, too, understand Beethoven only from when I first scented the poetic object of his compositions and eventually tracked it down: Coriolan demonstrates this to me quite clearly. (*SB* IV, p. 299)

With this discovery of the 'poetic object', Wagner had evidently reached a new inner conviction that in principle, such an 'object' was behind Beethoven's works, although it might vary from one to another. Admittedly it is an open question as to whether he could trace it in every composition.[7]

But what did Wagner really mean by Beethoven's 'poetic object'? What is its essence? Much as he discussed and invoked it, Wagner never made a definitive statement about this. If we look at his programmes, we will notice that basically his remarks do no more than outline or point to particular emotional areas. Hence they are substantially different from a great many other attempts, whose authors were concerned with interpreting individual works as a musical depiction of actual events. An enlightening statement in this respect is the introduction to Wagner's 'programmatic explanation' of Beethoven's 'Eroica' Symphony, written in 1851.

This ... tone poem – the Master's third symphony, and the work with which he struck out in an entirely personal direction – is in many ways not as easy to understand as its name might suggest, and that is because the title 'Heroic Symphony' automatically misleads us into seeing a sequence of heroic connections somewhat in the spirit of an historical drama, portrayed in musical forms ... First of all the term 'heroic' must be taken in the widest sense and not simply as relating to a military hero. If we understand by 'hero' the whole, complete *man* who is in possession of all purely human feelings – love, pain and vigour – at their richest and most intense, we shall comprehend the right object the artist is communicating to us in the movingly eloquent tones of his work. The artistic area of this work is occupied by all the manifold ... feelings of a strong, fully rounded individuality to which nothing human is alien, and containing within itself everything that is truly human... (*GS* v, pp. 169f.)

The above is a clear rejection of any attempt to see Beethoven's music as illustrating specific historical features or events. The same is true of the letter to Uhlig of 13 February 1852, the document in which we find those remarks on the 'poetic object' in Beethoven's music we have already quoted. Here Wagner writes of 'fantasy striving for comprehension' with the help of 'all kinds of arbitrarily invented exploits and fanciful pictures' – readings which he describes as grotesque and trivial.

Wagner rejected 'heroic connections ... in the spirit of an historical drama' in favour of the representation of feelings. Thus he adopts the same standpoint in his 'Eroica' programme as he does in *A Happy Evening*. In the novella, however, he promptly excludes the 'philosophical idea' as an irrelevance, whereas there is a basic emphasis in the letter to Uhlig on the significance of the 'poetic object'. This seems to be at odds with the common emotional basis, making it less clear how things stand. But the conflict is resolved by an important nuance to Wagner's interpretation which shows what was new about it. The programme for the 'Eroica' refers not to generalized feelings but to 'purely human feeling' embodied by the ideal of a 'strong, fully rounded individuality'.

What this 'purely human feeling' in Beethoven's compositions entails was explained in detail by Wagner in another letter of 1852. On 30 January he wrote to Hans von Bülow. In the following passage he appraises an overture planned by Bülow in the light of his programme for Beethoven's *Coriolan* Overture. He says of the latter:

I was delighted to observe that this entire piece of music is no more and no less than the accompaniment to a graphic – almost mimic – scene between C. and his mother and wife in the camp outside Rome. You, too, should conflate the whole of the poem of R. & J. [Romeo and Juliet] to produce a similar moment of graphic intensity: if you continue to plan the work along philosophical lines, your music can only become increasingly incomprehensible. For – once again – absolute music can express only feelings, passions and moods in their antitheses and degrees of intensity, but not relationships of a social or political nature. Beethoven has a splendid instinct for this: I almost prefer *his* poem of Coriolanus to Shakespeare's in its graphic unity and succinctness, which almost allows the subject-matter to achieve the sensuality of myth... (*SL*, p. 249, slightly amended)

It is worth pointing out that Wagner's use of the word 'graphic' [*plastisch*] is significant. Taken in conjunction with one another, his 'Eroica' programme and the letter to Bülow make the following point clear. Beethoven's 'poetic object' or 'poetic content', the constellation of expression reduced to its essence, is identical with the 'purely human expression of feeling', with those emotional qualities of myth that constitute the heart of drama. Now we can fully grasp Wagner's exclamation in his letter at the climax of his apotheosis of the 'poetic object': 'The aim of this endeavour?? – *Drama*!!' (*SL*, p. 253).

For Wagner, drama was simply a realization of Beethoven's 'poetic object' by other means. And the crucial difference between Wagner's view of music during his Paris years and in the Zurich letters and essays we have quoted is this. In the first case, emotional values are grasped and organized in purely musical terms, independently of poetic aims. In the second, however, music is announcing a 'poetic object' condensed into the emotional qualities of what is 'purely human'. Granted, music was still the medium of the 'inexpressible', but its determination had changed.

Beethoven's 'poetic object' and its transformation into drama helps to illustrate the conversion of instrumental music into a musico-dramatic quality contradicting the notion of a Wagner permanently driven by 'symphonic ambitions'. And it underlines Wagner's idea that the traditional symphony had come to an end as an historically feasible genre. Or else he could not have said the following (14 April 1873) to Cosima:

I clearly feel that what I said in *The Art-Work of the Future* is true: that the 9th Symphony is also the last. Now all the young people pin their hopes on excessive accents, which can only be understood through the action, and the result is a mess. It is frightful.

The way Wagner developed his aesthetic reflections on Beethoven's symphonies up to and during his first years in Zurich also illustrates something else. Contrary to Voss's belief, it was not the painful recognition of his own inability in the purely instrumental, symphonic field which drove Wagner to compose music dramas; moreover the above reflections were being developed at a time when he was fully concentrating on the *Ring* he was going to compose. Rather, Wagner had the special talent he describes in the letter to Gaillard – a talent that was stretched by his difficulties in construing Beethoven's symphonies. This was a talent for combining musical events with poetic and even theatrical images in his mind. And what it led to was his 'dramatic' view of the Beethoven symphony as music which delimited and also transcended purely instrumental music. Hence it is not surprising that Wagner should be making visually orientated comments on Beethoven's Seventh Symphony at a time when, according to Voss, he was already concentrating more and more on the symphonies he had yet to compose. It was not because he really wanted to write symphonies that he arrived at the *Ring des Nibelungen, Tristan und Isolde, Meistersinger* and *Parsifal*. That came about because he needed to compose music dramas as *dramas*. Such is the conclusion to be drawn from a thorough scrutiny of his understanding of Beethoven.

In his interpretation of the overture to *Coriolan*, Wagner still saw it as 'absolute music'. But this concept had undergone a surreptitious change. It already foreshadows that larger concept of music which appears in the essay on Liszt's symphonic poems, and which the *Beethoven* essay underpins philosophically.

The broader concept that Wagner visualized was music in the sense of the Greek *mousikē*, based upon a 'purely human' primal ground of feelings. This is evident from what he wrote in 1852 to Franz Brendel:

If we are to free our music from the false position which a literary mediation of its interpretation is forcing it into, I believe we can only achieve this by assigning it the extremely broad meaning that the original name implies. We have got used to regarding 'music' as simply the art of sound [*Tonkunst*] – or even the 'artificiality of sound' [*'tonkünstelei'*] these days. We know this notion is an arbitrary one because the race which invented the name 'music' used it to mean not only *poetry* and the art of sounds, but every artistic manifestation of the inner man insofar as he expressively conveyed his feelings and ideas in the ultimate, most convincing sensory form through the organ of resonant speech. Accordingly, the education of young Athenians was divided into just two parts: music and – gymnastics.

(*SB* IV, p. 263/*GS* V, pp. 59f.)

So it was only logical of Wagner to describe the *Coriolan* Overture as 'the accompaniment to a graphic – almost mimic – scene', and to write the following in *On Franz Liszt's Symphonic Poems*: 'Hence a symphony's meaning cannot be expressed in a programme, which tosses the awkward question of Why? around rather than settling it. The meaning can only be expressed in the actual drama played out on the stage' (*GS* VII, p. 129).[8]

(d)   The 'programmatic explanation' and 'programme music'

In his *Esthetics of Music* (p. 63), Carl Dahlhaus observes that it is hardly exaggerating 'to regard the symphonic poem as a musical realizing, by composers, of a literary principle that had determined descriptions and expositions of music ever since the beginning of the century'. And Wagner's Beethoven 'programmes' were certainly pioneering contributions to the development of this principle.

In turn, Wagner's practice of supplying Beethoven's works with programmatic explanations to make them clearer was inspired by Berlioz, whose 'Roméo et Juliette' symphony, *Symphonie fantastique* and *Grande symphonie funèbre et triomphale* he had heard in Paris. Moreover, Berlioz remarked in reviews on the incomprehension with which Beethoven's Ninth was being greeted. He tried to make the symphony accessible to the general public by translating its text and by interpreting the content. Nonetheless Wagner sharply criticized Berlioz's compositions in *Opera and Drama*, not least the *Symphonie fantastique* together with the programme for it. As Wagner saw it, Berlioz was emulating Beethoven's 'sketches', i.e. those works of his that were problematic and hard to understand. '*Hector Berlioz* is a direct and very energetic scion of Beethoven on the very side which the latter abandoned as soon as he progressed (as I put it earlier) from the sketch to the real painting' (*GS* III, p. 282).

Wagner was not revoking earlier standpoints with this judgment. Admittedly he had said in 1841, à propos of the *Symphonie fantastique*, that Berlioz had not only known Beethoven's symphonies but also understood them. But the 'French method', he remarked, dominated the way that Berlioz utilized this understanding as a composer. And that was sufficient to condemn him: 'That tendency prevented him, however, from approaching the genius of Beethoven directly. It is a tendency to face outwards, the search for common accords in the extremities' (*GS* XII, pp. 86f.).

Wagner accused Berlioz of 'fantastic arbitrariness and caprice', brought about by copying external details, and resulting in an artistically unconscionable obscurity which it took a programme to illuminate. These were the points that subsequently made up his specific judgment of Berlioz – and of any other composers who were following Beethoven in the 'wrong' way. He attacked musicians who used programmes like labels in the following words:

But if there was only an external side [of Beethoven] to be copied, because the content of those curious features was destined to remain what was really the Master's *unexpressed* secret, then it was imperative to find for it, with regard to content, some kind of object which would allow one to utilize the features pointing towards the particular and individual in spite of its inherent generality. Naturally this object could only be found outside music, and as far as purely instrumental music was concerned it could only exist once more in the imagination. The pretence of the musical depiction of an object taken from nature or from human life was conveyed to the listener in the form of a programme, and it was up to the imagination to use it to explain all the musical curiosities that could now be let loose in a totally arbitrary way, until there was the wildest chaos and confusion.

(*GS* III, p. 281)

But although Wagner rejected Berlioz's programme works firmly and consistently, he did not always reject programme music on principle. His essay of 1857 on Liszt's symphonic poems is an apologia on behalf of Liszt's programme symphonies and the branch of programme-oriented composition he stood for.

The contrast between Berlioz and Liszt accounts for the nuances Wagner gave to the term 'symphonic poem'. He sees Berlioz's music as lacking in continuity and overall clarity, using the 'Roméo et Juliette' Symphony to illustrate the listener's experience, the loss of the 'musical thread':

the extreme fascination which the development of the principal motif had had for me was dissipated and diluted in the course of the movement until I felt distinctly uneasy; I immediately guessed that now that the musical thread had disappeared (i.e. the consistently clear alternation of certain motifs), I was obliged to go by scenic motifs of which I was not aware, and which were not listed in the programme, either. (*GS* v, pp. 193f.)

In contrast to the raggedness of Berlioz's works, Wagner maintained, there was a unity to Liszt's. Liszt obtains the form of his symphonic works from the central motif on which each composition is based.

I question whether the march or dance, with all the mental images that convey this action to us, is a better motif for formal shaping than, for instance, the idea of the characteristic aspects of the deeds and sufferings of Orpheus, Prometheus etc. I would also ask this. If the form has such a dominating effect on what music declares as I proved to you earlier, would music not find it nobler and more liberating to derive that form from the idea of an Orpheus or Prometheus motif than from the idea of a march or dance motif? (*GS* v, p. 192)

The above viewpoint seems to correspond to what modern analysis of Liszt's music sums up as 'motivic combination through transformation'. In his 'Eroica' analysis, Uhlig had shown that a composition does not begin with complete themes; these themes and hence the musical form are developed from a motif or configuration of motifs. Wagner had probably first noticed this process in Liszt's music in July 1853, when the two of them went through 'several of his latest symphonic poems ... in particular his *Faust* Symphony' (*ML*, p. 495). But, obvious though it may be to us nowadays, to apply the same analytical criteria to Berlioz's music requires a degree of abstraction that was still foreign to music analysis in the mid-1860s. It may seem strange to us that Wagner failed to recognize the chromaticism in the first movement of the *Symphonie fantastique* as a contrasting theme to the *idée fixe*. Dahlhaus suggests that Wagner suppressed the thought on account of his evolutionary perspective, which Berlioz was impeding, but this need not have been the case. (See Dahlhaus [1988], pp. 228ff.)

Wagner was judging from a less lofty perspective. Without a musical working-up and more overt linking together of the poetic or dramatic motifs, it did not seem possible to him to organize the musical material clearly and intelligibly into a unified musical form that was inherently consistent and meaningful. Detachment with regard to the dance or march form, and the conversion of purely dramatic ideas into emotional values which can be portrayed and developed in music – these are both part of the same technique. Following his criticism of 'Roméo et Juliette' Wagner writes:

> Without question these [scenic] motifs were there in Shakespeare's famous balcony scene; but the composer's great mistake was to abide by the way the dramatist had laid them out. The moment he planned to use this scene as the theme of a symphonic poem, the composer ought to have sensed that a dramatist has to resort to quite different means than the musician in order to express roughly the same idea ... The musician ... takes no account whatever of the business of ordinary life. He eliminates all its contingencies and individual details, sublimating everything in them in accordance with its concrete affective content, which by virtue of its unique designation can only be presented in music. Hence a really musical poet would have shown Berlioz this scene in an eminently concrete ideal form...
>
> (*GS* v, p. 94)

Wagner was asking that the poetic theme of a symphonic poem be derived from 'purely human' affective qualities. And here his starting-point was the method he had recognized as being decisive to Beethoven's 'poetic object'.

(e) The Beethoven centenary essay and Schopenhauer
Wagner's essay on the Liszt symphonic poems reflects the influence of Schopenhauer. On a superficial level, this is clear from such phrases as 'the idea [*Vorstellung*] of an Orpheus or Prometheus motif' and 'the idea of a march or dance motif'. Moreover Wagner's aforementioned statements on 'absolute music' indicate the presence in the essay of ideas he had taken from Schopenhauer's 'metaphysics of music'. He now denied that there was such a thing as 'absolute' music existing for its own sake, and added in parentheses 'as regards its manifestation in life, mind you'. The qualification suggests that he was now positing the absoluteness of music in a quite different, more far-reaching sense. Like Schopenhauer, he was setting music above 'manifestations in life'. It will now be clear how Wagner's view of music had changed. Music had become an element reaching beyond all appearances but at the same time ennobling them.

Thirteen years later Wagner produced his Beethoven centenary essay. Here he made Schopenhauer's ideas on the essence of music the corner-

stone of his argument. The stated aim of the essay was 'a written exposition
... of the meaning of Beethoven's music', but over and beyond this,
Wagner was aiming at a 'contribution to the philosophy of music' (*GS* IX,
p. 61). That this involved some amending of Schopenhauer is an acknowledged fact. But these revisions seemed vital to Wagner if he was to keep his
conception of music drama intact on the theoretical level, and so far this
has never been sufficiently remarked on and discussed. (Even Ernest
Newman merely notes in *Wagner as Man and Artist* that 'Wagner has been
expounding the Schopenhauerian theory of music'. Although Stein [1960]
examines the subject in more detail, he largely ignores the importance to
the essay of Wagner's special view of Beethoven.)

True, Wagner said that he had found a 'quietus' in Schopenhauer's philosophical system, in its denial of the will-to-life. Schopenhauer's aesthetics of
music, too, satisfied him completely to begin with. *My Life* mentions the
particular pleasure Wagner derived from the 'surprising and significant
conception of music' (p. 509). But very soon he discovered some 'alarming
weaknesses' in the system which he was 'able to remedy' (*ML*, p. 579).

On receiving the poem of the *Ring*, Schopenhauer had not only made
some caustic notes in the margin. He had also remarked to the composer's
friend Dr François Wille that Wagner ought to give up music and had
more genius as a poet. (See also CW, 16 January 1869.) This was not
simply a passing mood; it logically followed from Schopenhauer's 'metaphysics of music'. He asked Wille to tell Wagner that he himself would stay
loyal to Rossini and Mozart. From this we might even conclude that he
knew *Opera and Drama*, since Rossini is portrayed there as a musical
anti-Christ in the realm of opera. Nearly two years after the *Beethoven* essay,
Wagner spoke to Cosima of Schopenhauer's 'quaint worship' of Rossini
and wanted 'to have the piano scores of this curiously talented composer'
(CW, 8 March 1872).

Schopenhauer's aesthetics of music – and this point cannot be emphasized too strongly – automatically exclude the music drama of Wagner.
There are passages in the *Parerga and Paralipomena* which, without being
explicitly couched in terms of Wagner's aesthetic axioms, nonetheless read
like a commentary on them.

Strictly speaking, therefore, we could call the opera an unmusical invention for the
benefit of unmusical minds into which music must first be smuggled through a
medium that is foreign to it, possibly as the accompaniment to a long, spun-out,
vapid love-story and its wishy-washy poetry. For the text of the opera cannot
possibly endure a poetry that is condensed and full of spirit and ideas, because the
composition is unable to keep up with this. But to try to make music entirely the
slave of bad poetry is the wrong way which is taken especially by Gluck whose opera
music, apart from the overtures, is, therefore, not enjoyable at all without the
words. Indeed it can be said that opera has become the ruin of music.

([1974] II, pp. 433–4)

Felix Gotthelf in particular has regarded Schopenhauer's thesis of the ruination of music through opera as a parallel to Wagner's attack on traditional opera, indicating an inner agreement between them. But this misses the essence of Schopenhauer's musical aesthetics. What the philosopher said to Karl Hebler, who visited him in August 1855, obviates any speculations of this kind. Hebler confirms the attitude we have noted from the conversation with Wille. Schopenhauer had a high regard for the composer of the *Ring* as a dramatic poet. On the other hand he objected to the 'trade association' between poetry and music, arguing that each of those arts produced its own special effect. And in his published statements on opera Schopenhauer discusses in detail the relationship of music to such 'external' matters as 'text, action, march, dance, sacred or worldly ceremony'. Here again we have the same story. All these appendages are basically alien to music. Music is not a means to an end but an end in itself.

Wagner, then, had ample reason for revising Schopenhauer's aesthetics of music. On 8 December 1858 he wrote to Mathilde Wesendonck that as a result of reading the philosopher, he had had some wonderful trains of thought and had been prompted to correct some of Schopenhauer's deficiencies. Wagner goes on to say:

> I am finding the theme more interesting with each day because answers are needed which only I can provide, since there was never previously anyone who was both a poet and a musician in my sense of the phrase, and who could thus obtain a unique insight into inner processes... (Wagner [n.d.], pp. 107f.)

What is especially notable about this letter is that the association of poetry and music [and action] – exactly that point on which he fundamentally differed from Schopenhauer – played an important part in Wagner's intended revisions. Moreover the letter makes it clear that Wagner was already thinking about a revision in 1858. Soon afterwards, on 2 March 1859, he mentions the 'grand results' of his extensive studies of philosophy, results which were 'complementing and correcting Schopenhauer'. For the time being, however, he was not disposed to write down his findings; he preferred, he said, to ruminate on that kind of thing in his head. Wagner went on 'ruminating' for a good ten years before he set down his ideas on paper. When writing to Ludwig II in 1868, he was still talking of the 'very fascinating thoughts' with which he would one day provide a profound insight into music – an insight that so far, philosophy had only come close to attaining through Schopenhauer. And here again he added that he would have to correct Schopenhauer 'on many points' (*BLW* ii, p. 222, n. 2).

Wagner takes up Schopenhauer's aesthetic system at the stage where the philosopher is expounding music's significance as follows:

> If I have been at pains throughout this account of music to make it clear that music expresses in a very universal language the inner essence, the intrinsic nature [*das*

An-sich] of the world ... if moreover, in my opinion and aim, philosophy is nothing else than a complete and accurate repetition and expression of the essence of the world ... then anyone who has been following me will not find it so very paradoxical when I say that, assuming one managed to provide in conceptual terms a wholly accurate, comprehensive and detailed explanation of music, i.e. a detailed recapitulation of what it expresses, this would straight away also be a sufficient recapitulation and explanation of the world in concepts, or the exact equivalent of one, and thus be true philosophy ...   (Translated from Schopenhauer II [1938], p. 312)

Wagner made it his aim to resolve Schopenhauer's (supposed) paradox. For all its profundity, this paradox revealed its author's limited knowledge of music. And the limitations were clearly illustrated by his interpretation of Beethoven – from which Wagner distances himself as much as he does from his own view of thirty years earlier. Schopenhauer saw Beethoven's symphonies in the same terms as Wagner had used to describe 'absolute music' in *A Happy Evening*. But Wagner himself was now far from permitting so restricted a view. Hence Dahlhaus is mistaken in his hypothesis that because of an admiration for Schopenhauer (and in agreement with Liszt's ideas), Wagner returned unconditionally to a concept of music which fitted the framework of 'absolute music'.

Wagner bypasses Schopenhauer's interpretation of the symphony. He combines his solution to the other's paradox with an explanation of Beethoven which is a corrective to Schopenhauer's.

While presenting this hypothetical explanation of music as a paradox, since it cannot really be elucidated with concepts, Schopenhauer nonetheless supplies the uniquely extensive material that might shed further light on the correctness of his deeply pondered explanation. Perhaps the only reason why he did not do so himself was that as a layman, he lacked a sufficient command of music, or familiarity with it; besides which, his knowledge of it could not yet be related firmly enough to an understanding of the very musician whose works had first revealed to the world that deepest of music's secrets. For *Beethoven* himself cannot be fully assessed either until Schopenhauer's deeply pondered paradox has been correctly explained and resolved for the benefit of philosophical knowledge.   (*GS* IX, pp. 66f.)

Wagner's method was to bring together several areas of ideas from Schopenhauer's writings; Schopenhauer was thus being applied to himself. The 'uniquely extensive material' the philosopher had provided was chiefly his theory of dreams. Wagner used this to explain the musician's creativity, taking into account Schopenhauer's hypothesis that there is an outward-looking consciousness and an inward-looking one to match it. The creative will of the musician and the universal Will coincide:

As must now be evident from scrutinizing what we have quoted from Schopenhauer's magnum opus, the musical conception, since it can have nothing in common with the conceiving of an idea ... can only originate in that side of consciousness which Schopenhauer calls inward-looking ... Schopenhauer also helps us to make further progress along these lines with his . . . hypothesis about the physiological phenomenon of clairvoyance and the theory of dreams which he bases on this. For if that phenomenon means that inward-looking consciousness becomes really clairvoyant . . . *sound*, on the other hand, presses forward out of this darkness into really wide-awake apperception, being the direct expression of will.

(*GS* IX, p. 68)

As Wagner envisaged it, the creative musician turns into a sleep-walking clairvoyant, and the 'essence of things' in its most direct manifestation then grows on him as a kind of dream-image. This clairvoyant state is also typical with regard to the adequate reception of music on the listener's part. And one important aspect of Wagner's method is his adoption of Schopenhauer's division of the dreaming faculty into 'direct', 'theorematic' and 'allegorical' dreaming. Theorematic dreaming is, in Wagner's words, 'the dream of the deepest sleep, totally removed from the waking state of cerebral consciousness'. This dreaming comprises the deepest layer of the world's essence as manifested in music. Allegorical dreaming, by contrast, denotes the lighter kind of dream which 'directly precedes waking up', and in a sense it represents the borderland of musical utterance. Wagner associates this distinction between different levels of dreaming with a grading of music's components. There is an internal zone, and there is also an external one to provide a link with the 'visual, graphic world'. Harmony, Wagner maintains, represents the internal side of music, whereas rhythm denotes the periphery and the link with the outside world. He assumes that there are a great many gradations between the two areas. For in striving to communicate the innermost dream-image in an intelligible way, the musician will approach 'the ideas of the waking mind' just as allegorical dreaming does. This brings into play the category of time, within which rhythm develops.

While the *harmony* of tones, which is something that belongs to neither space nor time, continues to be music's most essential element, the creative musician will use the *rhythmic* temporal sequence of his utterances to come to an agreement with the waking world of appearances . . . By organizing his tones *rhythmically*, the musician thus comes into contact with the visual, plastic world . . . Human gesture, which seeks to make itself understood in dance through expressively changing regular movement, appears to be to music what solids are to light. For light could not shine without solids to refract it, and similarly we can say that without rhythm, it would not be possible for us to perceive music. (*GS* IX, p. 76)

How does Beethoven fit into this aesthetic conception? The significance of Beethoven is that he drives forth from music's innermost essence the outer layer in which music as form is condensed:

To have penetrated to the innermost essence of music through these forms [the 'systematic framework' of 'rhythmical periodic construction'] so as to be capable, in turn, of projecting the clairvoyant's innermost light outwards from that angle,

133

and to show us this form again solely in terms of its inner meaning – this was the work of our great *Beethoven*, whom we have therefore to think of as the very epitome of a musician. (*GS* IX, p. 79)

Here Wagner is referring to Beethoven's revival and renewal, with formal modifications, of the calcified structure of the symphony and sonata. Beethoven, he says, fills the calcified 'periods of contrast and return' in the musical framework with 'the essential spirit of music', thereby initiating a basic process of regeneration. This makes him the embodiment of all that music means and embraces. If, however, the essence of music is manifest in the artistic phenomenon of Beethoven, then so too, according to Schopenhauer's precept, is the essence of the world. Thus it was not illogical of Wagner to combine an interpretation which suggested Beethoven's paradigmatic musical qualities with a 'detailed explanation of music' that would help to resolve Schopenhauer's aforesaid paradox.

But what Schopenhauer had in mind was an 'explanation of the world in concepts', based on a detailed account of the essence of music. And Wagner's revision of the Schopenhauerian system in fact nips this in the bud. In revising Schopenhauer with the help of Beethoven, the embodiment of the musical spirit, Wagner was aiming ultimately at an aesthetic justification of the music drama. Wagner perceived in music 'man's *a priori* talent for dramatic design in general', because

it is not just that the movement, shaping and transformation of these [musical] motifs are related by analogy to drama alone; in reality the drama portraying the idea [of the world] can only be understood perfectly clearly through those musical motifs as they move and are shaped and transformed. (*GS* IX, pp. 105f.)

There is an obvious difference between the above and Wagner's earlier view of music. On the other hand it is obvious from the 'details' of his explanation of music that his 'contribution to the philosophy of music' included important elements of his system as stated in *Opera and Drama*.

As in *Opera and Drama*, harmony is the 'most essential' element in music, while rhythm is similarly associated with the 'visual, plastic world', i.e. with physical gestures. But with this grading Beethoven develops the essence of music from 'within', thus laying the basis for drama. This constitutes the crucial difference from *Opera and Drama*, which pointed up the discrepancy between the composer's aims and the powers of 'absolute' music. This difference is a vivid illustration of the change we have mentioned in Wagner's view of music. It also illustrates the part Beethoven played in this. Wagner's notion that the basis of drama has an *a priori* existence in music derives from his interpretation of Beethoven's music.

The starting-point for Wagner's aesthetic exposition of the structure of drama varies accordingly. In the conception of drama he set forth in *Opera and Drama*, 'absolute' music and a dramatic action had to complement one another to produce musical drama (i.e. music drama). Now, however, music and dramatic action are seen as simply different – but at the same time interlocking – products of the same creative impulse. Beethoven and Shakespeare embody these complementary phenomena. Like Beethoven, Shakespeare was bound up with the interior of the consciousness in a creative and visionary way. 'His dramas', Wagner writes, 'seem to be such a direct illustration of the world that the artist's hand in the presentation of the idea is quite imperceptible.' The complex of Shakespeare's characters is paralleled by the complex of Beethoven's motifs; the 'sleepwalking' Beethoven corresponds to Shakespeare, who saw and exorcized spirits.

As soon as we avail ourselves of this analogy with all that it entails, we may describe Beethoven – whom we compared to a sleep-walking clairvoyant – as effectively underlying the Shakespeare who saw spirits: whatever produces Beethoven's melodies also projects the spirit-shapes of Shakespeare; and the two will jointly work their way through to the same essence if we let the musician enter the world of light at the same time as he emerges into the world of sound.   (*GS* IX, pp. 109f.)

By comparison with *Opera and Drama*, the relationship between poet and composer has now been reversed. Speech is no longer the primary, generative element. Rather, the embodiment of music that was Beethoven is seen as a precondition of the poet, as underlying the Shakespeare who saw spirits. (For Wagner, the special thing about the Ninth Symphony was no longer the introduction of words, but of the human voice as such.) The relationship of music to poetry in general is now an 'altogether illusory' one, and the dramatic action is the 'visual counterpart' of the music. In fact, of course, both Wagner's accounts of the relation between words (or dramatic action) and music are extreme theoretical positions that do less than justice to the creative process. Following his statements on the specific correlation between Beethoven and Shakespeare, Wagner writes:

To explain the artistic problem which faces us, we can apply this hypothetical explanation of an otherwise inexplicable physiological process from different angles, in order to achieve the same result. Shakespeare's spirit-shapes would be induced to sound forth through the complete awakening of the inner musical faculty. In other words, Beethoven's motifs would inspire the weakened vision to a clear apprehension of those characters, as embodiments of which they would act out their parts in front of us with our clairvoyant powers.   (*GS* IX, p. 110)

Here Wagner is once again adumbrating the structure of his own creative process. If we look at the earlier document, the 1844 letter to Carl Gaillard, we will find basically the same interrelation between the verbal-cum-mimic-cum dramatic component on the one hand and the musical component on the other. Neither of these always provides the trigger; rather the relation is reversible. This is confirmed by the fact that while Wagner made musical 'jottings' alongside his texts, there are also instances of 'primarily musical invention' (e.g. in *WWV* 443, 551) to which he only gave a dramatic charge or 'specification' at a later date. We must always bear in mind, of course, that even a musical jotting-down without a verbal text may have stemmed from the idea of a dramatic situation. That would illustrate that Wagner was not re-imposing the 'idea of absolute music' on drama with comments like 'the drama is ... projected from this magic lantern [i.e. music]', (to Cosima, 7 March 1873). Rather, what Wagner had said on 16 August 1869 holds true: 'In me the accent lies on the conjunction of poet and musician, as a pure musician I would not be of much significance.'

To be sure, this 'poet' was no longer just a poet with words. Wagner was referring to the musico-*dramatic* poet, who designs every layer of the drama. In his letter to Franz Brendel, he had called gymnastics the 'epitome of all the arts that relate through actual physical representation to the most perfect expression'. Music, by contrast, embraced the arts of poetry and musical composition. Now, however, Wagner's thoughts were on the Beethoven centenary and his revision of Schopenhauer; and as part of a still broader notion of *mousikē*, 'gymnastics' in the context of the 'deeds of music made manifest' was being integrated within the latter framework of ideas.

Here again, Wagner takes his bearings from Beethoven. He goes on to state that the 'most perfect drama' – as initiated by the model of Beethoven's Ninth – can only proceed from a fusion of Beethovenian and Shakespearean drama. As the 'most perfect art form' it will emerge from that 'boundary point ... at which those laws [of the two 'forms of drama'] would be able to come into contact with one another'. There can be no doubt that for Wagner, his own music drama represented this ideal.

(f) The Beethoven essay and Hanslick
The Beethoven centenary essay is not only a revision of Schopenhauer. Although Wagner does not say so directly, it also contains a reply to Eduard Hanslick's *On the Beautiful in Music*, published sixteen years before. So far commentators have completely overlooked this latent anti-Hanslick polemic and the role that Wagner assigns to the concepts of 'the sublime' [*das Erhabene*] and 'inner form'. Understandably, he was not prepared to ignore his critical arch-enemy,[9] who frequently attacked his music; there are several pieces of evidence to support this. In 1869, for instance, Wagner addressed to Marie Muchanoff a preface to the second edition of his *Jewry in Music*, in which he dismissed Hanslick's publication as a one-sided concoction. And around the turn of the year 1870 he wrote a letter to Friedrich Stade containing an appreciation of Stade's treatise *Vom Musikalisch-Schönen* (1869), which was conceived as a counterblast to Hanslick's.

Despite the elevated tone of Wagner's *Beethoven* essay, the anti-Hanslick feeling becomes obvious on closer scrutiny. On the simplest level, certain turns of phrase are already some indication of it. For example, Wagner refers to a prejudice against the 'pathological element' in music which, he asserts, has often led to a wrong aesthetic outlook. This was surely a reference to Hanslick, who had condemned music's 'emotional effect' as an 'intensive influence on the *nervous system*', a 'physically overwhelming' artistic effect, and thus 'pathological'. The fifth chapter of Hanslick's famous work even has the title 'The aesthetic reception of music compared to the pathological'. Wagner also has Hanslick in mind when he comments as follows on the 'systematic framework' of 'rhythmical periodic construction':

The ability merely to play around in these conventional forms with music's enormous powers in order to evade its real effect – the manifestation of the inner essence of everything – as though there was a risk of being swamped by it: this was long considered by the aestheticians to be the true and only desirable product of the cultivation of the art of music. (*GS* IX, p. 79)

The repeated rejection of a mere 'pleasure in beautiful forms' is also clearly aimed at Hanslick. This attitude, Wagner remarks, expects nothing of music beyond 'an effect similar to that which is achieved in the visual arts'. But Wagner was not content with an (implicit) rejection of Hanslick. He developed some counter-ideas that are focused on two thematic areas: 'the sublime' and 'inner form'. Here the 'sublime' is more concerned with the effect of music, and 'inner form' with the artistic shaping process. The 'sublime' is Wagner's reply to Hanslick's concept of the 'beautiful in music':

Music which speaks to us solely by animating for us, as distinctly as it can, the most general concept of inherently mysterious feeling in every imaginable shade can only be judged in essence by the category of the *sublime* . . . Conversely, music would be exhibiting a downright trivial character if it were to dwell colourfully on the effect of its first appearance, thereby continually restricting us to the relations wherein the most outward side of music is turned to the concrete world. (*GS* IX, p. 78)

Here two aesthetic concepts are deliberately being contrasted. This becomes even clearer if we observe how Wagner, having started out from Schopenhauer in his notion of the 'sublime', abruptly departs from the philosopher's argument. Only then is the 'sublime in music' established as a counter-idea to Hanslick's aesthetic precept.

Schopenhauer uses the term 'sublime' solely to describe the element of 'self-elevation' beyond the will's last tie with the object. The purpose is to overcome this lingering resistance and achieve a state of pure contemplation:

What therefore distinguishes the feeling of the sublime from that of the beautiful is this: with the beautiful, pure perception has gained the upper hand without a struggle . . . whereas with the sublime, that state of pure perception is only achieved through a conscious and violent breaking away from the same object's relations to the will, which are recognized as being unpropitious. . .

Schopenhauer also writes:

it was simply a particular modification ... which separated the sublime from the beautiful. Whether, that is to say, a state of pure perception devoid of will ... [was achieved] without resistance ... or whether it was striven for first ... that is the difference between the beautiful and the sublime. Within the object, the two are not fundamentally different...

Thus Schopenhauer distinguishes between pure perception and a vision of the beautiful which is only achieved through an 'elevation via the will'. He only expounds this distinction with regard to those realms of art – and, incidentally, natural beauties – where the 'will', or the 'thing-in-itself', is lit up by (platonic) ideas. Schopenhauer never discusses the sublime in music; only once, in *The World as Will and Representation*, does he refer in general terms to the 'beauty, purity and sublimity' of musical composition. This could be attributed to the thesis that 'sublimity' in music does not need proving inasmuch as music, being a direct objectivation of the will, 'jumps over' the realm of (platonic) ideas. All the other arts inspire the pure perception of ideas 'by portraying individual things (for this is what works of art themselves invariably are)'. Since music, by contrast, transcends ideas, it is quite independent of the world of appearances and ignores it altogether. The act of elevation for the sake of pure contemplation of the idea, and of the beautiful, was irrelevant to music as a non-representational art. On the other hand, to quote Carl Dahlhaus:

The fact that music 'acts directly on the will, that is, a listener's emotions, passions and affections' is more a disgrace than an excellence. Without Schopenhauer's having made this explicit, it is only consistent with his metaphysics.

(Dahlhaus, *Esthetics of Music*, p. 43)

It may be for this reason that in connection with music's 'physical' basis – the relative vibrations of the intervals – Schopenhauer claimed it was necessary to overcome the will's arousal in switches between dissonance and consonance. For this arousal was hindering a 'pure recognition' of music:

Here, then, we see the agitation of the will being carried across to the realm of mere *representation*, which is the sole arena for the achievements of all the fine arts; since these always ask that the will *itself* should remain uninvolved, and that we should always be in the position of purely *perceiving*. Hence the affections of the will itself, namely true pain and true pleasure, must not be evoked but only their substitutes: that which is suited to the *intellect*, as an *image* of the will's satisfaction and ... and *image* of greater or lesser pain. It is only in this way that music will never cause us real affliction and always give us pleasure, even in its painful chords...

Schopenhauer calls for a detachment from a direct influencing of the emotions in the reception of music. This can be set alongside the concept of the 'sublime' in the other arts. If these need to overcome the will which is obstructing pure recognition, music must keep away from the 'affections of the will itself'. It is significant that Wagner does not take this as a starting-point for a more detailed account of the 'sublime' in music. Rather he transfers the concepts of both the beautiful and the sublime to music, taking account of the formal aspects. And the relationship between them is now reversed. For in Wagner's view the act of 'elevation' does not bring about a pure perception of the 'beautiful' but a detachment from it in favour of the 'sublime'. Within the musical field the beautiful and the sublime thereby become a contrasting pair of concepts. Wagner's concept of the sublime is thus opposed to Hanslick's idea of 'the beautiful in music', which now became a byword for superficiality. It never went, according to Wagner, beyond a 'prismatic toying with effects'. The mark of true music, on the other hand, was its progression 'from the effect of a beautiful appearance, which is music's very first effect when it simply comes in, to the revelation of its essential character, through the effect of the sublime' (*GS* IX, p. 78).

Hanslick's *On the Beautiful in Music* was aimed against the aesthetics of feeling. It was thus directed against Wagner, because when he had published *Opera and Drama* three years earlier, he had stressed that music was a language of feelings. Hanslick's polemically sharpened thesis was that music was 'form animated by sounds' [*tönend bewegte Form*]. Wagner now countered this by taking Beethoven as an example and using Schopenhauer to support his argument. He perceived the metaphysically established 'content' of all music as lying in feeling, since 'all human passions and affections' (Schopenhauer's phrase) are contained in the 'will' which music directly reflects.

To be sure, this reply did not cover one of Hanslick's polemical points, and that was the accusation of formlessness. For to dwell on a beauty of form as the 'content and object' of music automatically suggested that music which was chiefly concerned with emotional expression was 'formless'. And it logically followed that in later editions of his work, Hanslick would describe Wagner's 'infinite melody' as 'formlessness elevated to a principle, a narcotic delirium of singing and fiddling, for the cult of which a temple has been specially opened in Bayreuth'.

Wagner did defend himself against the charge of formlessness in his Beethoven centenary essay and, even more clearly, in both *Franz Liszt's Symphonic Poems* and *'Music of the Future'*. This defence was based on the criterion of 'inner form', corresponding to Schopenhauer's view of music as a direct objectivation of the will. It is no contradiction to say that the term 'inner form' does not appear in Wagner's actual writings in this or any other context. Reinhold Schwinger has remarked that although deeply rooted in Western ideas and frequently influencing them, the phrase has seldom been used. Several of Wagner's formulations come very close to the term 'inner form', and the signs are that he was following earlier writers in his conception of it.

In the Beethoven essay Wagner applies the idea of inner form in the following way. Starting with the sonata, he argues, Beethoven filled the mould of sonata form with the actual essence of music. It was a process of regeneration from 'within'. 'Within those forms in which music was only meant to be seen as an agreeable art, he [Beethoven] had to proclaim the message of the innermost vision of the world of sound [*der innersten Tonweltschau*]' (*GS* IX, p. 83). The art of Beethoven represented the German reforming mentality, the 'peculiarity of the German nature'. This, unlike the revolutionary mentality, did not destroy the 'outward form' but was able 'to endow every form with its essence by reshaping it anew from within'. A German obtains 'a wealth of forms unmatched by any other nation ... to communicate his inner essence' (*GS* IX, p. 85). These and similar statements indicate that Wagner was in fact using the idea of inner form. Beethoven's composing – and ultimately Wagner's as well – was determined by the 'inner form', and thus superior to 'outward form'.

Wagner gives a quite particular slant to this statement by describing the reshaping of forms from within as typical of the German attitude, and the destruction of the outward form as typifying the French attitude, as regards both the State and the arts. It is possible that Goethe was the inspiration for this. For in his appendix to the German version of *Du théâtre ou nouvel essay sur l'art dramatique* by Louis Sébastien Mercier (Amsterdam, 1773), Goethe had expounded the need for 'the sense of inner form' against the background of the French drama's formal rigidity. Goethe's influence seems even more probable if we turn to Wagner's *'Music of the Future'*, for there Wagner contrasts the German with the Romance cultivation of form. What he calls the agreeable [*gefällig*] form, by virtue of its nature, to be found in Italy, Spain and France is compared with the form of Goethe and Schiller, to which he attributes unique historical value as an 'ideal, purely human' art form. And it should be noted that in the passage which follows, Wagner is alluding chiefly to the theoretical writings on art of Goethe and Schiller.

The distinctive significance of Goethe and Schiller, Germany's two greatest poets, was that, as never before in the history of art, they concerned themselves for the first time with the problem of an ideal, purely human art form in its most comprehensive sense – indeed one might almost say that the quest for such an ideal art form was also the main ingredient of their works. Although they chafed against the tyranny of the form which among the Latin nations had the authority of law, they evaluated it objectively, taking cognizance both of its virtues and its defects; from this standpoint they then ... arrived at a full comprehension of the antique form. This led to the conception of an ideal, purely human art form, liberated from narrow national conventions and yet at the same time capable of developing and transforming those very conventions into purely human, eternally valid laws.

(*TWE*, p. 17, rev. Kropfinger)

The 'purely human' quality mentioned in the above passage does in fact fulfil the criteria of 'inner form'. This becomes clear if we bear in mind that the epithet 'purely human' also applies to the subsoil of myth that underlies Wagner's music drama, and that in '*Music of the Future*', form based on the music drama's 'purely human content' is plainly being described in terms of 'inner form'. Thus in connection with the realization of a subject taken from myth, or 'saga', Wagner speaks of a 'manifestation of the inner motives of the action . . . these inner psychic motives' (*GS* vi, p. 121). And he was surely referring to 'inner form' as a prerequisite of the 'outward form' when he wrote of *Tristan*: 'Completely confident, I immersed myself in the depths of the psyche and from this innermost centre of the world boldly constructed an external form' (*TWE*, p. 35).

Wagner was almost certainly using the notion of 'inner form' to defend himself against Hanslick's accusation of formlessness. He interprets the 'beautiful in music' as the external form. And Hanslick's precept of 'form animated by sounds' is countered with the thesis that if it is to be true to music's essence, formal design must start with the 'inner form' in order to achieve the 'outward form'. Regarding Hanslick as the advocate of mere 'outward form', Wagner banishes him to the mere sidelines of music and brands him as a formalist.

Wagner's concept of inner form helped to justify not only the music drama but also the symphonic poems of Liszt. Liszt's conquest of formal schematicism in his tone poems was based on 'inner form'. In every case, according to Wagner, the 'novel form' grew out of the object, from the 'poetic motif' (see *GS* v, p. 191).

Although Wagner regarded both music drama and the symphonic poem as deriving from an 'inner form', he was not prepared to set them on a par with one another. Liszt's socially motivated aim of putting literary masterpieces into music – see Dahlhaus's *Esthetics of Music*, p. 61 – was alien to Wagner. All the same he could see that the other composer was taking a road which he himself had once rejected as impossible. Probably it was also Liszt who made the ageing Wagner think of writing symphonies again: instrumental music to match his substantially altered, integral view of his art.

Beethoven exegesis and the theory of the music drama

In certain of his earlier writings, Wagner is obviously paving the way for later, more strongly focused ideas. But equally obviously, *Opera and Drama* marks the beginning of his theory of the music drama. It is, moreover, Wagner's most comprehensive work on the subject. Here he was palpably trying to cover and investigate it systematically, albeit at the expense of clarity. Thus there is some justification for regarding this treatise as the real theoretical heart of Wagner's aesthetics. Wagner himself encouraged this view. Ten years afterwards he wrote in *'Music of the Future'*:

In the third part of the work [meaning *Opera and Drama*] I finished by attempting to describe in more detail the technical laws governing this innermost fusion of music with poetry within the drama. (*TWE*, amended, p. 29)

It has rightly been said that in *'Music of the Future'* Wagner had moved away from his theoretical standpoint in *Opera and Drama*, and that this affected his view of the union of the arts in music drama. But *Opera and Drama* does not concentrate on the relation between music and poetry as exclusively as is generally supposed. The dramatic action is in fact dealt with at length, and the first appearance, the exposition, of the 'leitmotifs' is by no means reserved in theory for the 'verse melody'. Finscher has claimed that the dramatic function of the leitmotifs was 'largely disconti- nued' after *Rheingold* and *Walküre*, i.e. in *Tristan* and especially in *Meister- singer*. To this we would reply that the fact that Wagner wrote an introduction [*Einleitung*], or 'prelude' [*Vorspiel*], to *Tristan* and *Meistersinger* does not in itself rule out the leitmotivic function. For it is precisely the 'presentiment' [*Ahnung*] which is associated with the prelude in *Opera and Drama* that is an integral part of the functioning leitmotivic system. Only the nature of the function had changed, inasmuch as this changed from one work to the next.

To some extent Wagner's response to Beethoven was involved in this change. As the forerunner of 'infinite melody', Beethoven was already being examined far more from the viewpoint of form and compositional technique in *'Music of the Future'* than in *Opera and Drama*. But in the Beethoven centenary essay and the 1871 lecture *On The Destiny of Opera*, Wagner bases his theory of music drama on the idea that it was with Beethoven that music first fulfilled itself as the bedrock of drama. The viewpoint and overall conception within Wagner's broader definition of music (the Ancient Greek *mousikē*, uniting verse, song, instrumental accompaniments and dancing) had shifted in music's favour. Nonetheless some of the essential aims expounded in *Opera and Drama* still applied. On the one hand instrumental music needed elucidating; on the other, the emotional values of the poetry, the dramatic action were to be delegated to music. The function of Beethoven's 'powers of speech' [*Sprachvermögen*] remained in force within the framework of a 'symbiosis of the arts'.

Despite the aforesaid changes it will be useful to look at the way Wagner included Beethoven in his plan of the music drama, particularly with regard to *Opera and Drama*. For here he first states in aesthetic terms his belief that drama has 'resolved' [*aufgehoben*] (instrumental) music. We shall now discuss the ideas in the treatise that matter most in this context.

'Verse melody'; 'orchestral melody'; the orchestra's 'powers of speech'

In his theory of the poetic and compositional process, Wagner was aiming at a seamless union of the linguistic and musical elements. 'Verse melody' performs the function of a contact part, as it were: it is 'the binding and mediating link between verbal and musical language' (*GS* IV, p. 171). And this is the case in a twofold sense. With *Stabreim* as the basis, the conjunction of music and poetry will be already achieved in the verse melody. 'But 'verse melody' is also the means whereby speech (poetry), gesture, dramatic action and the orchestra (music) are connected up. In the first instance we can speak of a fusion of the different elements, whereas in the second it is a matter of how they correspond. It is the second, mediating function of 'verse melody' which bears upon the association between Wagner as a dramatist and the 'tone-poet' in Beethoven.

A central theoretical requirement in *Opera and Drama* is the conversion of intellect into feeling. This is expressed both in Wagner's *Stabreim* theory and in his statements on the leitmotivic network of the 'musical components'. The relation between 'inside' and 'outside' is an important part of this, and Wagner resorts to an eye/ear metaphor to describe it. The root syllables of *Stabreim* words have consonants (= the eyes of hearing) on the outside, and vowels (= the ears of hearing) on the inside. The composer transfers the potential vowel sound in the music to the actual vowel sound in the 'verse melody'. *Stabreim* becomes the hinge between speech and music. In this way the verse melody acquires the emotional qualities of the *Stabreim*'s root words, but not what is inexpressible in words, namely the actual emotional content of the 'original communication in speech'. Now, however, this emotional element which words cannot express is added to the verse melody twice over: firstly through the visual gesture accompanying the song, and then through the aural motifs of the orchestral melody, which are the products of the orchestra's powers of speech. Thus the eye/ear metaphor establishes a direct connection between Wagner's *Stabreim* technique, his verse melody (or poetico-musical period) and the motifs in the orchestral melody that correspond to the verse melody and visual gestures.

The gestural content which is inexpressible in the auditory language of words can, however, be conveyed to our ears by that orchestral speech which is wholly detached from the aforesaid verbal speech, just as gesture itself displays the inexpressible to our sight. (*GS* IV, pp. 175f.)

The above passage indicates the possibility of introducing 'leitmotifs' not only in the form of 'verse melody', as the theory requires, but also as orchestral motifs. 'Orchestral melody' as it has just been described, wholly detached from verbal poetry, corresponds to gesture and to nothing else. This admits of the exposition of motifs which are bound up solely with gestures. And it is only a short step from here to the successive deployment of verse melody, gesture and orchestra, which originally functioned simultaneously. Thus Wagner does not state or even suggest the Hunding motif in association with Sieglinde's words 'Diess Haus und diess Weib sind Hundings Eigen' (*Walküre*, I: 1). Rather, it occurs at the moment when the returning Hunding is stabling his horses. His motif effectively complements Sieglinde's physical movement as she starts with alarm and silently listens. So Wagner had already established in theory that 'the exposition of a leitmotif as "verse melody" . . . is the exception and not the rule in the *Ring*" (Dahlhaus).

One aspect of the mediating role of 'verse melody' is the presentation of thoughts in music. This involves a special dramaturgical tool, so to speak, whereby the individual elements in the drama – the emotions, words, gestures and actions of the characters – are related to one another and interwoven in both recollection and anticipation. On this level the judicious poet-cum-composer intervenes in the drama as a kind of higher-ranking actor. Another important thing about 'thoughts' is that they are to be communicated in the form of feelings and not as a reflective element. Hence Wagner defines a thought as a sensation that is stored in the memory [*Gedenken*] rather than actually present. It is, then, a reminiscence which the music needs to reawaken in the form of a feeling, needs to 'actualize'.

The poet's verse melody will now, before our very eyes in a way, realize the thought – i.e. a feeling which is not a present one but is being depicted from memory – a present, really perceptible sensation. It contains in its pure word-poetry the feeling which is being portrayed from memory, being thought and described and not actually present, yet a *determining* sensation... (*GS* IV, p. 183)

Here again, however, the 'speech of the orchestra' is needed to support or complement the 'verse melody'. This is when 'the present verse melody, as the declaration of a mixed and not yet wholly unified feeling, cannot and will not' express the thought, but it is even less possible for a gesture to convey this thought visually.

In his conception of music drama, Wagner attached great importance to the orchestral motifs. This is closely connected with his interpretation of Beethoven and the way Wagner derived the symphony from the dance. The graphic motif, he believed, sprang from Beethoven's 'poetic intention', and the musical shapes were dance gestures converted into rhythm and sonority. The orchestra's 'heightened powers of speech' resulting from this could be justified in the music drama 'by the word and the word-conditioned gesture' (*GS* IV, p. 177). Beethoven had developed an 'immense capacity' for melodic expression; although this was being merged with drama, music was now acquiring the 'intelligibility' it had previously lacked.

Admittedly there is an implicit paradox in Wagner's application of

Beethoven's orchestral language to drama. On the one hand he was very keen to bring to the drama the orchestra's 'powers of speech' as extended by Beethoven, but on the other hand he was equally set on purging this language of some of the excesses that Beethoven had actively cultivated. This can be gleaned from *Opera and Drama*:

> We have seen these powers of speech develop in Beethoven's symphonies to a point at which they felt impelled to express even what they are by nature unable to express. In the verbal verse melody, we have supplied orchestral language with precisely what it was unable to express, and as the carrier of this kindred melody it has been allowed to work – in complete contentment – by expressing only what it is, by nature, uniquely able to express. This achieved, these orchestral powers of speech must clearly be described as the capacity for proclaiming the *inexpressible*.
>
> (*GS* IV, p. 173)

If we are to take Wagner literally, the aforesaid 'powers of speech' fall into two different categories. One is the Beethovenian type based on a consciously intended transcending of limits; the other is a variant which has been completely 'pacified' by being absorbed within drama. Although wanting to bring out Beethoven's 'powers of speech', Wagner excludes the actual preconditions of these powers, and this amounts to an aesthetic reductionism. In Wagner's theory the true state of affairs is distorted by his account of the orchestra's function, which is too concerned with the relationship to the 'verse melody'. Wagner in fact presented the majority of his 'leitmotifs' as 'orchestral melody' and not directly as 'verse melody', which indicates that there can be no question of 'pacifying' the music. There is a notable plasticity about the orchestrally deployed, poetically inspired motifs of music drama. It shows how far away Beethoven really was from the 'poetic object' which Wagner imputes to him, and which Wagner himself tried to achieve by dint of the 'poetic intention'. Adorno has written of this difference between the thematic–motivic shapes of Beethoven and Wagner. He aptly if exaggeratedly sums up the one type as the elaborate empty 'idea' (*Einfall*), the other in the phrase 'vehement grandeur' (*pathetische Gebärde*). And this is the language of Wagner the musical dramatist – not of an ambitious instrumental composer lurking in the background to his own artistic career, however well disguised.

The 'actualization' of a 'thought' as an emotional quality and the elucidation of the 'language of instrumental sound', with its expressive vagueness, were simply two aspects of the same thing. Every motif bound up with the musico-dramatic context functioned as a 'melodic moment' retrieving thoughts from the past, 'resolved' into emotional values. As such, it constituted one joint in a motivic structure covering the whole drama. Wagner sought to make not only the individual musical elements plain, but also the musical structure. This was to be fully squared with the 'poetic intention', while the receptive listener for his part would be fully able to follow it – a structure calculated to silence the question, 'Sonate, que me veux-tu?'

To accomplish this, Wagner evolved his own particular system. It was to bring together those emotional qualities which are combined in the musical motif as 'presentiment' (*Ahnung*), 'actualization' (*Vergegenwärtigung*) and 'reminiscence' (*Erinnerung*). These three different human attitudes within the dimension of time are interlocked in such a way that in the course of the drama, elements of both the past and the future will, at given points, be lit up within present events. Thus, as Nicolai Hartmann has outlined in his *Philosophie der Natur*, synchronic and diachronic features interact.

At first glance there is a contradiction here. For, as Hartmann observes, it is illogical to expect of different moments in time that they should exist together, i.e. simultaneously. But we can resolve this contradiction by taking into account that 'the categorial structure of time consciousness' is based on 'the overlaying of two kinds of time, namely real time and ideal time [*Anschauungszeit*]'. Real time ties us to a particular point in time which, while part of a succession, excludes any possibility of our experiencing this in 'the present'. But ideal time, not being tied to the present, leaves us free to look into the past or future. This depends on the 'extended present' of ideal time, since our apprehension is actually in the nature of a progression.

This very fact enables us to grasp the difference between 'pure' music and 'music drama'. With the latter, the listener takes his bearings from a greater variety of points within the 'extended present'. Because several time-layers correspond, these points are 'clearer' and reach beyond the present in a more exact way. Diachronic and synchronic features are linked to the combination of 'verse melody', 'orchestral melody', gesture and dramatic action, along with the stage and lighting design.

The unity of presentiment, actualization and reminiscence – being closely connected with the relation between verse melody and orchestral melody – has, however, been questioned. Dahlhaus maintains that because Wagner presents his motifs largely in the form of 'orchestral melody', the 'verse melody' becomes secondary. But the composer envisaged a much more flexible, adaptable design than might be supposed from the exaggerated way he stressed the complementary roles of poetry and music. Granted: in connection with the verse melody's mediating function, his theory will be found to include the necessity of a purely orchestral deployment. But then this instrumental motif developed with the actor's gesture will also be found to fit into the referential scheme of presentiment, actualization and reminiscence.

The life-giving centre of the dramatic expression is the performer's *verse melody*: to this is related, as a *presentiment*, the preliminary absolute orchestral melody; from it is derived, as a *reminiscence*, the 'thought' of the orchestral motif. Presentiment is like a spreading area of light which, upon striking an object, turns the colour that is peculiar to that object and conditioned by it into a manifest truth; reminiscence is like the actual colour thus achieved, just as a painter will take it from the object with a view to transferring it to related objects. The visually meaningful, ever present appearance and movement of the person declaiming the verse melody, namely the actor, is the dramatic gesture; this gesture is made clear in an audible way through the orchestra, itself completing its earliest and most crucial function as harmonic bearer of the verse melody. – Thus the *orchestra* has a continuous share, and one which has a clarifying effect all round, in the overall expression of everything the actor is imparting to both the ear and the eye: it is the highly active womb of music, and from it grows the uniting bond of expression. (*GS* IV, p. 190)

Wagner's 'presentiment' [*Ahnung*] has different nuances of meaning. It may arise because in the light of the momentary dramatic situation, an actualized reminiscence is at the same time creating an expectation of something. (See *Oper und Drama* [1984], pp. 383f.) Wagner used the end of Act II of *Lohengrin* to illustrate this in his letter to Liszt of 8 September 1850 and in *Opera and Drama*. But 'presentiment' also embraces the 'vague sense of anticipation' with which the poet–composer makes ready for the appearance of a natural setting and/or human character in the first place, before proceeding to the 'verse melody'.

Presentiment is the declaration of a feeling that is unstated because in terms of our verbal speech it is still inexpressible. An inexpressible feeling is one that is not yet defined, and a feeling will be undefined if it is not yet defined by the object which corresponds to it ... The poet has to awaken such a mood of anticipation in us, in order for *its longing to give us the necessary share of our own in creating the work of art.* (*GS* IV, pp. 186f.)

To awaken this presentiment [*Ahnung*] is the central function of the prelude or introduction. It ties in with the exposition of orchestral motifs which will play an important part in the further course of the drama. The 'poetic intention', Wagner states, relating to a particular phenomenon to be realized,

[is able] to gather the sensual elements in the preparatory piece of music from this phenomenon in advance, thereby obtaining so complete a correspondence that when it is finally presented, it will live up to the expectations that the music which anticipated it aroused in us. (*GS* IV, p. 189)

The above principle is put fully into practice in *Tristan*. The first four motifs in the 'introduction' form a thematic complex attuning the listener's presentiments to that which will follow. It reappears several times in the course of the first act, and also later on, thereby illustrating the 'present-iment' in line with the 'poetic intention' and giving it a fresh actuality each time to further the dramatic development. As the drama develops, the initial 'vague' sense of anticipation becomes more definite, more clearly focused, for a reminiscence is now becoming a presentiment. This combin-ation of the two is the second meaning of *Ahnung*. And it indicates the absurdity of always referring to the Wagnerian 'leitmotif' as simply a motif of reminiscence (see Dahlhaus, *NGW*, p. 152).

At this stage, however, we also need to clarify the meaning of the term 'reminiscence' [*Erinnerung*] – particularly in the sense used by Wagner to define the word 'thought'. In that context 'reminiscence' would mean more than simply the 'actualization' of something that has 'just been *thought* by the performer' within the dramatic action. It leads to a further, extended area of meaning beyond the confines of the drama. For here we have a reminiscence from the distant, mythical past, only to be revived by means of the presentiment aroused by the prelude. Once again the first act of *Tristan* provides an example. Isolde's words 'Mir verloren, mir erkoren' at the beginning of Scene 2 plumb the dramatic significance of the Yearning motif for the first time. They also summon up the whole spiritual dimension of a legendary past already intimated musically in the prelude, and hence the mythical foundations of the conflict that will develop in the course of the drama.

We have seen that the dramatic gesture and orchestral motif go together, and also that 'presentiment' and 'reminiscence' perform a second function. In view of this it is fair to assume that ultimately, 'verse melody' was only one element in the overall musico-dramatic conception – not that central integrating factor which Wagner, to align it with his words-and-notes doctrine, sometimes presents it as. In the notes on performance he included in *Opera and Drama*, he appreciably modified this doctrine. The 'presentiment' needs to be illustrated step by step, in an organic way, enabling the dramatic setting and the human presence to correspond to the 'verse melody'.

True, 'verse melody' has the final say in the illustrative process because of the thought-element which is both contained by and tied to the verbal poetry. But the way the musical motifs are coloured in line with the 'poetic intention' does not have to be directly dependent on it. In many respects this takes place indirectly in correlation to the other elements in the drama. One example of this is the statement of the Rheingold motif in the *Ring*. There are no less than thirty-three bars between the first visual sign of the gold (as noted in a stage direction) and the point where its significance is conclusively established by the Rhinemaidens ('Rheingold! Rheingold!'). During this passage there is a mounting expectancy, and finally a feeling of certainty. First we have the awakening of a presentiment, the combination of the glinting gold and the preparatory fourth interval (oboe, cor anglais, bar 511) as well as rhythmic pointers (semiquaver upbeat, bass trumpet in E flat, bars 510, 512), followed by the Rheingold motif's appearance on the horns. Immediately afterwards, Woglinde's 'verse melody' comments on this ('Lugt Schwestern! Die Weckerin lacht in den Grund!'), in obvious imitation of the Rheingold motif (sequence of a fourth and third). Wellgunde and Flosshilde in their turn back up Woglinde's song, but all this is vaguely descriptive rather than unequivocal, thus increasing the expectancy. Only when they sing 'Rheingold! Rheingold!' do we hear the word that really clarifies the point and resolves it. For that reason it is doubtful whether we can pin down the statement of the Rheingold motif to the figure on the horns. Rather than appearing at a single point, it occurs in the course of a development in which the dramatic action, stage picture, music and language are jointly involved.

The Rheingold motif, then, is made up of a whole set of components, and the content of the phrase is only discovered in retrospect. There is a steady progression from the awakening of *Ahnung* to the final identification of the feeling by way of the action and verse melody. Evidently Wagner saw in this a basic formal unit upon which the structure of the whole drama is built. In *Opera and Drama* he outlines a dramatic cell of this kind and goes on to say:

A situation proceeding from this basis and growing to such a pitch inherently forms what is manifestly a separate link in the drama, which in its form and content is made up of a chain of such organic links. These must condition, complement and support one another like the organic limbs of a human body, which will be complete and alive when it has all the limbs that go to make it up through the way they condition and complement one another – not a link too few, and not a link too many.   (*GS* IV, p. 196)

From the viewpoint of form, the above account of the 'dramatic situation' gives a far better picture of what is actually going on in music drama than we get from the 'poetico-musical period'. Although the latter is an important formal unit, it is only a structural unit of 'verse melody'. And this in its turn constitutes the referential framework of the 'dramatic situation' along with 'orchestral melody' and the dramatic action (gesture, etc.). The drama as Wagner conceived it was really built on a motivic framework spread over the 'poetico-musical period' and rooted in the interaction of all the various representational levels.

Myth and music: structural aspects

Myth is the foundation of music drama as Wagner outlined it in *Opera and Drama*. And he regarded the 'purely human' as being the core both of the mythical and of the 'poetic object' in the music of Beethoven. Can it be that this will provide us with additional ways of examining Wagner's response to Beethoven?

One starting-point for an answer is stucturalism. In *Le cru et le cuit*, Lévi-Strauss has called Wagner the undeniable father 'de l'analyse structurale des mythes (et même des contes, e.g. les Maîtres)' – an analysis to be carried out with the help of music. Myth and music come together, for Lévi-Strauss, in a meshing of the synchronic and diachronic elements and by dint of the fact that both are 'languages' which go beyond spoken language, each in its own particular way. In an orchestral score, the permeation of the synchronic and the diachronic is represented by the association of a horizontal (diachronic) axis with a vertical, harmonic (synchronic) axis.

But this will seem an unsatisfactory approach precisely when we try to find a structural perspective that covers both myth and music in the drama of Wagner. For if we apply Lévi-Strauss's structural definition to the music drama, it will be a case not simply of establishing relations but of identifying the structural model which those relations produce. Applied to Wagner's dramatic structures, this means we have not only to establish the motivic relations but also to discover their formula, the structural model.

Lévi-Strauss's observations with regard to the synchronic–diachronic complex in myth are of relevance here. Myth, he says, invariably relates to past events, as is illustrated by phrases like 'before the world was created' and 'a long time ago'. These reflect a temporal distance, an historical and therefore diachronic element, but what is peculiar to myth is that it also transcends time, i.e. it is a-historical and therefore synchronic as well; it forms a 'permanent structure'. This, says Lévi-Strauss, relates to the past, present and future simultaneously.

Wagner comes remarkably close to this view of the nature of myth. Let us recall something he described a number of times: the step from the historical subject to the mythical 'object'. Here he was passing from an object bound up with time to one that transcended it, from the outward, adventitious circumstances and attendant features of human actions and factions to their essential inner motives. In *Opera and Drama* he states:

The unique thing about myth is that it is true at all times and its content, being very tightly compressed, is inexhaustible for all eras. The poet's task was simply to interpret it.　　　　　　　　　　　(*GS* IV, p. 64; see also VI, p. 267)

Wagner does in fact see myth as combining a synchronic with a diachronic element. In saying that myth is true at all times, he is agreeing that it forms a 'permanent structure'. Conversely, the reference to the poet's interpretation indicates the historical dimension. Myth can only be realized within a temporal framework.

It might be inferred from its supra-temporal character that the 'purely human' was the primary ground of human existence and the essence of man, a ground set free from history. This was the view of Schelling, for instance. Schelling states that it is not things at all with which man deals in the process of myth, but powers welling up within his own consciousness. But although the 'purely human' thus guarantees the supra-temporal, permanent character of myth, it still unfolds within time in the drama. Despite the fact that the 'purely human' transcends time and is permanent, it should not be regarded as something petrified (see Dahlhaus, *NGW*, p. 75). Rather, there is in its stability a store of opportunities for development, and these have to be brought to life in musico-dramatic terms.

What is the significance of the two temporal co-ordinates for the interpretation, i.e. the refashioning, of the original mythic material? The answer to this yields the true structural model. It is the scheme comprising 'presentiment', 'actualization' and 'reminiscence'. For in interpreting the original mythic material which is 'true at all times', the dramatist does not simply recount something which is far off in time. Rather he is actualizing something from the past; in other words, 'actualization' and 'reminiscence' start to interact. It is, however, 'presentiment' that guides the progressive re-creation of the material.

Here we can speak of the application of a more highly placed structure to the dramatic action itself. The two structural levels then merge: the poet's 'actualizing' reminiscence merges with that of his dramatic characters, while mythic time is projected into the real time of the drama. This process is suggested in *My Life*. Wagner was discussing *Die Sieger*, a drama he was planning in 1856 but never carried out:

Apart from the beauty and profound significance of the simple tale, I was influenced to choose it as much by its peculiar aptness for the musical procedures that I have since developed. To the mind of the Buddha, the previous lives in former incarnations of every being appearing before him stand revealed as clearly as the present. The simple story owed its significance to the way that the past life of the suffering principal characters was entwined in the new phase of their lives as being still present time. I perceived at once how the musical remembrance of this dual life, keeping the past constantly present in the hearing, might be represented perfectly to the emotional receptivities, and this decided me to keep the prospect of working out this task before me as a labour of especial love.   (*ML*, pp. 528–9)

The 'reminiscence' stretching back beyond the limits of the actual plot recalls the previous history of the main characters and hence of the action. In every instance the characters in the drama will have their own legend, from which the action will grow.

As *Tristan* illustrates, the prelude mediates between the antiquity of myth and the dramatic present. The prelude itself stands for 'presentiment', 'actualization' and 'reminiscence': the presentiment leading into the drama is based on an actualizing reminiscence of the mythic material. Thus the presentiment of the prelude also represents an account of the previous history. First apprehended in the form of a vague feeling, it will be clarified in the drama through reminiscence, which is an actualization of 'what had happened previously'.

We can go further than Lévi-Strauss and say that Wagner analysed the structure of myth, but not just because his cultivation of it combined a diachronic and a synchronic element. More than that, he was organizing the dramatic structure in accordance with the system of presentiment, actualization and reminiscence.

There is confirmation from various quarters that this is nothing short of a structural model. Ernst Cassirer points out – and psychological research backs him up in this – that the mind perceives both 'past' and 'future' in an 'actualization'. This intermingling of the temporal modes also influenced the writer Novalis in a quite extraordinary manner, and he may have been one model for Wagner.

A particularly graphic representation of the model of interlocking times is to be found in the 'Allegory of Time'. Since Macrobius, writers from Petrarch and Giordano Bruno to Cesare Ripa have seen it as an extensive transposition into visual terms of the idea of the structural interlocking of past, present and future. Visually the allegory is presented as a figure comprising three animal's heads (wolf, lion and dog), or the heads of three men of various ages. Two of these are shown in profile, facing right or left, while the third is seen full face. This allegory represents not only Time but also Prudence. One of Titian's late works combines animal shapes and a group of human heads in a pyramid-like arrangement under the heading 'Ex praeterito praesens prudenter agit ni futura actione deturpet'. In *Meaning in the Visual Arts* (p. 149), Erwin Panofsky says of this 'Allegory of Prudence':

> The elements of this inscription are so arranged as to facilitate the interpretation of the parts as well as the whole. The words *praeterito, praesens* and *futura* serve as labels, so to speak, for the three human faces in the upper zone, viz., the profile of a very old man turned to the left, the full-face portrait of a middle-aged man in the centre, and the profile of a beardless youth turned to the right; whereas the clause *praesens prudenter agit* gives the impression of summarizing the total content after the fashion of a 'headline'. We are given to understand, then, that the three faces, in addition to typifying three stages of human life (youth, maturity and old age), are meant to symbolize the three modes or forms of time in general: past, present and future. And we are further asked to connect these three modes or forms of time with the idea of prudence or, more specifically, with the three psychological faculties in the combined exercise of which this virtue consists: memory, which remembers, and learns from, the past; intelligence, which judges of, and acts in, the present; and foresight, which anticipates, and provides for or against, the future.

Wagner's categories of presentiment, actualization and reminiscence are variants of the 'psychological faculties' – 'memory', probing and active 'intelligence', and 'foresight'. 'Prudence', however, is the product of a combination of all three. Possibly under Novalis's influence, Wagner was employing categories of time-consciousness that permeate the structure of myth. These corresponded on the deepest level to his own consciousness of the future, succoured by the constant critical actualization of art from the past.

By using the structure of myth as a basis for dramatic construction, Wagner was of course introducing a structural element characteristic of music itself into dramatic design. It is precisely in music that the anticipation of things to come and the recollection of past events – Husserl's terms for these are protention and retention – are a characteristic form-giving element. Active listening involves a simultaneous vision of the past and future at given points during the piece of music. By the same token, the opening conveys an expectation of things to come, and the conclusion draws past events into an 'extended present'. But for Wagner these elements lacked the clarity, the explicitness of a perceptibly developing and constantly actualizing train of events. Formally and aesthetically, there is a distinction between the 'structuralistic' component in Wagner's drama – the interlocking of presentiment, actualization and reminiscence – and this combination of the three forms of time in the sonata, which is both shadowy and tied to a frame. Once released from the abstract framework connecting them and made to tie in with poetico-scenic events, themes and motifs acquire a meaning we can follow. What will be banished along with the abstract scheme is, to put it crudely, the regimentation of the musical events, the limitation on the form. The reprise in particular will also go because each configuration, being open to both the past and the future, now points beyond itself and the present moment. Thus the association of myth and music signifies an 'unleashing' of that structural component which in sonata writing is tied to the formal scheme.

Aesthetically, however, the other side of the coin to this release is a new motivation for the formal design. For Wagner, it was the course of events governed by the pre-established outline which determined the matter of 'Why?' But this question became redundant in the drama, because the motivic configuration was linked to the dramatic context by means of presentiment, actualization and reminiscence. Charged with meaning by the theatrical and verbal context, the musical motifs grew intelligible. As his definition of the 'poetic object' in Beethoven's music indicated, Wagner acknowledged the 'purely human' as the basis of both the symphony and the 'drama of the future'. But he outstripped symphonic structure with the structural model of presentiment, actualization and reminiscence, on the lines of the 'Allegory of Prudence'.

The Wagner we are looking at in this 'Allegory' is *not* a frustrated or secret instrumental composer. He is master of the stage setting and is turning it into a reality. And this embraces much more than just the theatrical setting Wagner organized in terms of music drama – it is also the setting for the ruling artistic message. It extends to the audience that is being (or is conceived as being) guided by the leitmotivic structure, i.e. the '*vis-à-vis*' whom Wagner is directly addressing and leading.

Wagner used the phenomenology of the idea of time, depending on the model of the three modes of time called past, present and future, not only as a way of designing his artistic effect and reception, but also as a framework within which to co-ordinate and portray his own experience and biography, as well as for his view of mankind in general.

Certainly Wagner's visual ideas, his ideas about stage design, were not very advanced. But far more important is the structural conception whereby he could integrate every element of drama, including the scenic elements. It positively invites us to tackle innovatory stagings. For the leitmotivic network, that system of 'infinite' reciprocity, admits of a long-term effect of any initiative, however isolated the changes it makes. We must remember, too, that every performance is an appeal to the spectator's imagination, and that by virtue of his knowledge of the music drama, he should be capable of rising to the challenge.

5

WAGNER'S THEORY AND CONSTRUCTION OF MUSIC DRAMA

The theory

Opposed critical viewpoints

One of the particular difficulties of studying the arts is that of tracing an artist's ideas in his works. We must first have a clear picture not only of the theory but also of the relationship between theory and practice. It was basically for want of this that inapposite judgments were passed on Wagner's works right from the beginning. At the time of his Zurich writings on artistic questions, critical discussion was already being determined by the mistaken idea that in *Opera and Drama*, Wagner wanted to sum up in theoretical terms what he had previously achieved as a composer–dramatist in *Tannhäuser* and *Lohengrin*. In actual fact, *Opera and Drama* was influenced by the works Wagner had in view as much as by his past projects. (To his credit, Raff observed in 1854 that the Dresden works could not be judged by the standards of *Opera and Drama*.) In trying to map out in his head the new works he vaguely envisaged, the composer would draw on the experience of previous works and at the same time distance himself from them. It follows from this that as a creative artist, Wagner did not, indeed could not, adhere rigidly to his theoretical precepts – and that goes not only for *Opera and Drama*. But the compositional statement is often hard to fathom from an aesthetic viewpoint; this is probably the biggest methodical problem. So we need to make aesthetic statements susceptible of analysis and reduce them to a nucleus that bears on investigations into the composer's techniques and forms. Recently Voss has come up with the reservation that Wagner's theory involved an element of make-believe. The superseding of the symphony by the drama was, he claims, an intention far more than a fact. But in the guise of a musical fact, it eventually became part of the Bayreuth ideology.

The way Wagner invoked Beethoven as a starting-point and jumping-off point is especially bound up with these problems. This is reflected in the diametrically opposed critical views which already became apparent at an early stage, particularly after the publication of *'Music of the Future'*. Here Wagner expressed his indebtedness to Beethoven from a formal and technical angle more emphatically than he had in *Opera and Drama*. In so doing, he led people to measure him by that composer. In 1861 Ludwig Bischoff wrote in the *Niederrheinische Musik-Zeitung*:

In his projected application of the Beethovenian symphony to the drama, Wagner has left out just one small factor which does seem fairly essential. We refer to Beethoven's genius – combined with his supreme musical ability – for creating out of one or two musical motifs a piece of music that can indeed be described as 'a single coherent melody'. As long as the poet–musician fails to show us Beethoven's brilliant inventiveness – and not just that, but also *the brilliant work* that went with his *musically active* creativeness –, this writer's rhetoric and the impudent way he assumes the mystical aura of a priest of the Beethovenian symphony-drama will only ever convince us of his arrogant *desire*, not of his genuine *ability*. We grant the validity of Wagner's observations on the Beethovenian symphony, but they implicitly acknowledge a thematic working-out which is not routinely contrapuntal but brilliantly handled, and without which Beethoven's approach would not have been possible. And where can we find the slightest trace of this in anything that Wagner has written? ([1861], p. 11)

Possibly Bischoff was referring not only to '*Music of the Future*' but also, by implication, to a letter from Hans von Bülow which had been leaked to the press. Bülow had written it to Franz Brendel in 1859. In expressing his enthusiasm for *Tristan*, he had particularly remarked on the analogy with Beethoven's late quartets and on Wagner's 'knowledge of pure music':

This is directly connected with late Beethoven – it no longer compares with Weber or Gluck. 'Tristan' relates to 'Lohengrin' as 'Fidelio' is related to the 'Seraglio', or as the C sharp minor Quartet relates to the first of Beethoven's opus 18, in F. I confess it threw me into a perpetual state of surprise and delight. Any musician who won't believe that this is an advance has no ear. Wagner impresses on every page with his vast knowledge of pure music. It's impossible to overestimate his sense of architecture, his handling of musical detail. (Bülow IV [1898], p. 263)

For a long time, these contradictory views on Wagner's position in relation to Beethoven were typical of Wagner criticism as a whole. They have persisted up to the present day. There have also been attempts to substantiate these views by means of analysis. Theodor Adorno, representing the negative critical pole, has followed Guido Adler in examining the differences between Wagner's and Beethoven's compositional methods. Adler thought Wagner's sequences were all too similar to the rosalia which Wagner criticized in Schumann's music. Adorno goes further and suggests that on the small scale, 'there is really nothing to analyse in Wagner's music'. Wagner, he says, 'knows about motivs and large-scale forms – but not about themes. Repetition poses as development, transposition as thematic work' (p. 41). Adorno was more subtle than this in *Wagners Aktualität* (1978).

Even the main point of Adorno's criticism, the fixed allegorizing he always associates with Wagner's motifs, had a tradition behind it. As early as 1854, Otto Jahn was remarking that Wagner's motifs of recollection were like the symbol of the pointing hand in newspapers, indicating what should be noted and how to interpret it. And A. B. Marx – who was no enemy of progress – wrote only a year later:

> For his own part Wagner could not bring himself and his chosen art to do it. What he objected to in the form of working-up (the artistic dialectical fashioning, expansion, reshaping of motivs etc.) because he gave priority to the word and action – this wriggles its way in as bald repetition... (Marx [2/1872], p. 114)

Walter Engelsmann is one recent exponent of the unreservedly positive viewpoint reflected in Bülow's letter. Engelsmann exaggerates the technical similarity between Wagner and Beethoven. He sees Wagner's music as being organically 'grown' in the same way as Beethoven's. Both composers, he claims, employ the same evolutionary technique: starting with the main theme as the 'germ cell' of the whole composition, they proceed to spin an 'inexhaustible' melodic thread.

But these extreme views are open to question. Even where Beethoven is concerned, Engelsmann's position is not unassailable. Kurt von Fischer has rightly commented that 'anything can be read into anything as a result of more or less arbitrary omissions, reductions and contractions of themes and motifs' (K. v. Fischer [1948], p. xxiv). Moreover, Lockwood has drawn attention to the way Engelsmann distorts Draeseke's account of Wagner's 1859 discussion of the 'Eroica' in Lucerne. Wagner never said that the opening of the 'Eroica' contained the melody of the whole symphony, as Engelsmann would have it. Rather, according to Draeseke, Wagner maintained 'that in Beethoven's symphonies the melody flowed on inexhaustibly, and one could vividly recall the whole symphony with the help of this melody' (Lockwood [1982], p. 87n; Draeseke [1907]).

Two alternative possibilities are suggested by the idea of tracing a whole composition or at least one movement of it back to an 'organic primary cell'. In the one case the whole work will have been developed from the primary cell, while in the other, the work's unity is achieved from several different thematic or motivic starting-points. But Engelsmann considers only the first possibility. He believes that the process whereby Wagner's 'infinite melody' comes into being is analogous to biological growth. It is evident from an essay written for the 1951 Bayreuth Festival ('Wagners musikalisches Kompositionsverfahren') that Engelsmann derived the idea from Goethe's *Metamorphosis of Plants*. This, however, is not a valid approach to musical analysis. The mere fact that the parts of a music drama fit together organically does not tell us anything about the genesis of the motifs, about their derivation. Wagner suspended work on his *Ring* cycle for twelve years, and when he returned to *Siegfried*, he incorporated in its third act (Ewig war ich, ewig bin ich...') some thematic material he had jotted down in 1864. This in itself makes nonsense of Engelsmann's claim. Now that Cosima's diaries are completely accessible to us, we know that Wagner could favour either of the viewpoints we have mentioned in his references to Beethoven's melody. The following statement indicates a development from one basic theme: 'Beethoven is the first composer in whom everything is melody; it was he who showed how from one and the same theme a succession of new themes arise which are complete in themselves' (10 June 1870). But there is also this contrasting statement, referring to the development section of the first movement of the 'Eroica' in particular: 'I know of nothing so perfect with regard to structure, the architecture of music. The way the themes intermingle, they are like garlands linked to each other!' (4 October 1882).

Here, probably, Wagner was referring in particular to the interlocking of different thematic motifs and accompanying phrases or counter-motifs – a development proceeding in several stages. It is clear evidence that here he was indeed thinking of different melodic 'components' woven together into a single entity.

Adorno took steps to protect Beethoven against Wagner's claim concerning the drama's absorption of the symphony. But this depends on an acceptance of the analyses of Alfred Lorenz, which do not do justice to Wagnerian forms. And the flimsiness of such analysis calls into question Adorno's judgment that Wagner's forms are simply a collection of prefabricated sections, to be filled out with sequential work later on. The matter of Wagner's work within and upon 'small-scale forms' has not been disposed of; it arises afresh. Adorno's opinion, however, (he subsequently revised it) that Wagner's 'leitmotifs' were musical gestures which had become ossified through mechanical repetition, ignores the fact that these motifs are woven into a many-layered dramatic context and take part in its configurations, which are ever-changing. And this in turn dictates changing thematic–motivic formations. The question to be asked is whether, in creating these, Wagner followed specific structural principles in Beethoven's symphonic writing.

The gap in the material

It is, of course, easy to understand how Wagner, by preaching in 'Music of the Future' the idea of applying to drama Beethoven's melodic spinning-out of thematic–motivic material, provoked his readers. The differences between the two composers are obvious. Maybe, however, we have been reading Wagner in too general a sense.

But if we look for passages in his writings that specify the similarities and differences between his own technique and Beethoven's, we will run up against serious difficulties. Above all it is Wagner's language which limits us in this respect. This applies both to his description of Beethoven's compositional style and to remarks on points of contact between Beethoven and himself.

What analytical insight really lies behind Wagner's thesis of dance melody split up into its smallest components? Wagner says that Beethoven's technique was a 'demonstration of the act of giving birth to melody'. He refers to melody which has been broken up into its component parts, whose individual elements Beethoven bound together in a new whole by having 'the components of different melodies come into varying contact with one another', thus proclaiming 'the organic affinity between the apparently most diverse components of this type' (GS III, p. 315). These partially metaphorical statements too contain several layers of meaning. It is far from clear that they could imply – to quote Engelsmann – 'a composition theory of the Beethoven–Wagnerian art of evolution'. Bearing in mind Wagner's actual words, there is more justification for supposing that he was thinking of a technique based on the convergence, the limited and exactly matched 'evolution towards one another' of even the most different melodic elements.

There is an obvious gap in the theoretical material. We could rely on statements like 'I always maintain that we, Beethoven and I, are the twin melodists, we both have the grand line' (CW, 3 February 1880). But that would only be masking the absence of concrete details to go on.

An attempt at exactitude

There is one point that the various commentators on Beethoven's influence on Wagner have failed to consider. While praising Beethoven's technique, which he described as exemplary, Wagner nonetheless indicated the differences that exist between a musical dramatist's technique and that of an instrumental composer. He expressly rebutted the idea of a seamless link between Beethoven and himself.

Newspapers from Vienna; a passage in which it is maintained that the *Eroica* foretells Wagner particularly displeases R.: 'I find it horrible when people compare me to Beethoven; I always feel like saying, "What do you know of B.?"'
(CW, 7 May 1870)

Bischoff would not have made the kind of comment he did if he had looked at Part III of *Opera and Drama*. Here there is a section dealing with the function of the orchestra in drama. Wagner makes the point 'that the orchestra's matching expressive elements must never be determined by the musician's whim', which would make them just an artificial sound overlay; the 'intention of the poet' must be the sole determining factor (GS IV, pp. 199f.). Wagner sets his face against the 'musically motivated choice' of design, the motivic working and organization that inform a 'piece of absolute instrumental music' (GS IV, p. 202). In the light of such statements, it would seem a mistake from the very beginning to want to compare Wagner's working-up technique directly with Beethoven's, or to detect behind it something like an excess of intention.

The gap dividing the symphony from the music drama is considerable. But we can still try to establish the exact points of reference between the works of Wagner and Beethoven via the medium of theory. In connection with Uhlig's essays and his commentary on *Opera and Drama*, but also drawing on later statements by Wagner (and not forgetting the special features of dramatic design), we can sum up Wagner's debt to Beethoven under four separate headings. Firstly, there is the way Wagner pointed up the kind of short, malleable motif to be found in Beethoven's music. Secondly, we have the connections between the problems of musico-dramatic design Wagner was facing at the start of his Zurich exile and Uhlig's observations on Beethoven's choice and treatment of his motifs – plus the commentary on *Opera and Drama*. The gist of what Wagner said to Draeseke in 1859 on the subject of the 'Eroica' comes very close to Uhlig's ideas. It is an obvious conclusion that Wagner's remarks were inspired by Uhlig, and not taken from *'Music of the Future'* (1860) to be presented 'later' – as Dahlhaus writes [1988, p. 225] – to Draeseke. Thirdly, we have Wagner's statements in *On the Application of Music to Drama* concerning the musico-dramatic variation of themes. On the one hand these correspond to Uhlig's statements on Beethoven's motivic treatment; on the other they clearly distinguish between instrumental music and drama. This brings us to our fourth point, which is Uhlig's thinking on the subject of an association of themes extending beyond a single movement, as in Beethoven's Fifth. We now begin to see the connection between a kind of cyclical thematic working in the symphony and a working-up of dramatic themes linking several individual dramas together.

Let us start by examining the role of the short motif. Around 2 September 1851 Wagner informed Uhlig that he was making a start on the composition of *Der Junge Siegfried*:

I am now starting work on the music ... the musical phrases fit in with these verses and periods without any effort on my part ... The beginning I already have in my head; also a number of plastic motifs like the Fafner motif. (*SB* IV, p. 99)

This is strikingly reminiscent of Wagner's comments to Bülow on the way Beethoven condensed Shakespeare's drama into a 'plastic moment' in his *Coriolan* overture. It also recalls Wagner's comments on the motivic figure at the start of the Fifth Symphony. We are reminded, too, of the fact that he used the words 'theme' and 'motif' as musical synonyms, both when discussing his own music and when he was talking about Beethoven.

There is plainly a connection between the stress Wagner laid on the concise design of Beethoven's motifs and the 'plastic motifs' in the *Ring*. But it would be an over-simplification to say that Wagner was 'influenced' by Beethoven in the popular sense of the term. That Wagner should recall Beethoven in his composing was the product of an inner readiness, of certain tendencies in his output. By his own account, Wagner had abandoned historical subjects in favour of myth with *Der Fliegende Holländer*. But he was not yet pursuing a thought-out dramatic conception, because he lacked the right musical form. The transformation (already being implemented) of poetic motifs into musical motifs, the exposition of productive, self-sufficient motifs was still at odds with the periodic layout it remained tied to. At this juncture Wagner attained to a new stage of artistic awareness. He discarded the historical subject of Friedrich Rotbart, and his *Nibelung Myth – as a Sketch for a Drama* of 1848 saw the beginning of a new creative phase, his 'period of conscious artistic willing' (*GS* IV, p. 320). He had developed a new artistic consciousness, and he started to realize that in the realm of myth, there was a correlation between a poetic and a musical disposition for expression. And this larger awareness was paralleled by his response to Beethoven. In 1849, at a time of revolution, he discovered anew the effect that Beethoven's music could have, and he continued his search for the 'poetic object' in Beethoven's works. But this search was bound up with Wagner's thoughts about his own creative work, with the writing of his theoretical essays and with the shaping of the *Ring* material – which was a slow and gradual process.

It will be evident from the above remarks that Wagner was taking his bearings from Beethoven in more than one respect. He was doing so in a more general sense, in accordance with the 'poetic object', but also in his endeavour to adapt Beethoven's musical formulations of that object in the way he wanted.

Indirectly, the quotation from the letter to Uhlig also shows that musically speaking, Wagner's 'plastic motifs' were sure to be quite different from Beethoven's motifs as regards their specific gravity. Fafner's motif is just one among many, coined in various ways. It would not be appropriate to refer to *the* plastic motifs in Wagner's music drama. Because of the way they are tied to the dramatic subject, they are much more diverse and at the same time 'individual'. They are principal characters but also bear the responsibility for the dramatic function and development.

We now come to our second point of reference. With Uhlig's encouragement, Wagner looked to Beethoven both when he was designing his musical 'moments', or elements, and in connection with technical problems posed by the music drama, in the course of its realization. Music drama involved the linking together of the 'basic', 'principal' or 'nature' motifs: a projected fabric of central themes covering not just the one scene, as was the case with earlier opera's individual lyrical sections, but 'the whole of the drama, in the closest accordance with the poetic intention' (*GS* IV, p. 322). As we have mentioned, this created fresh problems for Wagner with regard to the thematic and/or motivic working-out. Uhlig had

examined Beethoven's composition technique in connection with specifically designed themes and their continuous development, and it gave
Wagner some important ideas for his own working-up technique. There is
an indication of this in Wagner's remarks to Draeseke about the 'Eroica',
for he was obviously quoting from Uhlig's discussion in the *Neue Zeitschrift
für Musik* of Part I of *Opera and Drama*. The passage in question was Uhlig's
description of Beethoven's thematic–motivic work as the expansion into a
'completely finished melody' of 'a short motif's principal motif'.

It might be objected that this was sending Wagner back to the idea of a
melodic thread developed from one basic motif: the idea Engelsmann made
his formal criterion *par excellence*. But this is not necessarily true. As the two
quotations from Cosima's diaries illustrate, Wagner's later comments on
Beethoven's melody adumbrate one or the other aspect of the melodic
procedure. Besides the development from one basic motif, there is also the
meaningful interaction of various motifs. Rather, these statements were
made at a greater distance in time, but Wagner is speaking to the point in
his commentary. He perceived both methods of melodic development that
Beethoven applied in his music – and in essence, his perceptions were
surely consistent. And Wagner adumbrated the same position in respect of
his own creative output.

In his *Communication to My Friends*, Wagner speaks quite unambiguously
of different 'principal moods'. Each of them, he says, determines 'a
particular musical theme'. It was, however, a case of developing these
moods from one another and of obtaining the drama's unity of expression,
which was the universally recognizable sign of this development. Thus the
unified design of the various principal moods (which the poet had
established beforehand) and their motivic expression was achieved by a
technique which involved the evolution and the convergence of clearly
distinguished motivic areas, their interlocking, superimposition and combination.

The third of our four points concerns the 'single main musical idea' that
Uhlig propounded. This, he said, generally appears as a short motif at the
beginning and supplies the listener with a guiding thread. We can tell that
it became an important compositional element for Wagner from his treatise
On the Application of Music to Drama. He examines the Rhinemaidens' motif,

Ex. 1 Wagner, Rheingold, *scene 1 (bars 540–1)*

whose recurrence can be traced 'through all the changing passions that
agitate the whole four-part drama, up to the song of Hagen's watch in the

first act of *Götterdämmerung*'. He points out how it differs from a purely musical variation in its 'various connections with nearly every other motif in the far-ranging dramatic action' (*GS* x, p. 189). Characteristic transformations of this kind would be impossible in instrumental music, because they would spoil its 'inherent lucidity'.

In his letter to Röckel of 1854 (see p. 81) Wagner asserts the 'close-knit unity' of *Rheingold*, saying that the orchestra does not play a single bar which is not developed from previous motifs. But how far does this square with the musical facts? If we assume that everything is derived from a 'germ cell', as Voss puts it, the statement becomes an exaggeration. But the way Wagner puts it, it is much more likely he was referring to several motifs each functioning as points of departure or reference. If we think of the link not only between the 'Nature' and Erda motifs but also between the 'Renunciation' and 'Woman's Bliss and Worth' (*Weibes Wonne und Wert*) motifs, the Ring and Valhalla motifs, this reading matches the facts – and Wagner's dictum – very closely. And a rough similarity, if not an actual affinity, can be readily established between the different motivic filiations. So examples proliferate of the idea of the germinal motif and also of a reciprocal relationship.

In the treatise *On the Application of Music to Drama* Wagner was much concerned with the contrast between the symphony and music drama. All the same (and this is the fourth point of contact with Beethoven), he proceeded to compare his own kind of thematic work with the classical variation form in a thoroughgoing way. Unlike the symphonist, who restricts the return of his principal theme to a single movement, normally the first, Wagner was out to illustrate the expansion of the thematic fabric across the entire drama. A purely instrumental set of variations is based on one theme from beginning to end. This is in marked contrast to the opportunities for thematic change in the drama, the spinning of a thematic thread and the weaving of it into the dramatic whole.

What now becomes clear is this. For all Beethoven's merits, and over and above Wagner's criticism of the reprise, he also regarded the symphony and sonata as outmoded forms from the viewpoint of the overall cyclical construction of music.

Yet there are also some examples in Beethoven of themes that are repeated or recalled in the course of a symphony as a whole. Later Wagner noted this element with regard to the Fifth Symphony on at least two occasions, although his attitude to it changed drastically. In 1882 (CW, 18 December) he criticizes it on account of the scherzo, which Beethoven 'runs into the last movement'. Barely ten years before, however, he was moved by the 'melancholy little march'. Interpreting it in theatrical terms, Wagner sees 'everything here' as 'dramatic' (CW, 20 January 1873). Uhlig had already remarked on this interlocking of movements in his essay *Beethovens Sinfonien im Zusammenhange betrachtet*:

The linking of the 3rd and 4th movements is highly significant for the object of the symphony, and accordingly this second half forms a truly dramatic whole. Here, that type of scherzo whose character is the most dance-like logically takes on a thoroughly anomalous expression. But with the return of the minor section it already appears in a substantially modified form, and eventually, in the finale, it turns into a march of triumph, in the major key. By virtue of its rhythmic main theme, incidentally, this finale has a connection with the first movement, albeit a hidden one – which is a clear indication of the composer's efforts to create an inner connection between the individual movements.   (Uhlig [1913], pp. 198, 214)

E. T. A. Hoffmann had previously noted both these points in his review of Beethoven's Fifth – the incorporation of parts of the third movement in the finale, and the reappearance of a characteristic bass figure from the first movement.[1] But Uhlig interprets them in a way that patently relates to Wagner. This is more evident still from an essay of 1851–2 in which he contrasts Schumann with Beethoven:

In his Eroica Symphony Beethoven is not yet basically questioning the original character of the individual movements . . . but in the C minor Symphony he attacks the very heart of symphonic form, and he completely demolishes the 'essence' of tradition based on the established form . . . for the first time . . . he links two separate movements directly together. In this way he tries to give musical shape to a moral necessity, and to develop one mood from another by purely musical means. Here, for the first and only time (and in a very modest way), he uses a purely musical motif which is initially a rhythmic one to produce and encourage the relationship between the individual movements, and hence the inner connection between them. Such an artistic device could only have been prompted by a higher ideal intention on the part of the tone-poet.   (Uhlig [1913], pp. 241f.)

Uhlig uses a concrete example to supplement his remarks on the way Beethoven designed and handled his themes. It is safe to assume that Wagner, like Uhlig, saw these motivic relationships that extended beyond the individual movement as a further clue to Beethoven's poetic intention. In his centenary essay, Wagner wrote that the 'lyrical pathos' of Beethoven's Fifth lay 'very close to that of an ideal drama in the more precise sense' (*MET*, p. 66). This merits particular attention. Here Wagner is seen to be aware of a first step towards the technique of bringing back the same themes not only in different scenes and acts of a music drama but throughout a dramatic cycle.

We are suggesting that Wagner took note of the way themes could be linked together in the successive movements of a symphony. This seems even more likely if we bear in mind that there were contemporary works where this technique had been already applied. Wagner knew these works, but he criticized them because he did not think they succeeded in benefiting by Beethoven's example. Here again, what Uhlig wrote about Schumann aroused Wagner's interest and won his approval:

In his second symphony, Schumann already shares with Beethoven in general and the composer of the C minor Symphony in particular firstly the higher artistic aim, but also the ambition of manifesting the inner connections between the symphony's individual movements through purely musical correspondences (such as the use of the same idea in several movements). In this respect we need only recall the following motif,

Ex. 2 Schumann, Symphony no. 2, C major, 1st movement

which appears in both the first and the last movement of his previous symphony. But in spite of this affinity between Schumann and Beethoven, the former's actual musical style is not rooted in Beethoven's; indeed it seeks to counteract the latter's revolutionary daring. This we intend to demonstrate another time, thereby offering the most constructive criticism of the whole modern trend in composition. (Uhlig [1913], pp. 243f.)

So Uhlig perceives common ground between Schumann and Beethoven as regards the 'higher' artistic intent and 'use of the same idea in several movements'. At the same time he thinks that Schumann's art is calculated to counteract rather than carry on Beethoven's 'revolutionary daring'. This view is clearly in line with that held by Wagner. He thought it wrong-headed to borrow Beethoven's technique to compose purely instrumental music, as is evident from his condemnation of Berlioz, whose *idée fixe* similarly recurs all through the *Symphonie fantastique*. (Wagner knew the work intimately – see CW, entry of 1 December 1879. In *My Life*, p. 191, he writes of being 'particularly impressed by the musical genre painting'.) What he regarded as misconceptions about Beethoven, whether by Schumann or by Berlioz, must have been a further incentive for Wagner to treat Beethoven's composition technique as an important preliminary step. It was, however, something that needed to be converted to the specific requirements of music drama.

Musical and dramatic construction

The question of influences

In endeavouring to bridge the gap in the theoretical material, we shall bring some basic principles and precepts of composition into sharper focus. What we can only go a little way towards achieving by this method is the identification of a potential link between theory and practice with the aid of an individual, concrete example. The matter of the solid connections that may exist between Wagner and Beethoven as composers can only be clarified further if we can succeed in detecting more extensive and intensive traces of them in the actual music. This question of musical influences has yet to be studied comprehensively, in such a way as to take account of all its systematic and historical aspects. All we can attempt to do here is shed more light on some aspects of the problem as it relates to Wagner's 'reception' of Beethoven.

One cliché about artistic creativity is that everything comes to a genius through inspiration. Wagner is one of the most frequently cited examples. Thus Ernst Kurth saw a 'basic psychological trait' behind the technical features of 'infinite melody'. This led him to say it was pointless asking 'whether and how far Wagner consciously depended on earlier models', because he was enough of a genius 'to re-create intuitively what had belonged to entire earlier ages and was now lost and buried'. There is, however, no reason for ignoring Wagner's own remarks on the subject in *A Communication to My Friends*, which paint a quite different picture. And they continue to matter even when compared with later, diverging statements. Wagner had this to say:

I associate the power which we commonly call genius only with that faculty I described in detail a moment ago. What works on this power so strongly that eventually it will always attain to full productiveness of its own accord must in fact be seen as the real creator and designer, the sole enabling condition of this power's effectiveness. I am referring to the art already developed outside of this individual power, a universal substance formed from the art works of our forerunners and contemporaries, and combining with real life ... to influence ... the individual.

(*GS* IV, p. 248)

In Wagner's view, therefore, genius only develops when stimulated from outside. Influence means the power of pre-existent art works to awaken, develop and mould a talent – on the basis of a particular predisposition. The moment the 'receptive faculty' is 'totally considerate towards what it is going to receive', this faculty in its fullest strength must necessarily finish up by becoming a creative power. Genius proves itself by absorbing influences and transforming them creatively. Wagner does not say in his essay whether this process always occurs on the conscious level. But in his letter of 1 January 1847 to Eduard Hanslick he wrote:

the unconsciously created work of art belongs to periods remote from our own: the work of art of the most advanced period of culture can be produced only by a process of conscious creation. (*SL*, p. 134)

This suggests that he did not 'underestimate the power of reflection' with regard to influences, either.

All the same, Wagner's thoughts kept revolving around the subject of 'opera and drama', and this raised some special problems. Was opera as a genre not bound to resist being influenced by purely instrumental forms such as the symphony, sonata or string quartet? The answer to this is no; not if we perceive Wagner's intention. What he wanted to do was open up the barriers between genres. His 'music drama' was the result of an effort to transform the ossified genre of opera into a qualitatively new genre with the help of instrumental music – and the Beethoven symphonies, sonatas and string quartets took pride of place here. So there was no question of an instrumental urge, of a symphony dressed up as drama. Wagner stood, he thought, at the end of a development that covered a whole millennium, and not only the different art forms but also the different genres of music were to be merged in the music drama. Surely this was the point of that sentence in *'Music of the Future'* which speaks of 'guiding the whole rich stream' of German music as enlarged by Beethoven 'into the bed of this musical drama'? In addition, the projected regeneration of the drama could never be primarily a matter of quotation, thematic borrowing or stylistic imitation. Rather, it had to do with principles of design and construction, with formal matters which transcended genres. Wagner's intentions are sufficient reason for trying to locate such principles within the *œuvre*.

The above continues to apply when we consider the fact that Wagner saw the basic conditions of musico-dramatic design as lying in its 'intimate relationship to the poetic intention'. In *Tristan*, the connection became so strong that the 'whole expansion of the melody' was already prefigured in the 'fabric of words and verses'. Even evidence of a structural correspondence between the text and the course of the music would require an extremely subtle approach to aspects of this correspondence before we could rule out any other influence on the musical structure. And even then, it would still be possible that Wagner was following musical principles, since this might have been already going on whilst he was putting the text together. We must always remember that Wagner regarded Beethoven's compositions as tone poems whose 'poetic object' extended to that realm of myth which governed his own 'poetic intention'. All this – in the sense of the Greek concept of music – transcended purely instrumental music.

One other point is worth considering in connection with the issue of the intrinsic 'self-sufficiency' of musico-dramatic construction. It concerns the following question. How far do we need to apply parameters of an historical process embracing a number of individual styles in order to explain resemblances between different composers? This appears to relate not least to stylistic principles that are part of the thematic–motivic working-up technique. We need only mention the adoption of a Beethovenian manner by Berlioz, Schumann and Brahms, deplored by Wagner and members of his circle. Clearly, personal stylistic features conjoin in a process transcending individuals. Yet the individual forms those features take are so plainly embedded in the crucial early phase of Wagner's Beethoven reception that they must be described as influences up to a point. So Beethoven's influence on Wagner is not in doubt; it is more a question of how and in what ways it was exerted. And here we must distinguish between what Ulrich Weisstein has called direct, indirect and negative influences.

Wagner had got to know two of Berlioz's works in Paris, the dramatic symphony *Roméo et Juliette* and the *Symphonie fantastique*. In part this music directly influenced him (as in the thematic construction and instrumentation of the *Faust* Overture), but there was also an indirect reaction to Berlioz's *idée fixe* which reinforced some of Wagner's own tendencies (in both the *Faust* Overture and *Der Fliegende Holländer*). Wagner seems to have been greatly impressed at the time by Berlioz's instrumentation and also his *idée fixe*, inasmuch as it was a personal adaptation of the Beethovenian technique. Nonetheless Berlioz, Schumann and, at a later date, Brahms exerted an influence which was chiefly 'negative'. They prompted a move in the opposite direction. Wagner's *Der Fliegende Holländer*, which caused him to stop work on a *Faust* symphony, and his *Pilgrimage to Beethoven* are anything but mere pieces of musico-dramatic pretence. He was being sent in the direction of music drama as well as back to Beethoven. Admittedly, towards the end of his life Wagner conceived a desire to write symphonies again – a final, jaded reaction to instrumental music which, through the symphonies of Bruckner and Brahms, had finally declared Wagner's conception of history invalid.

The general reception of Beethoven is bound up with a particular spectrum of influences, whose different categories are interwoven. Similarly, Wagner's changing reception of Beethoven dictates a quite specific differentiation. As we can see from his first great Beethoven experience, Wagner's early reception of the composer was naive and spontaneous. Only gradually did it begin to be governed by firm conceptions. Basically we can distinguish between a phase where the influence was unaffected by Wagner's theories, and a phase where it was substantially determined by theoretical reflections bearing upon music drama. Up to the beginning of the 1840s Wagner's relationship to Beethoven was comparatively unthinking. The Zurich writings ushered in a period of conscious probing and self-orientation. Of course these statements need qualifying. The years from 1840 to 1849 – and especially the period between 1846 and 1849 – were a time of transition. They saw the crystallization of thoughts which Wagner only recorded later, when they had matured. And no doubt he had also thought about Beethoven during his early years – though on a quite different level and starting with quite different intentions.[2] At the other end of the scale, he continued to absorb impressions spontaneously after the 1850s, and directly to work over musical data stored by his 'involuntary memory' (the term is Adorno's).

This brings us to another distinction with a strong bearing on the question of influence. We refer to the difference between conscious and unconscious influence. In their different ways, both types simultaneously condition and conceal the dependence on the model. Unconscious influence scarcely goes, as a rule, beyond small-scale forms the size of a motif or group of motifs, which is why it can seldom be clearly demonstrated. Together with stylistic features, on the other hand, principles of structure and form come mainly under the heading of conscious influence. The transformation is usually such that the borrowed features will be concealed by the restructuring, or only vaguely discernible.

It is hard to say exactly how these two types of influence relate to the different phases in Wagner's career. At all events it was not the case that when the influences were unaffected by his theorizing, they were entirely or even predominantly unconscious ones. Conscious influences – and even deliberate imitation – may certainly be surmised in early Wagner behind thematic–motivic, general stylistic and, in particular, overall formal characteristics that only approximate to those of the model. Wagner had a marked desire to be original from early on, and this permeates his relationship to compositional models. During his early, 'absolutely musical period', he recalled, he had often had an inspiration for initially devising 'really original melodies that would bear my special, personal stamp' (*GS* IV, p. 324). As this shows, his object was to acquire an artistic profile of his own from the model in question.

It will already be apparent that often enough, the influences are difficult to make out and even more difficult to prove. But the practical problem of proving such influences should not be used as an argument against attempting to track them down. As Ulrich Weisstein remarks, influence is by no means the same thing as literal borrowing. This sanctions what we are trying to do, especially as literal correspondences are generally superficial forms of influence – where they have not come about by pure accident. Influences affecting the construction of a piece are profounder and more interesting.

The above point is a crucial one. While it is impossible to miss the kind of influence that can be read straight from the notes, the essential elements are correspondingly hidden, being absorbed by the structure. So it would be fundamentally wrong to say that because music drama evinces traces of genuine thematic–motivic work only in a fragmentary, sporadic way (if at all), this technique was unproductive as far as Wagner is concerned. Rather – as indicated by the account of the 'Eroica' Symphony's melody that he based on Uhlig – Wagner attached a special meaning to this component, which he creatively transformed.

Everything depends on the available methods and on how they are employed. We are not primarily interested in individual pieces of evidence or in the number of examples; our main concern is rather with the exploration of influences and their components, and with the way that the different levels and facets are combined and concentrated. Among the 'surface manifestations', we can distinguish between the thematic and

motivic reminiscences and more broadly-based formal and stylistic similarities. What may be termed 'essential' influence covers the technical sides
of composition, the structural and architectonic aspects. In Wagner's early
works it is the motivic–thematic, sporadic influences which predominate.
So we are entitled to discuss these mainly early surface details separately
from the profounder, essential elements. Next we shall discuss the formal,
stylistic and sundry aspects of more essential similarities. There are
parallel manifestations which might not constitute a strong case indi-
vidually but serve to reinforce one another. It is important, too, starting
with Wagner's reception of Beethoven, to consider the concrete situation in
which specific works originated. Often a scrutiny of the background
problems and motives can shed some light on matters which would
otherwise seem merely incidental, or at any rate unconnected. In spite of
the problematic relationship between the theory and the œuvre, we must
also be constantly considering the theoretical 'context', the context of the
reception history and background problems.

Thematic–motivic reminiscences

If there is one category of influence that typifies the period when Wagner
was responding to Beethoven naively, it is the thematic–motivic reminiscence. In order to grasp this correctly we must refer back to Wagner's
early Beethoven experience. It produced a readiness to absorb things from
Beethoven which was bound to affect the works he wrote in his youth. In
1838 Heinrich Dorn wrote a report from Riga for the *Neue Zeitschrift für
Musik*. He described the young Wagner's enthusiasm for Beethoven in the
following terms:

I doubt if there has ever been a young composer who was more familiar with
Beethoven's works than the then 18-year-old Wagner. He possessed the Master's
overtures and larger instrumental compositions mostly in the form of scores he had
specially copied. He went to bed with the sonatas and rose with the quartets, he
sang the songs and he whistled the concertos (for as a player he wasn't making
much progress).   (See Kirchmeyer [1967], II, p. 9)

This obsession on Wagner's part can be described as a kind of 'Beethoven craze'. It accounts for his knowledge of the works, for the fact that
where Beethoven was concerned, he was so 'well read'. By 1832 or so
Wagner must have already known an appreciable number of Beethoven
compositions of every possible kind. As is clear from *My Life* and his letters,
he was conversant with not only the symphonies and several overtures but
also piano sonatas, string quartets, the music for *Egmont*, the song cycle *An
die ferne Geliebte, Adelaide, Fidelio* and the *Missa Solemnis*. Cosima's diaries
refer to his early acquaintance with the Gellert Lieder. In addition he
probably knew some other works that are not specifically mentioned.

Wagner's constant involvement with Beethoven's works is one important reason why thematic–motivic reminiscences are discernible in Wagner's early music, and even in later works.

Later on, Wagner never denied these influences. In retrospect he saw himself as one of those 'followers in music' who from time immemorial had trotted out what they regarded as original tunes, but who were really just mimicking their favourite models. And Wagner gives individual examples. The Overture in B flat major (*WWV* x) of 1830, which Dorn had performed the same year, derived from a study of the Ninth Symphony, in the sense that he ascribed a 'mystical significance' (see *ML*, p. 51) to the orchestra. Wagner also confirms a connection with Beethoven in the case of other early compositions like the Overture in D minor (*WWV* xx) and the overture to Raupach's drama *König Enzio* (*WWV* xxiv). He saw Beethoven's Seventh and Eighth Symphonies as having 'greatly influenced' (*My Life*, p. 91) the style and construction of his Symphony in E major (*WWV* xxxv), of which he drafted only the first movement. Traces of Beethoven's influence were also mingled with traces of other composers. Wagner set the opera libretto for *Die Feen* (*WWV* xxxii) to music under the impact of Beethoven, Weber and Marschner. And Mozart as well as Beethoven influenced him when he was composing his Symphony in C major (*WWV* xxix).

It must, of course, be asked how accurate Wagner was with his information. And in conjunction with this, we must also look into the amount of freedom that allows us to speak of influences in spite of divergences from the model. Let us take Wagner's remarks on his Symphony in C, since they are more specific than other remarks. 'Without the andante of the C minor Symphony and the allegretto of the Symphony in A,' he wrote in his *Report on the Revival of an Early Work* (*GS* x, p. 314), 'the melody of the second movement (andante) ... would probably have never come about.' How clear, then, are the connections that Wagner suggests, and at what levels is the work affected by them?

Let us look at the 'melody' of the movement Wagner headed 'Andante ma non troppo, un poco maestoso'. We will see that neither whole themes nor longer paragraphs are modelled on the aforesaid movements by Beethoven. Wagner did not even reproduce motivic figures note for note, and yet it is

Ex. 3 Wagner, Symphony in C major, Andante ma non troppo, un poco maestoso, theme (bars 17–25)

these which – like chemical trace elements – point to Beethoven. Melted
down, as it were, into the melodic context, they intersperse original detail
with Beethoven-like 'colouring'. This is illustrated at the beginning of the
'melody' by the combination of dotted semiquaver, demisemiquaver and
quaver, reminiscent of the Andante con moto from Beethoven's Fifth
Symphony:

*Ex. 4a Wagner, Symphony in C major, Andante ma non troppo, un poco maestoso,
theme (bars 17–18)*

Ex. 4b Beethoven, Symphony no. 5, C minor. op. 67, Andante con moto (bars 1/2)

It could be said that since this rhythmic echo is only a sporadic one, it is
not sufficient evidence of Beethoven's influence. But it is qualitative rather
than quantitative considerations that matter. Even though the detail we
have described appears only from time to time (whereas with Beethoven it
is always present), it does so in an interesting way. The notation in itself
tells us something. Instead of appearing in isolation, the motif is tied to the
first quaver. This makes it fit in with the 3/4 rhythm, but the notation of the
3/8 rhythm from the Beethoven Andante is still perceptible; normally with
3/4 rhythm, the double-dotted quaver would be connected to the demisemiquaver. Furthermore, attached to the quaver, the motif gives the
impression of being something Wagner regarded as immutable, a detail he
had remembered and adopted. In the course of the twelve-bar theme, the
motif is repeated another three times in its rhythmic structure. The
repetition in the fourth bar is particularly important. Here the correspondence with Beethoven's theme is not only rhythmic but harmonic (half-
close) and metrical (end of initial phrase):

*Ex. 5a Wagner, Symphony in C major, Andante ma non troppo, un poco maestoso,
theme (bars 29–32)*

Ex. 5b Beethoven, Symphony no. 5, Andante con moto (bars 1–7)

A further point of comparison is that the two motifs are themselves matching inasmuch as they enclose the first phrase. At the same time the difference becomes particularly evident, but it tends to confirm Beethoven's influence rather than disprove it. For in the first half-phrase of the Beethoven theme an upbeat and a downbeat motif are correlated (the latter, which closes the half-phrase, being relatively accentuated). In Wagner's case, by contrast, the first motif is also associated with a downbeat, but both rhythmically and melodically it is basically an upbeat motif, which makes it look like an interpolation. It appears to have been forced into the bar – an impression which is underlined by the notation. This alerts us to a significant stylistic element in Wagner's writing: a lack of homogeneity in the musical substance as well as the design. The motif is not fully integrated. Wagner was obviously striving to create something original, but the fact is that it has been crystallized from elements of borrowed material.

The connections with the Allegretto of Beethoven's Seventh confirm our impression. Some typical features of the theme that starts in Beethoven's bar 27 – especially in the order of two quavers, slide, crotchet with quaver joined on, followed by two semiquavers – seem to form part of a fresh melodic context but have not been fully assimilated:

Ex. 6a Wagner, Symphony in C major, Andante ma non troppo, un poco maestoso, theme (bars 29–32)

Ex. 6b Beethoven, Symphony no. 7, A major, op. 92, Allegretto (bars 40–4)

Here the thematic–motivic reminiscence is again only partial. There are changes in the note values (two quavers instead of two crotchets) and the rhythmic–metrical proportions. This apart, however, the diastematic values largely agree, as do the rhythmic–melodic outlines; this is emphasized by the same degree of the scale (in A minor).

So, even going only by individual elements of the Andante theme, we can endorse Wagner's later statement about the connections between his C major Symphony and the Fifth and Seventh Symphonies of Beethoven. And this will be supported by other, more general similarities which we shall examine presently. But we have also seen that there is considerable scope for adjustment to our first impressions with regard to influences. This leads us to investigate further – although caution is necessary.

We particularly need to be cautious, it would seem, in the matter of conscious or unconscious influence. But we cannot ignore the distinction. The probability of thematic–motivic reminiscences on Wagner's part increases when we remember that his familiarity with Beethoven's works produced a store of possible recollections. Even where they were unconscious ones, such recollections were strong enough to affect Wagner's composing. Influences of this kind, though unconscious, are not accidental. We must also distinguish between more than one kind of conscious influence. It is conceivable that as he was composing, reminiscences which the composer could identify came into his mind unbidden, and were then consciously worked into his music. We cannot rule out such a combination of conscious and unconscious influences in Wagner's case.

More far-reaching than the reminiscences in our last example are those connecting the Larghetto of Wagner's Piano Sonata in B flat major with a second theme from the Larghetto of Beethoven's Second Symphony.

Ex. 7a Wagner, Piano sonata in B flat major, Larghetto (bars 40–4)

Ex. 7b Beethoven, Symphony no. 2, D major, op. 36, Larghetto (bars 32/3–6)

There are, however, differences in the melodic profile. In particular, the twofold rising motion within Beethoven's two-bar phrase contrasts with a rise and fall in Wagner's:

Ex. 8a Wagner, Piano sonata in B flat major, Larghetto

Ex. 8b Beethoven, Symphony no. 2, D major, op. 36, Larghetto

Moreover Beethoven requires two steps to bridge the intervals of the sixth and seventh respectively, whereas Wagner bridges them with a single step. But underlying these differences are some important formal and structural parallels. Both Larghetto movements are in 3/8 time; and the periodic construction of their themes is based on two four-bar units, divided up by means of the change to the dominant in the second bar and the return to the tonic in the fourth (in Wagner's second four-bar unit, only after the second degree of B flat major). With both themes the minor version of the tonic appears in the second four-bar unit (not until the close in Wagner's case,

175

whereupon it is heard twice more in a 'spinning-out'). Apart from the divergences mentioned, the rhythmic–melodic material corresponds in its more significant features, and the same applies to the accompaniment. Lastly, the articulation of this material from bar to bar and from one two-bar group to the next also corresponds in the two examples. The perceived similarity is now such as to raise the question of whether Wagner was not deliberately copying the Beethoven theme, especially as it was a second theme in each instance. The thematic reminiscence evokes the formal shaping power of this Beethoven second theme.

The same movement's main theme is a different matter. This contains only a sporadic echo of Beethoven. It is based on the subdominant on A flat with added sixth; here the position, harmonic progression and motivic tie-up suggest a reduction of the initial six bars of the first movement of Beethoven's Piano Sonata in E flat, op. 31(iii):

Ex. 9a Wagner, Piano sonata in B flat major, Larghetto (bars 1–4)

Ex. 9b Beethoven, Piano Sonata in E flat major, op. 31, no. 3, Allegro (bars 1–4)

For all the similarity of the detail, there is a palpable difference as far as the status and function of the chord are concerned. With Beethoven it constitutes the initial motif of his first movement, providing the basis not only of the main theme but also of large portions of the movement. With Wagner, it amounts to no more than a chordal interpolation in the first theme of his slow movement.

The above could be interpreted as an unconscious influence, and so could various similarities with Beethoven in other works by Wagner. Take, for instance, the bass triplets in the Adagio molto e cantabile of Wagner's Fantasy in F sharp minor. They automatically suggest those passages in the Adagio of the D minor Sonata, op. 31(ii), in which the melodic line is supported and continued by demisemiquaver triplets followed by a quaver. Wagner's triplet figure is similarly inserted between the phrases of the melody. But Beethoven's triplets – quite unlike Wagner's – really offset the melody and add to the expressive intensity.

Ex. 10a Wagner, Fantasy in F sharp minor (bars 249/5–299)

Ex. 10b Beethoven, Piano sonata in D minor, op. 31, no. 2, Adagio (bars 17–19)

Again, in the F sharp minor Adagio of Wagner's Piano Sonata in A, a couple of bars in the A major section are reminiscent of the Largo e mesto from Beethoven's Sonata in D, op. 10(iii). There are some more or less extensive similarities. They include the harmonic drop (in each case in the order dominant⁷–tonic = supertonic–dominant⁷–tonic, related to D minor and F sharp minor respectively); the broken chords in the accompaniment; and above all the basic notes of the melody:

Ex. 11a Wagner, Piano sonata in A major, Adagio (bars 24/5–6)

Ex. 11b Beethoven, Piano sonata in D major, op. 10, no. 3, Largo e mesto (bars 11/12–13)

There are also other connections between this Wagner adagio movement and compositions by Beethoven. Characteristic features of the main theme suggest a link both with the Adagio e sostenuto of the 'Hammerklavier' Sonata and with the Adagio of the Sonata in A flat, op. 110. Here, an important role may have been played by the falling third in the initial motif of the theme – a feature which still interested Wagner in his later years:

Ex. 12a Wagner, Piano sonata in A major, Adagio (bars 1–2)

Ex. 12b Beethoven, Piano sonata in B flat major, op. 106, Adagio e sostenuto (bars 1–3)

Ex. 12c Beethoven, Piano sonata in A flat major, op. 110, Adagio ma non troppo (bars 9–13)

These two connections are not, however, of equal weight. The only reminiscence of the 'Hammerklavier' theme is the falling fifth, C sharp^2–F sharp^1, that proceeds via the third-interval of C sharp^2–A^1 (the fact that both movements are in the key of F sharp minor constitutes another link, of course). The reminiscences of the Arioso dolente from Beethoven's Sonata in A flat go deeper. Wagner's writing shows that he was striving for expressive richness and broad melodic lines, and Beethoven's magnificent depiction of the soul appears to have served as a model. This particular early piece by Wagner illustrates the extent to which it is non-literal borrowing that represents the profounder influence, for it is hard to discern any precise details of the Beethoven melody in Wagner's. There are also obvious differences in the melodic structure: whereas Beethoven's broad, arching melody over-rides the periodic scheme, Wagner forces his melody into a straitjacket of two bars to two. Nonetheless, the curves of the melody (between wide intervallic leaps, and descending stepwise) show that he wanted to capture something of the quality of Beethoven's melodic construction. This is underlined by the fact that the framework for Wagner's melody – 12/16 rhythm and the chordal accompaniment's perpetual semiquaver triplets – is modelled on Beethoven's theme.

The young Wagner's enthusiasm about Beethoven must be regarded as preconditioning a favourable climate for influences. And this is true of the Beethoven experience triggered off by Habeneck's performance of the Ninth Symphony, whatever the circumstances. Let us recall the lasting impression which hearing the open fifths made on Wagner, an impression which riveted him to the symphony. In view of his particularly desperate existence during his Paris stay of 1839–42, there can be little doubt that the response mechanism triggered off by hearing the fifths was reactivated when he heard the Ninth under Habeneck. In the process of establishing his leitmotif principle, Wagner needed vivid experiences that would help him relive again and again the attachment of expressive qualities – what he called *Hauptstimmungen*, principal moods – to specific themes and motifs. And the reawakening of this very first experience surely fulfilled such a role. (This is not to say, of course, that Wagner's leitmotif technique derives entirely from his reception of Beethoven.)

There is a connection between the motif of a fifth and fourth at the beginning of the first movement of the Ninth Symphony and the Dutchman's motif in *Holländer*:

Ex. 13a Wagner, Der Fliegende Holländer, *Overture (bars 1–6)*

Ex. 13b Beethoven, Symphony no. 9, D minor, op. 125, Allegro ma non troppo, un poco maestoso (bars 1–5)

This again is hardly fortuitous; rather, it is very likely to have been the reworking as a leitmotif of an experience that was central to Wagner's artistic development. At the start of the overture to *Holländer*, the Dutchman motif is a motif of a fifth and fourth embedded in the sound of the open fifths on the strings (minus cellos and basses) and winds (flute, oboe, clarinet and trumpet). A personal experience that fused at once with a musical impression has now been artistically transformed and heightened.

The above effect of Wagner's Beethoven experience in Paris was simply one outlet for an impulse whose immediate repercussions can be felt in the *Faust* Overture (Berlioz's influence aside). As we have seen, the Beethoven experience specifically serves to design a motif in *Der Fliegende Holländer*. This becomes even more apparent if we bear in mind that it had already fulfilled the same function in the *Faust* Overture, on much the same level of expression. We can see it at work in the following echoes of the first phrase of the main theme from the opening movement of the Ninth,

Ex. 14a Wagner, Faust *Overture (bars 73–80)*

Ex. 14b Beethoven, Symphony no. 9, D minor, op. 125, Allegro ma non troppo, un poco maestoso (bars 16–22)

but especially in the quaver motif for the strings, which is reminiscent of the *Coriolan* Overture:

Ex. 15a Wagner, Faust *Overture (bars 52–6)*

Ex. 15b Beethoven, Coriolan *Overture, op. 62 (bars 13–19)*

Here the motif has been shown in a form already derived from its first appearance in the slow introduction (bar 3). The dark colouring in itself is quite striking. But the quasi-'leitmotivic' character is particularly brought out by the way the motif is repeated over large portions of the overture. These are standard repetitions, but the intervallic steps and direction are modified nonetheless. The motivic connections with Beethoven can be seen as a different mixture of conscious and unconscious influences. On the one hand we may assume that Wagner was fundamentally aware of the links with Beethoven. On the other hand he would scarcely have been really conscious as yet of the incipient leitmotivic tendency, which his Beethoven experience had intensified. Not until the second half of the 1840s did this come to dominate Wagner's thinking more and more. It eventually attained an aesthetic and compositional profile in connection with his quest for Beethoven's 'poetic object' and with his execution of the drama and music of the *Ring* cycle.

We can now see the importance of weighing up the 'conscious' and 'unconscious' influences. From the viewpoint of Wagner's early instrumental works, particularly the overtures to dramas, the 'unconscious' aspect shows that as yet it is quite impossible to speak of actual leitmotifs. A work like the *Faust* Overture illustrates that Wagner was already displaying a talent which aimed at combining music with a context of ideas, or of a dramatic action. According to Voss, such compositions are good examples of his 'symphonic ambition', but they can surely be taken as proving the opposite.

Wagner's *Faust* Overture is (additionally) orientated to the overture as a genre. This confirms the importance to him of musico–dramatic considerations and not modish operatic ones. It is already a sign that he was moving away both from the operatic manner and from purely instrumental music. The connections with the symphony – here it is Beethoven's Ninth, among others – do not rule this out, indeed they back it up. The four-movement plan, the function of the slow introduction and certain motivic features point to the symphony in general, and to this one in particular. And Wagner was, demonstrably, overwhelmed by Beethoven's musical language precisely with regard to those mystic and arcane associations which also underlie the *Faust* Overture.

Wagner's early attraction to the overture actually constitutes an argument against his alleged symphonic ambition. His subsequent publication of the *Faust* Overture can be ascribed mainly to his contact with Liszt. But he turned down Liszt's suggestion that the second theme should provide a real contrast. And his reason for rejecting it indicates how much he was viewing the work in the light of its literary subject – and to what extent this affected its form. For on 27 November 1852 he wrote to Uhlig:

With this piece of music I in fact had in mind only the first part of a Faust symphony. Here the subject is Faust, and the woman is only a vague, amorphous object of longing that hovers before him, and therefore unattainable, not to be grasped: hence his despair, his execration of all tormenting visions of beauty, his headlong plunge into bewitching, delirious sorrow. – It was only in the second part that the woman would actually materialize; its subject was to be Gretchen, just as the subject of the first movement was Faust. I had already found the right theme and atmosphere; but then I gave it all up and – true to character – started work on the 'flying Dutchman', whereby I made good my escape from the haze of instrumental music [*aus allem Instrumental-Musik-Nebel*] to the clear-cut world of the drama. (Wagner [1888], 248)

This account, and the phrase 'haze of instrumental music', seem altogether consistent with the structure and formal plan of the work. This is especially the case if we bear in mind the (partial) model of Berlioz. Had Berlioz not already impressed Wagner both positively and negatively with his *Roméo et Juliette*? From that viewpoint, is it not evident that Wagner – who always basically rejected Berlioz's approach to composition, despite the many striking details – was in two minds about his own piece of 'Berliosophy'? Was he not forced to recognize that what he was planning was simply incompatible with these techniques? The sentiment expressed in his letter agrees with the drift of his Zurich writings; rather than being a revelation, as Voss would have it, it confirms a trend.

The deliberate and full-scale theoretical study on which Wagner embarked in his Zurich writings signified a shift in his relationship to Beethoven. Thematic connections gave way to a fresh coming to grips with compositional techniques and forms. A naive type of borrowing was replaced by a process of exploration and systematization with drama as the envisaged goal.

The relationship that John Deathridge has discovered between the *Rienzi* overture and Beethoven's Ninth can be regarded as a step in this direction. The observation that the overtures to *Rienzi* and *Der Fliegende Holländer* 'were somehow related in Wagner's mind' is an important point in itself. But the link with the Ninth Symphony underlines the extent to which Beethoven's music had absorbed Wagner around the time of the *Faust* Overture. And the novella *A Pilgrimage to Beethoven* surely comes within the same context. For the *Gazette musicale* began publishing it on 19 November 1840, while Deathridge assigns the *Rienzi* overture to the period between January and September 1840.

All the same, thematic–motivic reminiscences were not disappearing altogether. One illustration of this is the main theme of the 'Wesendonck' Sonata. As William Ashton Ellis noted, it is reminiscent of the variation theme from Beethoven's Piano Sonata in A flat, op. 26:

Ex. 16a Wagner, 'Wesendonck' Sonata (bars 1–9)

Ex. 16b Beethoven, Piano sonata in A flat major, op. 26, Andante con Variazioni (bars 1–4)

Stylistic similarities in their formal aspects

As we have already suggested, to delineate Wagner's early orientation to Beethoven (and other composers) solely with the help of thematic reminiscences would be placing an undue restriction on the areas of influence. And while the thematic echoes already reflect a patently conscious borrowing, this applies still more to broader similarities of structure and design. As yet these may not have been established in Wagner's mind on a theoretical level, in a conception that was drama-orientated, but they probably arose from his attempt to obtain insights into the construction of Beethoven's works that he could use in his own composing.

In that respect, Wagner found both inspiration and guidance in the lessons he received from Theodor Weinlig between the autumn of 1831 and some time in 1832. (His first teacher, Gottlieb Müller, has also been mentioned in this connection.) He learnt the techniques of counterpoint and also – judging by what he told the London critic Edward Dannreuther – the rudiments of musical analysis.

The C major Symphony in particular shows traces of Wagner's studies with Weinlig and of 'Beethoven's example, which I now understand somewhat better' (*SB* 1, p. 99). Here the approximations are not only thematic–motivic ones. Both the Andante theme and the layout of the beginning of the movement point to the Allegretto of Beethoven's Seventh Symphony. The appearance of the 'tune' is preceded by an (almost motto-like) four-bar passage, and this is repeated.

Ex. 17 Wagner, Symphony in C major, Andante ma non troppo, un poco maestoso (bars 1–8)

This is followed by a few bars of *Fortspinnung* or spinning-out. Its function is similar to the function of the first theme in the Beethoven Allegretto. Like that theme, it prefaces the movement, and the 'tune' which comes soon after stands out from it. True, Beethoven's introductory theme is an enduring metrical–harmonic structure securing the melody, and Wagner's prefatory bars do not have the same effect. All the same, Wagner was evidently at pains to combine the function of the 'introduction' with that of a continuous 'background'. This can be seen from the staccato quavers that punctuate the course of the 'tune'. They are even included in the middle section (bars 62–105), together with a metrically dislocated motif:

Ex. 18 Wagner, Symphony in C major, Andante ma non troppo, un poco maestoso (bars 62–5)

It is as though Wagner also wanted to suggest something of the rhythmic steadiness which in Beethoven's movement links the main section and the middle section.

Another aspect of Wagner's style that merits attention is the distribution of the various melodic entries. Like the Beethoven 'tune', Wagner's makes three appearances on the strings in the first section (bars 17–53). And except for the first repeat (where Wagner gives the melody to the violas as well as second violins), the distribution is the same as Beethoven's: on cellos and violas the first time round, and on first violins the third. As to Wagner's second section (bars 106–72), the imitative thematic development from bar 126 onwards seems to have been freely modelled on the Beethoven fugato (from bar 183).

In his early years Wagner was already fascinated by rhythm – which dominates, more than anything else by Beethoven, his Seventh Symphony. This fascination is reflected in the C major Symphony's first movement in particular. Admittedly there is a difference, in terms of the rhythmic–metrical grouping and internal structuring, between the chains of notes attached to the 'head' of the allegro theme and the structure in the Beethoven Vivace:

Ex. 19 Wagner, Symphony in C major, Allegro con brio (bars 78–83)

But the particular way these are used, the fact that they permeate large chunks of the Wagner Allegro in an unchanging pattern, suggests the Vivace as a model. Moreover, the standard rhythmic pattern also comes to affect the second theme. This is partly because of the rhythmic connection with the main theme, and partly because the succession of notes attached to the head of the theme again expands in a 'persevering' manner:

Ex. 20 Wagner, Symphony in C major, Allegro con brio (bars 109–18)

Later on, Wagner was to perceive connections with the 'Eroica' Symphony as well as the Fifth and Seventh. The 'passionate and bold elements of the *Sinfonia eroica*, and particularly its first movement,' he writes in *My Life* (p. 58), 'were not without obvious influence on my conception'. Possibly he was alluding to the diastematic profile of the head of the theme, the pattern of a rising and falling third. In Beethoven's case this is followed by a fourth-step, whereas with Wagner (in association with the theme's entry on the mediant) it is followed by a major third:

Ex. 21a Wagner, Symphony in C major, Allegro con brio (bars 55–8)

Ex. 21b Beethoven, Symphony no. 3, E flat major, op. 55, Allegro con brio (bars 1–8)

186

Of greater weight, however, are such broader issues as the thematic head's particular function in the course of the music. The formal accents this gives rise to are quite specific. In the development there are two passages (from bar 231 and bar 276 respectively) where the head comes after the second theme. The resulting contrast might have been taken from Beethoven's development. In the form of a drastic confrontation, it would come from bars 300ff., which usher in the 'principal motif ... in its complete original form' (Walter Riezler [5/1942], p. 285) after the new melodic episode – which functionally speaking may be regarded as representing the second theme; and in its 'conciliatory' form, the effect would derive from bars 338ff.

Finally, Wagner's coda is a noteworthy one from the viewpoint of symphonic writing. Significantly, it is announced by an appearance of the head of the theme on the brass (trumpet, bars 420ff.). This is reminiscent of the horn entry prior to Beethoven's coda (bar 535). In both cases, moreover, the coda begins with the imitative entry of the main theme. Evidently Wagner was trying not only to capture something of the heroic character of Beethoven's theme but also to accentuate its development on similar lines, at least from the formal standpoint. It is hardly necessary to add that his development does not match the 'Eroica' movement in magnificence. It would be unjust to dismiss Wagner's efforts for that reason, but the underlying compositional factors are instructive. Wagner conspicuously adheres to his established thematic–motivic shapes. This approach rules out a Beethovenian type of development, and we shall examine it in greater detail presently.

It is possible that Beethoven's 'Eroica' in particular was Wagner's source for certain scherzo elements as well. Bars 5–8 and 13–16 of his third movement read like an abridged and modified version of the rocking motif – 'Schaukelmotif' (Gustav Becking [1921], pp. 39ff.) – in Beethoven's scherzo; see bars 1–3 and the incipient rise in bar 4. But it is more the broader, structural features that reveal a stylistic similarity. True, Wagner did not compose a genuinely Beethovenian scherzo; the construction of his theme does not have the same lucidity and regularity. But the phrases' relationship to one another shows typical scherzo features. These are manifested in the rhythmic lack of proportion existing between a^1–b^1 and a^2–b^2, as regards the relationship between strong and less strongly marked rhythm,

Ex. 22 Wagner, Symphony in C major, Allegro assai (bars 5–12)

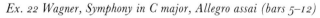

and also in the relationship between the half-phrases. For whereas the phrases in a^1–b^1 are moving in different directions, the phrases of a^2–b^2 show a rising motion in both cases.

Ex. 23 Wagner, Symphony in C major, Allegro assai (bars 5–20)

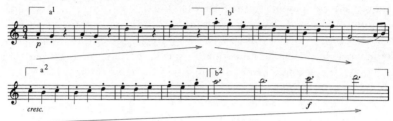

A quite different aspect of Beethoven's stylistic influence probably lies behind the formal problems presented by Wagner's Piano Sonata in A major. Again it transcends thematic–motivic reminiscences, yet it actually crops up in association with them.

The work dates from 1832, and it has been rated far higher than the Sonata in B flat major composed a year earlier. There is an unmistakable increase in compositional skill, in Wagner's command and shaping of musical ideas. But precisely these elements lead to breaks in the work. In the sonata Wagner evidently wanted to compose, the first movement would correspond to the normal pattern, but in addition, the fugue principle would be incorporated in the design of the final movement, along the lines of Beethoven's late sonatas. This hypothesis is supported by the source-findings published in the piano volume of the *Gesamtausgabe*, edited by Carl Dahlhaus. Originally the maestoso introduction to the finale was to have been followed by a fugued passage, Tempo moderato e maestoso, but this was later deleted.

Whatever we think of this cut, we cannot simply ignore it. Nor is it irrelevant to enquire into the technical reasons for it. (Daube relegates this important point to a footnote; even the *Werkverzeichnis* mentions it only in passing.) The evidence of the autograph indicates that it was Wagner himself who made the deletion. A comparison of the joins also supports this view. The demisemiquavers before the second main section (Allegro molto) are more convincing when they follow on from the demisemiquaver quintuplet of the maestoso section than when they carry on after the fermata of the fugued Tempo moderato e maestoso. These demisemiquaver figures signal a reorganization. Voss connects this with the intended publication of the work in 1877–8, a project which fell through. But can we be sure that the cut – which, like the opus number '4', is inscribed in red ink – was made as late as that? It seems fair to assume that the composer, after originally planning a fugued finale, turned to an extended sonata movement with coda because he could not sustain his initial conception. The hybrid form engendered by the 39 (41) bars of the fugued section was ultimately something repugnant to Wagner's sense of form.

There is also something else to suggest that Wagner was originally aiming at a fugued (or a fugal) finale. This has not been previously considered in Wagner studies. It is the connection with the maestoso opening of Beethoven's Sonata in C minor, op. 111, followed by an Allegro con brio ed appassionato in which the writing is solidly contrapuntal. Not only Wagner's heading and the 4/4 time but also some rhythmic – not melodic – details point to Beethoven's introductory Maestoso. Here we are referring to the combination of double-dotted quavers and demisemi-quavers, and particularly the alternation between one bar where the rhythm is built in this way and one bar of looser figuration (consisting of passage work with Wagner, arpeggiated triads with Beethoven):

Ex. 24a Wagner, Piano sonata in A major, Maestoso (bars 1–5)

Ex. 24b Beethoven, Piano sonata in C minor, op. 111, Maestoso (bars 1–7)

Compared with Beethoven, Wagner's grouping of dotted quavers and demisemiquavers looks naive, and he does not keep it up. With Beethoven all the subsequent events are evolved from this opening, in an atmosphere of taut suspense. Wagner supplies a fifth bar, and this is followed by the makings of a recitative as far as bar 10 (8), which leads to a fermata. Then the fugue theme makes its appearance.

Taken together, the maestoso opening and the ensuing 'fugue' once more justify the thesis that Wagner was influenced by Beethoven in the conception of his finale. The slow movement and last movement suggest what we might call an orientation towards the late piano sonatas of Beethoven's op. 106, op. 110 and op. 111 combined. But Voss is incorrect in saying that in the last movement, Wagner departed 'a little' from the overall order of Allegro – Adagio – Allegro; and the 'fugue', together with the maestoso introduction, is certainly not a substitute for a minuet or scherzo. Rather, the maestoso, fugal and allegro molto sections are all part of an attempt to integrate the characters of several movements and types of expression within one complex design. Wagner undertook this against the background of the late Beethoven sonatas, especially op. 111 and op. 110. The result was a hybrid construction, so to speak. Wagner wanted to live up to his model, and to surpass it if possible. This reflects a pupil's eagerness, not 'symphonic ambition'.

Compositional technique: motivic persistency

The streak of persistency in Wagner is one of his most interesting features. (We are not applying the word in any pathological sense.) It would seem to be the common denominator in various manifestations of his personality. It covers his proverbial eloquence as a speaker and writer, the way he would harp on ideas and concepts. It also covers his tendency as a composer to hang on to themes and motifs once he had found them, and his fondness for sequences. This applies both to the compositional detail and to motivic relationships in the broader context of music drama, the leitmotif technique. Wagner's idiosyncrasy can be traced right back to his early works. And at this point we must consider the question of the correlation between personal temperament and outside influences.

Any attempt to identify elements of the mature composer's style in the early works does of course present problems. It is only too easy to read things into works. Nonetheless there are certain individual points that encourage this kind of examination. It is also helpful to know that even contemporary critics of Wagner discovered things in his early compositions which must strike the later observer as heralding future characteristics.

In what Dorn describes as the 'first overture (B flat major, 6/8)', Wagner is already stubbornly hanging on to a musical 'idea'. Wagner intended to use different colours in his manuscript for different sections of the orchestra (see *My Life*, pp. 51, 53). The drum-beat, that fixed thematic component which kept following the 'red' allegro theme at the fifth bar, like an exclamation mark or acoustic signal (Strohm), is a clear enough indication of the persistent streak in Wagner. When the overture was performed, this 'persistent and regularly recurring effect soon began to excite the attention and then the amusement of the audience'. Later it would become a target for criticism. As Wagner developed as an artist, his musical compulsion to repeat things was developed to the point of perfection. But although it achieved the status of a first-class artistic device, it was one on which the critics differed.

A look at one or two of the instrumental works will help us to sketch in some of the stages in the above development. We shall find that the sequences and the chains of leitmotifs in the Wagnerian music drama cannot be wholly attributed to the 'poetic intention' and dramatic context. For one of their sources lies in Wagner's purely musical development. Something else that will emerge, however, is the correlation between temperament and outside influence. It would hardly be true to say that the example of Beethoven already lay behind the specific cut of the theme of the B flat major Overture. Beethoven's example took effect only little by little, serving to guide and to speed up Wagner's progress. Let us now begin to retrace this progress.

The thematic–motivic reminiscences, formal similarities and aspects of the working-up technique vary in emphasis from one piece to another. In Wagner's Piano Sonata in A, for instance, the element of thematic–motivic development is relatively slight, compared with individual thematic and formal approximations to Beethoven. What is especially pronounced is a tendency simply to hang on stubbornly. The upbeat extension of the main theme following on from the initial motif

Ex. 25 Wagner, Piano sonata in A major, Allegro (bars 1–6)

is repeated separately and sequentially in the first movement's development section. This is associated with a continuous reduction of the thematic material. Let us divide the first five bars of the main theme into the two segments a and b, using x and y to represent those motivic particles of a and b which are split off in the development and deployed in fresh combinations. This produces the following series of combinations for bars 106/7–123 and 146/7–163:

$$a^{x+y} \; b^{x+y} \; b^{x+y}, \; a^{x}b^{x+y} \; b^{x+y}, \; a^{x}b^{x}, \; a^{x}b^{x}, \; a^{x}.$$

Although following the principle of motivic fragmentation, Wagner never combines this with any development, any extension of thematic–motivic material. Instead he favours a succession of segments whose progressive shortening, in conjunction with a variable combination of motifs, never does more than merely repeat the same thing. Basically this is a process of shrinkage, not an evolution. And the monotonous regularity this implies is particularly obtrusive because the main theme, like the bridge passage and second theme, makes two appearances in the development.

Things are different in the C major Symphony. Significantly, though, one contemporary review criticized the 'persistent development of the one idea' and another for being 'still used too long, and too much'. In fact the paratactic, motivically short-winded technique of the Sonata in A major gives way to features of a more extensive development. This is reflected in the aforementioned chains of notes in the Allegro, the rhythmic–motivic relations between the two main themes and the appearance of a part of the second theme which corresponds to the first theme before the second theme actually enters.

Ex. 26 Wagner, Symphony in C major, Allegro con brio (bars 91–97)

Even here, the unfolding of the musical events is based not on a Beethoven-type development but on the insistent recurrence of the one idea. All the same, in his compositional technique Wagner was now approaching a new type of melodic development with the help of expanding sequences – instead of shrinking ones. This is probably attributable to Beethoven's influence. So here that influence was having an active, perceptible effect with the support of a tendency inherent in Wagner himself. But it should also be noted that the 'persistent development of the one idea and another' already conveys something of that solidifying of thematic and motivic figures which would eventually be looked upon as a negative (because overworked) feature of Wagner's 'leitmotifs'.

Wagner's 'Wesendonck' Sonata is a vivid example of the further development of long-lasting sequences in his instrumental writing. It is a work in one movement. After the leap of a sixth (b^x) has paved the way, thus:

Ex. 27 Wagner, 'Wesendonck' Sonata (bars 76–7)

the development eventually brings b^x in full (from bar 85):

Ex. 28 Wagner, 'Wesendonck' Sonata (bars 85–7)

and then (in a modified version) b^{x+y} from bar 92:

Ex. 29 Wagner, 'Wesendonck' Sonata (bars 92–100)

Up to bar 114 this is repeated five times. Then come b^x and a new combination which recurs three times and is formed out of two downward leaps of the sixth.

Ex. 30 Wagner, 'Wesendonck' Sonata (bars 117–21)

After this (from bar 130) we have b^{x+y} once more, turning into passages in stepwise motion which lead to a kind of apotheosis of the leap of a sixth from b^x plus the adjoining step of a second.

Ex. 31 Wagner, 'Wesendonck' Sonata (bars 131–34)

This sonata shows an intensive and multifarious spinning-out of thematic–motivic material. That it reflects Wagner's particular problems as a composer at the start of the 1850s is hardly deniable in the light of our earlier remarks on the subject. We shall discuss it further in connection with some thoughts on Wagner and sonata form.

Sonata form: traditional mould; modification; music drama

(a) The traditional mould: B flat major and A major Sonatas
As a musical dramatist Wagner was to proclaim an emancipation from sonata form, but in his early writing he closely conformed to the traditional pattern. In so doing he was guided by various models. The sonatas in D minor and F minor and the sonata for piano duet in B flat major which are mentioned in *My Life* have not survived. Next came the B flat major Sonata, op. 1, a product of Wagner's lessons with Weinlig. *My Life* says of it that Weinlig gave him 'one of the most childlike sonatas of Pleyel ... as a model' (*ML*, p. 56).

This work can indeed be regarded as an imitation of the style of Pleyel; at all events there seems to be more of him than of Mozart in it. Quite recently (1977), Voss has even proposed Beethoven as a model. We have already mentioned the somewhat superficial reminiscences in the slow movement and some occasional ones, such as the triplet motif, in the first movement. But just where in this sonata can we find more deep-seated connections with Beethoven? In the four-movement layout? That would be the most likely possibility – were it not for the flimsy construction of the musical blocks, and for a development which resembles nothing so much as a prayer wheel. The example of Pleyel, on the other hand, is suggested by the trite construction in general, the jerky and incessantly recurring ductus of the first movement's main theme, and the hackneyed construction of note-groups and themes, particularly in the development section. Much more than the way the second theme is included in the development section – a feature which could well derive from Haydn, who was Pleyel's teacher, the double occurrence, in this section, of both the first and second theme has that obviously schematic look which clearly separates Pleyel from either Haydn or Mozart. In *My Life* Wagner expressed regret at the fact that Breitkopf & Härtel had recently reprinted the piece. He also con-trasted it with the merits of some early overtures. So later on this stylistic imitation was clearly an embarrassment to him.

There are obvious advances when we come to the first movement of the Sonata in A. Nonetheless the construction is scarcely less conventional than the construction of the Sonata in B flat. True, the thematic design is more individual, and the working-up of the material shows more variety, but the schematic nature of the writing reveals that Wagner looked on sonata design as a special assignment. What is particularly noticeable is that the formal features reminiscent of Pleyel are still in evidence. This sonata too has a development containing parts of the first and second theme, and they appear twice. Even the bridge passage is built into the development, at the same place as it occurs in the exposition.

Another salient feature also betrays something of a Pleyel-like standardization. Rather like a children's box of bricks, the whole movement is made up of individual components which appear over and over again. It is true that in the development (see bars 107–22 and 147–62), Wagner was evidently trying to arrive at some kind of evolution by progressively reducing motivic material from the main theme. He also expanded the bridge passages in the development. But there is still no sign of the Beethovenian technique of evolving themes and motifs, and indeed whole paragraphs, from what has gone before, as elements that move the music onwards. Even a motif which has split off from the principal theme in the exposition (bars 41–7) still serves to lead back to it and looks conventional in respect of the writing as a whole. Beethoven's approach to development meant an organically evolving whole; Wagner organizes the thematic elements additively. But the harmony of his sequences is interesting. It at once proceeds (bars 4/5, 8/9) within the area of the dominant upon the varying bass octave A_1–A, ending up on a fermata of the dominant in bar 11; and then, starting with the bridge-passage figuration (bar 25), it reaches the 'double dominant' in the key of the dominant, E major. This 'F sharp major' (bar 39) on the one hand and the erosion of the function of the dominant on the other lend a great deal of conviction to the introduction of the second theme in C sharp minor (the relative key of the dominant). This element breaks away from the traditional mould. It is reminiscent of, say, Beethoven's Piano Sonata in G, op. 31(i). There, after we have already heard plenty of the D major key in bars 39–45, the second theme enters in the major-key version of the mediant, i.e. B major.

The above element is a pointer to the future, and by no means in a negative sense. It seems like a very rudimentary form of something that was to become so typical of Wagner: a combination of sequential technique and wide-ranging harmony – to which, of course, he would later apply all his cunning.

(b) A modification: the 'Wesendonck' Sonata

On 20 June 1853 Wagner sent Otto Wesendonck the piano sonata he had written for Mathilde. The accompanying letter includes the following noteworthy phrase: 'my first composition since the completion of Lohengrin (that was 6 years ago)'. The fact that it was his first composition after a long interval was obviously important to Wagner, but so was the inner creative process which had gone on in the meantime. It covers the period in which his theory of music drama was taking shape and especially the period between 1850 and 1853, when he could begin to sense that his theoretical reflections and his efforts to reach a final design for the *Ring* cycle were aspects of the same process of clarification and were closely connected.

Longer still – and this is correspondingly evident from the sonata itself – is the period separating it from the Sonata in A major. There is no longer any sign of an attempt to produce a stylistic imitation, a sonata according to type, in spite of the thematic reminiscences of Beethoven's Sonata, Op. 26. Carl Dahlhaus remarks that the 'Wesendonck' Sonata stands out among the piano compositions as a 'work' in the fullest sense of the word. This, however, could refer to the intention rather than the finished product.

Along with certain improvisatory touches, the one-movement layout may have influenced the publisher's original plan to issue the piece under the title 'Sketch of a Sonata for the Album of Frau M.W.' Wagner objected to this heading. On the other hand, as a letter from Cosima to Schotts indicates, he wanted the piece to be readily recognizable as one that was written for an occasion. Even later on, he seems to have accepted it as a fully rounded and valid composition, while trying to stop people from regarding it as being up to his usual standard.

The basic formal pattern may be described as a^1-b^1-c-b^2-a^2, i.e. sonata form with the first and second themes changing places in the reprise. This could mislead us into speaking of 'arch form', which is not an accurate description. The work's structure is proof that sonata form had become 'problematic' for Wagner, the main problem being the reprise or recapitulation.

By beginning his reprise with the return of the second theme, Wagner upsets the recapitulatory principle in two respects. Firstly, the change of order means a major departure from the exposition, and in the second place, Wagner's second theme contains bits of the principal theme:

Ex. 32 Wagner, 'Wesendonck' Sonata (bars 173–80)

Thus the developmental character extends beyond the middle section (c). And the same goes for the conclusion (a²). Although the main theme appears again from bar 206 onwards, it is strongly modified in comparison to the exposition. It leads to a triplet motion, but in the end Wagner brings back the motif which held the development (section c) together as the principal link in the sequential chain.

From the development section to the close, the piece is palpably determined by the principle of (sequential) thematic–motivic working, in the sense of a linking of themes and motifs. An important role is played by the motivic material of the principal theme, which also creeps into the second theme. This state of affairs corresponds to Uhlig's observations on the 'Eroica'. There are in fact – to paraphrase Wagner's remark on the composition of *Rheingold* – only a few bars which we cannot relate to previous motifs. Thus the melodic line of the transition (bars 39ff.) is connected with the sequential motivic chain in the previous bars (32/3ff.), an ascending sequence derived from the initial theme. In the second theme, the direction of these transitional phrases is reversed, and there are melodic extensions and modifications. We can regard this motivic–melodic linking as a practical commentary on what Wagner expounded in his letter to Röckel. Increasingly we see a direct connection with melodic phrases which are more and more remote from the starting-point (the first theme) but immediately adjacent to the relevant point in the development. This produces a multi-layered quality – in abstract terms, a 'stemma' of genealogical relations. There are various motivic 'degrees of affinity'; but since everything is connected with something else at one level or another, it is perfectly feasible to inject material that has not been derived genetically into the criss-crossing relationships. The ideal of deriving everything from a single nucleus becomes eroded in Wagner's practice.

The 'Sonata for the Album of Frau M.W.' is a latent technical study. As such it must be seen within the context of the problems that were occupying

Wagner before he composed *Rheingold* and which his orientation to Beethoven played a major part in solving. This technique was complemented by a form which may be described as strongly modified sonata form. The 'Wesendonck' Sonata is proof that Wagner associated more with sonata form than just the notional A-B-A scheme, or even that combination, variation and alternation of themes and motifs which his own composing was inclined to dictate.

The above point becomes particularly evident in the light of his later statements, when he was expressing an inclination to start writing symphonies again:

> At breakfast he talks about symphonies, how one might perhaps do something in this form of music if one did not feel obliged to compose in four movements, and if one shaped the motifs – first, second, return to the first – into movements.
>
> (CW, slightly revised, 18 October 1878)

This indicates how much Wagner associated formal ideas relating to sonata form with his individual themes and their reappearance. In addition, it was evidently not until now that he hit on the idea of combining several linked movements within the form of a single movement.

But there are also other reasons why it would be wrong to regard the 'Wesendonck' Sonata as combining several movements in one, despite the time-signature and change of tempo in the development section. It is not merely that the tempo change is designed to achieve a continuous intensification – the (single) change of rhythm being connected with this. Later on, Wagner was very rightly concerned to create specific thematic characters and movement areas as intrinsic types of expression within the single-movement framework, and thus to compose the movement in, as it were, cyclical form. But this does not happen with the 'Wesendonck' Sonata because of the way segments are reversed in the recapitulation. It is an exaggeration to say that this sonata represents several movements rolled into one.

What obviously lies behind such a claim is the desire to boost Wagner's merits as an instrumental composer, in spite of his own remarks on the subject. Was it really the case that he later set a low valuation on the piece he had written 'for the Album of Frau M.W.' out of consideration for Cosima? There is an entry in her diary which suggests otherwise:

> I tell him [Richard] I should like to hear the sonata which Frau Wesendonck had. 'It is nothing much,' he says, 'for I wrote it for her, and always when I sit down to do something, it turns out miserably . . .'   (CW, 23 September 1871)

The Sonata was an 'occasional' piece with 'Frau M.W.' as its cause and addressee. But significantly, Wagner attached the motto 'Wisst ihr wie das wird?' (the Norns' question in the *Ring*), and this was ambiguous. It referred partly to the uncertain nature of Wagner's future direction as a composer, and only this aspect of the question continued to interest him. The composition study had swallowed up the personal 'message'. So for Wagner, the Sonata had become a workshop piece – something private and yet of more general interest. As the instrumental sketch it was, it could not stand alongside the later music dramas that constituted Wagner's 'real' compositions. Self-criticism led him to resist the publication of other early works; it was also guiding him in this particular instance.

(c) Sonata form and music drama
Even though Wagner announced that he had conquered the schematicism of sonata form, this does not make the question of the 'sonata within the drama' redundant. Rather, it arises precisely because Wagner's feelings about the sonata were ambivalent, a mixture of familiarity and detachment. The question also remains relevant in view of the problematic relationship between theory and practice, and on account of the development that Wagner's sonata works actually illustrate.

Are there formal parallels with these sonatas in the music dramas? One point that needs making clear from the start is that we cannot hope to find more or less complete sonata forms within Wagner's drama. It is more a matter of particular structures, of the principles underlying the co-ordination and status of the separate parts within the whole even where they amount to mere fragments of what is commonly regarded as a sonata.

This is not an entirely novel perspective. It has figured in Alfred Lorenz's efforts to elucidate the 'secret of the form' in Wagner's music dramas. And on the face of it, this already removes the problem, since some of the formal patterns that Lorenz adduces also embrace sonata form. In fact, however, it renders Lorenz's own analysis problematic. Abstract forms like his *Reprisenbar* (recapitulatory strophe) and *Bogenform* (arch form) are basically products of the recapitulatory principle. And for Wagner this was the main drawback with sonata form; it was incompatible with a dramatically developing design. Further analysis is therefore needed, the central question being whether such concepts as the *Reprisenbar* and *Bogenform* – which feature recapitulation – can do justice to the musico-dramatic forms of Wagner's music drama.

In respect of bars 81–96 of the Prelude to *Rheingold*, Lorenz takes the *Reprisenbar* scheme for granted, i.e. a structure with the pattern m-m-n-m-(o). Two 'Stollen' each of two bars are followed by a twelve-bar 'Abgesang' divided into ten bars of development and two of recapitulation. It is germane to an appraisal of his analysis that Lorenz regards these sixteen bars as comprising the second variation in a set of four variations plus coda, underpinning an intensification 'by melodic and figurative means and through instrumental filling-in' that runs right through the prelude. This is doubtless correct, and it emphasizes the dynamic character of the prelude. But it consorts ill with the attempt to classify individual components of the whole as a recapitulation of formally self-contained units. Here Lorenz was categorizing against his own better judgment. The first figuration takes up two bars and is repeated once. Where this occurs (from bar 81), there is after the preceding quavers a new bout of development, spreading in semiquaver motion. This gradually takes hold of the full orchestra, in groupings of 4:6:6 bars. And the two 'recapitulatory' bars that come at the end of the second six-bar group represent a fresh dynamic impulse, not the return of anything that has appeared before.

What accounts for the weaknesses in Lorenz's analysis? They seem to have stemmed from the fact that he included dramatic and theatrical considerations only when he was forced to. At bottom he did not regard them as essential factors in the overall form. And as a result there is a wrong emphasis on recapitulation. Let us take just one of many instances where the *Reprisenbar* scheme is of doubtful validity: bars 3458–521 in Scene 4 of *Rheingold*. After fourteen introductory bars during which the Norns' motif is first heard, there are, according to Lorenz, two 'Stollen' which repeat the motif sequentially, followed by an 'Abgesang' containing a development and recapitulation. In fact, however, the one repeat of the Norns' motif is followed by a further development of it in the 'Götterdämmerung' motif, and this already conflicts with the idea of a recapitulation. The musico-dramatic status of this transformation is clear from the context. The entry of the 'Götterdämmerung' motif is assisted by the syncopated motif which precedes it, embodying the destructive work of the Nibelungs, although Lorenz only mentions this in passing ('insertion of new motifs'). It corresponds to Erda's ominous words 'Doch höchste Gefahr führt mich heut' selbst zu dir her.' This, if we relate it to Alberich, points far beyond Fafner's impending murder of his brother. The ensuing warning, however, is part of the actual 'Götterdämmerung' motif: 'Alles, was ist, endet! Ein düsterer Tag dämmert den Göttern: dir rath' ich, meide den Ring!' Suddenly the negative dimension of things to come is made more apparent.

The above links not only help us to sense the fateful shadows lurking behind the 'Götterdämmerung' motif that frames the warning. There is already a suggestion that the stages on the path of destiny will be basically determined by the immediately preceding, syncopated motif. This represents Alberich, who is plotting to destroy the gods and recover the ring. What Lorenz classifies as the 'reprise', or recapitulation, is really part of one of those nodal points in Wagner's music drama where some further development is implied. At such points there is a telescoping or 'actualizing' of the past (in the form of 'reminiscence') and the future (in the form of 'presentiment'), in addition to their being brought into focus as things far off in time.

There are, of course, other configurations – irrespective of the *Reprisenbar* and *Bogenform* – behind which we can discern fragments of sonata form. The Valkyries scene that opens Act III of *Die Walküre* can be regarded as a modified sonata form divided as follows: main theme–second theme–development–recapitulation–second development–coda. Here again, however, the recapitulation points beyond orthodox limits, since it leads to a second development section. The coda, on the other hand, has no recapitulatory function inasmuch as it is only a fragment, both motivically and in terms of its range (see Dahlhaus [1969], pp. 102f., 121).

We see from the above that not only individual motifs and motivic associations but also larger formal connections are bound up with the dramatic context. These larger connections have their own particular structure, while also forming part of the overall structure. And once again, a study of the musical form and dramatic 'environment' seems the right way to solve questions of formal relationships.

The question of a relationship between musical construction and the dramatic implications becomes especially urgent when certain elements in the drama may not fit in with an analysis oriented towards purely musical design. There has been a many-sided attempt by Carl Dahlhaus [1985] to show how the 'Wahnmonolog' in *Meistersinger* reflects the 'classical and post-classical tradition in instrumental music' (Beethoven plus Liszt); the 'developing variation' and combinations of themes in line with the 'art of transition'; 'vagrant tonality' and scherzo stylization in the design of the development. But this approach cannot demonstrate how motifs which do not fall within the area of purely musical 'developmental forms' might be comprehended in analytical terms as integral elements. Take Wagner's 'Lenzgebot' ('spring's command') motif. It can certainly be linked to other motifs on the level of 'submotivic' association, but it does not have a function in terms of form orientated to the symphonic model.

But the problem is not insoluble. We must cast aside the prejudiced idea that Wagner based all his music on purely musical principles of design and give due weight to the 'verse melody' and the 'surplus' motifs as well as orchestral melody. For these motifs are far from being 'secondary' – providing they are accorded serious consideration as part of the associative network of 'presentiment' [*Ahnung*], 'actualization' [*Vergegenwärtigung*] and 'reminiscence' [*Erinnerung*].

There is good reason for the 'Lenzgebot' motif to come as a 'nodal point in the web of submotivic association'. For is not 'spring's command' the cause of the confusion that Sachs, in his monologue, recognizes as one particular form of human folly [*Wahn*]? And surely the 'pre-history' of the motif goes back to its first palpable appearance in Walther's trial song (I:3, bars 1719ff.), when it is still a song motif? There, it is heard in the context of a spring song, but Sachs clarifies its meaning in his 'Fliedermonolog' (II:3). This 'elder-tree' soliloquy tells of Sachs's own folly, the love for Eva that he finds so hard to renounce. The 'Lenzgebot' motif from the 'Fliedermonolog' is the bridge to the 'Wahnmonolog' – both spacious and poetically motivated. And it is woven into the 'Wahnmonolog' musically as a motif of reminiscence, dramatically reliving the event. In this musico-dramatic capacity, however, it corresponds within the 'Wahnmonolog' to the lyrical motif, whose significance is far from marginal. The lyrical motif derives from the overture and the initial exchange of glances between Walther and Eva. In the 'Wahnmonolog', though, it is connected with Sachs's resolve to be in control of folly and to 'do some noble deed'. And in the form of a 'presentiment', it also points forward to the passage (III:4) containing the quotation from *Tristan*. At that point Sachs is delivered from his folly and carries out his deed with the help of a reminiscence of mythical profundity.

This shows that Wagner's symphonic techniques and forms in the 'Wahnmonolog' are interspersed with motifs whose motivation is primarily poetic. Such motifs are linked to the 'verse melody' and the network of 'presentiment', 'actualization' and 'reminiscence', and they take on a meaning that conforms to the 'poetic intention'. Here we have a mixture of the most different working-up techniques. Moreover the music results partly from a symphonic and partly from a musico-dramatic approach; and both must be taken into account if it is to be fully susceptible of analysis.

The aforesaid mixture of musical and dramatic structures is also the only explanation for the special position of the 'reprise' in Wagner's music dramas. True, he strongly advocated dispensing with recapitulation. But there is no mistaking the reappearance of larger structural and formal units, as well as the ever-recurring individual motifs. One example is the song of the Rhinemaidens that wells up 'from deep in the valley' at the end of *Rheingold*. From a purely musical viewpoint, this could certainly be described as a recapitulation. But the song occurs within a series of events that jerk the listener out of his retrospection. The lament is for the theft of the gold, which has already brought a curse and bloodshed, but it is also implicitly marked by the impending dramatic catastrophe.

This is why even the worthiest study will be too narrow in scope if it excludes the vital dramatic dimension. To concentrate on the purely musical areas because of textual shortcomings (see Poos [1987]), for instance, would be missing the point. Within the dramatic context the recapitulation takes on a double function: whilst looking backwards it also helps us to anticipate the future. Janus-like, the recurring material is both like and unlike itself. The history of Wagner's composing activities is an illustration in itself of this double function.

In *Lohengrin* the drama and the music were still two separate areas. In the *Ring* cycle, Wagner brought them together (see Dahlhaus [1970], pp. 23f.). There is a fundamental difference between his leitmotif technique up to *Lohengrin* and the technique he first adopted in the *Ring*. In the latter the leitmotifs become an integral part of the overall drama, of the poetic, musical and theatrical events combined. They are no longer fragments that have been interpolated into elements of musical forms, as they were in *Der Fliegende Holländer* and *Lohengrin*. Instead they constitute the actual formal points of reference, components and joints in the dramatic edifice. And when the function of the leitmotif was extended in this way, there were implications for the 'reprise'. What had been the 'recurrence of the same' (Adorno) became now, within the associative web of the music drama, the same in the guise of modification and for the sake of dramatic change and development.

Wagner took a step forward with the *Ring*; and this step corresponds both to his objections to a purely musical schematicism and to the stress he laid on Beethoven's compositional technique. And the two aspects are reflected in the 'Wesendonck' Sonata as well as in the *Ring* cycle. These parallels are too striking to be purely accidental. It really does seem to be the case that when Wagner was planning a new approach to drama, his orientation to Beethoven exerted some influence on the achievement of that plan.

The superseding of the reprise led to a new formal tautness in the *Ring*. To be sure, it was the leitmotivic technique that was chiefly responsible for this. Specifically formal considerations were of lesser weight, particularly those taking sonata form as their starting-point. This can be deduced from the fact that Wagner's first explicit attack on the recapitulation in the sonata came in 1857, in his essay *On Franz Liszt's Symphonic Poems*. And the musical evidence supports this. If we examine the function of the prelude (*Vorspiel*) or introduction (*Einleitung*) from *Tristan* onwards, we will observe a tendency to blend certain principles of musical architecture with principles of leitmotif technique. In the *Ring* cycle the preludes are generally built into the first scene of the drama concerned. This enables them to remain 'mobile' and to represent links of associative significance in the overall drama. By comparison, the introductions to Wagner's subsequent music dramas again reflect a certain stabilization.

In this respect the combination of leitmotif usage and introductory function in the first act of *Tristan* is particularly interesting. There is a complex of four motifs, comprising the themes of sorrow and yearning, destiny and the 'glance'. This represents the core of the introduction, and with its modifications it supports the inner, spiritual development. The complex recurs three times in Act I and once in each of the second and third acts. Wagner was probably inspired to bring back the introduction in this way by Beethoven's String Quartet in B flat, op. 130 (first movement) – and perhaps by the quartets of op. 127 and op. 132 as well. This is a point worth noting because the repeated introduction in these quartets includes some evolving thematic–motivic work. It means that Beethoven was superseding the rigid framework of the sonata, along with the one-sided, wholly backward-looking reprise. It is very tempting to interpret the reappearance in *Tristan* of the introductory motivic complex as a 'return', which it is from the viewpoint of the 'reprise' within the introduction (Poos [1987], p. 82n.), i.e. from the purely musical angle. But from the viewpoint of the dramatic configuration, this reading seems out of place.

The formal principle described above is one which transcends genres. And it is not just the formal parallels that lead us to think that Wagner adapted Beethoven's principle to the music drama. For he was realizing the idea of the repeated introduction at a significant time. It was when he was criticizing the recapitulatory principle in his essay devoted to Liszt, taking the sonata as a starting-point. It was also when he was completing a first series of explorations of the Beethoven string quartets with the Heisterhagen-Schleich Quartet.

Structures of quartet writing

It is fair to stress the point that Wagner applied the symphonic style to the music drama. But there is also important evidence that he drew on structures taken from string quartet writing; *Tristan und Isolde* and *Die Meistersinger* are particularly relevant in this context. And in Act III of *Siegfried* he uses a theme and possibly longer passages that he had sketched in the Villa Pellet by Lake Starnberg – thematic material which was also the basis for the *Siegfried Idyll*.[3]

As we have noted, the principle of the repeated introduction influenced *Tristan* in respect of the architectonics, the extensive motivic connections and their function. Another aspect of Beethoven's influence can be observed in the detail of the quartet – or quintet – style. This is evidence that with regard to small-scale forms, Wagner was by no means content with a string of formularized sequences. Taking Beethoven's late quartets as a point of departure, he was also capable of finely shaded, many-layered quartet writing.

Although it is hard to identify the links precisely, there are nonetheless passages that suggest a connection. We can immediately set Isolde's 'story of the ailing Tristan' in Act I of the music drama alongside the beginning of the finale of Beethoven's String Quartet in A minor, op. 132. A direct influence is suggested by the polyrhythmic construction, i.e. the simultaneous realization of varied sustained rhythms which, moreover, are complementary to each other. And then there is the fact that the rhythm in the inner parts runs counter to the stressed beats:

Ex. 33a Beethoven, String Quartet in A minor, op. 132, Allegro (bars 1–6)

Ex. 33b Wagner, Tristan und Isolde, *Act 1, scene 3 (bars 119–24)*

Ex. 33c Wagner, Tristan und Isolde, *Act 1, scene 3 (bars 138–44)*

When Hans Sachs sings 'Mein Freund, in holder Jugendzeit' in Act II of *Die Meistersinger*, the increasingly condensed string writing is reminiscent of the second theme in the opening movement of Beethoven's op. 132, with the complementary rhythms of the accompaniment.

Ex. 34a Beethoven, String Quartet in A minor, op. 132, Allegro (bars 48–51)

Ex. 34b Wagner, Meistersinger, *Act III, scene 2 (bars 123–5)*

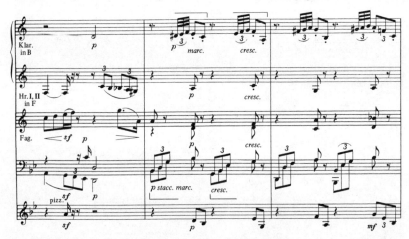

Ex. 34c Wagner, Meistersinger, *Act III, scene 2 (bars 130–3)*

The second act of *Tristan* contains an even more striking example of a chamber-music style that recalls Beethoven. It occurs in the closing section of Scene 2: Sink 'hernieder, Nacht der Liebe…' Here matters are more complicated than in our last example. Beethoven's influence is mixed up with two other things. One is the song *Träume*, which Wagner wrote as a 'study' for this passage on 4–5 December 1857, and the other is the 'love's rest' (*Liebesruhe*] motif already noted down under the heading '(Love scene. Tristan and Isolde)' on 19 December 1856.

In his diary Heinrich Porges states that the musical prototype of 'Sink hernieder, Nacht der Liebe' was the Adagio of Beethoven's E flat major Quartet, op. 127. Very probably he learnt this from Wagner himself. Op. 127 is described in Cosima's diaries as a favourite quartet of Wagner's. And when Porges wrote a book on *Tristan und Isolde* for King Ludwig II in 1866–7, Wagner certainly kept an eye on the project. Since it was intended as a gift for his royal patron, the text needed to have Wagner's approval. Moreover he wrote to Porges (15 May 1867) setting forth his views on that part of the text which dealt with the second act of *Tristan*.

The influence of this particular Beethoven Adagio is in any case fairly obvious. Of course, there is no question of a literal borrowing. The elements of the Beethovenian 'prototype' have been combined with the *Tristan* style and the lyrical 'study' in such a new and truly idiosyncratic way that it is difficult to examine them in isolation. Once again it is only when all the features are put together that a full picture begins to emerge.

Something that is particularly illuminating is the development of the idea we can trace – albeit only roughly – from what Otto Strobel identified as the 'love's rest' motif. Wagner first jotted it down on 19 December 1856 without any words:

Ex. 35 Wagner, Tristan und Isolde, *'Motiv der Liebesruhe', sketch*

Extract 35 (cont.)

But, as a pocket-book entry tells us, Wagner provided a text for the motif not long before August 1857. They are the words we hear at the beginning of the scene on the 'bank of flowers' – 'Sink' hernieder, Nacht der Liebe...'

Ex. 36 Wagner, Tristan und Isolde, *'Motiv der Liebesruhe', sketch*

Sink' hernie - der Nacht der Lie - be nimm mich auf in dei-nen Schoss Hell dann leuchten Ster - ne der Wonne
Glüht im Busen mir die Sonne

This continues with the phrase 'nimm mich auf in deinen Schoss'. The words for the motivic variant that Wagner noted down next are 'Hell dann leuchten Sterne der Wonne / Glüht im Busen mir die Sonne.' As we see from all this, the text is a half-way house between a prose draft and dramatic poetry. In the final version of the work, Wagner proceeded to separate the 'love's rest' motif from the words 'Sink' hernieder...' The motif is now heard for the first time fifty-two bars later on, in a simplified form (a preliminary stage, as it were), to the words 'Herz an Herz dir, Mund an Mund...':

Ex. 37 Wagner, Tristan und Isolde, *Act II, scene 2 (bars 627–32)*

Isolde

Herz an Herz __ dir, Mund an Mund;

T.

dei - nen Au - gen süß zer - ron - nen; ei - nes A -

Vc. *p* *p* *p*

In the very first version Wagner noted down, it makes its first appearance even later, just before Tristan's 'soll ich lauschen' (i.e. after 314 bars). There must have been a serious reason for this change. The crucial consideration must have been the need for a musical framework within which the whole scene could be properly developed. And with this in mind, Wagner surely looked at the Adagio, ma non troppo e molto cantabile from Beethoven's op. 127. This conjecture is supported by the following factors. First there is the curtain-like unfurling of the writings for strings. Then there are the rhythmic–melodic relations. Thirdly, there is the way these melodic factors are incorporated in the musical context, along with the alternation of time-signatures (3/4 and 9/8 time). Fourthly, there is the quartet style's rhythmicality, and lastly there are certain principles of variation to consider.

The similarity with regard to the curtain-like impression will be obvious if we compare the two scores:

Ex. 38a Beethoven, String Quartet in E flat major, op. 127, 2nd movement, Adagio, ma non troppo e molto cantabile (bars 1–3)

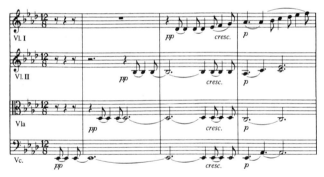

Ex. 38b Wagner, Tristan und Isolde, Act II, scene 2 (bars 573–8)

In the case of *Tristan* the cellos (which are divided here, like all the strings) are silent for a moment when the 3/4 rhythm begins, and the actual 'unfurling' starts on the violas. This may be attributed to Wagner's exceptional care and economy in his treatment of the instruments, and to his efforts to achieve a chamber-music sound.

Rhythmic–melodic reminiscences will be evident if we compare bars 3–4 of the quartet movement (Vln I) with the melodic dialogue of the vocal parts from 'gib Vergessen' to 'löse von der Welt mich los!':

Ex. 39a Beethoven, String Quartet in E flat major, op. 127, 2nd movement, Adagio, ma non troppo e molto cantabile (bars 1–4)

Ex. 39b Wagner, Tristan und Isolde, *Act II, scene 2 (bars 584–94)*

These reminiscences can also be found in the passage 'welterlösend aus. Barg im Busen uns sich die Sonne':

Ex. 39c Wagner, Tristan und Isolde, *Act II, scene 2 (bars 614–20)*

In the two vocal parts 9/8 time alternates with 3/4 time. It is noticeable that this change of rhythm is connected with a succession of musical structures which are completely different from one another. A rising or falling melodic line (in 9/8 time), divided into groups of three quavers, is succeeded by a long-drawn suspended note which is not 'resolved' until the next bar (3/4 time). It is obvious where these suspensions come from: they originate in the song *Träume*:

Ex. 40a Wagner, 'Wesendonck' song 'Träume' (bars 5–9)

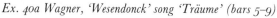

Ex. 40b Wagner, Tristan und Isolde, *Act II, scene 2 (bars 585–90)*

But it is not just by virtue of the melody and the figurative division of the beat into three that the 9/8 phrases point to the Beethoven adagio movement (12/8 time). The main resemblance is that these phrases seem like interpolations, considering the 3/4 rhythm that prevails in all the other parts. Since, however, the alternating 3/4 and 9/8 segments are being shifted one against the other in the two voices, the melodic line in 9/8 time runs right through the vocal parts, the dialogue between Tristan and Isolde. Wagner has shared the first violin's rising and falling melodic phrases in Beethoven's variation theme between the two voices. This might have been inspired by the way Beethoven turned the variation theme into a dialogue – the second variation being based on that principle:

Ex. 40c Beethoven, String Quartet in E flat major, op. 127, 2nd movement, Andante con moto (bars 40–2)

Wagner's actual string quartet writing is similar to the theme of Beethoven's variation movement in its rhythmic structure, in its continuous series of groups of three. The differences are that Wagner is writing in 3/4 time and the groups of three are constructed with triplets, rather than by means of a notional division of the beat into three. Moreover the last quarter of each bar is divided into two quavers. In this way, however, Wagner commutes precisely between 9/8 and 3/4 time. The effect is reinforced by the syncopated shift in the triplet rhythm, forming a kind of hazy continuum in the background which coincides only here and there with one or other of the melodic segments. The rhythmic construction is an indirect sign that Wagner was blending melodic–motivic material from various sources.

As we have observed, the dialogue form of the 9/8 phrases suggests the influence of Beethoven's second variation. The working-up of the 'love's rest' motif indicates that Wagner also drew on another variation technique that Beethoven used in his op. 127. This is the varying of individual motifs belonging either to the theme or to its context. (See bars 97ff., 111ff., 120/1ff. in the Beethoven movement. For the purposes of our comparison we do not need to decide whether each of these is a new and separate variation.) True, Wagner noted down some variations on the theme among his 1856 sketches, but this was more a case of establishing the best form of the idea for the time being, or of giving himself a choice later. And even if he already had variation technique in mind, there was nothing to stop him from varying in accordance with this new approach later on, when the Beethoven Adagio had made him think again, and drawing on earlier sketches in the process. In keeping with this, the 'love's rest' motif as first stated is a simplified and abbreviated preliminary form of the motif proper. (Here we could adopt Karl H. Wörner's term 'motivic variations'.) Wagner takes it up several times in passages like the following:

Ex. 41a Wagner, Tristan und Isolde, *Act II, scene 2 (bars 689–91/694–6)*

Eventually it becomes more sharply delineated and is developed further:

Ex. 41b Wagner, Tristan und Isolde, *Act II, scene 2 (bars 714–18)*

Next, at this stage in its evolution, the motif is worked sequentially:

Ex. 41c Wagner, Tristan und Isolde, *Act II, scene 2 (bars 741–8)*

until the initial part is finally split off:

Ex. 41d Wagner, Tristan und Isolde, *Act II, scene 2 (bars 766–72)*

Ex. 41d (cont.)

and this soon leads to a line of 'spinning-out':

Ex. 41e Wagner, Tristan und Isolde, *Act II, scene 2 (bars 792–6)*

And the form in which the motif last appears comes closest to the one that Wagner sketched first.

This analytical outline illustrates the complexity of the compositional process. It shows that Beethoven's influence was just one element in a whole complex of related factors.

'Leitmotifs'

(a) The term

As is well known, it was not the composer himself but Hans von Wolzogen who introduced the term 'leitmotif' into the literature on Wagner's music.[4] In *On the Application of Music to Drama*, Wagner mentions the younger friend who 'scrutinized the characteristics of what he called the "leitmotifs" more with regard to their dramatic meaning and effectiveness than . . . in respect of their role in the musical construction' (*GS* x, p. 185). For his part,

Wolzogen remarked in the *Bayreuther Blätter* of 1897 that he had first referred to 'leitmotifs' in the introduction to his essay on the *Motifs in Wagner's Götterdämmerung* (1877).

It was Wolzogen's aim to demonstrate the 'organized form of the drama' – namely the 'ordering of certain *basic ideas*' – from the way that the musical 'leitmotifs' succeeded one another and were mutually related. For the recurrent leitmotifs, he wrote, expressed the 'volitional content' of the basic dramatic ideas. Here Wolzogen was carrying on from two analyses (of *Rheingold* and *Walküre*) that Gottlieb Federlein had published in the *Musikalisches Wochenblatt* in 1871 and 1872. The Wagner circle at Tribschen knew of these, and the composer himself had read the *Rheingold* analysis, if not both. This can be inferred from a letter of 24 May 1870 to an unnamed correspondent (see Wagner [1953]). The recipient will surely have been Federlein, who had evidently sent Wagner a manuscript copy of his work and asked for the score in return, so that he could follow the deployment of the themes more closely. Cosima subsequently checked both his analyses – the *Rheingold* analysis on 23 October 1870, i.e. evidently after Federlein had worked over his essay with the aid of a score. In her diaries she comments: 'Read Herr Federlein's essay on *Das Rheingold*, which I find very good, and I suggest to R. that he have it printed as articles.'

Wolzogen was cautious in the *Bayreuther Blätter* about the origin of the word 'leitmotif'. 'It no longer seems possible to tell who "invented" it. Legend may have it that I was responsible, but I could not honestly claim that I was conscious of that.' In fact Friedrich Wilhelm Jähns had already used the term in 1871, at the beginning of his thematic catalogue of the works of Weber. And prior to that, Friedrich Stade comes very close to it in his essay *On the Wagner Question* (1870):

The music embodies [*plastificirt*] these characters and dramatic motives from the viewpoint of their emotional manifestation in the form of so-called typical leading themes [*'Leitthemen'*], and takes their development as a basis. In the process it reveals to us the entire workings of the inner life, the most private urges and impulses, whereas poetry *on its own* lacks the ability to portray these exhaustively. This interaction, this mutual illumination from within of the poetic and musical statements allows the characterization to take on an extraordinary wealth of shadings and nuances. At the same time the continuous use of principal motifs to underpin the musical development results in a unity which the old type of opera could never achieve. (Stade [1870], p. 563)

There was an important anticipation of all such writings – in other words, the idea of outlining the dramatic plot with the aid of characteristic motifs – even earlier than this. For Heinrich Porges had charted the 'principal motifs' of the music to the drama in his study of *Tristan und Isolde*. As Ernest Newman observed, he and Wolzogen were really doing the same thing. And significantly, the letter in which Wagner gives his opinion of Porges' study similarly uses the term 'principal motif' [*Hauptmotif*] in the musico-dramatic sense, where the meaning is close to that of 'leitmotif'. We might add that Porges's study was probably prompted by a letter which Ludwig II's secretary, Franz Pfistermeister, wrote to Wagner on 26 October 1864. The king, it said, wanted to know which were the 'principal musical motifs' [*die musikalischen Haupt-Motive*] for *Ring des Nibelungen* and *Tristan und Isolde*.

There remains the question of whether the leitmotif is basically of literary origin. Voss and Borchmeyer have recently answered this with an emphatic 'Yes'. But perhaps the answer is not that straightforward. Doubtless there exist parallels and correlations here between music drama and literature. Even so, the structural underpinning by means of 'present-iment', 'actualization' and 'reminiscence' (Thomas Mann, late in his life, was to stress the importance of this) is an undoubted achievement on Wagner's part. It is what gives real meaning to the concept of the leitmotif. The question of a literary provenance or context returns us to the heart of the problem.

(b) Distinctions regarding the 'leitmotif'

The guides that were published to Wagner's 'leitmotifs' were one cause of the exaggerated criticism which they had to face. After Wolzogen, such 'guides' became a rapidly expanding industry. Wolzogen himself had been against the idea of Wagner's motifs as a 'musical attempt to represent a concept' or the 'tonal painting of a phenomenon'. But that was the very idea he unwittingly encouraged: others were to define the music drama's 'melodic moments' in conceptual and pictorial language. As a result of such labelling, people tended to overlook the spiritual and musical variation to which Wagner submitted his motifs, and hence the dramatic evolution in which these motifs are simply one element.

Scepticism and reservations about the names given to the various leitmotifs are as old as the guides to them. Yet commentators still go on speaking of 'leitmotifs' and making use of the labels – which, we may note, are used anything but consistently. Initially these names may help us to find our bearings and understand what is happening. In the long run, however, distinctions will be needed if we are to do justice to the reality of the music drama with its multiplicity of outward forms.

As we have already suggested, there are certain differences which are based on the origins of the leitmotif principle. Carl Dahlhaus has written of the qualitative leap between *Lohengrin* and the *Ring* in both the forging and the deployment of the motifs. This leap shows that the 'early forms' of the leitmotif idea gave little indication of its essence. And we have not yet covered all the changes in the leitmotifs and their deployment in Wagner's output as a whole. In his 1970 study of the counterpoint in *Meistersinger*, Ludwig Finscher deliberately avoids the term 'leitmotif'. It was, he says, the composition technique in *Rheingold* and *Walküre* to which it was most readily applicable, and that technique had been largely over-ridden in *Meistersinger*. There, disregarding their musical character, the majority of the motifs hardly retain the dramatic function of leitmotifs as Wagner envisaged it in theory. Finscher's view is in accordance with that of Jack M. Stein, who remarks that because of the twelve-year interruption, there are distinct differences even within the *Ring* cycle:

The new motifs, those which first appear in Siegfried, Act III on, are of a quite different nature from the earlier Ring motifs. They are broader, longer, more independently musical, with less emphasis on characteristic pictorialization than the briefer, more fragmentary earlier ones. They are unsuitable for the kind of psychological commentary Wagner had used the earlier motifs for.

(*Richard Wagner and the Synthesis of the Arts*, p. 192)

Not just twelve years lay between the composition of the second and third acts of *Siegfried*. They were also separated by two works as self-contained and as individual in style as *Tristan* and *Meistersinger*. And while there is a remarkable stylistic consistency in the way Wagner carried on with the *Ring*, the artistic experience he had acquired in the meantime did affect his composing. It is, however, a moot point whether the somewhat longer motifs are really less suitable for psychological commentary, as Stein asserts.

The above divergences were caused by changes and pauses in the course of the creation of the *Ring*. But the motifs of the tetralogy have also been divided into various groups according to the particular level of dramatic expression and reference. Max Lamm makes a basic distinction, although not always convincingly, between what he calls concrete motifs (such as the motifs of the waves and the ring), conceptually determined motifs (those of becoming, of sleeping, death and the curse) and motifs of feelings and moods. This reflects the influence of Guido Adler, who in his 1904 lectures on Wagner proceeded to draw a contrast between specific 'families' of motifs representing different degrees of affinity. And, as we have suggested, the individual music dramas show considerable differences in respect of the motivic design and function. Ernst Kurth makes a point about the 'personal motifs' that appear in the *Ring* in particular, but also in *Meistersinger* and *Parsifal*. These, he observes, give way in *Tristan* to 'simply the encircling of the people involved with their spiritual and destiny motifs; here there is an unusually strong concentration on the spiritual side of the motifs'.

The factors we have mentioned so far include the history of a work's creation and the level of dramatic meaning and reference. One other means of differentiation is according to features of musical technique. As we said earlier, this particularly applies to the period when Wagner's awareness of Beethoven was being governed by his plans in the field of music drama. Obviously the *Ring* cycle is the main work to be examined in this context, being the first drama that Wagner completed after setting down his theory of music drama. And what should be equally obvious is that there are no demonstrable 'influences' in the sense of motivic–thematic reminiscences and features of the musical style. Earlier we established a connection between Wagner's ambivalent attitude to the sonata and the principle of dramatic development, i.e. the interaction of musical and poetic-cum-theatrical elements. The next question to answer is this. Does the *Ring* drama involve principles of musico-dramatic design which can be regarded as a transference and transformation of certain features of Beethoven's compositional technique?

(c) Developmental motifs; technique of musico-dramatic development
Adorno lumped Wagner's leitmotifs together in the epithet 'allegorical inflexibility'. But if we examine the facts closely, this label will prove to be unwarranted. This is particularly evident from a group of motifs which can be classified as developmental motifs. In keeping with the music drama's special requirements, Wagner evolved a type of motif which basically corresponds to Beethoven's celebrated malleable figures, but which resembles from the outset the kind of fragmented motif that Beethoven used in development sections, as well as in transitional passages. The stage between the presentation of the themes and the formation of fragmented motifs, of developmental models, was eliminated. Being specifically musical, this stage in the process was irrelevant and indeed a distraction from the dramatic viewpoint. One of the aforementioned developmental motifs is the so-called Nibelung motif:

Ex. 42a Wagner, Rheingold, *scene 2 (bars 710–12)*

The motif is built such that it can be used in various ways. Being both primitive and fertile, it trumpets its importance; it readily fits in with requirements. It will blend with other motifs, is amenable to transformation and can also be used as an accompanying motif. The motif first appears in its dramatic role at Loge's words 'Zwerge schmieden, rührig im Zwange des Reif's' in *Rheingold*, Scene 2. As a rhythmic unit, however, it has been already stated in the first scene, following Alberich's 'Fing' eine diese Faust!':

Ex. 42b Wagner, Rheingold, *scene 1 (bars 504–7)*

At the end of Scene 2 it grows out of the driving rhythmic accompaniment
to the descent into Nibelheim of Wotan and Loge:

Ex. 42c Wagner, Rheingold, *scene 2 (bars 1079–86)*

Strings and winds take it up as a rhythmic force, while the Rhinegold motif
is played by the trumpets. Soon afterwards the Nibelung motif is given
solid form, as it were, by the addition of anvils. It takes refuge in the strings
for the closing bars of the scene. The motif plays a quite different role in the
next scene, where it provides a rhythmic 'continuo' to Mime's report to
Wotan and Loge ('Sorglose Schmiede, schufen wir sonst wohl...'). In *Die
Walküre* the motif is heard during Wotan's argument with Fricka ('O, was
klag' ich um Ehe und Eid') in the first scene of Act II. In Scene 2 it is bound
up with the destructive task of the Nibelungs (at Wotan's remark to Hagen,
'des Hasses Frucht hegt eine Frau'). This again is a typical developmental
motif:

Ex. 42d Wagner, Walküre, *Act II, scene 2 (bars 379/80–382)*

Subsequently the Nibelung motif has an important and flexible role in *Siegfried*, particularly in the first act. In Act I, Scene 2 of *Götterdämmerung*, Wagner quotes it like a catchphrase (Hagen's 'Doch des Nibelungenhortes nennt die Märe dich Herrn?'). We hear it again just before Scene 3, in the Nibelungs' work of destruction. In the scene between Alberich and Hagen at the beginning of Act II, it is blended in music based on semiquaver triplets with the 'rhythms of destruction'. And finally, it appears in a modified version in Scene 5 of this act (Gunther: 'Hilf, Hagen! Hilf meiner Ehre!').

This outline of the dramatic stages through which the Nibelung motif passes demonstrates its technical adaptability. It also reflects a process that is of equal importance to Wagner's musico-dramatic development technique. This could be described as a functional fluctuation. That interaction between the musical and poetic-cum-theatrical levels which is crucial to the drama becomes responsible for the action's development – which is achieved through a varying, greater or lesser emphasis on the one level or the other. The method invites comparison with Beethoven's development technique. In Beethoven's case the evolutionary and functional compass extends from thematic to developmental motifs. With this kind of Wagnerian leitmotif, however, the practical scope could be roughly described as poetic-cum-theatrical in both the engaged and (for the time being) relatively disengaged sense.

The above applies to what Wagner himself called the Rhinemaidens' motif:

Ex. 43a Wagner, Rheingold, scene 1 (bars 540–1)

The motif permeates the entire *Ring* cycle, appearing in the most varied reworkings and combinations imaginable. Only in quite specific places does it reappear in the original context and in something resembling its original shape. If we are to comprehend the motif as an *Absplitterungsmotif*, as one lending itself to fragmentation and therefore mutable, we must be careful not to confuse it with the 'drudgery' motif, which would reduce its scope and give it an inappropriate symbolism. It would be in many ways a mistake to identify it with the 'drudgery' motif; this is evident from Wagner's *On the Application of Music to Drama*. There he writes of the transformations undergone by the 'simple motif of the "Rhinemaidens"' . . . up to Hagen's watch song in the first act of "Götterdämmerung"' (*GS* x, p. 190). Wagner is referring to the version of the motif in Hagen's watch song which Alfred Lorenz followed Wolzogen in interpreting as part of Alberich's lordly call:

Ex. 43b Wagner, Rheingold, scene 3 (bars 399–404)

So it is not the 'drudgery' but the Rhinemaidens' motif that twice reappears in this combination at the beginning of Hagen's watch song:

Ex. 43c Wagner, Götterdämmerung, *Act 1, scene 2 (bars 564–7)*

Soon afterwards the motif occurs in new couplings – first with a motif that recalls Gutrune's (Act I, bars 924–34), and then with the ring motif:

Ex. 43d Wagner, Götterdämmerung, *Act 1, scene 2 (bars 628–33)*

Later still the Rhinemaidens' motif is coupled once more with the ring motif (bars 956–64), and finally with the last Valhalla motif (bars 1329–35). But prior to this Wagner had worked it up in all kinds of 'variations', notably in *Rheingold* at the start of Scene 3 (bars 1894–925). We hear it again at Alberich's 'Ho-ho! Ho-ho!' (bars 1987f.) and shortly before the arrival in Nibelheim of Wotan and Loge (bars 2017ff. and 2030ff.). The motif also figures in *Walküre* (for instance bar 1373 of Act I and bars 852ff. and 1773f. in Act II) and *Siegfried* (see bars 2321f. in Act I, bars 284f., 1352f. and 1823–31 in Act II, bars 51ff. in Act III). The Rhinemaidens' motif is therefore anything but an example of allegorical inflexibility. It is a developmental motif and is subject to all kinds of working-up processes. Harmonically it is modified in many different ways, and the composer links it together with a great many other motifs. This particular motif shows what a mistake it is to obscure Wagner's repeatedly new and varied deployment of his motifs by pinning labels on them. Lists of leitmofits can blind us to all the evidence of Wagner's thematic–motivic working-up.

How close Wagner comes to some of Beethoven's thematic construction is illustrated by the Rhinemaidens' motif itself on its first appearance. It is stated together with the motif of the waves and may be described as a twin-layered theme, analogous to the allegro theme of Beethoven's Quartet in B flat, op. 130:

Ex. 44a Beethoven, String Quartet in B flat major, op. 130, 1st movement (bars 14/15–16)

Ex. 44b Wagner, Rheingold, *scene 1 (bars 540–1)*

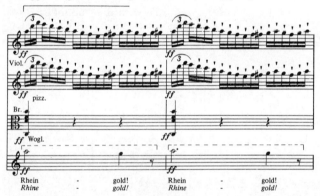

In both cases a short motif is 'carried' by the surrounding motion in semiquavers. But in spite of the similarity to Beethoven, our chosen example will now reveal some fundamental differences. In the Beethoven quartet the two parts of the theme – a concise upbeat and upward-moving motif, and a sharply delineated, initially downward-moving and figuratively articulated line of semiquavers – are set in contrast to one another. In the case of Wagner, however, the semiquavers supply the harmonic and melodic tension in the Rhinemaidens' motif. 'Harmony' is the governing factor, not contrast.

These differences are preserved in the working-up of the thematic and motivic segments. In the Beethoven quartet the semiquavers are carried on in passages of motivic development (bars 32–44), with the second theme and closing group to follow. Then comes the working-up of fragmented and contrasting thematic or motivic particles in the main development areas – the development section proper (bars 104–31) and the coda (bars 222–34).

This is combined (bars 94–103 and 214–22) with the reappearance of the introductory passages, and here too there is contrast and hence an evolution. In the *Ring*, on the other hand, the semiquaver motion of the motif of the waves is largely a colourful grounding of the dramatic developments for much of the first scene of *Rheingold* (and also many times later on). And throughout the cycle, the Rhinemaidens' motif remains an harmonically and melodically flexible detail, to be worked up in the manner we have outlined.

The reappearance of the whole motivic complex (waves and Rhinemaidens combined) does not signify a Beethovenian working in contrasts. Instead it mirrors the evolution of the drama. There are centres of dramatic development where both past and future flare up in the present, in the light of the immediate situation. Loge's narration in Scene 2 of *Rheingold* relives or 'actualizes' the theft of the gold. And by relaying the Rhinemaidens' plea for its return, he is indicating positive future opportunities. Or so it seems; in fact the way Wotan reacts ('Thörig bist du, wenn nicht gar tückisch') already gives us an inkling of impending disaster, in view of his own situation. Soon afterwards the calamitous turn of events is confirmed (bars 1555–63). This is in Wotan's 'Des Rheines Töchter? Was taugt mir der Rath?', which too is heard in conjunction with a modified version of the motifs of the Rhinemaidens and waves, and Loge's memory of the beseeching Rhinemaidens. The end of Scene 4 reveals how established the fateful chain of events already is. When we hear the Rhinemaidens singing this time, it is after Wotan has seized the gold that Alberich had forged into the ring, which he proceeded to curse; after the ransoming of Freia, which meant passing on the ring to the giants; and after the slaying of Fasolt, which confirmed Alberich's curse. This situation already precludes the ring's recovery. So when Loge calls to the Rhinemaidens 'in der Götter neuem Glanze sonnt euch selig fortan!', this is merely an ironic comment on the gods' illusory glamour. There is a parallel here with the soliloquy that directly precedes it ('zur leckenden Lohe mich wieder zu wandeln spür' ich lockende Lust. Sie aufzuzehren, die einst mich gezähmt . . . und wären's göttlichste Götter'). And so even Wotan's 'great idea', the motif of the sword, is overshadowed by Loge's words, which already hint at the eventual outcome. The first appearance of the sword motif is a latent indication of the fateful chain of events that will follow.

In *Götterdämmerung*, the motifs of the Rhinemaidens and the waves combine in an evocation of the gloomy outlook during Siegfried's Rhine journey. At the same time the combination arouses a vague presentiment which will be 'actualized' dramatically through the plot that Hagen is hatching at the court of the Gibichungs. And when, upon Siegfried's arrival there, the combined motifs are played again, a calamity which could only be vaguely sensed up to now turns into a certainty which will be realized in a very specific series of actions. The beginning of Act III brings back the scene of the Rhinemaidens in a modified form, almost the length of the first scene of *Rheingold*. This marks the moment of decision for Siegfried. His confrontation with the Rhinemaidens, who are demanding the ring's return, signifies the final, decisive combination of actualizing reminiscence and presentiment. The dramatic climax involves a compression of the motivic material. It is characterized by the contrast between the workings of fate and an apparent freedom of choice, between seriousness and playfulness. Siegfried's downfall is indicated all the more clearly by the prophecy of his death and by his whole carefree way of life, which is condensed, as it were, into a series of impulses. Wagner quotes a great many motifs and works them into his musical fabric: Hagen's hunting-horn, the summons to the wedding, the boy in the woods, the Rhine-maidens, the Rhinegold, the ring, the renunciation, the curse and Siegfried motifs, Wotan's blessing on the Nibelung offspring. This piling up of motivic material represents the fateful climax, the accumulation of the past in the present. It heralds Siegfried's forthcoming death and also the end of all that remains. And the motivic richness that is closely linked with this dramatic compression reflects the special intensity of the thematic working-up in Wagner's dramatic centres of development. It is similar to the intensity we find in Beethoven's development sections, the centres of his motivic–thematic working-up. By this we do not mean a working-up of musical contrasts, but the interweaving of motifs in a context of dramatic development.

Our typical example of a motivic complex and the way it develops in the course of the drama suffices to show the points of contact between Wagner and Beethoven. It is true that there is no working-up of contrasting elements, no waging of a conflict inherent in the theme. Nonetheless individual motifs that have been designed as *Absplitterungsmotive* are extracted from the complex and then modified or varied, being musical details with a changing dramatic status. But it is the whole recurring complex that establishes the dramatic structure's long-range connections, in the sense of 'presentiment', 'actualization' and 'reminiscence'. Both these aspects – the working-up of motivic detail, and modification by virtue of the return of the whole motivic complex – play their part in the drama's development. The accumulation of motifs in Act III of *Götterdämmerung* shows the extent to which even the tectonic associations include and indeed determine motivic working-up in just such a context. Once again, these musico-dramatic points disprove the claim that all Wagner did was to reiterate musical gestures that stood for fixed images. At the same time they confound any attempt to propound the reprise, and hence the schematicism of circular form, as a basic structural principle in Wagner's works.

(d) Motivic transformation

Wagner's dramas are not simply the spinning-out of an 'infinite' melodic thread created by the permanent metamorphosis of a nuclear melody. All the same, the way that Wagner redesigned his motifs in a linked succession affects the drama's development and its formal substance.

Characteristic elements of Wagner's motifs provide a nucleus for the crystallization of new motivic shapes. This technique may be described as motivic transformation. It reconciles theory and practice particularly well, since it obviously amounts to that 'development of moods separately' that the composer wanted. Moreover, he was solving the associated composition problems with Beethoven's methods in mind. So here Beethoven's influence emerges via Wagner's theoretical reflections.[5]

The 'primordial element' motif in the prelude to *Rheingold* is the first link in an important chain of affiliated motifs. This will be evident without our needing to refer to the symbolic content. Granted, in addition to the rising version, which is easily the more frequent one, there is also one moving downwards at a number of points in the prelude. Both these versions must be taken into account before we can perceive that the ring motif probably originates in a fresh conjunction of these two 'halves of one motif':

Ex. 45a Wagner, Rheingold, *Introduction and scene 1 (bars 177–9)*

Ex. 45b Wagner, Rheingold, *Introduction and scene 1 (bars 180–2)*

The progression from the ring motif to the Valhalla motif is obvious enough not to require special analysis. A further dramatic ramification is the reappearance, almost note for note, of an early form of the initial motif (bars 81f.). It now constitutes the Norns' motif:

Ex. 45c Wagner, Rheingold, *scene 4 (bars 602–16)*

From it is derived the motif of the twilight of the gods:

Ex. 45d Wagner, Rheingold, *scene 4 (bars 644–7)*

In *Walküre* Wagner combines both motifs in that of the 'gods' penury' [*Götternot*]:

Ex. 45e Wagner, Walküre, *Act II, scene 2 (bars 250–2)*

Wolzogen describes the new version of the aforementioned motif that we find in *Siegfried* as the motif of the 'might of the gods' [*Göttermacht*]:

Ex. 45f Wagner, Siegfried, *Act 1, scene 2 (bars 274–8)*

This motivic reshaping does not play a purely musical role. Rather, the principal function is dramatic, and at this level it is a formal one as well. The dramatic function will be evident from the mere fact that occasionally it is not so much the musical shape as the dramatic meaning that is being reformulated. Over and beyond this, the dramatic status of these motivic reshapings is illustrated by the relevant points of reference within the dramatic framework. And they confirm the formal role of thematic transformation at the same time. Thus the transition from the ring motif to the Valhalla motif represents the link between Acts I and II of *Rheingold*. It is the link between the theft of the gold – the point at which Alberich starts forcing his way to power with the ring's assistance – and the display of 'dubious power' which marks the beginning of Wotan's guilty involvement. As for the Norns' motif, this first suggests the gloomy prospect of the imminent downfall of the gods that will permeate *Rheingold, Walküre* and *Siegfried*. In formal terms the development can be perceived from the connection between the Norns' motif and the prelude at the beginning of *Götterdämmerung*.

Wagner's motivic transformation in a musico-dramatic context was not limited to the *Ring* cycle. Being dictated by the dramatic substance and status of the dramatic idea, the transformation and formal function of the leitmotifs play a very particular part in the *Ring*; nobody would deny that. But an evolving motivic reshaping is also far more prominent later on in Wagner's output than it was before the tetralogy. Take *Tristan und Isolde*, for instance, for which he interrupted his work on the *Ring*. There are extensive affinities of substance in the chromatic ductus of significant melodic features throughout the drama. This aside, however, Wagner's technique of using specific details or features of a motif as the starting-point or nucleus of a new one can be seen in the way he connects the 'yearning' [*Sehnsucht*] and 'doom' [*Verhängnis*] motifs:

Ex. 46a Wagner, Tristan und Isolde, *'Sehnsuchtsmotiv', Prelude (bars 2–3)*

Ex. 46b Wagner, Tristan und Isolde, *'Verhängnismotiv', Prelude (bars 16–17)*

the motifs of 'doom' [*Verhängnis*] and of death [*Todesmotiv*]:

Ex. 47a Wagner, Tristan und Isolde, *'Verhängnismotiv', Prelude (bars 16–17)*

Ex. 47b Wagner, Tristan und Isolde, *'Todesmotiv', Act 1, scene 2 (bars 31–7)*

of 'the glance' [*Blick*] and 'custom' [*Sitte*]:

Ex. 48a Wagner, Tristan und Isolde, *'Blickmotiv', Prelude (bars 19–23)*

Ex. 48b Wagner, Tristan und Isolde, *'Sittemotiv' Act 1, scene 5 (bars 4–8)*

as also in the linking of King Marke's motif with that of 'love's rest' in Act II of *Tristan*:

232

Ex. 49a Wagner, Tristan und Isolde, *'Motiv der Liebesruh', Act II, scene 2 (bars 714–16)*

Ex. 49b Wagner, Tristan und Isolde, *'Markemotiv', Act II, scene 3 (bars 120–2)*

And the same technique is employed in *Die Meistersinger.* There is the connection between the Knight and Marker motifs:

Ex. 50a Wagner, Meistersinger, *'Rittermotiv', Act I, scene 3 (bars 443–7)*

Ex. 50b Wagner, Meistersinger, *'Merkermotiv', Act I, scene 3 (bars 627–30)*

between the Lyric motif and the Nuremberg motif:

Ex. 51a Wagner, Meistersinger, *'Lyrisches Motiv', Act III, scene 1 (bars 354–6)*

Ex. 51b Wagner, Meistersinger, *'Nürnbergmotiv', Act III, scene 1 (bars 350–2)*

and between the Lyric motif and Midsummer Day motif:

Ex. 52a Wagner, Meistersinger, *'Lyrisches Motiv', Prelude (bars 27–9)*

Ex. 52b Wagner, Meistersinger, *'Johannistagmotiv', Act III, scene 1 (bars 369–71)*

(e) 'Contrasting derivation'

For all Wagner's analytical acumen, we can hardly credit him with 'anticipating' such specific concepts as that of contrasting derivation. The idea comes from Arnold Schmitz, who in 1923 published a study called *Beethovens 'Zwei Prinzipe'.* If it also lends itself to Wagner's music dramas, that is because Wagner was cultivating a very specific form of evolving motivic reshaping based on motivic transformation. Wagner stated that while 'the new form of dramatic music' must display the unity of symphonic writing, the 'laws of separation and union' would be determined by the dramatic action as realized and performed in the theatre (see *GS* x, p. 185). And the kind of motivic reshaping we have mentioned illustrates this in a particular way.

One instance of the dramatically determined 'contrasting derivation' of musical motifs is the special reshaping of Siegfried's horn call. At the beginning of *Götterdämmerung,* following the Norns' scene, Siegfried's heroic theme is evolved from a fresh nucleus, so to speak. In spite of the rhythmic and melodic affinity with the horn call, it differs from it enough for us to regard it as a 'contrasting derivation':

Ex. 53a Wagner, Siegfried, *'Hornruf' Act II, scene 2 (bars 435–7)*

Ex. 53b Wagner, Götterdämmerung, *Prelude (Act I) (bars 311–13)*

Ex. 53c Wagner, Götterdämmerung, *Prelude (Act I) (bars 326–9)*

The 'guardian of the sword' [*Schwertwart*] motif stands somewhere between 'contrasting derivation' and a thematic amalgam. It is clearly made up of the sword motif and the horn call.

Ex. 54a Wagner, Siegfried, *'Hornruf', Act II, scene 2 (bars 435–7)*

Ex. 54b Wagner, Rheingold, *'Schwertmotiv', scene 4 (bars 922–4)*

Ex. 54c Wagner, Siegfried, *'Schwertwartmotiv', Act I, scene 3 (bars 358–63)*

A further example of contrasting derivation is the connection between the motifs of the ring and the curse:

235

Ex. 55a Wagner, Rheingold, *'Ringmotiv', scene 1 (bars 669–71)*

Ex. 55b Wagner, Rheingold, *'Fluchmotiv', scene 4 (bars 270–4)*

there is also the link between the renunciation motif and Siegfried's motif:

Ex. 56a Wagner, Rheingold, *'Entsagungsmotiv', scene 1 (bars 617–24)*

Ex. 56b Wagner, Walküre, *'Siegfriedmotiv', Act III, scene 3 (bars 377/8–381)*

and especially the link – Wagner himself pointed it out – between the renunciation motif and that of 'woman's bliss and worth' [*Weibes Wonne und Wert*]:

Ex. 57a Wagner, Rheingold, *'Entsagungsmotiv', scene 1 (bars 617–24)*

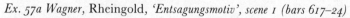

Ex. 57b Wagner, Rheingold, *'Weibes Wonne und Wert', scene 2 (bars 570–2)*

A similar connection can be observed between the stormy motif of Siegfried ('Da hast du die Stücken, schändlicher Stümper') and Mime's persistent quaver motif ('Was ich ihm Gutes schuf'):

Ex. 58a Wagner, Siegfried, 'Da hast du die Stücken . . .', Act I, scene I (bars 342–7)

Ex. 58b Wagner, Siegfried, 'Was ich ihm Gutes schuf . . .', Act I, scene I (bars 434–40)

Examples of contrasting derivation also occur in Wagner's other music dramas. Let us just mention the transformation of the motto 'Durch Mitleid wissend, der reine Tor' in Act III of *Parsifal*. Lorenz's name for this reshaping of the motivic nucleus is the Black Knight's motif:

Ex. 59a Wagner, Parsifal, 'Durch Mitleid wissend . . .', Act I, scene I (bars 624/5–628)

Ex. 59b Wagner, Parsifal, 'Motiv des schwarzen Ritters', Act III (bars 28–30)

(f) Motivic linking through rhythmic convergence
The associative magic whereby everything is connected with everything
else in Wagner's music dramas does not depend entirely on thematic
derivation, on an amalgam and reshaping of certain themes. It is also
based on a convergence of initially distant motivic and thematic formations. The best way of demonstrating this is by means of the rhythmic
unification (see Wörner [1969], p. 241) that Wagner was obviously
striving for. There were models for this in Beethoven's output – we need
only mention the Fifth Symphony and its principal theme. With such
connections it is sometimes difficult to say whether we are dealing with a
case of derivation or of convergence. We shall ignore this question as far as
the following examples are concerned. The degree of rhythmic approxi-
mation is the crucial consideration. The binding elements are dotted
rhythms and triplet rhythms. These effect a connection between motifs
which from a dramatic viewpoint are, in part, variously localized.
Examples include the destructive work of the Nibelungs and the Nibelung
rhythm:

Ex. 6oa Wagner, Rheingold, *'Vernichtungsarbeit der Nibelungen', scene 4 (bars
291–2)*

Ex. 6ob Wagner, Rheingold, *'Nibelungenrhythmus', scene 2 (bars 1094 sqq.)*

the Nibelung rhythm and the Valkyrie motif:

Ex. 6oc Wagner, Rheingold, *'Nibelungenrhythmus', scene 2 (bars 1094 sqq.)*

Ex. 6od Wagner, Walküre, *'Walkürenmotiv', Act III, scene 1 (bars 12–13)*

and Hunding's motif, the Valhalla motif and the giants' motif:

Ex. 61a Wagner, Walküre, '*Hundingmotiv*', *Act 1, scene 2 (bars 1–2)*

Ex. 61b Wagner, Rheingold, '*Walhallmotiv*', *scene 2 (bars 1–4)*

Ex. 61c Wagner, Rheingold, '*Riesenmotiv*', *scene 2 (bars 215–16)*

This rhythmic convergence is particularly striking where Wagner puts the rhythm of several motifs one on top of another, as in the prelude to Act II of *Walküre*. Here the music comprises the Ride motif, Hunding's rhythm and the Valkyrie motif.

Ex. 62 Wagner, Walküre, *Act II, Introduction (bars 64–8)*

Ex. 62 (cont)

Another pointer to the convergence is that the sword motif appears in triplet form at the beginning of the prelude:

Ex. 63 Wagner, Walküre, *Act II, Introduction (bars 1–2)*

A similar instance is a variant of the 'love greeting' [*Liebesgrüß*] motif in Act I of *Götterdämmerung*:

Ex. 64 Wagner, Götterdämmerung, *'Motiv des Liebesgrußes', Act I, scene 3 (bars 134–6)*

Now and then, however, rhythmically pregnant motifs are placed in contrast to each other, as in the third act of *Walküre*, where the gods' motif alternates with the Ride motif (see bars 283–307. Dahlhaus regards this as a working-up of the motif of the gods' penury, along the lines of Beethoven's development technique). There is a similar contrasting, albeit within a shorter space, of the Nibelung rhythm and the horn call in Act II of *Siegfried*. The resemblance between the motifs creates a rhythmic continuity in spite of the contrast:

Ex. 65 Wagner, Siegfried, *Act II, scene 3 (bars 430–2)*

(g) 'Durchbrochene Arbeit'[6]
Beethoven's working-up technique must not be used as an exact yardstick by which to assess Wagner's development technique and the way he derives and works up his motifs. We must bear in mind any divergences from orthodoxy that are dictated by the drama. This will apply if we examine the music dramas for evidence of *durchbrochene Arbeit*. Very probably Wagner was familiar with the technique, but for him it had less to do with differentiating or ramifying motifs than with instrumentation and nuances of timbre. Thus the 'song of death' [*Sterbegesang*] motif in Act II, Scene 4, of *Walküre* is divided between the oboe and clarinet:

241

Ex. 66 Wagner, Walküre, *Act II, scene 4 (bars 266–7)*

It must, of course, be remembered that Wagner uses horns to accompany the motif that the clarinet takes over, the destiny motif (this is a kind of motivic analysis through instrumentation). The result, as Egon Voss has noted, is another strong blend of sounds in the motivic facture. There is a more distinct motivic differentiation in the third scene of Act I of *Walküre*. Here the sword motif is played successively on the trumpet, flute (plus oboe, clarinet and horn), oboe, horn, oboe (plus clarinet and horn), trumpet, oboe (plus clarinet and horn again), clarinet, cor anglais and trumpet. Such fine distinctions and poetic nuances make it virtually impossible to speak of a motivic 'inflexibility' – even with a fanfare motif like this. Something else that can be described as *durchbrochene Arbeit* is the way a melodic phrase is divided among the violins, clarinet and horns at the beginning of *Walküre*, in bars 279–85. This is first heard when the listening Sieglinde bends over the motionless Siegmund (the 'pity' [*Mitleid*] motif).

Wagner's *durchbrochene Arbeit* takes a specifically dramatic form. It is particularly in evidence where the aim is to elaborate musically on the spiritual nuances of a dramatic situation, through a melodic linking or dissection of motifs that has many instrumental facets. This is also true, for instance, of Act I, Scene I of *Meistersinger*. Here instrumental melodic phrases (the Lyric motif, youth motif, Eva's motif and the love melody) are blended with the chorale. They accompany the gestures of Walther and Eva, unfolding on woodwind and stringed instruments alternately.

6

WAGNER AS BEETHOVEN'S
HEIR

Wagner's philosophy of history

The three stages of history

Wagner saw history from the viewpoint of the evolving history of the arts.
This he envisaged as a progression in three stages, which he described as
follows: (1) the arts are united in the 'total art-work of tragedy' (*GS* III,
p. 12); 2(i) the 'decline of tragedy', entailing the dissolution of the original
unity of the arts, and (ii) a 'renaissance of the arts' (*GS* III, p. 29) 'among
the Christian nations of Europe' (*GS* VII, p. 105); (3) at a new and final
stage in history the original unity is regained in the 'art-work of the future'.
Wagner deals with this in Parts II and III of *Opera and Drama* in particular.

In his account of the first historical stage and its decline, Wagner makes
it clear that his concept of art is bound up with a concept of society:

> For through the medium of tragedy he [the Ancient Greek] rediscovered himself –
> the noblest part of his being, which was combined with the noblest parts of the
> whole nation's collective being ... The decline of tragedy is intimately connected
> with the dissolution of the Athenian city-state. Just as the spirit of unity divided into
> a thousand and one egoistic impulses, so the great 'Gesammtkunstwerk' of tragedy
> was broken down into its separate, inbuilt artistic components ...   (*GS* III, p.12)

A notable feature of Wagner's second stage is that with the development
of the individual arts, there was a gradual emergence of trends that
represented a mutual drawing together. Language as 'poesy' in the broad
sense of the term was moving in the direction of music, while the latter was
tending towards the kind of compression which is really the exclusive
property of language. When we come to Wagner's third stage, however, the
main thing is that he was projecting it into the future as being the absolute
conclusion of the whole development of history.

> The variety of our natural inclinations will cause the most diverse arts – and the
> most diverse directions within these – to develop into a treasure house beyond
> anyone's imaginings. In the end, all human knowledge will find religious expres-
> sion in the single, active science of free, united humanness; and similarly, all these
> richly developed arts will find their most sympathetic conjunction in drama, in the

splendour of the human tragedy. Tragedies will be the celebrations of mankind . . .
This art will be *conservative* once more; but in reality, and on account of its genuine
tenacity and vigour, it will endure through its own efforts and not just clamour to be
preserved for some extraneous purpose . . .   (*GS* III, p. 35)

It is significant that the above standpoint is already very firmly established
in Wagner's *Art and Revolution*. For at the time his mind was being ruled by
revolutionary ideas, and any cementing of future gains in a definitive way
must have seemed a remote prospect.

The philosophy of history that Wagner conceived can be described as
dialectical – without our needing to prove a direct dependence on Hegel.
As we have seen, his projected drama was to be the core of the developing
history of art, and also of human evolution generally. This 'synthesis'
would follow on from the period of the original unity of the arts and the
subsequent period when the individual arts were dominant (analogous to a
'thesis' and 'antithesis' respectively). Although he looked upon Greek
tragedy as a model for the 'art-work of the future', Wagner was a long way
from contemplating its revival. He spoke out against the 'foolish restoration of a pseudo-Hellenism' in contemporary art. He also believed that he
understood the deeper reason for the Grecian decline – and this was a
central issue for Wagner. It involved something that would need to be
eliminated in and through the medium of the 'art-work of the future':

No, we do not wish to live as the Greeks did; for what the Greeks did not know, and
the reason why they were doomed, is something we do know. After a long period of
misery, and as a result of the worst universal affliction, we can perceive the cause of
their downfall. It clearly shows us what we need to turn into: it shows that we must
love all humanity if we are to be capable of loving ourselves again and of once again
taking pleasure in ourselves.   (*GS* III, p. 30)

It was a case of getting rid of slavery, the expression of this dearth of love.
In ancient times it was manifested in a Greek's relationship to a 'non-
Greek'; in Wagner's time, in the position of the 'haves' as against the
'have-nots'. And the desired victory of love would be crystallized within the
drama of the future. This is where the artistic and social motives of the
revolutionary in Wagner coincide.

Ideas of utopia and progress

Wagner stated in *Art and Revolution* (*GS* III, pp. 35ff.) that he did not want
his ideas and intentions regarding the history of the arts and mankind to be
labelled utopias. But he had created a typical utopia, all the same.
Wagner's concept was one more attempt to visualize and strive towards an
ideal society projected upon the future. Moreover his statements are
typically utopian inasmuch as they avoid giving an exact picture of this
new society. Rather, they are so phrased as to put the emphasis on the new

forms of human behaviour and human relations for which Wagner was aiming. He envisaged the society of the future primarily as a function of an art that had undergone revolutionary changes. (Of course he was aware that art alone cannot change society; see *GS* iii, p. 40.) Such terms as 'love', 'all-embracing art' [*allgemeinsame Kunst*] and the 'fellowship of all arts' – to name but three – play a major part in his forward-looking vocabulary.

Over and beyond this, the underlying scheme of Wagner's philosophy of history comes close to some specific and, where much of his writing is concerned, ruling utopian conceptions. Without wishing to suggest that this influenced Wagner, let us look at the Joachimite doctrine of the three ages. It uses typological connections as a basis for projecting a 'final age': a 'third age' in which there will be a revival of humanity. This idea is far more relevant than may appear at first glance. Joachim of Floris created expectations of a future state of earthly perfection on the basis of the thesis that all history was divided into three stages. Ernst Benz tells us that his influence extended right up to the German Romantic 'theology of history' as taught by Franz von Baader, Fichte, Hegel and Schelling.[1] By combining the idea of progress and development with the prophecy of the imminent redemption of mankind, Joachim of Floris 'provided the model of the modern age's utopia – religious, social, political and philosophical'.

It also seems to be typical of these utopian readings of history that they can survive any setbacks created by inimical historical developments. They will prove to be tenacious and 'elastic'. In this respect, too, Wagner's ideas were utopian in character. Even after he had built the Bayreuth Festspielhaus and mounted his festival, Wagner was forced to acknowledge the shipwreck of his original aims and plans. These had been particularly directed towards making his art something that would provide a focal point for society and transform it. The 'public collectivity' which the true drama produced by the 'combined impetus of all the arts' (*GS* iii, p. 150) was originally meant to address had dwindled to a 'community'. Just as he had done earlier, Wagner regarded the state as barbaric and unfit 'to promote art' (*GS* x, p. 121). The public, he found, was still being corrupted by bad or mediocre performances, and his own works were out of place where 'all one comes across is mediocrity' (*GS* x, p. 64). Wagner's hopes for the future had been dashed by now. For a long time the revolutionary élan had increasingly given way to an attitude fluctuating between a profound cultural pessimism and the question 'Shall we hope?' (see *GS* x, pp. 118–36). Combined with Wagner's anti-semitism, of course, this attitude becomes extremely distasteful.

In the circumstances, Wagner proceeded to transfer his objective, and the hopes attaching to it, to a far-away future. He mentions in *The Public and Popularity* (1878) that the present barbaric epoch will terminate in about another six hundred years (in a manner resembling the decline and fall of the Roman Empire; *GS* x, p. 89). And it is interesting that this demolition

245

of his short-term hopes goes hand in hand with a reference to the early Church's disappointment over the Second Advent and a reference to the Apocalypse. (See also CW, 15 June 1878.)

Can you imagine what a barbaric condition we shall have fallen into if this world of ours carries on for another six hundred years or so along the lines of the Roman Empire during its decline? The early Christians expected the Second Advent during their own lifetime, and it subsequently took root as a mystical dogma. I believe it might have a meaning for that age that we can foresee – even, perhaps, amid the events depicted in the Apocalypse, which are not entirely dissimilar.

Wagner now regarded his art as a potential means of re-establishing a link with art in the ideal sense, after this 'apocalyptic' period was over:

A true art addressing itself to the as yet ideal nation [*Volk*], in the finest sense of the word, might very well seem destined to anticipate repairing, in one way or another, the inevitable damage to the development of the human race, rather like the way Schiller's conception of Joan of Arc anticipated the evidence of the historical documents. (*GS* x, p. 90)

Clearly Wagner was not only postponing what he conceived to be the 'final age' of history, and therefore revising his expectations of the future. He was also thinking of ideas taken from Christian eschatology, especially those of Joachim of Floris.

For all his harking back to Greek tragedy, Wagner's concept of history had nothing to do with restoration, as we have already implied. He observes in *Art and Revolution* that the only way to regain the highest achievement is via a revolution and not a restoration. He continues as follows:

The task facing us is infinitely greater than the one which was once solved by our ancestors. If the Greek work of art comprised the spirit of a handsome nation, the art-work of the future is meant to comprise the spirit of all free men, irrespective of national boundaries... (*GS* iii, p. 30; see also iv, p. 150)

But although the idea of progress and development seems closely associated with Wagner's thoughts on history, his concept of 'progress' is an ambiguous one. On the one hand he speaks of the human race's progress in the history of civilization as signifying the 'cultivation of its inherent abilities' (*GS* iii, p. 208). On the other he speaks of the 'anti-human' progress of civilization, whose one merit is that it will eventually lend the 'immortal Nature' thus squashed together the necessary resilience. And the form of action this will take is revolution.

'Progress' only means something to Wagner as long as it is orientated towards the 'final age' from the viewpoint of his historical system. Later on he continued to abide by the views he had expressed in his revolutionary aesthetic writings, although they acquired a new slant. It is noticeable that the word 'progress' now occurs more often, particularly in the sense of the 'constant progress' (*GS* x, p. 123) of natural science. To Wagner's mind this was 'progress' in the wrong direction, since it was driving a wedge between his art and society. Like his earlier use of 'absolute', Wagner's increasing use of this word contains a value judgment. To him, 'progress' in the humdrum, material sense represented an aberration, and it needed to be resisted and treated with irony.

Beethoven's art as an historical threshold value

Real, authentic progress, in Wagner's view, is of a special quality: its immediate objective is the 'art-work of the future'. Where Wagner's writings use the word in this unreservedly positive, indeed emphatic sense, it serves to underline Beethoven's historical achievement. Wagner wrote that no further progress was possible after Beethoven's last symphony; its only possible sequel was the 'universal drama' (*GS* iii, p. 96). This shows that he regarded Beethoven's music as constituting an historical threshold value, because the way it transcended artistic limits was historically decisive. With the last symphony of Beethoven, music had finally achieved its 'task in the universal history of art' (*GS* iii, p. 100). Consequently the 'art-work of the future' was simply an obligatory final step, and basically the concept of 'progress' did not cover it adequately. This is why Wagner showed an exaggerated aversion to the word 'progress' later on; people were using it too often and too lightly. For him, the attitude it signified was merely a shallow faith in the perspective of modern civilization.

Wagner saw himself as Beethoven's successor and heir on more than one count. Not only had he been blessed with a talent for intuitive sympathy and deciphering that made him aware of the tone-poet's dramatic intentions. First and foremost he was Beethoven's heir in terms of a philosophical conception of the arts and history which held that Beethoven had achieved the decisive step towards the drama of the future, and towards the 'final age'.

The insubordination of history

The 'battle for Beethoven'

It was the musicologist Adolf Sandberger who coined the phrase 'der Kampf um Beethoven'. Other composers besides Wagner claimed that they were Beethoven's 'successors' (or were categorized thus by the critics). We must realize just how exaggerated and exclusive Wagner's ideas were on the history and future of the arts in order to grasp his intransigence *vis-à-vis* these rival claimants.

The intransigence has been already illustrated, in Chapter 4, by Wagner's attitude to Berlioz. At the outset, however, and in the latter half of the 1850s, he regarded himself as still in transit in respect of the music drama; it was not yet finished or fully 'functioning'. Accordingly his judgments were somewhat provisional. Later on, by contrast, he was to assess the compositions of others through the eyes of one who was in a paradoxical situation. The paradox was that he had arrived at his objective without having actually achieved it. Measured against his original hopes, and faced with a history that was impervious to his aims and had gone on evolving, Wagner's viewpoint was now an aloof one – not to mince words. And more than ever, prejudice and indignation were ruling his judgments on particular composers.

Keen disciples of Wagner expressed this outlook in a particularly forthright way. Probably the most vehement was Joseph Rubinstein in his pamphlet *On the Music of Schumann*. He accused Schumann of taking Beethoven's late works as a starting-point without following things through to their conclusion. Unlike Liszt, he wrote, Schumann was incapable of adopting the only logical course, which was programme music; instead he had vacillated between 'vague, ill-defined' goals and a return to the use of sonata form. As far as Schumann's composition technique was concerned, all Rubinstein could see in it was an 'extremely loose stringing together of unconnected themes, phrases, rhythms and ornaments'. He also referred to 'almost uninterrupted strings of simple-minded cobbler's patches [sequences]'. A letter that Cosima Wagner wrote to Ludwig Schemann on 16 June 1881 is evidence that Rubinstein's pamphlet had Wagner's personal approval:

We are, I think, all agreed on the fact that the form of the essay on Schumann did not come up to the subject-matter. But the fact it was prompted by my husband and written with his complete approval was something that H. v. Bülow understood so well that while finding it irresponsible of Rub. to put his name to such comments, he applauded him all the same, because behind them he could see all the things he had once read in a letter from my husband.

If Cosima found formal weaknesses in the essay, this was probably in response to the indignant reactions that it had provoked. In a piece entitled 'Hie Wagner! Hie Schumann!' (1870), Hugo Riemann spoke out particularly strongly. He criticized the attempt not just to discredit Schumann as a model for younger composers but also to write off the works themselves at all costs. Above all, he pointed out the similarity that existed between Schumann and Wagner. This, he said, lay not only in the pithiness of their short motifs but also in the very 'cobbler's patches' for which Rubinstein was reproaching Schumann:

The similarity goes much farther still: the motivic manipulation, the transpositions of brief phrases to the upper fourth or upper fifth and other intervals are said by

248

Herr Rubinstein to be 'cobbler's patches' when they occur in Schumann, but surely nobody uses them as often as Wagner. And yet these formations would be much more readily dispensable and avoidable in Wagner's music than in Schumann's, where the structural laws of absolute music demand them.

(Riemann [1901], p. 209)

Wagner's claim to exclusiveness as stated by his followers also spread into the realms of scholarly debate. It is reflected in the views that lay behind the attacks on Thayer and Nottebohm by Ludwig Nohl (who in 1865 dedicated his publication *Beethoven's Letters* to Wagner). It also accounts for some of Nohl's misreadings of his source material. Nohl's objections to Thayer's Beethoven biography read like a revised version of the criticisms Wagner had once made of Schindler's biography. Wagner had criticized Schindler for failing to enter the mind of Beethoven, as any true biographer ought to. And what Nohl missed in Thayer was a knowledge of the 'human factors':

Truly, people should not be discussing human factors when they know and understand so little about them. From the psychological angle in particular, this 'historical school' has never explored and experienced anything proper, for all the relish with which it is normally blowing its own trumpet in the history of art and literature as well. Similarly, no 'school' whatever has ever really explored human life. (Nohl [1874], p. 74)

It was only logical of Nohl to attack Gustav Nottebohm as well:

One of the most industrious and overweening 'piece-workers' in our branch of artistic studies is the aforementioned Herr G. Nottebohm in Vienna, who has certainly corrected many a minor error and established many points of fact in his *Beethoveniana* (Leipzig 1872). (Nohl [1874], p. 71n)

Admittedly Wagner was by no means in agreement with all the interpretative excesses of Nohl. Cosima's intermittent reading of Nohl's Beethoven study was accompanied by critical remarks from her husband:

R. objecting to the bringing together of *Fidelio* and the real-life love episode: 'I shall have to write something one day about the manner in which the life of the spirit goes its own way and has nothing to do with actual experiences – indeed it is, rather, the things one does not find which provide the images.' (CW, 16 August 1879)

Naturally Nohl did not regard 1814 as marking the climax of Beethoven's development. For him this climax was reached in the late works: the *Missa Solemnis*, the Ninth Symphony and the late string quartets (on this point Nohl was strongly contradicting Thayer). He saw Beethoven's Ninth as representing 'the true conclusion and actual end-result' of the composer's life. It was also the essential starting-point for 'any further activity in the life of the mind, insofar as it means to be fruitful and lasting' (Nohl [1870], pp. lxxx f.).

Significantly, Wagner's idea of a development leading up to the Ninth

249

Symphony as the culmination and termination of instrumental music misled Nohl into confusing an envisaged '2nd symphony' – which was initially planned in tandem with the Ninth – with Beethoven's projected Tenth Symphony. No doubt this was because the sketches for the '2nd symphony' provided for human voices. In line with Wagner's ideas on the evolutionary history of music, Nohl regarded a symphony with human voices as the only possible sequel to the Ninth. In fact, however, Beethoven's plan for this other symphony coalesced with his Ninth; it had nothing to do with the 'Tenth'. A similar scholarly failing on Nohl's part may again be attributed to Wagner's influence. This was Nohl's interpretation of the words 'Herr, wir danken dir' ['Lord, we thank You'] on a sketch for the 'Pastoral' Symphony as a projected choral entry.

Wagner must have virtually ceased to be surprised by attacks on his exegesis of Beethoven's Ninth in terms of the 'universal history of art'. Riemann too, in his reply to Rubinstein's article, finished by rejecting the claim that Beethoven's historical mission as set forth in the Ninth Symphony had been accomplished in the music drama. But there were also critics and defectors from within the Wagnerian camp. In these instances Wagner must have wondered if they were not symptomatic of profound and significant changes and counter-movements.

Such a symptom was the standpoint that was eventually adopted by Hans von Bülow. For a long time he had supported Wagner's interpretation of Beethoven unreservedly and had strongly publicized it. But in 1888 (five years after Wagner's death), he wrote to Siegfried Ochs summarizing his new standpoint:

I have no stomach, no enthusiasm any longer for this finale, the public harmfulness of which – since, after all, the whole confounded 'New German' movement [*'Neudeutsche' Richtung*] I had the misfortune and stupidity to belong to for so long was based on this trespassing over music's boundaries – has become more obvious to me with every year that goes by.

Was Bülow aware that Wagner had described the finale of the Ninth Symphony to Liszt as not really all that perfect, and had later (25 April 1880) described the form in the same terms to Cosima? At all events Wagner's admiration for this composition was at one time motivated by the history of musical developments, later on by an historical ideology!

Bülow's change of heart was undoubtedly motivated by various factors. It is likely that personal reasons played an appreciable part. But such a marked reorientation would never have been possible if circumstances had not paved the way for it. Bülow's new attitude towards Beethoven's Ninth – and the way he expresses it is clearly an attack on Bayreuth – went hand in hand with his advocacy of Brahms. He had already knocked the Ninth off its pedestal in Bayreuth when he hailed Brahms's First Symphony as Beethoven's 'tenth'. (This occurs in his 'Travel Reviews' of 1877.)

WAGNER AS BEETHOVEN'S HEIR

Wagner used this epithet ironically in his 1879 essays on the writing of texts and music (*Über das Dichten und Komponieren*). Passing the composers of the time in a kind of fancy-dress review, he included among them a 'sterling symphonist masquerading in a number ten'. He also awarded the palm to one composer as being the first (*erster*) and also a serious (*ernster*) 'prince of music', although there was an ordinary-looking face behind the mask (*GS* x, p. 148). This may have been another sally against Bülow's reverence for Brahms. Wagner interpreted Bülow's particular comment as an insult to his own conviction that he was the genuine heir to Beethoven. How much it rankled with him can be discerned from his *Open Letter to Herr Friedrich Schön of Worms* (1882). It paints a gloomy picture of the future. Drawing a parallel with the survival of Euripidean tragedy, instead of the works of Sophocles and Aeschylus, Wagner feared that no more than two Beethoven symphonies might be preserved for posterity, as opposed to about nine Brahmsian symphonies. This was because 'the plagiarists were invariably on the side of progress' (*GS* x, p. 293). Bülow refers to this statement in a letter to Brahms dated 17 July 1882.

Wagner placed the works of Schumann and Brahms on a par with those results of cultural developments which he dismissed as being mere pseudo-progress. Beethoven's historically binding 'progress' had already found its inevitable sequel in the music drama, but composers like the above, Wagner believed, were distorting this progress to the point of caricature.

The spirit of Beethoven and the Beethoven manner

Wagner was never in any doubt that through music drama, he had fulfilled Beethoven's artistic testament. Cosima's diaries are evidence of that. But it must have been difficult for him to persist in his claim when others were obviously far more entitled to say they were composing 'in the spirit of the Master' with regard to the thematic design, thematic working-up and command of purely musical form. Hanslick as well as Bülow had put forward the case for Brahms, and Eduard Hanslick also pointed out Schumann's importance. Wagner referred to Hanslick in *Observations on Jewry in Music*. It was, he said, only through the libel about 'the beautiful in music' that Hanslick had succeeded in adding Mendelssohn 'to the ranks of Haydn, Mozart and Beethoven as a matter of course', and finally placing 'some Christian worthies like Robert Schumann' alongside him (*GS* viii, pp. 243f.). This was inspired by anything but 'pure' criticism. Wagner was only too conscious of Mendelssohn's abilities. Part of him was willing to acknowledge them, while part of him rejected them.

In order to counter Hanslick's argument, Wagner accused such composers of mere 'landscape painting' (Mendelssohn) or stylistic imitation. He described Schumann to Cosima as 'a very fragile talent; when he does

251

produce a theme, it is a Beethovenian one' (CW, 28 February 1878). With regard to Brahms, he wrote of his 'apparent enjoyment of *Weltschmerz*' – a *Weltschmerz* that was based musically on little scraps of melody 'like stale tea-leaves mixed with hay', and sold as the genuine article. According to Wagner, Brahms was just copying Beethoven in his thematic working. The object of this polemicizing is stated unequivocally in the following lines:

Quite seriously, we cannot believe that instrumental music has been assured of a thriving future by the creations of its latest masters. First and foremost, however, we could be doing ourselves some harm by unthinkingly assigning these works to the Beethovenian legacy because we should actually come to realize the completely un-Beethovenian things about them. And that ought not to be too difficult, considering how unlike Beethoven they are in spirit, despite the Beethovenian themes that we still come across... (*GS* x, p. 182)

So in Wagner's opinion, a thematic design and working-up technique in the Beethovenian manner is irreconcilable with composing in the spirit of Beethoven. In his essay *On the Application of Music to Drama*, he pointed out that his own thematic design and working-up technique differed from Beethoven's. By so doing, Wagner was actually underlining his closeness to Beethoven in spirit, and his inheritance of Beethoven's mantle.

Basically Wagner was defending himself against the insubordination of history. Historical events had failed to realize the end of the symphony which he had announced, or that 'final age' which he had expected. But it was not just a matter of defending the claim that he alone had understood Beethoven's mission and carried out his historical assignment. He wanted to do more than this in view of the 'symphony compositions' of the 'Romantic–Classical' school. He tolerated the programme music of Liszt, but he needed to show the contrast with music drama, which marked the termination and culmination of a development. That is why he modified his own earlier view of history, introducing the model of a continuous development which began with Beethoven and carried on irresistibly through the symphonic poem and 'musical melodrama' [*Melodram-Musiken*] before finally culminating in music drama. With Liszt, who toned down the excesses of Berlioz, we are looking at the way that purely instrumental music acquires unlimited abilities 'with the help of a dramatic picture of events'. It was the 'programmaticist' urge to illustrate 'a poetic shape or design' that lured him into his 'eccentric characterizations'. Eventually, this compulsion led to 'whole musical melodramas for which one had to imagine the mimed action'. So all that remained to be done, after these birth-pangs, was 'to deliver the new form of musical drama itself' (*GS* x, pp. 180–1).

It is typical of the way Wagner juggled with the historical facts that now he no longer linked the birth of music drama directly to Beethoven's works. Instead he introduced the development of 'programme music' as an intermediate stage – although it really went hand in hand with the development of music drama.

Equally telling is the way that Wagner resisted the temptation 'to apply the fruits of musical innovations in the dramatic field to the symphony, etc.' (*GS* x, p. 191). This attitude is somewhat at odds with his jovial attitude towards Bruckner, for Bruckner's symphonies include some stylistic features which – either as a result of Wagner's influence or in line with the course of history – demonstrate precisely what Wagner was objecting to. (As H. F. Redlich has observed, it is hard to decide 'whether Wagner was serious when he promised Bruckner ... to perform his symphonies at Bayreuth'.) Bruckner figures just twice in Cosima's diaries, first as 'the poor Viennese organist' (8 February 1875) and later in a dream of a pope who shared his physical features (22 April 1881). Thus he played a remarkably meagre part in Wagner's everyday conversation. Wagner condemned the fact that 'all the young people' were associated with 'excessive accents which can only be grasped through the action'. Why was this? Once again an answer is suggested by Cosima's diaries: '"I clearly feel," he says, "that what I said in *The Art-Work of the Future* is true: that the 9th Symphony is also the last..."' (see entry for 14 April 1873).

In melting down the symphony into music drama, Wagner had originally declared this act a sign of progress, to be regarded in that spirit. In the end, however, it became the antithesis of everything else, anything pointing beyond music drama. In the last years of his life Wagner was collecting symphonic themes more and more, but without really working out any of them, even after he had finished *Parsifal*. Although he mulled over the form of these imaginary symphonies, he never came to a firm decision or tried out his ideas. (The 'one-off' exception was the *Siegfried Idyll*, and this constituted a plunge into compositional privacy, rather than a formal and structural test.) He got out his early symphony and gave it a ceremonious, intimate performance. But none of this affected the real core of Wagner's artistic personality. It was just a means of reassuring himself in a field that in his view had long been fallow from the historical standpoint. He was still in opposition to Schumann, Mendelssohn and Brahms.

Contrary to those composers, and in spite of Liszt and Bruckner, Wagner saw music drama as the one and only way of executing the legacy of Beethoven. There was a time when he had envisaged it as fulfilling history; now it would creatively refute history. Music drama finally came to represent, for him, not only the end of a development but also the consummation of everything that was yet to come.

NOTES

2 Wagner's experience of Beethoven

1 See Newman's *Wagner as Man and Artist* (1952), pp. 9ff. Doubtless Wagner's other writings are sporadically on a par with his letters as regards factual accuracy (see *NGW*, p. 88).

2 Published in the *North American Review*. [The text was actually prepared by Wolzogen and only signed by Wagner. Cosima records Richard's dissatisfaction with it in a diary entry for 1 May 1879. See J. Kühnel's final remarks in his contribution to the *Richard Wagner Handbook* (forthcoming) – Translator's note].

3 By 'response pattern' [*Erlebnisstruktur*] we mean a vibrating of musical and extra-musical emotional states on the same spiritual wavelength, as it were. Thus the impressions responsible for producing the emotions and the emotional states themselves form part of a single response-complex.

4 This extract is open to misinterpretation if we concentrate too much on the passage 'even before I set about writing a single line of the text ... I am already thoroughly immersed in the musical aura of my new creation ...' As Wagner has in fact stated, this depends on his being attracted only to subjects 'which reveal themselves ... not only as poetically but, at the same time, as musically significant'. What follows has to do with the interplay between the poetic and musical components in the creative process, neither component having any discernible priority in the creative order. Dahlhaus observes (*NGW*, p. 116) that the *Ring* evolved out of a poetico-dramatic scheme which was 'accompanied to only a very small extent by tangible musical ideas'. This does not conflict with the pattern of reception and creation described in the letter to Gaillard; with the *Ring* cycle, it was a case of achieving the poetico-dramatic scheme to begin with. After that, Wagner had numerous motifs for *Rheingold* at his fingertips (see, for instance, *SL*, pp. 238–9).

5 There is a well-known psychological connection between frustration and aggression (see Dollard). This would explain Wagner's aggressive – and totally unjustified – attitude towards Meyerbeer, as well as the extreme tone of his letter of 22 October 1850 to Uhlig (*SL*, pp. 217–20). Hence what Knepler calls his anarchist's jargon is the aggressive language of a person who could not forget the frustration he had experienced in Paris ten years earlier. Deathridge notes in *NGW* (pp. 19f.) that Wagner's jobs as a musical arranger were spread over a longer period than is generally realized, and that Schlesinger did not force them on him, as *My Life* implies. But this does not alter the fact that Wagner was often faced with nothing to live on in Paris, and was making no headway as an artist.

6 Wagner directed the Ninth Symphony in London on 26 March 1855 as part of a series of eight invitation concerts. This performance was peripheral in terms of quality, significance and function, for both external and internal reasons. According to Wagner the two rehearsals he was allowed were insufficient, the choir was mediocre if not wretched, and the soloists were unbearably bad. On the other hand, Wagner did impress the Ninth on the minds of his London audience as being an important composition.

7 This passage may contain an echo of Schindler's account of Beethoven's creative transports. Wagner's 'wild sobs' and 'crying' are reminiscent of Beethoven's 'singing, howling and stamping' when engaged on the fugue in the Credo of the *Missa Solemnis*.

8 The passage reads in full: 'and with the heaven-shaking cry, "*I am a human being!*", the millions, active revolution, God become man, hurtle down to the valleys and plains, and announce to the whole world the new gospel of happiness!" (see *GS* XII, p. 249).

9 In 1857 the *Neue Zeitschrift für Musik* (46) published the third in a series of 'Musikalische Briefe aus der Schweiz'. This includes a revealing description of how Wagner, the creator of music dramas, realized Beethoven the 'tone-poet'. Based on his 1856 concert in St Gall, it tells us what he achieved as a conductor:

> Above all *Wagner's* style of conducting helped enormously to heighten the audience's receptiveness to the work; that enchanting power and authority over the players, and the enthusiasm emanating from a noble artist's soul which carries everyone away with irresistible force, to the highest peaks of rapture ... To use his profound grasp of Beethoven to develop in the attentive listener the growing feeling that the music can, and must, be conceived and sound exactly like this and no other way: that is *Wagner's* artistic portion, and it has a mighty effect all round. His very programme for the *Eroica* deserves to be called a symphony in words; and the two, the work and the programme, complement each other by virtue of the spirited presentation.

3 The Romantic background and Beethoven biography

1 The piece is unsigned but given as being by Marx in the index. Moreover Marx expressly refers to it in his signed essay *Etwas über die Symphonie und Beethovens Leistungen in diesem Fache*. [For a full appraisal of both Hoffmann's and Marx's writings on Beethoven, see R. Wallace's *Beethoven's Critics* (1986) – Translator's note]

2 Wagner's first contact with Marx's activities probably dates back to 1828. Marx had translated Logier's *Thoroughbass*, which is mentioned in the *Red Pocket-Book*. Wagner did not lose track of him after his visit, and he possessed the score of Marx's *Moses*, dating from 1841.

3 Schindler writes that although Beethoven was unable to see Schröder-Devrient's performance, the reports he had of it led him to reject her interpretation of the role. The singer's own later account contradicts this. According to her, Beethoven saw her on stage and expressed his recognition and thanks to her after the performance. See Thayer, ed. Forbes (1970), pp. 811f., and Solomon (1977), p. 268.

4 No doubt periodicals also brought new publications about Beethoven to Wagner's notice. Thus he would have learnt of the appearance of W. von Lenz's *Beethoven. Eine Kunststudie* (I: *Das Leben des Meisters*) from the *Rheinische Musik-Zeitung* 46 in 1855. In 1857 the *Niederrheinische Musik-Zeitung* 13 carried a review of *Beethoven, ses critiques et ses glossateurs* by Alexandre Oulibicheff. L. Bischoff reviewed A. W. Thayer's *Ludwig van Beethoven's Leben* (Berlin, 1866) in the same journal (41) in 1866.

5 W. A. Ellis's *Life* (1900–8, p. 137) also connects the novella with Wagner's journey in 1832. In later life Wagner continued to voice his regret that he had not been able to see Beethoven in the flesh (see CW, 26 May 1871).

6 In 1823 the Englishman Edward Schulz visited Beethoven, his account being printed in the *Harmonicon* (10) the following year. The same journal published a similar account by an Englishwoman in 1825. Cipriani Potter, who visited Beethoven in 1817, published his 'Recollections of Beethoven' in *The Musical World* in 1836. Wagner's novella gives a completely distorted impression of Beethoven's relations with the English; see, for instance, Magnani (1967), pp. 35, 37, 205–22.

4 Beethoven's role in Wagner's writings on art

1 Wagner (like Uhlig) does not take into account the harmonic framework of the sonata scheme. This is a trend which goes back to the beginning of the nineteenth century. The 'pragmatic sonata form' of the theorists (see Ritzel [2/1969], pp. 196ff.) represented the development of a view which emphasized thematic–motivic details and aspects at the expense of harmonic aspects.

2 Rightly or wrongly, this aspect still carries particular weight compared to the harmonic–metrical aspect. To accuse Wagner of one-sidedness here would be to ignore the historical background.

3 [*The New Harvard Dictionary of Music* defines *durchbrochene Arbeit* as a technique, 'often encountered in works of the Classical period, in which melodic material is broken into fragments and distributed among two or more instruments or parts' – Translator's note]

4 Wagner had his objections to the phrase 'music drama' (*GS* IX, pp. 302–8). He himself had used the term 'musical drama' (V, p. 147), but subsequently rejected this as well (IX, p. 303). See *Wagners Aesthetik*, selected and introduced by C. Dahlhaus, V: *Ueber die Benennung 'Musikdrama'*, Bayreuth Festival 1970, pro-gramme booklet VI, *Götterdämmerung*, pp. 40ff.

5 One could compile a whole list of phrases in which Feuerbach assigns the same function to the word 'absolute', albeit in a different thematic context. Wagner was particularly attracted by Feuerbach's anti-Hegelianism (see *ML*, p. 431). This again is a pointer to Feuerbach's *Kritik der Hegelschen Philosophie*; it also points to the *Grundsätze der Philosophie der Zukunft* (1843). This title was in the air at that time. Along with Ludwig Feuerbach's work, G. Adler cites two publi-cations by Friedrich Feuerbach: *Die Religion der Zukunft* (1838) and *Die Kirche der Zukunft* (1847).

6 All the same, Wagner was not uncritical of certain of Beethoven's later works. According to Glasenapp he said of the third 'Rasoumovsky' Quartet that it was not Beethoven but pure Hellmesberger and still 'the half-way music of the sonata

style', calling for 'virtuosic dexterity in the execution of the fioriture'. To Cosima he said of Beethoven's Fourth Symphony that the scherzo was splendid, but that the adagio always made him think 'Yes, I know', and that the theme of the first movement meant nothing to him. A. B. Marx had already classified the Fourth Symphony in a similar way in 1830. He described it as 'one of the works ... in which the artist has not yet risen to a higher consciousness, to a particular idea' (*BAMZ* [1830], p. 92). Wagner was against those of Beethoven's quintets, trios, concertos and duets where the music 'never pierces you like a dagger'. The first movement of the C sharp minor Quartet seemed to him bewildering; it did not '*sound* well'. (See CW, 26 February 1878 and 29 January 1879.)

7 Wagner wrote 'programmatic explanations' for the 'Eroica' and the Ninth Symphony, the *Coriolan* Overture and the C sharp minor Quartet, op. 131. The comments on Beethoven's Fifth Symphony and especially the Seventh Symphony and *Leonore* Overture No. 3 are programmatic references. In his account of *Coriolan*, Wagner furthermore describes 'nearly all the Master's symphonic works as representing scenes between man and woman as regards the plastic object of their expression' (*GS* v, pp. 173f.).

8 The fact that Wagner included his 'programmes' for the C sharp minor Quartet and the *Coriolan* Overture in the Beethoven centenary essay does not signify a return to his earlier viewpoint. In the essay, the account of op. 131 is like the condensed image of an inner, spiritual life, in which the deaf hero's spiritual range is developed through the successive moods of a single day. *Coriolan* reflects the extent to which Beethoven and Shakespeare are referring to the same material (*GS* ix, p. 107): their motives are essentially identical.

9 The relationship between Wagner and Hanslick was initially a friendly one. Hanslick wrote as many as eleven articles about Wagner within a short space of time in 1846. But the review of *Tannhäuser* for which Wagner thanked him on 1 January 1847 already contained passages of criticism that were not to Wagner's liking. Wagner also held it against Hanslick that he supported the music of Meyerbeer. His later antipathy towards Hanslick was explicitly connected with his unfortunate and embarrassing anti-Semitism, as references in Cosima's diaries bear out. See, for instance, CW, 27 June 1870 and 18 June 1879.

5 Wagner's theory and construction of music drama

1 [For a translation of Hoffmann's review of Beethoven's Fifth Symphony, see the Norton Critical Score (ed. Elliot Forbes, 1971); also *E.T.A. Hoffmann's Musical Writings* (ed. D. Charlton, Cambridge 1989) – Translator's note]

2 In *My Life* (pp. 175, 429) Wagner speaks of the mystical 'constellations' or 'influence' that had determined his thinking at the time. But he also says (p. 91) that as early as 1834 he was coming to the conclusion 'that to go beyond Beethoven in the symphonic area and to do anything new and noteworthy was an impossibility'.

3 The theme comes eight bars before Brünnhilde's 'Ewig war ich, ewig bin ich...' But Gerald Abraham's and Ernest Newman's supposition that the Starnberg sketches were for a string quartet has now been discredited. On the connection between the *Meistersinger* prelude and Beethoven's late string quartets, see Finscher (1970), p. 307 and n. 8; concerning details of the connection between

NOTES TO PAGES 205–45

the *Tristan* introduction and Beethoven's String Quartet op. 130, see Kropfinger (1970), pp. 26off.

4 Let us reiterate that in the present study, the term 'leitmotif' and references to Wagner's leitmotif technique do not imply the kind of wholesale concept that is suggested by catalogues of leitmotifs. Moreover the use of specific names (they are taken from Wolzogen or Lorenz) is purely for the sake of convenience.

5 E. Newman (1952), p. 381, rightly regards this technique as dependent on Bach or as a rediscovery of Bach's compositional techniques. In his views at the time, however, Wagner was being guided by that exaggerated interpretation of Beethovenian composition technique that goes back to Uhlig. Later on, to be sure, Wagner regarded Bach's handling of melody – along with Beethoven's – as an important preliminary to 'infinite melody' (see Geck [1969], pp. 134–42).

6 See n. 3 to Chapter 4.

6 Wagner as Beethoven's heir

1 See Benz (1965), pp. 58f. Elements of Joachim of Floris are already to be found in Lessing's *Erziehung des Menschengeschlechts*. According to Grundmann ([1955], p. 10), there are traces of Joachim's thinking in the eighteenth and nineteenth centuries among 'minds as different as Lessing and Schelling'. But the real upsurge of interest in Joachim of Floris has occurred in the twentieth century, and particularly since around 1930. This upsurge is rooted in work stretching back into the nineteenth century. Ernst Bloch describes Joachim's teaching as the 'medieval social utopia that had the greatest consequences' (Bloch [1969], p. 49). According to Bloch, a statement made by the young Engels in 1842, a few years before the *Communist Manifesto*, carries an echo of Joachim. Engels writes: 'The self-awareness of mankind, the new grail around whose throne the nations are jubilantly gathering . . . It is our mission to become knights of the grail, to gird a sword round our loins for it and cheerfully to risk our lives for the last holy war, which will be followed by the millennium of freedom.'

BIBLIOGRAPHY

Abraham, Gerald, 1924. 'The Influence of Berlioz on Richard Wagner', *Music &*
Letters 5, 239–46
1925. 'The Leit-Motif since Wagner', *Music & Letters* 6, 175–90
1939. 'The Flying Dutchman': Original Version, *Music & Letters* 20, 412–19
1940. Marschner and Wagner, *The Monthly Musical Record* 70, 99–104
1945. Wagner's String Quartet: An Essay in Musical Speculation, *The Musical*
Times 86, 233f.
Adler, Guido, 1904. *Richard Wagner*, Lectures given at the University of Vienna,
Leipzig
1911. *Der Stil in der Musik* I: *Prinzipien und Arten des musikalischen Stils*, Leipzig
1919. *Methode der Musikgeschichte*, Leipzig
Adorno, Theodor W., 1952. Versuch über Wagner, Frankfurt a. Main, or
Collected Writings 13, Frankfurt a. Main 1971
1955. 'Tradition', in *Dissonanzen. Musik in der verwalteten Welt*, Göttingen, or
Collected Writings XIV, Frankfurt a. Main (1973), 127–42
1978. Wagners Aktualität in Collected Writings XVI, 543–64
Allemann, Beda, 1969. Strukturalismus in der Literaturwissenschaft?, in *Ansich-*
ten einer künftigen Germanistik 1969, edited by Jürgen Kolbe, Munich
Altmann, Wilhelm, 1905. *Richard Wagners Briefe nach Zeitfolge und Inhalt. Ein*
Beitrag zur Lebensgeschichte des Meisters, Leipzig, reprinted 1971
Ambros, August Wilhelm, 1856. *Die Grenzen der Musik und der Poesie*, Prague
Anders, Godefroid-Engelbert, 1838. Beethoven est-il Hollandais?, *Gazette musicale*
de Paris 5
1839. *Détails biographiques sur Beethoven d'après Wegeler et Ries*, Paris
Arro, Elmar, 1965. Richard Wagners Rigaer Wanderjahre, in *Musik des Ostens* III,
Kassel, 123–68
Bagge, Selmar, 1880. Die geschichtliche Entwicklung der Sonate, in *Sammlung*
musikalischer Vorträge, edited by Paul Graf Waldersee, Leipzig
Bailey, Robert, 1968. Wagner's Musical Sketches for 'Siegfrieds Tod', in *Studies*
in Music History: Essays for Oliver Strunk, Princeton, 459–95
1969. *The Genesis of Tristan and Isolde, and a Study of Wagner's Sketches and Drafts*
for the First Act, diss., Princeton University
1972. The Evolution of Wagner's Compositional Procedure after Lohengrin, in
IMSCR 11, Copenhagen, 240–6
1977–8. The Structure of the 'Ring' and its Evolution, *19th Century Music* 1,
48ff.
Barzun, Jacques, 1958. *Darwin, Marx, Wagner: Critique of a Heritage*, New York

Baudelaire, Charles, 1954. *Œuvres complètes*. Texte établi et annoté par Y.-G. Le Dantec, Paris

Bauer, Hans-Joachim, 1977. *Wagners 'Parsifal'. Kriterien der Kompositionstechnik* (Berliner musikwissenschaftliche Arbeiten 15), Munich and Salzburg

Bause, Renate, 1951. Probleme der Musikkritik bei Richard Wagner, diss., Münster

Bayreuther Blätter 1878–1938. 1–61

Bebington, Warren A., 1984. *The Orchestral Conducting Practice of Richard Wagner,* diss., New York

Becking, Gustav, 1921. *Studien zu Beethovens Personalstil: Das Scherzothema,* Leipzig (Abhandlungen des Sächsischen Staatlichen Forschungsinstituts für Musikwissenschaft 2)

1924. Zur musikalischen Romantik, in *Deutsche Vierteljahresschrift für Literaturwissenschaft und Geistesgeschichte* 2

1928. *Der musikalische Rhythmus als Erkenntnisquelle,* Augsburg

Beethoven, Ludwig van, 1923. Complete Letters, edited by E. Kastner, new edition by J. Kapp, Leipzig

1961. *The Letters of Beethoven,* edited by Emily Anderson, 3 vols., London and New York

Bekker, Paul, 1905. Die Musik im Lichte Schopenhauerscher Philosophie, *Allgemeine Musikzeitung* 32, 638

1924. *Wagner. Das Leben im Werke,* Stuttgart and Berlin

Bélart, Hans, 1900–1. *Richard Wagner in Zürich,* 2 vols., Leipzig

1912. *Friedrich Nietzsches Freundschafts-Tragödie mit Richard Wagner und Cosima Wagner–Liszt,* Dresden

1914. *Richard Wagners Beziehungen zu François und Eliza Wille,* Dresden

Benz, Ernst, 1934. *Ecclesia Spiritualis. Kirchenidee und Geschichtstheologie der Franziskanischen Reformation,* Stuttgart

1965. *Schöpfungsglaube und Endzeiterwartung,* Munich

Berlioz, Hector, 1843. *Musikalische Reise in Deutschland,* Leipzig

1924. *A Travers chants,* Paris

(n.d.) *Mémoires comprenant ses voyages en Italie, en Allemagne, en Russie et en Angleterre, 1803–1865,* 2 vols., Paris

Besseler, Heinrich, 1957–9. *Das musikalische Hören der Neuzeit,* Berlin (Berichte über die Verhandlungen der šachsischen Akademie der Wissenschaften, 103, 104)

Birtner, Herbert, 1937. Zur Deutschen Beethoven-Auffassung seit R. Wagner, in *Beethoven und die Gegenwart,* Berlin and Bonn, 1–40

Bloch, Ernst, 1959. 'Paradoxa und Pastorale in Wagners Musik', *Merkur* 13, 405–35; reprinted in *Verfremdungen* I, Frankfurt a. Main 1962, *Literarische Aufsätze,* Frankfurt a. Main 1965; English translation in *Essays on the Philosophy of Music,* Cambridge 1985

1969. *Freiheit und Ordnung,* Hamburg

1973. *Geist der Utopie,* Frankfurt a. Main

Blume, Friedrich, 1958. Art. 'Klassik', *MGG* VII (1958), 1027–90

1963. Art. 'Romantik', *MGG* XI (1963), 785–845

Blümer, Hans, 1958. *Über den Tonartencharakter bei Richard Wagner,* diss., Munich

Bohe, Walter, 1933. *Die Wiener Presse in der Kriegszeit der Oper*, diss., Würzburg

Borchmeyer, Dieter, 1982. *Das Theater Richard Wagners. Idee–Dichtung–Wirkung*, Stuttgart

Boschot, Adolphe, 1945. *Le Faust de Berlioz*, Paris

Boucher, Maurice, 1947. *Les Idées politiques de Richard Wagner*, Paris

Boulez, Pierre, 1976. Die neuerforschte Zeit, in *Rheingold* programme book, Bayreuth, 19–36

Boyer, Jean, 1938. *Le 'Romantisme' de Beethoven. Contribution à l'étude de la formation d'une légende*, Paris

Breig, Werner, 1973. *Studien zur Entstehungsgeschichte von Wagners 'Ring des Nibelungen'*, Freiburg

Breitkopf, Rudolf Maria, 1903–4. Richard Wagners Klaviermusik, *Die Musik* 3, 108–34

Brelet, Gisèle, 1949. *Les Temps musicales*, 2 vols., Paris

Brenneis, Clemens, 1979. Das Fischhof-Manuscript. Zur Frühgeschichte der Beethoven-Biographik, in *Zu Beethoven. Aufsätze und Annotationen*, edited by Harry Goldschmidt, Berlin, 90–116

1984. Das Fischhof-Manuskript in der Deutschen Staatsbibliothek, in *Zu Beethoven. Aufsätze und Dokumente*, edited by Harry Goldschmidt, 27–87

Brescius, Hans von, 1898. *Die königlich sächsische musikalische Kapelle von Reissiger bis Schuch (1826–1898)*, Festschrift zur Feier des 350 jähr. Kapelljubiläums, Dresden

Brinkmann, Reinhold, 1971. Szenische Epik. Marginalien zu Wagners Dramenkonzeption im Ring des Nibelungen, in *Richard Wagner – Werk und Wirkung*, edited by Carl Dahlhaus, Regensburg (Studien zur Musikgeschichte des 19. Jahrhunderts, 26), 85–96

1978. Mythos – Geschichte – Natur. Zeitkonstellationen im 'Ring' in *Richard Wagner. Von der Oper zum Musikdrama*, edited by Stefan Kunze, Berne and Munich, 61–77

1985. Musikforschung und Musikliteratur. Eine Nachschrift von Improvisationen über ein so nicht gegebenes Thema, in *Wagnerliteratur – Wagnerforschung. Bericht über das Wagner-Symposium in München 1983*, edited by Carl Dahlhaus and Egon Voss, Mainz, London, New York, Tokyo, 150–5

Bücken, Ernst, 1933. *Richard Wagner*, Potsdam

Bülow, Hans von, 1860. *Über Richard Wagners Faust-Ouvertüre*, Leipzig

1898–1908. *Briefe und Schriften* iv–viii, Leipzig

²/1899. *Briefe und Schriften* i and ii, Leipzig

²/1911. *Briefe und Schriften* iii, Leipzig

1927. *Neue Briefe*, edited by R. Graf Du Moulin-Eckart, Munich

Bülow, Hans von and Richard Strauss, Correspondence. 1953, edited by Willi Schuh and Franz Trenner, London

Bülow, Paul, 1916. *Die Jugendschrifte Richard Wagners*, diss. Gießen

Burbidge, P., and Sutton, R. (eds.), 1979. *The Wagner Companion*, London

Burke, Edmund, 1773. *Burkes philosophische Untersuchungen über den Ursprung unsrer Begriffe vom Erhabenen und Schönen*, fifth English edition translated by Christian Garve, Riga

1956. *Vom Erhabenen und Schönen*, edited and translated from the first English edition (1756) by Friedrich Bassenge, Berlin (Philosophische Bücherei, 10)

Bus, Antonius Johanna Maria, 1947. *Der Mythos der Musik in Novalis' 'Heinrich von Ofterdingen'*, Alkmaar

Carlsson, A., 1955. Das mythische Wahnbild Richard Wagners, *Deutsche Vierteljahrsschrift für Literaturwissenschaft und Geistesgeschichte* 29, 237ff.

Carse, Adam, 1929. *Orchestral Conducting*, London

  1948. *The Orchestra from Beethoven to Berlioz*, Cambridge

Cassirer, Ernst, 2/1957. *The Philosophy of Symbolic Forms* I, London

  1955. Vol. II, London

  1957. Vol. III, London

Champfleury (pseud. of Jules François Felix Husson), 1856 *Contes posthumes d'Hoffmann traduits par Champfleury*, Paris

  1860. *Richard Wagner*, Paris

Chop, Max, 1906. Richard Wagner im Spiegel der Kritik seiner Zeit, *Richard Wagner-Jahrbuch* I, Bayreuth

Coren, D., 1977. Inspiration and Calculation in the Genesis of Wagner's 'Siegfried', in *Studies in Musicology in Honor of Otto E. Albrecht*, Kassel

Cox, Hugh Bertram, and C.L.E., 1907. *Leaves from the Journals of Sir George Smart*, London

Culshaw, J., 1976. *Reflections on Wagner's Ring*, London

Curzon, H. de., 1920. *L'œuvre de Richard Wagner à Paris et ses interprètes, 1850–1914* (Paris)

Dahlhaus, Carl, 1964. Musikalische Prosa, *NZfM* 125

  1965. Wagners Begriff der 'dichterisch-musikalischen Periode', in *Beiträge zur Geschichte der Musikanschauung im 19. Jahrhundert*, edited by Walter Salmen, Regensburg (Studien zur Musikgeschichte des 19. Jahrhunderts 1), 179–87

  1967a. *Musikästhetik*, Cologne

  1967b. Eduard Hanslick und der musikalische Formbegriff, *Die Musikforschung* 20, 145–53

  1969. Formprinzipien in Wagners 'Ring des Nibelungen', in *Beiträge zur Geschichte der Oper*, edited by Heinz Becker, Regensburg 1969 (Studien zur Musikgeschichte des 19. Jahrhunderts 15), 95–129

  1970a. Soziologische Dechiffrierung von Musik: zu Theodor W. Adornos Wagnerkritik, *International Review of Music Aesthetics and Sociology* 1, 137–47

  1970b. Zur Geschichte der Leitmotivtechnik bei Wagner, in *Das Drama Richard Wagners als musikalisches Kunstwerk*, edited by Carl Dahlhaus, Regensburg 1970 (Studien zur Musikgeschichte des 19. Jahrhunderts 23), 17–40

  1970c. *Die Bedeutung des Gestischen in Wagners Musikdramen*, Munich

  1970d. Wagner and Program Music, *Studies in Romanticism* 9, 3; in German as Wagner und die Programmusik, *Jahrbuch des Staatlichen Instituts für Musikforschung Preußischer Kulturbesitz*, Berlin 1973, 50–63

  1971a. *Die Musikdramen Richard Wagners*, Velber; in English as *Richard Wagner's Music Dramas*, Cambridge, 1979

  1971b. *Wagners Konzeption des musikalischen Dramas*, Regensburg

  1972. Wagners dramatisch-musikalischer Formbegriff, in *Colloquium 'Verdi–Wagner', Rom 1969*, edited by F. Lippmann, Cologne and Vienna, 290–301

  1974. Wagners Berlioz-Kritik und die Ästhetik des Häßlichen, in *Festschrift Arno Volk*, Copenhagen 1974, 107ff.

1975. Beethovens 'Neuer Weg', *Jahrbuch des Staatlichen Instituts für Musikforschung Preußischer Kulturbesitz*, Berlin 46–52

1976. Liszts Bergsymphonie und die Idee der Symphonischen Dichtung, *Jahrbuch des Staatlichen Instituts für Musikforschung Preußischer Kulturbesitz*, Berlin, 96–159

1978a. *Die Idee der absoluten Musik*, Kassel

1978b. 'Tristan' – Harmonik und Tonalität, *Melos/NZfM* 4, 215–19

1978c. Was ist eine 'dichterisch-musikalische' Periode?, *Melos/NZfM*, 224f.

1983. Wagner's 'A Communication to my Friends': Reminiscence and Adaptation. *The Musical Times* 124, 89–91

1984. Wagner und die musikalische Moderne, in *Richard Wagner*, Wissenschaftliche Buchgesellschaft, Darmstadt, 361–70

1985. Der Wahn–Monolog des Hans Sachs und das Problem der Entwicklungsform im musikalischen Drama, *Jahrbuch für Opernforschung*, 9–25

1987. *Ludwig van Beethoven und seine Zeit*, Laaber

1988. Zur Wirkungsgeschichte von Beethovens Symphonien, in *Gattungen der Musik*, edited by Hermann Danuser, Laaber, 221–33

Damrosch, Walter, 1924. *My Musical Life*, London

1927. Hans von Bülow and the Ninth Symphony, *The Musical Quarterly* 13, 280–9

Dannreuther, Edward, 1873. *Richard Wagner: His Tendencies and Theories*, London

Danuser, Hermann, 1975. *Musikalische Prosa*, Regensburg (Studien zur Musikgeschichte des 19. Jahrhunderts 46)

Daube, Otto, 1960. *'Ich schreibe keine Symphonien mehr', Richard Wagners Lehrjahre nach den erhaltenen Dokumenten*, Cologne

Davison, Henry D. (ed.), 1912. *From Mendelssohn to Wagner, being the Memories of J. W. Davison, Forty Years Critic of the Times*, London

Deathridge, John, 1974/5. The Nomenclature of Wagner's Sketches, *PRMA* 101, 75–83

1977a. *Wagner's Rienzi: A Reappraisal based on a Study of the Sketches and Drafts*, Oxford

1977b. Wagner's Sketches for the 'Ring', *The Musical Times* 118, 383–9

1978a. Eine verschollene Wagner-Arie?, *Melos/NZfM*, 4, 208–14

1978b. Fragmente über Fragmentarisches: zur 'Lohengrin'-Kompositionsskizze, in *Bayerische Staatsoper. Richard Wagner, Lohengrin*, programme book for new production, Munich

1979. Wagner und sein erster Lehrmeister. With an unpublished letter by Richard Wagner, in: *Bayerische Staatsoper. Richard Wagner. Die Meistersinger von Nürnberg*, programme book for new production, Munich

1980. 'Im übrigen darf ich wohl hoffen, dass Sie mich nicht eben gerade für einen Honorararbeiter halten . . .' Zur Entstehung der 'Tristan'-Partitur, in *Bayerische Staatsoper: Tristan*, programme book for new production, Munich, 42ff.

1982a. Richard Wagners Kompositionen zu Goethes 'Faust', in *Jahrbuch der Bayerischen Staatsoper*, Munich, 90–9

1982b. *An Introduction to 'The Flying Dutchman'*, London

Deathridge, John, and Dahlhaus, Carl, 1984. *The New Grove Wagner*, New York and London

Deathridge, John and Geck, Martin and Voss, Egon, 1985. *Wagner. Werkverzeichnis (WWV). Verzeichnis der musikalischen Werke Richard Wagners und ihrer Quellen. Erarbeitet im Rahmen der Richard Wagner-Gesamtausgabe*, Mainz, London, New York, Tokyo

Dessoir, Max, 1891. Richard Wagner als Ästhetiker, *Bayreuther Blätter* 14

Dinger, Hugo, 1892. *Richard Wagners geistige Entwicklung* 1: Die Weltanschauung Richard Wagners in den Grundzügen ihrer Entwicklung, Leipzig

Doernberg, E., 1965. Anton Felix Schindler, *The Musical Quarterly* 51, 373–86

Dollard, John (*et al.*), 1939. *Frustration and Aggression*, New Haven

Donington, Robert, 1963. *Wagner's 'Ring' and its Symbols: The Music and the Myth*, London

Dorn, Heinrich, 1870–86. *Aus meinem Leben*, Berlin

1877. *Ergebnisse aus Erlebnissen*, Berlin

Draeseke, Felix, 1907. Was tut in der heutigen musikalischen Produktion not?, *Signale* 65

Dubitzky, Franz, 1912. Von der Herkunft Wagnerscher Themen, *Musikalisches Magazin* 50

Dujardin, Edouard, 1855–6. Les Œuvres théoriques de Richard Wagner, *Revue Wagnérienne* 1, 62–73

1931. *Le Monologue intérieur*, Paris

Du Moulin Eckart, Richard, Graf, 1929–30. *Cosima Wagner. Ein Lebens- und Charakterbild*, 2 vols., Munich

1930. *Cosima Wagner*, translated by Catherine Alison Phillips, and with an introduction by Ernest Newman, 2 vols., New York

Eckart-Bäcker, Ursula, 1965. *Frankreichs Musik zwischen Romantik und Moderne. Die Zeit im Spiegel der Kritik*, Regensburg (Studien zur Musikgeschichte des 19. Jahrhunderts 2)

Edler, Arnfried, 1965. Zur Musikanschauung von Adolf Bernhard Marx, in *Beiträge zur Musikanschauung im 19. Jahrhundert*, edited by Walter Salmen, Regensburg (Studien zur Musikgeschichte des 19. Jahrhunderts 1), 103–12

Egermann, F., 1964. Aischyleische Motive in Richard Wagners Dichtung von 'Tristan und Isolde', *Deutsches Jahrbuch der Musikwissenschaft* 9, 40–8

Eggebrecht, Hans Heinrich, 1955. Das Ausdrucksprinzip im musikalischen Sturm und Drang, *Deutsche Vierteljahrsschrift für Literaturwissenschaft und Geistesgeschichte*, 29

1961. Musik als Tonsprache, *Archiv für Musikwissenschaft* 18

Ehinger, Hans, 1954. *E. Th. A. Hoffmann als Musiker und Musikschriftsteller*, Olten and Cologne

Eichberg, Iscar, 1887. *Richard Wagners Sinfonie in C-dur*, Berlin

Einem, Herbert von, 1956. *Beiträge zu Goethes Kunstauffassung*, Hamburg

Einstein, Alfred, 1921. Die deutsche Musiker-Autobiographie, *Jahrbücher der Musikbibl. Peters* 28

1950. *Die Romantik in der Musik*, Munich

1956. *Von Schütz bis Hindemith. Essays über Musik und Musiker*, Zürich and Stuttgart

Eisenbeiss, Hans, 1924. Schopenhauers Einfluß auf Richard Wagner, diss., Nuremberg

Ellis, W. Ashton, 1900–8. *Life of Richard Wagner. Being an Authorized English Version ... of C. F. Glasenapp's 'Das Leben Richard Wagners'*, 6 vols., London

Engel, Hans, 1948. Bearbeitungen in alter und neuer Zeit, *Das Musikleben* 1
  1955. Wagner und Spontini, *Archiv für Musikwissenschaft* 12, 167
  1956. Richard Wagners Stellung zu Mozart, in *Festschrift W. Fischer*, Innsbruck
Engelsmann, Walter, 1933. *Wagners klingendes Universum*, Potsdam
  1937. Von keinem Weib kam mir der Ruf, *Bayreuther Festspielführer*
  1938. Die 'Konstruktion' der Melodie in Wagners 'Tristan und Isolde', in
    Bayreuther Festspielführer, 145–56
  1939. Schaffenswende, *Bayreuther Festspielführer*, 109–20
  1951. Wagners musikalisches Kompositionsverfahren, *Das Bayreuther Festspiel-
    buch*, 96ff.
Ernst, Alfred, 1887. *Richard Wagner et le drame contemporain*, Paris
Ewans, M., 1982. *Wagner and Aeschylus: the 'Ring' and 'Oresteia'*, London
Federlein, Gottlieb, 1871. 'Das Rheingold' von Richard Wagner. Versuch einer
    musikalischen Interpretation des Vorspiels zum 'Ring des Nibelungen',
    Musikalisches Wochenblatt 2
  1872. 'Die Walküre' von Richard Wagner. Versuch einer musikalischen
    Interpretation des gleichnamigen Musikdramas, *Musikalisches Wochenblatt* 3
Fehr, Max, 1934. *Richard Wagners Schweizer Zeit*, 1, Aarau and Leipzig
  1954. *Richard Wagners Schweizer Zeit*, 11, Aarau and Leipzig
  1922. *Unter Wagners Taktstock*, Winterthur
Fellinger, Imogen, 1968. *Verzeichnis der Musikzeitschriften des 19. Jahrhunderts*,
    Regensburg (Studien zur Musikgeschichte des 19. Jahrhunderts 10)
Feuerbach, Ludwig, 1966. *Kleine Schriften. Theorie 1.* Frankfurt a. Main
Fischer, Kurt von, 1948. *Die Beziehungen von Form und Motiv in Beethovens
    Instrumentalwerken*, Strasbourg and Zürich (Sammlung Musikwissenschaftli-
    cher Abhandlungen 30)
Fischer, Wilhelm, 1915. Zur Entwicklungsgeschichte des Wiener klassischen
    Stils, in *Studien zur Musikwissenschaft* (Beihefte der Denkmäler der Tonkunst
    in Österreich, 3), Vienna
Frankenstein, Ludwig, 1912. Bibliographie der auf R. Wagner bezüglichen
    Buch-, Zeitungs-, und Zeitschriftenliteratur 1907–11, *R. Wagner-Jahrbuch* 4
Frey, Dagobert, 1946. *Kunstwissenschaftliche Grundfragen*, Vienna
Friedländer, Erich, 1922. *Wagner, Liszt und die Kunst der Klavierbearbeitung*,
    Detmold
Fries, Albert, 1910. *Zu Richard Wagners Stil in Vers und Prosa*, Berlin
Fries, Othmar, 1952. *Richard Wagner und die deutsche Romantik*, Zürich
Frimmel, Theodor v., 1905–6. *Beethoven-Studien*, 2 pts., Munich
Furness, R., 1982. *Wagner and Literature*, Manchester
Fürstenau, Moritz, 1849. *Beiträge zur Geschichte der kgl. sächsischen Kapelle*,
    Dresden
Gadamer, Hans-Georg, 3/1972. *Wahrheit und Methode. Grundzüge einer philosophischen
    Hermeneutik*, Tübingen
Galkin, Elliott, Washington, 1960. The Theory and Practice of Orchestral
    Conducting since 1752. diss., 2 vols., Cornell
Gassner, Ferdinand Simon, 2/1842. *Partiturkenntnis. Ein Leitfaden zum Selbstunter-
    richt*, Karlsruhe
Geck, Martin, 1968. *Die Wiederentdeckung der Matthäuspassion im 19. Jahrhundert*,
    Regensburg (Studien zur Musikgeschichte des 19. Jahrhunderts 9)

1969a. Richard Wagner und die ältere Musik, in *Die Ausbreitung des Historismus über die Musik*, edited by Walter Wiora, Regensburg (Studien zur Musikgeschichte des 19. Jahrhunderts 14), 123–46

1969b. Bach und Tristan – Musik aus dem Geiste der Utopie, in *Bach–Interpretationen*, edited by Martin Geck, Göttingen

1970. Musik und Musikleben im München Richard Wagners und Ludwig II, in Detta and Michael Petzet, *Die Richard Wagner-Bühne König Ludwigs II*, with contributions by Martin Geck and Heinrich Hebel, Munich

Glasenapp, Carl Friedrich, 1883. *Wagner-Lexikon, Hauptbegriffe der Kunst- und Weltanschauung Richard Wagners in wörtlichen Ausführungen aus seinen Schriften*, Stuttgart

1891. *Wagner-Encyklopädie. Haupterscheinungen der Kunst- und Kulturgeschichte im Lichte der Anschauung Richard Wagners. In örtlichen Anführungen aus seinen Schriften*, 2 vols., Leipzig

3/1894–1911. *Das Leben Richard Wagners*, 6 vols., Leipzig

Glaser-Gerhard, Ernst, 1929. Hermann Hettner und Gottfried Keller. Ein Beitrag zur Theorie des Dramas um 1850. Dargest. unter Benutzung von H. Hettners Briefnachlaß, diss., Weida

Glass, Frank W., 1983. *The Fertilizing Seed*, Ann Arbor

Goethe, Johann Wolfgang von. 3/1958. *Werke* XII: Schriften zur Kunst. Schriften zur Literatur. Maximen und Reflexionen. Annotated by Herbert von Einem (Schriften zur Kunst) and Hans Joachim Schrimpf (Schriften zur Literatur; Maximen und Reflexionen) Hamburg

Golther, W., 1902. *Die sagengeschichtlichen Grundlagen der Ringdichtung Richard Wagners*, Berlin

Gotthelf, Felix, 1915. Schopenhauer und Richard Wagner, *Viertes Jahrbuch der Schopenhauer-Gesellschaft* (issued on 22 February 1915), Kiel, 24–42

Graf, Max, 1946. *Composer and Critic: 200 Years of Musical Criticism*, New York

Greff, Paul, 1948. *E. T. A. Hoffmann als Musiker und Musikschriftsteller*, Cologne

Gregor-Dellin, Martin, 1969. *Das kleine Wagnerbuch*, Salzburg

1972. *Wagner Chronik: Daten zu Leben und Werk*, Munich

1980. *Richard Wagner. Sein Leben. Sein Werk. Sein Jahrhundert.* Munich and Zürich; English translation: London, 1983

Grempler, Ingeborg, 1950. Das Musikschrifttum von Hector Berlioz, diss. Göttingen

Grisson, R., 1934. *Beiträge zur Auslegung von Richard Wagners 'Ring des Nibelungen'*, Leipzig

Grossmann-Vendrey, Susanne, 1977. *Bayreuth in der deutschen Presse*, Regensburg

1977. *Bayreuth in der deutschen Presse*, II: *Die Uraufführung des Parsifal*, Regensburg

Grundmann, Herbert, 1927. *Studien über Joachim von Floris*, Leipzig and Berlin (Beiträge zur Kulturgeschichte des Mittelalters und der Renaissance 32)

1950. *Neue Forschungen über Joachim von Fiore*, Marburg

Grunsky, Karl, 1906. Wagner als Sinfoniker, *R. Wagner-Jahrbuch* I

1911. *Die Technik des Klavierauszuges, entwickelt am 3. Akt von Wagners Tristan*, Leipzig

4/1923. *Musikästhetik*, Berlin and Leipzig

1933. *Lessing und Herder als Wegbereiter Richard Wagners*, Stuttgart

Guggenheimer, Hedwig, 1907. E. Th. A. Hoffmann und Richard Wagner, *R. Wagner Jahrbuch* 2, 165–206

Guichard, Léon, 1964. *La Musique et les lettres en France au temps du Wagnérisme*, Paris

Gutman, Robert W., 1968. *Richard Wagner. The Man, his Mind and his Music*, London

Guttmann, Erich, 1934. *Die deutsche romantische Musikerzählung nach E. T. A. Hoffmann. Ein Beitrag zur Geschichte des historisch-biographischen Künstlerromans und der Künstlernovelle in Deutschland*, Breslau

Haefliger Graves, Marie, 1938. *Schiller and Wagner. A Study of their Dramatic Theory and Technique*, Michigan

Hansen, Bernhard, 1959. Variationen und Varianten in den musikalischen Werken Franz Liszts, diss., Hamburg

Hanslick, Eduard, 1869. *Geschichte des Concertwesens in Wien*, Vienna

1875. *Die Moderne Oper* (Berlin)

4/1911. *Aus meinem Leben*, 2 vols., Berlin

1854. *Vom Musikalisch-Schönen* (Leipzig)

Hapke, Walter, 1927. Die musikalische Darstellung der Gebärde in Richard Wagners Ring des Nibelungen, diss., Borna and Leipzig

Hartford, R., 1980. *Bayreuth: The Early Years*, London

Hartmann, Nicolai, 1950. *Philosophie der Natur*, Berlin

2/1966. *Ästhetik*, Berlin

Hausegger, Friedrich von, 1878. *Richard Wagner und Schopenhauer*, Leipzig

1887. *Die Musik als Ausdruck*, Vienna

Heckel, K., 1891. *Die Bühnenfestsspiele in Bayreuth*, Leipzig

Heine, Heinrich, 1964. *Zeitungsberichte über Musik und Malerei*, edited by Michael Mann, Frankfurt a. Main

Hettner, Hermann, 1852. *Das moderne Drama*, Leipzig

Heuss, Alfred, 1910–11. Zum Thema, Musik und Szene bei Wagner: im Anschluß an Wagners Aufsatz, Bemerkungen zur Aufführung der Oper 'Der fliegende Holländer', *Die Musik* 10, 3, 81

1912–13. Musik und Szene bei Wagner: ein Beispiel aus 'Tristan und Isolde' und zugleich ein kleiner Beitrag zur Charakteristik Gustav Mahlers als Regisseur, *Die Musik* 12, 20ff.

Hey, Julius, 1911. *Richard Wagner als Vortragsmeister*, edited by Hans Hey, Leipzig

Hildebrandt, K., 1924. *Wagner und Nietzsche: ihr Kampf gegen das 19. Jahrhundert*, Breslau

Hiller, Ferdinand, 1958–65. *Aus Ferdinand Hillers Briefwechsel 1826–1881*, edited by Reinhold Sietz, 4 vols., Cologne (Beiträge zur Rheinischen Musikgeschichte 28) 48, 56, 60.

1868. *Aus dem Tonleben unserer Zeit*, 2 vols., Leipzig

Hirth, Friedrich, 1950. Wagner, Meyerbeer und Heine, *Das Goldene Tor* 5, 383–7

Hoffmann, Ernst Theodor Amadeus, 1960–5. Complete Works, 5 vols., Munich

Hollinrake, R., 1970. The Title-Page of Wagner's 'Mein Leben', *Music & Letters* 51, 415

1982. *Nietzsche, Wagner and the Philosophy of Pessimism*, London

Hommel, K., 1963. *Die Separatvorstellungen vor König Ludwig II. von Bayern*, Munich

Hopkinson, Cecil, 1951. *A Bibliography of the Musical and Literary Works of Hector Berlioz 1803–1869*, Edinburgh

Hornstein, Robert von, 1908. *Memoiren*, edited by Ferdinand von Hornstein, Munich

Hotes, Leander, 1931. Das Leitmotiv in der neueren deutschen Romandichtung, diss., Frankfurt a. Main

Huber, Anna Gertrud, 1953. *Ludwig van Beethoven. Seine Schüler und Interpreten*, Vienna

Hubert, Jean, 1895. *Étude sur quelques pages de Richard Wagner*, Paris

Hueffer, F., 1872. *Richard Wagner*, London,

Hüffer, Eduard, 1909. Anton Felix Schindler, diss., Münster

Humperdinck, Engelbert, 1927. Parsifal-Skizzen. Persönliche Erinnerungen an die 1. Aufführung des Bühnenweihfestspiels am 25. Juli 1882, *Bayreuther Festspielführer*, 215–29

1975. *Briefe und Tagebücher*, 2 vols., Cologne

Husserl, Edmund, 1966. *Zur Phänomenologie des inneren Zeitbewußtseins (1893–1917)*, edited by Rudolf Boehm, The Hague

Ingarden, Roman, 1965. *Der Streit um die Existenz der Welt*, Tübingen

Ingenschau-Goch, D., 1982. *Richard Wagners neu erfundener Mythos: zur Rezeption und Reproduktion des germanischen Mythos in seinen Operntexten*, Bonn

Ipser, Karl, 1953. *Beethoven, Wagner, Bayreuth*, Bayreuth

Istel, Edgar, 1909. *Die Blütezeit der musikalischen Romantik in Deutschland*, Leipzig

Jäckel, Kurt, 1931–2. *Richard Wagner und die französische Literatur*, 2 vols., Breslau

Jackson, R., 1975. Leitmotive and Form in the 'Tristan'–Prelude, *Music Review* 36, 42ff.

Jähns, Friedrich Wilhelm, 1871. *Carl Maria von Weber in seinen Werken. Chronologisch-thematisches Verzeichnis seiner sämtlichen Compositionen ... mit ... kritischen, kunsthistorischen und biographischen Anmerkungen...*, Berlin

Just, K. G., 1978. Richard Wagner – ein Dichter? Marginalien zum Opernlibretto des 19. Jahrhunderts, in *Richard Wagner: von der Oper zum Musikdrama*, edited by Stefan Kunze, Berne and Munich, 79–94

Kähler, Guido, 1958. Studien zur Entstehung der Formenlehre in der Musiktheorie des 18. und 19. Jahrhunderts (Von W. C. Printz bis A. B. Marx), diss. Heidelberg

Kalischer, Alfred Christlieb, 1908–10. *Beethoven und seine Zeitgenossen*, 4 vols., Berlin

Kapp, Julius, 1911–12. Richard Wagner und Robert Schumann, *Die Musik* 11, 42–9, 100–8

Karbaum, Michael, 1976. *Studien zur Geschichte der Bayreuther Festspiele (1876–1976)*, Regensburg (Arbeitsgemeinschaft '100 Jahre Bayreuther Festspiele' 3)

Kerman, Joseph, 1957. *Opera as Drama*, London

Kiessling, Arthur, 1916. *Richard Wagner und die Romantik*, Leipzig

Kietz, Gustav Adolf, 1905. *Richard Wagner in den Jahren 1842–1849 und 1873–1875. Erinnerungen*, recorded by Maria Kietz, Dresden

Kindermann, William, 1980–1. Dramatic Recapitulation in Wagner's 'Götterdämmerung', *19th Century Music* 4, 101ff.

Kinsky, Georg, 1945. Eine Erläuterung Carl Loewes zu Beethovens 9. Symphonie, *Schweizerische Musikzeitung* 85, 181–94

Kinsky, Georg, and Halm, Hans 1955. *Das Werk Beethovens.* Thematic–bibliographical index, Munich and Duisburg

Kirchmeyer, Helmut, 1965. Ein Kapitel Adolf Bernhard Marx. Über Sendungsbewußtsein und Bildungsstand der Berliner Musikkritik zwischen 1824 und 1830, in *Beiträge zur Geschichte der Musikanschauung im 19. Jahrhundert,* edited by Walter Salmen, Regensburg (Studien zur Musikgeschichte des 19. Jahrhunderts 1), 73–101

1967. *Situationsgeschichte der Musikkritik und des musikalischen Pressewesens in Deutschland, dargestellt vom Ausgange des 18. bis zum Beginn des 20. Jahrhunderts. Das zeitgenössische Wagner-Bild* II: *Dokumente 1842–1845,* Regensburg (Studien zur Musikgeschichte des 19. Jahrhunderts 7)

1968. *Situationsgeschichte der Musikkritik und des musikalischen Pressewesens in Deutschland, dargestellt vom Ausgange des 18. bis zum Beginn der 20. Jahrhunderts.* IV. *Teil. Das zeitgenössische Wagner-Bild* III: *Dokumente 1846–1850,* Regensburg (Studien zur Musikgeschichte des 19. Jahrhunderts 7)

Kleefeld, Wilhelm, 1904–5. Richard Wagner als Bearbeiter fremder Werke, *Die Musik* 4, 326–37.

Kleinlercher, Herbert, 1948. Joseph Fischhof. Leben und Werk, diss. Vienna

Klugmann, Friedhelm, 1961. Die Kategorie der Zeit in der Musik, diss., Bonn

Kneif, Tibor, 1970. Wagner: eine Rekapitulation. Mythos und Geschichte im Ring des Nibelungen, in *Das Drama Richard Wagners als musikalisches Kunstwerk,* edited by Carl Dahlhaus, Regensburg (Studien zur Musikgeschichte des 19. Jahrhunderts 23)

Knepler, Georg, 1961. *Musikgeschichte des 19. Jahrhunderts,* 2 vols., Berlin

1963. Richard Wagners musikalische Gestaltungsprinzipien, *Beiträge zur Musikwissenschaft* 5, 33–43

Knopf, Kurt, 1931. Die romantische Struktur des Denkens Richard Wagners, diss., Jena

Koch, Max, 1907–18. *Richard Wagner,* 3 vols., Berlin

Kohut, Adolph, 1889. Richard Wagner und sein Dresdener Freundeskreis, *Die Gegenwart* 35, 187f.

1910. Richard Wagner und K. G. Reißiger, *Allgemeine Musikzeitung* 37, 53f.

Koppen, Erwin, 1973. *Dekadenter Wagnerismus,* Berlin and New York (Komparatistische Studien. Beiheft zu 'arcadia', Zeitschrift für Vergleichende Literaturwissenschaft 2)

Korte, Werner F., 1963, *Bruckner und Brahms. Die spätromantische Lösung der autonomen Konzeption,* Tutzing

Krehbiel, H. E., 1891. *Studies in the Wagnerian Drama,* New York, reprinted 1975

Kretzschmar, Hermann, 1910. Ein Abend bei den musikalischen Meinigern, in *Ges. Aufsätze über Musik und anderes*

Krienitz, Willy, 1943. Felix Mottls Tagebuchaufzeichnungen aus den Jahren 1873–1876, in *Neue Wagner-Forschungen. Veröffentlichungen der Richard-Wagner-Forschungsstätte Bayreuth,* edited by Otto Strobel, first series, Bayreuth, 167–234

Kroll, E., 1926. E. T. A. Hoffmann und Beethoven, *Neues Beethoven-Jahrbuch* 3, 125–42

Kropfinger, Klaus, 1970. Wagners Tristan und Beethovens Streichquartett op. 130. Funktion und Strukturen des Prinzips der Einleitungswiederho-

lung, in *Das Drama Richard Wagners als musikalisches Kunstwerk*, edited by Carl
Dahlhaus, Regensburg (Studien zur Musikgeschichte des 19. Jahrhunderts
23), 259–71

1974. Wagners 9. Symphonie – Das ambivalente Werk, in *IMSCR* 11,
Copenhagen (1972), 512–18

1975. *Wagner und Beethoven. Untersuchungen zur Beethoven–Rezeption Richard
Wagners*. Regensburg (Studien zur Musikgeschichte des 19. Jahrhunderts 29)

1983. Wagner und Brahms, *Musica* 37, S. 11–17.

1984a. Wagner – van de Velde – Kandinsky, contribution to the symposium
Richard Wagner 1883–1983. Die Rezeption im 19. und 20. Jahrhundert (Salzburg,
2–6 March 1983), Stuttgart, 181–206

1984b. Metapher und Dramenstruktur. Bemerkungen zur Sprache in Wagners
'Oper und Drama', *Musica* 38, 422–8

1984c. *Oper und Drama* edited, annotated and with an afterword by Klaus
Kropfinger, Stuttgart

1985a. 'Oper und Drama', Die Schrift und ihr Kontext, in *Wagnerliteratur –
Wagnerforschung. Bericht über das Wagner-Symposium in München 1983*, edited
by Carl Dahlhaus and Egon Voss, Mainz, London, New York, Tokyo,
131–7

1985b. Wagners Musikbegriff und Nietzsches 'Geist der Musik', *Nietzsche-
Studien* 14, 1–12

1988. Wagners 'Entsagungs-Motiv', in *Das musikalische Kunstwerk. Geschichte-
Ästhetik-Theorie. Festschrift Carl Dahlhaus zum 60. Geburtstag*, Laaber, 241–58

Krüger, Eduard, 1847. *Beiträge für Leben und Wissenschaft der Tonkunst*, Leipzig

Kruse, Georg Richard, 1911. *Otto Nicolai. Ein Künstlerleben*, Berlin

Kunze, Stefan, 1970. Über Melodiebegriff und musikalischen Bau in Wagners
Musikdrama, dargestellt an Beispielen aus Holländer und Ring', in *Das
Drama Richard Wagners als musikalisches Kunstwerk*, edited by Carl Dahlhaus,
Regensburg 1970 (Studien zur Musikgeschichte des 19. Jahrhunderts 23),
111–48

1978. Über den Kunstcharakter des Wagnerschen Musikdramas, in *Richard
Wagner: von der Oper zum Musikdrama*, edited by Stefan Kunze, Berne and
Munich, 9–24

1985. Dramatische Konzeption und Szenenbezug in Wagners 'Tannhäuser', in
*Wagnerliteratur – Wagnerforschung. Bericht über das Wagner-Symposium München
1983*, edited by Carl Dahlhaus and Egon Voss, Mainz, London, New York,
Tokyo, 196–210

Kurth, Ernst, 1920. *Romantische Harmonik und ihre Krise in Wagners Tristan*, Berne
and Leipzig

Lamm, Max, 1932. Beiträge zur Entwicklung des musikalischen Motivs in den
Tondramen Richard Wagners, diss., Marburg

Lanczkowski, Günther, 1947. Die Bedeutung des indischen Denkens für Richard
Wagner und seinen Freundeskreis, diss., Marburg

Lang, Paul Henry, 1941. *Music in Western Civilization*, New York

Langer, Susanne K., 1953. *Feeling and Form*, New York

Lenz, Wilhelm von, 1860. *Beethoven. Eine Kunststudie*, 5 pts., Hamburg

Leroy, L. A., 1925. *Wagner's Music Drama of the Ring*, London

Lévi-Strauss, Claude, 1964. *Mythologiques I. Le cru et le cuit*, Paris
  1969. *Strukturale Anthropologie*, Frankfurt a. Main
Levy, Albert, 1904. *La Philosophie de Feuerbach et son influence sur la littérature allemande*, Paris
Lichtenberger, Henri, 1899. *Richard Wagner der Dichter und Denker*. Authorized translation by Friedrich von Oppeln-Bronikowski, Dresden and Leipzig
Lichtenhahn, E., 1972. Die 'Popularitätsfrage' in Richard Wagners Pariser Schriften, *Schweizer Beiträge zur Musikwissenschaft* 1, 143ff.
Lippert, Woldemar, 1927. *Richard Wagners Verbannung und Rückkehr*, Dresden
Lippmann, E. A., 1958. The Aesthetic Theories of Richard Wagner, *The Musical Quarterly* 44, 209ff.
Liszt, Franz, 1851. *Lohengrin et Tannhäuser de Richard Wagner*, Leipzig
  1855. Richard Wagners 'Rheingold', *NZfM* 39.
  1910. Marx und sein Buch: 'Die Musik des neunzehnten Jahrhunderts und ihre Pflege', in Collected Writings by Franz Liszt IV, Leipzig
Lobe, Johann Christian, 1844. *Compositions-Lehre oder umfassende Theorie von der thematischen Arbeit und den modernen Instrumentalformen, aus den Werken der besten Meister entwickelt und durch die mannigfaltigsten Beispiele erklärt*, Weimar
Lockwood, Lewis, 1982. 'Eroica'-Perspectives: Strategy and Design in the first Movement, in *Beethoven Studies* 3, edited by Alan Tyson, Cambridge, 85–105
Loos, P. A., 1952. *Richard Wagner: Vollendung und Tragik der deutschen Romantik*, Berne and Munich
Lorenz, Alfred, 1924. Worauf beruht die bekannte Wirkung der Durchführung im 1. Eroicasatze?, *Neues Beethoven-Jahrbuch* 1, 159–83
  ²/1966. *Das Geheimnis der Form bei Richard Wagner*, 4 vols., Tutzing
Love, Frederick R., 1963. *Young Nietzsche and the Wagnerian Experience*, Chapel Hill
Lück, Rudolf, 1905. *Richard Wagner und Ludwig Feuerbach: eine Ergänzung der bisherigen Darstellungen der inneren Entwicklung Wagners*, Breslau
MacArdle, Donald W., 1963. Anton Felix Schindler, Friend of Beethoven, *Music Review* 24, 50–74
Magnani, Luigi, 1967. *Beethovens Konversationshefte*, Munich
Mähl, Hans-Joachim, 1965. *Die Idee des goldenen Zeitalters im Werk des Novalis. Studien zur Wesensbestimmung der frühromantischen Utopie und zu ihren ideengeschichtlichen Voraussetzungen*, Heidelberg (Probleme der Dichtung. Studien zur deutschen Literaturgeschichte 7)
Mainka, Jürgen, 1963. Sonatenform, Leitmotiv und Charakterbegleitung, *Beiträge zur Musikwissenschaft* 5, 11–32
Mann, Thomas, 1963. *Wagner und unsere Zeit. Aufsätze, Betrachtungen, Briefe*, Frankfurt a. Main
Marx, Adolf Bernhard, 1824a. Als Recension der Sonata Op. 111 von L. v. Beethoven ... Brief eines Recensenten an den Redakteur, *BAMZ* 1, 95–9
  1824b. Etwas über die Symphonie und Beethovens Leistungen in diesem Fache, *BAMZ* 1, 165–8; 20, 173–6; 21, 181–4
  1824c. Meeresstille und glückliche Fahrt von Ludwig van Beethoven. 112tes Werk, *BAMZ* 1, 391–6
  1828. Grand Quintetto pour 2 Violons, Alti et Violoncello par Louis van Beethoven ('Beurtheilung'), *BAMZ* 5, 445–7

1837–47. *Die Lehre von der musikalischen Komposition*, 4 vols., Leipzig

1841. *Die alte Musiklehre im Streit mit unserer Zeit*, Leipzig

1846. *Allgemeine Musiklehre*, Leipzig

1855. *Die Musik des neunzehnten Jahrhunderts und ihre Pflege. Methode der Musik*, Leipzig

1865. *Erinnerungen, aus meinem Leben*, 2 vols., Berlin

⁶/1902. *Ludwig van Beethoven. Leben und Schaffen*, 2 vols., Leipzig

Matter, Anne-Marie, 1959. Richard Wagner éducateur, diss., Lausanne

Mayer, Hans, 1954. *Richard Wagners geistige Entwicklung*, Düsseldorf and Hamburg

1959. *Richard Wagner in Selbstzeugnissen und Bilddokumenten*, Hamburg (rowohlts monographien 29)

1966. *Anmerkungen zu Wagner*, Frankfurt a. Main

Mehler, E., 1912–13. Beiträge zur Wagner-Forschung: unveröffentlichte Stücke aus 'Rienzi', 'Holländer' und 'Tannhäuser', *Die Musik* 12, 195

Metzger, H. K., and Riehn, H. (eds.), 1978. *Richard Wagner: wie antisemitisch darf ein Künstler sein?*, Musik-Konzepte 5, Munich

1982. *Richard Wagner: Parsifal*, Musik-Konzepte 25, Munich

1987. *Wagner. Tristan und Isolde*, Musik-Konzepte 57/8, Munich

Meysenbug, Malwida Freiin von, 1868–76. *Memoiren einer Idealistin*, Berlin 1953

Mey, Kurt, 1901. *Musik als tönende Weltidee*, Leipzig

1906. Richard Wagner als Ästhetiker, *R. Wagner-Jahrbuch* 1

Michaelis, Christian Friedrich, 1805. Einige Bemerkungen über das Erhabene in der Musik, *Berlinische Musikalische Zeitung* 1, 179–81

Michotte, Edmond, 1968. *Richard Wagner's Visit to Rossini and an Evening at Rossini's Beau-Séjour*, translated from the French and annotated with an introduction and appendix by Herbert Weinstock, Chicago and London

Misch, Ludwig, 1956. Sind Änderungen in Beethovens Instrumentation zulässig?, *NZfM* 117:11

Mohr, W. 1876. *Richard Wagner und das Kunstwerk der Zukunft im Lichte der Bayreuther Aufführungen betrachtet*, Cologne

Moniates, Maria Rika, 1969. 'Sonate, Que me Veux-Tu?': The Enigma of French Musical Aesthetics in the 18th Century, *Current Musicology* 9, 117–41

Moos, Paul, 1906. *Richard Wagner als Ästhetiker*, Berlin and Leipzig

1906/7. Hoffmann als Musikästhetiker, *Die Musik* 6, 67–84

Mosel, Ignaz Franz, 1813. *Versuch einer Ästhetik des dramatischen Tonsatzes* (Vienna). New edition with an introduction and explanatory notes by Eugen Schmitz, Munich, 1910

Moser, Max, 1938. *Richard Wagner in der englischen Literatur des XIX. Jahrhunderts*, Bonn

Muir, P. H., 1948. Ernest Newman's 'Life of Wagner', *Music Review* 9, 256–68

Müller von Asow, Erich H., 1943. *Johannes Brahms und Mathilde Wesendonck, ein Briefwechsel*, Vienna

Neumann, Angelo, 1907. *Erinnerungen an Richard Wagner*, Leipzig

Newman, Ernest, 1931. *Fact and Fiction about Wagner*, London

1933–46. *The Life of Richard Wagner*, 4 vols., New York, reprinted 1976

1952. *Wagner as Man and Artist*, London 1914, rev. ²/1924, reprinted New York

Nicolai, Otto, 1892. *Tagebücher nebst biographischen Ergänzungen*, edited by B. Schröder, Leipzig

1913. *Musikalische Aufsätze*. First edition by Georg R. Kruse, Regensburg (Deutsche Musikbücherei 10)

1924. *Briefe an seinen Vater*. First edition by W. Altmann, Regensburg (Deutsche Musikbücherei 43)

Nietzsche, Friedrich, 1954–65. *Werke* in 3 vols., edited by Karl Schlechta, Munich

Nohl, Ludwig, 1870. *Beethovens Brevier. Sammlung der von ihm selbst ausgezogenen oder angemerkten Stellen aus Dichtern und Schriftstellern alter und neuer Zeit. Nebst einer Darstellung von Beethovens geistiger Entwicklung*, Leipzig

1874. *Beethoven, Liszt, Wagner. Ein Bild der Kunstbewegung unseres Jahrhunderts*, Vienna

1884. *Das moderne Musikdrama*, Vienna

Nottebohm, Gustav, 1887. *Zweite Beethoveniana*, Leipzig

Novalis, 1965 and 1968. *Schriften*. Die Werke Friedrich von Hardenbergs. Das Philosophische Werk I and II, edited by Richard Samuel, Stuttgart

Nufer, Wolfgang, 1929. *Herders Ideen zur Verbindung von Poesie, Musik und Tanz*, Berlin (Germanische Studien 74)

Oesterlein, Nikolaus, 1882–95. *Beschreibendes Verzeichnis des Richard Wagner Museums*, 4 vols., Leipzig

Panofsky, Erwin, 1955. Titian's Allegory of Prudence: A Postscript, in *Meaning in the Visual Arts*, New York, 146–68

Panzer, F., 1907–8. Richard Wagners Tannhäuser: sein Aufbau und seine Quellen, *Die Musik* 7, 11ff.

Pascal, Roy, 1965. *Die Autobiographie. Gehalt und Gestalt*, Stuttgart and Berlin (Sprache und Literatur 19); English edition: *Design and Truth in Autobiography*, London, 1960

Peacock, R., 1934. *Das Leitmotiv bei Thomas Mann*, Berne

Petersen, Peter, 1977. Die dichterisch-musikalische Periode: ein verkannter Begriff Richard Wagners, *Hamburger Jahrbuch für Musikwissenschaft* 2, 105–23

1978. Was ist eine 'dichterisch-musikalische Periode'? Entgegnung auf die Kritik von Carl Dahlhaus, *Melos/NZfM*, 403f.

Petri, Horst, 1964. *Literatur und Musik*, Göttingen

Petsch, R. 1907. Der 'Ring des Nibelungen' in seinen Beziehungen zur griechischen Tragödie und zur zeitgenössischen Philosophie, *R. Wagner-Jahrbuch* 2, 284–330

Pfeiffer, Theodor, 5/1894. *Studien bei Hans von Bülow*, Leipzig

Phelan, John Leddy, 1956. *The Millennial Kingdom of the Franciscans in the New World. A Study of the Writings of Gerónimo de Mendietta (1525–1604)*, Berkeley and Los Angeles (University of California Publications in History 52)

Pohl, Richard, 1871. Bericht über das Konzert unter Richard Wagners Leitung in Mannheim am 20. 12. 1871, *Mannheimer Journal*, December

Poos, Heinrich, 1987. Die 'Tristan'–Hieroglyphe. Ein allegorischer Versuch, in *Richard Wagner. Tristan und Isolde*, Munich (Musik-Konzepte 57/8), 46–103

Porges, Heinrich, 1872. *Die Aufführung von Beethovens 9. Symphonie unter Richard Wagner in Bayreuth*, Leipzig

1877a. Ludwig van Beethoven's neunte Symphonie und das Stylprinzip der Musik des neunzehnten Jahrhunderts, *NZfM* 73, 351ff., 363ff. 369ff.

1877b. *Die Bühnenproben zu den Bayreuther Festspielen des Jahres 1876,* Leipzig
1906. *'Tristan und Isolde'. Nebst einem Brief Richard Wagners,* Leipzig
Prod'homme, Jacques-Gabriel, 1903–4. *Bibliographie berliozienne* (Sammelbände der Internat. Musikgesellschaft 5)
Prölss, Robert, 1879. *Beiträge zur Geschichte des Hoftheaters zu Dresden,* Erfurt
Pügner, Georg. 1960. *Johann Bernhard Logier. Leben und Werk. Ein Beitrag zur Entwicklung des musikalischen Gruppenunterrichts,* diss., Leipzig
Raff, Joachim, 1854. *Die Wagnerfrage: kritisch beleuchtet,* I: *Wagners letzte künstlerische Kundgebung im 'Lohengrin',* Braunschweig
Rayner, R. M., 1954. *Wagner and 'Die Meistersinger',* Cambridge
Reckow, Fritz, 1970. Zu Wagners Begriff der 'unendlichen Melodie', in *Das Drama Richard Wagners als musikalisches Kunstwerk,* edited by Carl Dahlhaus, Regensburg (Studien zur Musikgeschichte des 19. Jahrhunderts 23), 81–110
1971. 'Unendliche Melodie', in *Handwörterbuch der musikalischen Terminologie* (*HmT*), edited by Hans Heinrich Eggebrecht, Wiesbaden
Redlich, Hans Ferdinand, 1955. *Bruckner and Mahler,* London
Reimann, Heinrich, 1909. *Hans von Bülow* I: *Aus Hans von Bülows Lehrzeit* (first part of an unfinished biography), Berlin
Rellstab, Ludwig, 1825. Über Beethovens neuestes Quartett, *BAMZ* 2, 165f.
Réti, Rudolph, 1950. *The Thematic Process in Music,* London
Richter, K. F., 1956. Die Antinomien der szenischen Dramaturgie im Werk Richard Wagners, diss., Munich
Riedel, Herbert, 1959. *Musik und Musikerlebnis in der erzählenden deutschen Dichtung,* Bonn (Abhandlungen zur Kunst-, Musik- und Literaturwissenschaft, 12)
Riemann, Hugo, 1895–1901. *Präludien und Studien. Gesammelte Aufsätze zur Ästhetik, Theorie und Geschichte der Musik,* 3 vols., Leipzig
Riezler, Walter, 5/1942. *Beethoven,* Berlin and Zürich
Ritzel, Fred, 2/1969. *Die Entwicklung der 'Sonatenform' im musiktheoretischen Schrifttum des 18. und 19. Jahrhunderts,* Wiesbaden (Neue Musikgeschichtliche Forschungen 1)
Rochlitz, Friedrich, 1824–32. *Für Freunde der Tonkunst,* 4 vols., Leipzig
Roeckl, Sebastian, 1913–20. *Ludwig II. und R. Wagner,* Munich
1938. *Richard Wagner in München, ein Bericht in Briefen,* Regensburg
Roeder, Erich, 1932. *Felix Draeseke* I: Dresden
1937. *Felix Draeseke* II: Berlin
Rösch, Friedrich, 1897. *Musikästhetische Streitfragen,* Leipzig
Roth, Waltraut, 1951. Schopenhauers Metaphysik der Musik und sein musikalischer Geschmack. Ihre Entwicklung und ihr wechselseitiges Verhältnis, diss., Mainz
Rubinstein, Josef, 1879. Über die Schumann'sche Musik, *Bayreuther Blätter,* 8
Rühlmann, Adolf Julius, 1853. Theodor Uhlig, *NZfM* 38, 33ff.
[1854] Review, Beethoven's Symphonien nach ihrem idealen Gehalt mit Rücksicht auf Haydn's und Mozart's Symphonien, von einem Kunstfreund, (Dresden n.d.), *NZfM* 41, 114f.
Rummenhöller, Peter, 1965. Romantik und Gesamtkunstwerk, in *Beiträge zur Geschichte der Musikanschauung im 19. Jahrhundert,* edited by Walter Salmen, Regensburg (Studien zur Musikgeschichte des 19. Jahrhunderts 1)

Runciman, John F., 1913. *Richard Wagner Composer of Operas*, London
Ruprecht, Erich, 1938. *Der Mythos bei Wagner und Nietzsche*, Berlin
Sandberger, Adolf, 1924. Zur Geschichte der Beethovenforschung und des Beethovenverständnisses, in *Ausgewählte Aufsätze zur Musikgeschichte* II: *Forschungen, Studien und Kritiken zu Beethoven und zur Beethovenliteratur*, Munich, 11–80
Schadewaldt, Wolfgang, 1962. Richard Wagner und die Griechen, in *Richard Wagner und das neue Bayreuth*, edited by Wieland Wagner, Munich (*List*Bücher 237), 149–74
Schaefer, Hans Joachim, 1950, Gehalt und dramaturgische Gestaltung im Kunstwerk Richard Wagners, 2 pts., diss., Marburg
Schemann, Ludwig, 1902. *Meine Erinnerungen an Richard Wagner*, Stuttgart
Schenker, Heinrich, 1912. *Beethoven. Neunte Sinfonie. Eine Darstellung des musikalischen Inhaltes unter fortlaufender Berücksichtigung auch des Vortrages und der Literatur*, Vienna, reprinted 1969
    1925. *Beethoven. Fünfte Sinfonie. Eine Darstellung des musikalischen Inhaltes unter fortlaufender Berücksichtigung auch des Vortrages und der Literatur*, Vienna, reprinted 1969
Schering, Arnold, 1936. *Beethoven und die Dichtung*, Berlin
Schiller, Friedrich, 1961–2. *Philosophische Schriften*, edited by Benno von Wiese, 2 vols., Weimar (Werke, Nationalausgabe 20 and 21)
Schindler, Anton, 1840. *Biographie von Ludwig van Beethoven*, Münster, ²/1845, ³/1860 (new enlarged edition); reprint edited by A. C. Kalischer, Berlin and Leipzig 1909
    1842. *Beethoven in Paris, nebst anderen den unsterblichen Tondichter betreffenden Mitteilungen*, Münster
    1939. *Anton Schindler, der Freund Beethovens*. His diary for the years 1841–3, edited by Marta Becker, Frankfurt a. Main
    1966. *Beethoven as I Knew Him: A Biography*, edited by Donald W. MacArdle, translated by Constance S. Jolly, London
Schmerbach, Hartmut, 1926. *Stilstudien zu E. T. A. Hoffmann*, Berlin, reprinted 1967 (Germanistische Studien 26)
Schmidt-Görg, Joseph, 1935. *Katalog der Handschriften des Beethovenhauses und Beethoven-Archivs Bonn*, Bonn
    1949–51. Art. 'Beethoven', *MGG* I, col. 1505–65
    1964. *Beethoven. Die Geschichte seiner Familie*. Duisburg
Schmitz, Arnold, 1923. *Beethovens 'Zwei Prinzipe'. Ihre Bedeutung für Themen- und Satzbau*, Berlin and Bonn
    1926. Die Beethoven-Apotheose als Beispiel eines Säkularisierungsvorganges, in *Festschrift Peter Wagner*
    1927. *Das Romantische Beethovenbild*, Berlin and Bonn
    1937. Zur Frage nach Beethovens Weltanschauung und ihrem musikalischen Ausdruck, in *Beethoven und die Gegenwart* (Berlin and Bonn), 266–93
    1947–50. Der Mythos der Kunst in den Schriften Richard Wagners, *Beiträge zur christlichen Philosophie* 1–6, 3–22
Schnoor, Hans, 1948. *Dresden. Vierhundert Jahre Deutsche Musikkultur*, Dresden
Schopenhauer, Arthur, 1937–41. *Sämtliche Werke*, 7 vols., edited by Arthur Hübscher, Leipzig

Schrade, Leo, 1937. Das französische Beethovenbild der Gegenwart, in *Beethoven und die Gegenwart* (Berlin and Bonn), 41–113

1942. *Beethoven in France: The Growth of an Idea*. New Haven and London, German translation Berne and Munich 1980.

1964. *W. A. Mozart*, Berne and Munich

Schumann, Robert, [5]/1914. *Gesammelte Schriften über Musik und Musiker*, edited by Martin Kreisig, 2 vols., Leipzig

Schwinger, Reinhold, 1934. Innere Form. Ein Beitrag zur Definition des Begriffes auf Grund seiner Geschichte von Shaftesbury bis W. v. Humboldt, diss., Munich

Sedlmayr, Hans (ed.), 1957. *Über Sprache und Kunst* (1), Hefte des Kunsthistorischen Seminars, No. 3, Munich

Seidl, Arthur, 1887. Vom Musikalisch Erhabenen, diss., Regensburg. Leipzig [2]/1907

Seifert, Wolfgang, 1960. *Christian Gottlieb Körner, ein Musikästhetiker der deutschen Klassik*, Regensburg

Selle, G. F., 1898. *Aus Adolf Bernhard Marx' literarischem Nachlaß*, Berlin

Serauky, Walter, 1929. *Die Musikalische Nachahmungsästhetik im Zeitraum von 1700 bis 1850*, Münster

1958. Zur Neuinterpretation von Richard Wagners Werk, in *Internationale Gesellschaft für Musikwissenschaft. Bericht über den siebenten musikwissenschaftlichen Kongreß*, Cologne

Serow, Alexander, 1863. Der Status quo der Beethoven-Literatur und die Betheiligung Rußlands an demselben, *NZfM* 58, 4–6, 11f., 20f., 27–9, 37–40

Seyfried, Ignaz Ritter von, 1832. *Ludwig van Beethoven's Studien im Generalbaß, Contrapunkte und in der Compositions-Lehre*, collected and edited from his posthumous manuscript by Ignaz Ritter von Seyfried, Vienna; French translation: *Beethoven Études. Traité d'harmonie et de composition trad, et accomp. de notes critiques, d'une préface et de la vie de Beethoven par F. Fétis*, 2 vols., Paris, 1833

Shaw, George Bernard, 1898. *The Perfect Wagnerite: a Commentary on the Nibelungs' Ring*, London, [4]/1923, reprinted 1972

Siegel, Linda, 1965. Wagner and the Romanticism of E. T. A. Hoffmann, *The Musical Quarterly* 51, 597–613

Sokoloff, Alice, 1969. *Cosima Wagner*, New York

Solomon, Maynard, 1977. *Beethoven*, New York

Sonneck, Oscar George Theodor, 1897. *Protest gegen den Symbolismus in der Musik*, Frankfurt a. Main

1926. *Beethoven: Impressions of Contemporaries*, New York

Spohr, Louis, 1860–1. *Selbstbiographie*, 2 vols., Kassel and Göttingen; reprint edited by E. Schmitz, Kassel 1954/5

Stade, Friedrich, 1869. Vom Musikalisch-Schönen. Mit Bezug auf Dr. E. Hanslicks gleichnamige Schrift, diss., Freiburg

1870. Zur Wagner-Frage mit Bezug auf Dr. K. A. Pabst's Schrift: 'Die Verbindung der Künste auf der dramatischen Bühne', *Musikalisches Wochenblatt*, 1, 529ff., 546ff., 560ff., 580ff., 593ff.

Stange, Eberhard, 1954. Die Musikanschauung Eduard Hanslicks in seinen Kritiken und Aufsätzen. Eine Studie zur musikalisch-geistigen Situation des 19. Jahrhunderts, diss., Münster

Stein, Jack Madison, 1960. *Richard Wagner and the Synthesis of the Arts*, Detroit, reprinted 1973

Steiner, A., 1901–3. Richard Wagner in Zürich, 3 pts., *Neujahrsblatt der Allgemeinen Musikgesellschaft in Zürich*, 89/91

Stemplinger, Eduard, 1933. *Richard Wagner in München*, Munich

Stephan, Rudolf, 1970. Gibt es ein Geheimnis der Form bei Richard Wagner?, in *Das Drama Richard Wagners als musikalisches Kunstwerk*, edited by C. Dahlhaus, Regensburg (Studien zur Musikgeschichte des 19. Jahrhunderts 23), 9–16.

Stephani, Hermann, 1903. Das Erhabene insonderheit in der Tonkunst und das Problem der Form im Musikalisch-Schönen und Erhabenen, diss., Leipzig

Strauss, Richard, 1954. *Briefe an die Eltern 1882–1906*, Zürich and Freiburg

²/1957. *Betrachtungen und Erinnerungen*, edited by Willi Schuh, Zürich and Freiburg; English version: London, 1953

1964. Anmerkungen zur Aufführung von Beethovens Symphonien, *NZfM* 125

Strecker, Ludwig, 1951. *Richard Wagner als Verlagsgefährte*, Mainz

Strobel, Otto, 1925. Aus Richard Wagners Künstlerwerkstätte, *Bayreuther Festspielführer*, 162–6

1930. Die Kompositions-Skizzen zum 'Ring des Nibelungen'. Ein Blick in die Musikwerkstatt Richard Wagners, *Bayreuther Festspielführer*, 114–22

1933. Morgenlich leuchtend im rosigen Schein. Wie Walthers Preislied entstand, *Bayreuther Festspielführer*, 148–53

1934a. Richard Wagners 'Braunes Buch', *Bayreuther Festspielführer*, 113ff.

1934b. Das 'Porazzi'-Thema. Über eine unveröffentlichte Melodie Richard Wagners und deren seltsamen Werdegang, *Bayreuther Festspielführer*, 183ff.

1938. Geschenke des Himmels, *Bayreuther Festspielführer*, 157–65

1951. Eingebung und bewußte Arbeit im musikalischen Schaffen Richard Wagners, in *Bayreuther Festspielbuch*

1952. *Richard Wagner. Leben und Schaffen. Eine Zeittafel*, Bayreuth

Strobel, Otto (ed.), 1943. *Neue Wagner-Forschungen*, Karlsruhe

Strohm, Reinhard, 1977–8. Dramatic Time and Operatic Form in Wagner's 'Tannhäuser', *PRMA* 104

Szadrowsky-Burckhardt, Manfred, 1966. Heinrich Szadrowsky 1828–1878. Offprint from *Rorschacher Neujahrsblatt*, 75–86

Tappert, Wilhelm, 1887. Richard Wagner und die 'Neunte' von Beethoven, *Allgemeine Musikzeitung* 14, 375–7

Tenschert, Roland, 1954. Richard Wagner im Urteil von Richard Strauss. Aus Briefen und mündlichen Äußerungen des Meisters, *Schweizerische Musikzeitung* 94, 327–9

Thayer, Alexander Wheelock, 1917–23. *Ludwig van Beethovens Leben*. German adaptation by Hermann Deiters, revised edition by Hugo Riemann, 5 vols., Leipzig

1970. *Thayer's Life of Beethoven*. Revised and edited by Elliot Forbes, Princeton

Theens, Karl, 1948. *Geschichte der Faustgestalt vom 16. Jahrhundert bis zur Gegenwart*, Meisenheim

Tieck, Ludwig, 1911. *Phantasus I–III*, edited by Karl Georg Wendriner, Berlin

Tovey, Donald Francis, 1942. *Essays in Musical Analysis*, 4 vols., London

Truscott, Harold, 1963. Wagner's Tristan and the Twentieth Century, *Music Review* 24, 75–85

Uehli, Ernst, 1917. *Die Geburt der Individualität aus dem Mythos als künstlerisches Erlebnis Richard Wagners*, Munich

Uhlig, Theodor, 1849. Druckfehler in den Symphonie-Partituren Beethoven's *NBMZ* 3, 305ff.

1852a. Ein Kleiner Protest in Sachen Wagner's, *NZfM* 36, 277f.

1852b. Richard Wagner's Schriften über Kunst, v, Oper und Drama. Leipzig, 3 vols., *NZfM* 36, 4–6, 13–16, 25–9; vi, *NZfM* 36, 181–4; vii, *NZfM* 37, 53–7

1852c. Über den dichterischen Gehalt Beethoven'scher Tonwerke, *NZfM* 37, 131–3, 143–6, 163–6, 196–9

1852d. Lesefrüchte auf dem Felde der musikalischen Literatur, *NZfM* 37, 189f.

1912. Briefe von einer Schweizerreise mit Richard Wagner, *Süddeutsche Monatshefte* 2, 603–18, 689–700

1913. *Musikalische Schriften*, edited by Ludwig Frankenstein, Regensburg

Unger, Max, 1935–6. Beethoven und E. T. A. Hoffmann, *Zeitschrift für Musik* 102/3, 1204–211; 473ff., 855f.

Vetter, Isolde, 1978. Holländer–Metamorphosen, *Melos/NZfM* 4, 206–8

1982. 'Der fliegende Holländer' von Richard Wagner. Entstehung, Bearbeitung, Überlieferung, diss., Technische Universität Berlin (microfiche)

Vetter, Walter, 1956. Mozart im Weltbild Richard Wagners, in Ges. zur Herausgabe von Denkmälern der Tonkunst in Österreich. *IMSCR* (*Mozart Year*), Vienna

Vogel, Martin, 1962. *Der Tristan-Akkord und die Krise der modernen Harmonielehre*, Düsseldorf

1966. *Apollinisch und Dionysisch. Geschichte eines genialen Irrtums*, Regensburg (Studien zur Musikgeschichte des 19. Jahrhunderts 6)

Volkmann, Hans, 1942. *Beethoven in seinen Beziehungen zu Dresden*, Dresden

Voss, Egon, 1970a. *Studien zur Instrumentation Richard Wagners*, Regensburg (Studien zur Musikgeschichte des 19. Jahrhunderts 24)

1970b. Wagners fragmentarisches Orchesterwerk in e-moll – die früheste der erhaltenen Kompositionen?, *Die Musikforschung*, 23, 50–4

1977. *Richard Wagner und die Instrumentalmusik. Wagners symphonischer Ehrgeiz*, Wilhelmshaven

1982a. *Richard Wagner. Dokumentarbiographie*, revised and enlarged edition by Barth/Mack/Voss, Munich; English edition: London, 1975

1982b. *Richard Wagner. Eine Faust-Ouvertüre*. Munich (Meisterwerke der Musik, Werkmonographien zur Musikgeschichte 31)

1983a. Richard Wagner: Fünf Lieder nach Gedichten von Mathilde Wesendonck. 'Besseres, als diese Lieder, habe ich nie gemacht...', *NZfM* 144: 1, 22–6

1983b. Die Entstehung der 'Meistersinger von Nürnberg'. Geschichten und Geschichte, in *Richard Wagner. Die Meistersinger von Nürnberg. Faksimile der Reinschrift des Textbuchs von 1862*, Mainz

Wagner, Cosima, 1977. *Die Tagebücher 1. 1869–1877*, Munich (1976); *Die Tagebücher 2. 1878–1883*, Munich

1933. *Cosima Wagners Briefe an ihre Tochter Daniela v. Bülow 1866–1895 nebst 5 Briefen von Richard Wagner*, edited by Max Freiherr v. Waldberg, Stuttgart and Berlin

1934. *Cosima Wagner und Houston Stewart Chamberlain im Briefwechsel 1888–1908*, edited by Paul Pretzsch, Leipzig

1937a. *Cosima Wagners Briefe an Ludwig Schemann*, edited by Bertha Schemann, Regensburg

1937b. *Briefwechsel zwischen Cosima Wagner und Fürst Ernst zu Hohenlohe-Langenberg*, Stuttgart

1938. *Die Briefe Cosima Wagners an Friedrich Nietzsche*, Jahresgabe des Gesellschaft der Freunde des Nietzsche-Archivs 12–13, edited by Ernst Thierbach, Weimar

1978. *Cosima Wagner–Richard Strauss. Ein Briefwechsel*, edited by Franz Trenner, Tutzing (Veröffentlichungen der Richard-Strauss-Gesellschaft, Munich, 2)

Wagner, Franz J., 1910. *Beiträge zur Würdigung der Musiktheorie Schopenhauers*, diss., Bonn

Wagner, Richard, 4/1907. *Gesammelte Schriften und Dichtungen*, 12 vols., Leipzig

1879. *The Work and Mission of my Life*, North American Review. German title: *Richard Wagners Lebens–Bericht* (1884)

1963. *Mein Leben. Erste authentische Veröffentlichung.* Produced and with an afterword by Martin Gregor-Dellin, Munich

1871. *Richard Wagner an Friedrich Stade*, Musikalisches Wochenblatt 3, 33ff.

1888. *Richard Wagner's Briefe an Theodor Uhlig, Wilhelm Fischer, Ferdinand Heine*, Leipzig

1894. *Briefe an August Roeckel von Richard Wagner*, introduced by La Mara (pseud. of M. Lipsius), Leipzig 2/1912, revised edition 1908

1905. *Richard Wagners Briefe nach Zeitfolge und Inhalt: Ein Beitrag zur Lebensgeschichte des Meisters*, by August Wilhelm Altmann, Leipzig

6/1905. *Briefe Richard Wagners an Otto Wesendonk 1852–1870*, Berlin

1907. *Familienbriefe von Richard Wagner 1832–1874*, Leipzig

1907. *Bayreuther Briefe 1871–1883*, Berlin/Leipzig

1909. *Richard Wagners Briefe in Originalausgaben.* Second series, XVII: *Wagner an seine Freunde und Zeitgenossen*, edited by E. Kloss, Berlin and Leipzig

1910. *Briefe an Theodor Apel*, Leipzig

1911. *Richard Wagner an Ferdinand Praeger.* Second, newly revised edition with critical appendix by Houston Stewart Chamberlain, Berlin and Leipzig

3/1912. *Briefwechsel zwischen Wagner und Liszt*, 2 pts., Leipzig

1914. *Gesammelte Briefe*, edited by Julius Kapp and Emerich Kastner, I: 1830–43, II: 1843–50, Leipzig (only vols. to be published)

1916. *Briefe an Hans von Bülow*, Jena

1920. *Richard Wagners Briefe an Frau Julie Ritter*, Munich

1924. *Briefe an Hans Richter*, edited by Ludwig Karpath, Vienna

1930. *Richard Wagner an Mathilde Maier*, edited by Hans Scholz, Leipzig

1935. *Lettres françaises de Richard Wagner. Recueillies et publiées par Julien Tiersot*, Paris

1936. *Die Briefe Richard Wagners an Judith Gautier*, Erlenbach-Zürich and Leipzig

1936 and 1939. *König Ludwig II., und Richard Wagner, Briefwechsel*, edited by Otto Strobel, 5 vols., Karlsruhe

1953. *Richard Wagner Briefe. Die Sammlung Burrell*, edited and with commentary by John N. Burk, Frankfurt a. Main; English edition: London, 1951

Sämtliche Briefe, edited by Gertrud Strobel und Werner Wolf:

1967. I: 1830–42. Leipzig

1970. II: 1842–9, Leipzig

1975. III: 1849–51, Leipzig

1979. IV: 1851–2, Leipzig

1986. VI: January 1854–February 1855, Leipzig

(n.d.). *Tagebuchblätter und Briefe. Richard Wagner an Mathilde und an Otto Wesendonk*, edited by G. Will, Berlin

1877. *Wagner-Katalog. Chronologisches Verzeichnis der von und über Richard Wagner erschienenen Schriften, Musikwerke etc., etc., nebst biographischen Notizen.* Compiled by Emerich Kastner, reprinted Hilversum (1966)

1912. *Bibliographie der auf Richard Wagner bezüglichen Buch-, Zeitungs- und Zeitschriftenliteratur für die Jahre 1907–1911*, compiled and edited by Ludwig Frankenstein, Berlin

1956. *Internationale Wagner-Bibliographie 1945–1955*, edited by Herbert Barth, Bayreuth

1968. *Internationale Wagner-Bibliographie 1961–1966 und Wieland-Wagner-Bibliographie*, edited by Henrik (Herbert) Barth, Bayreuth

1975. *Das Braune Buch. Tagebuchaufzeichnungen 1865 bis 1882*, edited by Joachim Bergfeld, Zürich and Freiburg

Walzel, Oskar, 1913. *Wagner in seiner Zeit und nach seiner Zeit*, Munich

Wapnewski, Peter, 1981. *Tristan der Held Richard Wagners*, Berlin

²/1980. *Der traurige Gott. Richard Wagner in seinen Helden*, Munich

²/1983. *Richard Wagner. Die Szene und ihr Meister*, Munich

Weingartner, Paul Felix, 1895. *Die Lehre von der Wiedergeburt und das musikalische Drama*, Kiel

1896. *Bayreuth 1876–1896*, Leipzig

²/1901. *Die Symphonie nach Beethoven*, Leipzig

1906. *Ratschläge für Aufführungen klassischer Symphonien I: Ratschläge für Aufführungen der Symphonien Beethovens*, Leipzig

Weinstock, Herbert, 1968. *Rossini*, Oxford

Weißheimer, Wendelin, 1898. *Erlebnisse mit Richard Wagner, Franz Liszt und vielen anderen Zeitgenossen nebst deren Briefen*, Stuttgart and Leipzig

Weißmann, Adolf, 1930–1. Wagner und Brahms, *Der Türmer* 33, 2, 121–5

Wellek, Albert, 1939. *Typologie der Musikbegabung im deutschen Volke*, Munich (Arbeiten zur Entwicklungspsychologie xx)

Wellek, René, 1965. *Der Begriff der Romantik in der Literaturgeschichte*, in Grundbegriffe der Literaturkritik, German translation of the 1963 American edition titled 'Concepts of Criticism', Stuttgart and Berlin

Werner, Friedrich Zacharias (ed.), 1823. *Aus Hoffmanns Leben und Nachlaß*, 2 pts., Berlin

Westernhagen, Curt von, 1956. *Richard Wagner. Sein Werk, sein Wesen, seine Welt*, Zürich and Freiburg

1966. *Richard Wagners Dresdner Bibliothek 1842 bis 1849*, Wiesbaden

1968. *Wagner*, Zürich and Freiburg; English edition: Cambridge, 1978

Whittaker, William Gillies, 1940. Wagner's version of Gluck's Iphigenie in Aulis, Oxford (*Collected Essays* by W. Gillies Whittaker)

Williamson, Audrey, 1952. Wagner and Kundry, *Music Review* 13, 14–19

Winkel, Joseph, 1935. *Mallarmé – Wagner – Wagnerismus*, Münster

Wiora, Walter, 1965. Die Musik im Weltbild der deutschen Romantik, in *Beiträge zur Geschichte der Musikanschauung im 19. Jahrhundert*, edited by Walter Salmen, Regensburg (Studien zur Musikgeschichte des 19. Jahrhunderts 1), 11–50

Wolf, Werner, 1966. Richard Wagners geistige und künstlerische Entwicklung bis zum Jahre 1848, diss., Leipzig

Wolzogen, Hans von, 1876. *Thematischer Leitfaden durch die Musik zu Richard Wagner's Festspiel 'Der Ring des Nibelungen'*, Leipzig

1882. *Thematischer Leitfaden durch die Musik des Parsifal, nebst einem Vorwort über den Sagenstoff des Wagner'schen Dramas*, Leipzig

⁴/1889. *Thematischer Leitfaden durch die Musik zu Richard Wagner's Tristan und Isolde*, Leipzig

1891. *Erinnerungen an Richard Wagner*, Leipzig

1906. *E. T. A. Hoffmann und Richard Wagner*, Berlin

Wörner, Karl H., 1931–2. Beiträge zur Geschichte des Leitmotivs in der Oper, *Zeitschrift für Musikwissenschaft* 14, 151–72

1937. 'Das Leitmotiv als musikalisches Symbol', in *Bayreuther Festspielführer*, 172ff.

1969. *Das Zeitalter der thematischen Prozesse in der Geschichte der Musik*, Regensburg (Studien zur Musikgeschichte des 19. Jahrhunderts 18)

Wyzewa, Théodore de, 1898. *Beethoven et Wagner*, Paris, ²/1914 (Nouvelle Edition, entièrement refondue)

Zimmermann, L., 1910. *Richard Wagner in Luzern*, edited by G. Kauth, Berlin

Zinnius, Karl Wilhelm, 1936. *Die Schriften Richard Wagners in ihrem Verhältnis zur zeitgeschichtlichen Lage*, Heidelberg

INDEX OF NAMES

INDEX OF SUBJECTS